OBJECTIVE	CHAPTER
Catalyst 5000 Series Switch *(continued)*	
31) Describe Catalyst 5002 product features.	8
32) Describe Catalyst 5500 product features.	8
Catalyst 5000 Series Switch Product Architecture	
33) Describe the architecture and function of major components of the Catalyst 5000 series switch. Processors: NMP, MCP, and LCP; Logic Units: LTL, CBL, Arbiter, and EARL; and ASICs: SAINT, SAGE, SAMBA, and Phoenix	8
34) Trace a frame's progress through a Catalyst 5000 series switch.	8
Catalyst 5000 Series Switch Hardware	
35) Describe the hardware features, functions, and benefits of Catalyst 5000 series switches.	8
36) Describe the hardware features and functions of the Supervisor engine.	8
37) Describe the hardware features and functions of the modules in the Catalyst 5000 series switches.	8
Configuring Catalyst 5000 Series Switches	
38) Prepare network connections.	10
39) Establish a serial connection.	10
40) Use the Catalyst 5000 switch CLI to: enter privileged mode, set system information, and configure interface types.	10
Managing the Catalyst 5000 Series Switch Family	
41) Describe the different ways of managing the Catalyst 5000 series switch, including: out-of-band management (console port), in-band management (network connection using SNMP), RMON, SPAN, and CWSI	11
Troubleshooting the Catalyst 5000 Series Switches	
42) Upon completion of this module, you will be able to: describe the approach for tro[ ] Catalyst switches, describe the physical-layer problem areas, use the show commands [ ] problems, describe the switch hardware status, and describe network test equipment.	
Catalyst 5000 Series Switch FDDI Module	
43) Describe the major features and functions of the Catalyst 5000 FDDI/CDDI Module.	
44) Describe IEEE 802.10 VLANs.	9
45) Configure the Catalyst 5000 FDDI/CDDI Module.	9
Introduction to ATM LAN Emulation	
46) Define LAN emulation.	3, 9
47) Describe the LAN Emulation components.	3, 9
48) Describe the start-up procedure of a LAN Emulation Client.	3, 9
49) Describe how one LEC establishes communication with another LEC.	3, 9
50) Discuss how internetworking is achieved in a LANE environment.	3, 10
Catalyst 5000 Series Switch ATM LANE Module	
51) List the features of the Catalyst 5000 LANE module.	9
52) Outline the performance ratings for the ATM bus and the switching bus.	9
53) Describe how to access the CLI for the LANE module.	9
54) Describe the Simple Server Redundancy Protocol (SSRP).	9

D1417677

NOTE Exam objectives are subject to change at any time without prior notice and at Cisco's sole discretion. Please visit Cisco's Web site (http://www.cisco.com) for the most current listing of exam objectives.

NETWORK PRESS®
SYBEX

CCNP: Cisco LAN Switch
Configuration Study Guide

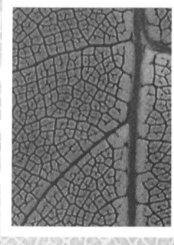

CCNP™: Cisco® LAN Switch Configuration Study Guide

Todd Lammle
Ward Spangenberg
Robert Padjen

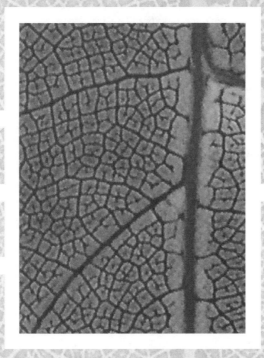

NETWORK PRESS®
SYBEX

San Francisco • Paris • Düsseldorf • Soest • London

Associate Publisher: Guy Hart-Davis
Contracts and Licensing Manager: Kristine O'Callaghan
Acquisitions & Developmental Editor: Neil Edde
Editor: James A. Compton
Technical Editors: Brian Horakh, John Swartz
Book Designer: Bill Gibson
Graphic Illustrator: Tony Jonick
Electronic Publishing Specialist: Robin L. Kibby
Project Team Leader: Leslie Higbee
Proofreaders: Theresa Mori, Blythe Woolston
Indexer: Ted Laux
Companion CD: Ginger Warner
Cover Designer: Archer Design
Cover Photographer: The Image Bank

Todd would like to dedicate this book to:

Dana Gertch, without whose help we could have never written this book! Thanks, bud.

Rob would like to dedicate this book to:

Tyler, for showing me that a smile can change the world. To Eddie, for reminding me that adults should be kids, too. And to my wife, Kristie, for years of support and caring that mean more to me each day.

Acknowledgments

Todd Lammle's acknowledgments: I would like to personally acknowledge Brian Horakh from www.networkstudyguides.com. As primary technical editor, he made sure everything was up to par and covered the CLSC exam to a tee. Thanks also to Dana Gertch, who helped me with the labs. Check out Dana's online lab at www.virtualrack.com.

Ward Spangenberger's acknowledgments: I would like to acknowledge several people for their time, patience and even the occasional swift kick to keep me in line. This illustrious list includes my wife, Laura, who put up with her own pain and suffering while I wrote and worked. I would like to thank my parents, Sam and Jean, for getting me this far and keeping their fingers crossed that I will go further. I would like to thank my own personal slave driver, Todd Lammle for giving me this opportunity. I am coming to Denver to get even with you. Finally, I would like to thank the old F'Liner crew, Bill Johnson, Chris Shaffer, Chet Puskarz, Nick Harris, Jim Chapman, Mark Schnabel, Mark Paukert, Raffi Tashjian, and, as I promised, special thanks to Scott Jensen for reading everything, even when it was bad.

Rob Padjen's acknowledgments: I wish to thank many people who have made an impact in my life and this project, but I want to specifically thank Todd, Neil, and the book team, for their assistance and support, in addition to the opportunity of working on this project. I also want to thank my parents for their guidance and strength. (And no, Dad, not this one either!)

Let us not forget all the wonderful editors: Jim Compton, the copy editor; and John Swartz, the second technical editor, who went tirelessly over and over the material. Check out John Swartz' certification Web site at www.boson.com. The Sybex production team that made this book a reality included electronic publishing specialist Robin Kibby, project team leader Leslie Higbee, and proofreaders Theresa Mori and Blythe Woolston.

We'd also like to thank the many terrific people who helped put the CD together:

James Chellis and Matt for creating and letting us use the Edge Test engine. (There are more CCNA/CCNP testing questions available. Check www.lammle.com for updates on Cisco testing questions and certifications.)

Janice Spampinato from AGGroup. Thanks to AGGroup, we were able to include network traces throughout this book with one of the best network analyzers on the market: EtherPeek.

Christy Delger from Visio Corporation provided an awesome product for the CD that can easily help you document your network plus more. Most of the figures in this book were produced in full or in part from Visio.

At Sybex, Ginger Warner and Hal Wakeling produced and tested the CD.

Contents at a Glance

Table of Contents

Introduction

This book is intended to help you continue on your exciting new path toward obtaining your CCNP and CCIE certification. Although you can take the tests in any order, you should ideally have taken the CCNA exam before reading this book to prepare for the CCNP: CLSC exam. At the very least, it is important to have read the Sybex *CCNA: Cisco Certified Network Associate Study Guide* (by Todd Lammle and Donald Porter with James Chellis). It would also be beneficial to read the Sybex *CCNP: Advanced Cisco Router Configuration Study Guide* (Todd Lammle, Kevin Hales, and Donald Porter). Many questions in the CLSC exam are extracted and/or built upon from the CCNA and ACRC material. However, we have done everything possible to make sure that you can pass the CLSC exam by reading this book and practicing with Cisco switches.

The new Cisco certifications reach beyond the popular certifications, such as the MCSE and CNE, to provide you with an indispensable factor in understanding today's network—insight into the Cisco world of internetworking.

Cisco—A Brief History

Many readers may already be familiar with Cisco and what they do. However, those of you who are new to the field, just coming in fresh from your MCSE, or maybe even with 10 or more years in the field wishing to brush up on the new technology may appreciate a little background on Cisco.

In the early 1980s, a married couple named Len and Sandy Bosack worked in different computer departments at Stanford University. They were having trouble getting their individual systems to communicate (like many married people), so in their living room they created a gateway server to make it easier for their disparate computers in two different departments to achieve communication using the IP protocol.

In 1984, they founded cisco Systems with a small commercial gateway server product that changed networking forever. (Notice the small *c*. One story is that the name was intended to be San Francisco Systems, but the paper got ripped on the way to the incorporation lawyers—who knows?) In 1992, the company name was changed to Cisco Systems, Inc.

The first product they marketed was called the Advanced Gateway Server (AGS). Then came the Mid-Range Gateway Server (MGS), the Compact Gateway Server (CGS), the Integrated Gateway Server (IGS), and the AGS+. Cisco calls these "the old alphabet soup products."

In 1993, Cisco came out with the amazing 4000 router, and then the even more amazing 7000, 2000, and 3000 series routers. These are still around and evolving (almost daily it seems).

Cisco Systems has since become an unrivaled worldwide leader in networking for the Internet. Its networking solutions can easily connect users working from diverse devices on disparate networks. Cisco products make it simple for people to access and transfer information without regard to differences in time, place, or platform.

Cisco's big picture is that it provides end-to-end networking solutions that customers can use to build an efficient, unified information infrastructure of their own or to connect to someone else's—an important piece in the Internet/networking-industry puzzle, because a common architecture that delivers consistent network services to all users is now a functional imperative. Because Cisco Systems offers such a broad range of networking and Internet services and capabilities, users needing regular access to their local network or the Internet can do so unhindered, making Cisco's wares indispensable.

Cisco answers this need with a wide range of hardware products used to form information networks using the Cisco Internetworking Operating System (IOS) software. This software provides network services, paving the way for networked technical support and professional services for maintaining and optimizing all network operations.

Along with the Cisco IOS, one of the services Cisco has created to help support the vast amount of hardware it has engineered is the Cisco Certified Internetworking Expert (CCIE) program, designed specifically to equip people to effectively manage the vast quantity of installed Cisco networks. The business plan is simple: To sell more Cisco equipment and have more Cisco networks installed, ensure that the networks you've installed run properly.

Having a fabulous product line isn't all it takes to guarantee the huge success that Cisco enjoys—many companies that offered great products are now defunct. If you have complicated products designed to solve complicated problems, you need knowledgeable people who are fully capable of installing, managing, and troubleshooting them. That part isn't easy, so Cisco began the CCIE program to equip people in supporting these complicated networks. This program, known colloquially as the Doctorate of Networking, has also been very successful, primarily because it is extremely rigorous. Cisco continuously monitors the program, revising it to make sure it remains pertinent and accurately reflects the demands of today's internetworking business environments.

Building upon the highly successful CCIE program, Cisco Career Certifications permit you to become certified at various levels of technical proficiency, spanning the disciplines of network design and support. So whether you're beginning a career, changing careers, securing your present position, or seeking advancement, this is the book for you!

Cisco's Network Support Certifications

Cisco has created new certifications that will help you get the coveted CCIE as well as aid prospective employers in measuring skill levels. Before these new certifications, you took only one test and were then faced with the lab, which made it difficult to succeed. With these new certifications that add a better approach to preparing for that almighty lab, Cisco has opened doors that few were allowed through before. So what are these new certifications, and how do they help you get your CCIE?

Cisco Certified Network Associate (CCNA)

The CCNA certification is the first in the new line of Cisco certifications and is a precursor to all current Cisco certifications. With the new certification programs, Cisco has created a type of stepping-stone approach to CCIE certification. Now you can become a Cisco Certified Network Associate for the meager cost of the Sybex CCNA Study Guide plus $100 for the test. And you don't have to stop there—you can choose to continue with your studies and achieve a higher certification called the Cisco Certified Network Professional (CCNP). Someone with a CCNP has all the skills and knowledge they need to attempt the CCIE lab. However, since no textbook can take the place of practical experience, we'll discuss what else you need to be ready for the CCIE lab shortly.

Why Become a CCNA? Cisco has created the certification process, not unlike Microsoft or Novell, to give administrators a set of skills, and to equip prospective employers with a way to measure skills or match certain criteria.

Becoming a CCNA can be the initial step of a successful journey toward a new, highly rewarding, and sustainable career.

The CCNA program was created to provide a solid introduction not just to the Cisco Internetworking Operating System (IOS) and Cisco hardware, but to internetworking in general, making it helpful to you in areas not exclusively Cisco's. At this point in the certification process, it's not unrealistic to imagine that future network managers—even those without Cisco equipment—could easily require Cisco certifications of their job applicants.

If you make it through the CCNA still interested in Cisco and internetworking, you're headed down a certain path to success.

To meet the CCNA certification skill level, you must be able to understand or do the following:

- Install, configure, and operate simple routed LAN, routed WAN, and switched LAN and LANE networks.

- Understand and be able to configure IP, IGRP, IPX, Serial, AppleTalk, Frame Relay, IP RIP, VLANs, IPX RIP, Ethernet, and access lists.

- Install and/or configure a network.

- Optimize a WAN using Internet access solutions that reduce bandwidth and WAN costs using features such as filtering with access lists, bandwidth on demand (BOD), and dial-on-demand routing (DDR).

- Provide remote access by integrating dial-up connectivity with traditional, remote LAN-to-LAN access as well as supporting the higher levels of performance required for new applications such as Internet commerce, multimedia, etc.

How Do You Become a CCNA?   The first step is to pass one "little" test, and poof—you're a CCNA! (Don't you wish it were that easy?) True, it's just one test, but you still have to possess enough knowledge to understand (and read between the lines—trust us) what the test writers are saying.

We can't say this enough—it's critical that you have some hands-on experience with Cisco routers. If you can get your hands on some 2500 routers, you're set. But if you can't, the Sybex *CCNA: Cisco Certified Network Associate Study Guide* (by Todd Lammle and Donald Porter, with James Chellis) provides hundreds of configuration examples to help network administrators (or people who want to become network administrators) learn what they need to know to pass the CCNA exam.

In addition to the Sybex *Study Guide*, there are other useful ways to supplement your studies for the CCNA exam.

Todd Lammle has created a router simulator that can help you practice on simulated router interfaces! Check out www.routersim.com.

Another way to get the hands-on router experience you'll need in the real world is to attend one of the seminars offered by Globalnet System Solutions, Inc. (www.lammle.com). Cyberstate University is providing hands-on Cisco router courses over the Internet using the Sybex Cisco Certification series books. Go to www.cyberstateu.com for more information. Keystone Learning Systems (www.klscorp.com) also offers the popular Cisco video certification series featuring Todd Lammle.

Also check out www.virtualrack.com for online access to Cisco equipment 24 hours a day!

It can also be helpful to take an Introduction to Cisco Router Configuration (ICRC) course at an authorized Cisco Education Center, but you should understand that this class doesn't meet all of the test objectives. If you decide to do that, reading the Sybex *CCNA Study Guide* in conjunction with the hands-on course will give you the knowledge you need for certification.

Cisco Certified Network Professional (CCNP)

This new Cisco certification has opened up many opportunities for the individual who wants to become Cisco certified but lacks the training, the expertise, or the bucks to pass the notorious and often failed two-day Cisco-torture lab. The new Cisco certifications will truly provide exciting new opportunities for the CNE and MCSE who just didn't know how to advance to a higher level.

So you're thinking, "Great, what do I do after I pass the CCNA exam?" Well, if you want to become a CCIE in Routing and Switching (the most popular certification), understand that there's more than one path to that much-coveted CCIE certification. The first way is to continue studying and become a Cisco Certified Network Professional (CCNP). That means four more tests, along with the CCNA certification.

The CCNP program will prepare you to understand and comprehensively tackle the internetworking issues of today and beyond—not limited to the Cisco world. You will undergo an immense metamorphosis, vastly increasing your knowledge and skills through the process of obtaining these certifications.

Remember that you don't need to be a CCNP or even a CCNA to take the CCIE lab, but to accomplish that, it's extremely helpful if you already have these certifications.

What Are the CCNP Certification Skills? Cisco demands a certain level of proficiency for their CCNP certification. In addition to those required for the CCNA, these skills include:

- Installing, configuring, operating, and troubleshooting complex routed LAN, routed WAN, and switched LAN networks, and Dial Access Services.

- Understanding complex networks, including such topics as IP, IGRP, IPX, async routing, AppleTalk, extended access lists, IP RIP, route redistribution, IPX RIP, route summarization, OSPF, VLSM, BGP, Serial, IGRP, Frame Relay, ISDN, ISL, X.25, DDR, PSTN, PPP, VLANs, Ethernet, ATM LAN emulation, access lists, 802.10, FDDI, and transparent and translational bridging.

To meet the Cisco Certified Network Professional requirements, you must be able to perform the following:

- Install and/or configure a network to increase bandwidth, quicken network response times, and improve reliability and quality of service.

- Maximize performance through campus LANs, routed WANs, and remote access.

- Improve network security.

- Create a global intranet.

- Provide access security to campus switches and routers.

- Provide increased switching and routing bandwidth—end-to-end resiliency services.

- Provide custom queuing and routed priority services.

How Do You Become a CCNP?   After becoming a CCNA, the four exams you must take to get your CCNP are as follows:

- Exam 640-403: Advanced Cisco Router Configuration (ACRC) continues to build on the fundamentals learned in the ICRC course. It focuses on large multiprotocol internetworks and how to manage them with access lists, queuing, tunneling, route distribution, route summarization, and dial-on-demand.

- Exam 640-404: Cisco Lan Switch Configuration (CLSC) tests your understanding of configuring, monitoring, and troubleshooting Cisco switching products.

- Exam 640-406: Cisco Internetwork Troubleshooting (CIT) tests you on the troubleshooting information you learned in the other Cisco courses.

- Exam 640-405: Configuring, Monitoring, and Troubleshooting Dial-up Services (CMTD) tests your knowledge of installing, configuring, monitoring, and troubleshooting Cisco ISDN and dial-up access products.

If you hate tests, you can take fewer of them by signing up for the CCNA exam and the CIT exam, and then take just one more long exam called the Foundation R/S exam (640-409). Doing this will also give you your CCNP— but beware, it's a really long test that fuses all the material listed above into one exam. Good luck! However, by taking this exam, you get three tests for the price of two, which saves you $100 (if you pass). Some people think it's easier to take the Foundation R/S exam because you can leverage the areas you would score higher in against the areas in which you wouldn't. Remember that test objectives and tests can change at any time without notice. Always check the Cisco Web site (www.cisco.com) for the most up-to-date information.

Cisco Certified Internetworking Expert (CCIE)

You've become a CCNP, and now you've fixed your sights on getting your CCIE in Routing and Switching—what do you do next? Cisco recommends that before you take the lab, you take test 640-025: Cisco Internetwork

Design (CID) and the Cisco authorized course Installing and Maintaining Cisco Routers (IMCR). By the way, no Prometric test for IMCR exists at the time of this writing, and Cisco recommends a *minimum* of two years on-the-job experience before taking the CCIE lab. After jumping those hurdles, you then have to pass the CCIE-R/S Exam Qualification (exam 350-001) before taking the actual lab.

To become a CCIE, Cisco recommends the following:

1. Attend all the recommended courses at an authorized Cisco training center and pony up around $15,000–$20,000 depending on your corporate discount.

2. Pass the Drake/Prometric exam ($200 per exam—so hopefully, you'll pass it the first time).

3. Pass the two-day hands-on lab at Cisco. This costs $1,000 per lab, which many people fail two or more times. (Some never make it through!) Also, because you can take the exam only in San Jose, California; Research Triangle Park, North Carolina; Sydney, Australia; Halifax, Nova Scotia; Tokyo, Japan; and Brussels, Belgium, you might just need to add travel costs.

The CCIE Skills The CCIE Router and Switching exam will include advanced technical skills required to maintain optimum network performance and reliability as well as advanced skills in supporting diverse networks that use disparate technologies. CCIEs just don't have problems getting a job. These experts are inundated with offers to work for six-figure salaries! But that's because it isn't easy to attain the level of capability mandatory for Cisco's CCIE. For example, a CCIE will have the following skills down pat:

- Install, configure, operate, and troubleshoot complex routed LAN, routed WAN, switched LAN, and ATM LANE networks, and dial-access services.

- Diagnose and resolve network faults.

- Use packet/frame analysis and Cisco debugging tools.

- Document and report the problem-solving processes used.

- General LAN/WAN knowledge, including data encapsulation and layering; windowing and flow control, and their relation to delay; error detection and recovery; link-state, distance vector, and switching algorithms; management, monitoring, and fault isolation.

- Knowledge of a variety of corporate technologies—including major services provided by desktop, WAN, and Internet groups—as well as the functions, addressing structures, and routing, switching, and bridging implications of each of their protocols.

- Knowledge of Cisco-specific technologies, including router/switch platforms, architectures, and applications; communication servers; protocol translation and applications; configuration commands and system/network impact; and LAN/WAN interfaces, capabilities, and applications.

Cisco's Network Design Certifications

In addition to the Network Support certifications, Cisco has created another certification track for network designers. The two certifications within this track are the Cisco Certified Design Associate and Cisco Certified Design Professional certifications. If you're reaching for the CCIE stars, we'd highly recommend the CCNP and CCDP certifications before attempting the lab (or attempting to advance your career).

This certification will give you the knowledge to design routed LAN, routed WAN, and switched LAN and ATM LANE networks.

Cisco Certified Design Associate (CCDA)

To become a CCDA, you must pass the CDS (Cisco Design Specialist) test (9E0-004). To pass this test, you must understand how to do the following:

- Design simple routed LAN, routed WAN, and switched LAN and ATM LANE networks.

- Use Network-layer addressing.

- Filter with access lists.

- Use and propagate VLANs.

- Size networks.

Cisco Certified Design Professional (CCDP)

If you're already a CCNP and want to get your CCDP, you can simply take the CID 640-025 test. But if you're not yet a CCNP, you must take the ACRC, CLSC, CIT, and CMTD exams.

CCDP certification skills include:

- Designing complex routed LAN, routed WAN, and switched LAN and ATM LANE networks, building upon the base level of the CCDA technical knowledge

CCDPs must also demonstrate proficiency in:

- Network-layer addressing in a hierarchical environment

- Traffic management with access lists

- Hierarchical network design

- VLAN use and propagation

- Performance considerations: required hardware and software; switching engines; memory, cost, and minimization

What Does This Book Cover?

This book covers everything you need to pass the CCNP: Cisco LAN Switch Configuration exam. It will teach you how to perform advanced configurations on Cisco 1900, 2820, 3000, and 5000 switches. Each chapter begins with a list of the CCNP: CLSC test objectives covered, so make sure to read over them before working through the chapter.

Chapter 1 starts with network congestion and ways to reduce it with segmentation using bridges, routers, and switches. You'll also learn about LAN switch types.

This provides an important background for Chapter 2's discussion of Virtual LANs (VLANs) and the role that switches play in implementing them. This chapter concentrates on how switches use frame filtering and describes how switches can be used with hubs to help extend your internetwork. It covers Token Ring VLANs and how Cisco VLAN architecture works.

Chapter 3 introduces ATM technology and shows how LANE works, concluding the general introduction to LAN switching concepts.

From there, the book moves on to the specific Cisco switch product "families" covered in the current 640-404 exam. For each family you'll find a discussion of the product features followed by installation/configuration instructions.

Chapter 4 presents the hardware, architecture, and features of the Cisco Catalyst 1900 and 2820 switches; this includes a discussion of controlling traffic with queuing. Chapter 5 shows how to install and configure the 1900 and 2820 switches.

Chapters 6 and 7 introduce the Cisco Catalyst 3000 series switches and show how to configure them.

Chapters 8 through 10 cover the Cisco Catalyst 5000 switches. In Chapter 8 you'll learn about the 5000 switch family's basic architecture and how it evolved. Chapter 9 introduces the advanced features of the switch, including its support for VLANs and LAN emulation (LANE). Chapter 10 shows how to configure the switch in an internetwork.

Chapters 11 and 12 complete the exam objectives by addressing troubleshooting and management issues.

Each chapter ends with review questions that have been specifically designed to help retain the knowledge presented. To really nail down your skills, read each question carefully, and if possible, work through the hands-on labs at the end of the installation and troubleshooting chapters.

We've included an objective map on the inside front cover of this book that will help you find all the information relevant to each objective in this book. At the beginning of each chapter, we've listed all exam objectives covered in that chapter.

Where Do You Take the Exam?

You may take the exams at any of the more than 800 Sylvan Prometric Authorized Testing Centers around the world. For the location of a testing center near you, call (800) 755-3926. Outside the United States and Canada, contact your local Sylvan Prometric Registration Center.

To register for a Cisco Certified Network Professional exam:

1. Determine the number of the exam you want to take. (The CLSC exam number is 640-404.)

2. Register with the nearest Sylvan Prometric Registration Center. At this point, you will be asked to pay in advance for the exam. At the time of this writing, the exams are $100 each and must be taken within one year of payment. You can schedule exams up to six weeks in advance or as soon as one working day prior to the day you wish to take it. If something comes up and you need to cancel or reschedule your exam appointment, contact Sylvan Prometric at least 24 hours in advance. Same-day registration isn't available for the Cisco tests.

3. When you schedule the exam, you'll be provided with instructions regarding all appointment and cancellation procedures, the ID requirements, and information about the testing-center location.

Tips for Taking Your CCNP Exam

The CCNP CLSC test contains around 70 questions to be completed in 90 minutes. You must schedule a test at least 24 hours in advance (unlike the Novell or Microsoft exams), and you aren't allowed to take more than one Cisco exam per day.

Many questions on the exam will have answer choices that at first glance look identical—especially the syntax questions! Remember to read through the choices carefully because close won't cut it. If you get commands in the wrong order or forget one measly character, you'll get the question wrong. So to practice, do the hands-on exercises at the end of the chapters over and over again until they feel natural to you.

Unlike Microsoft or Novell tests, the exam has answer choices that are really similar in syntax—some syntax will be dead wrong, but more than likely, it will just be very *subtly* wrong. Some other syntax choices may be right, but they're shown in the wrong order. Cisco does split hairs, and they're not at all above giving you classic trick questions. Here's an example:

- `access-list 101 deny ip any eq 23` denies Telnet access to all systems.

This looks right; most people will refer to the port number (23) and think, "Yes, that's the port used for Telnet." The catch is that you can't filter IP on port numbers (only TCP and UDP).

Also, never forget that the right answer is the Cisco answer. In many cases, the test presents more than one appropriate answer, but the correct answer is the one Cisco recommends.

Here are some general tips for exam success:

- Arrive early at the exam center so you can relax and review your study materials.

- Read the questions *carefully*. Just don't jump to conclusions. Make sure you're clear on *exactly* what the question is asking.

- Don't leave any unanswered questions. They count against you.

- When answering multiple-choice questions you're not sure about, use a process of elimination to get rid of the obviously incorrect answers first. Doing this will greatly improve your odds if you need to make an educated guess.

- Because the hard questions will eat up the most time, save them for last. You can move forward and backward through the exam.

- If you are unsure of the answer to a question, choose one of the answers and mark the question so that if you have time you can go back to it, and then go on. Remember that an unanswered question is as bad as a wrong one, so answer it because you may run out of time or forget to go back to it.

Once you have completed an exam, you'll be given immediate, online notification of your pass or fail status, a printed Examination Score Report indicating your pass or fail status, and your exam results by section. (The test administrator will give you the printed score report.) Test scores are automatically forwarded to Cisco within five working days after you take the test, so you don't need to send your score to them. If you pass the exam, you'll receive confirmation from Cisco, typically within two to four weeks.

Here's one more thing you can do: Go to Brian Horakh's Web site at www.networkstudyguides.com, and work through the exercise and practice test questions he has available. These will really help you keep abreast of any changes made to the test.

How to Use This Book

This book can provide a solid foundation for the serious effort of preparing for the Cisco Certified Network Professional CLSC (Cisco LAN Switch Configuration) exam. To get the full benefit from this book, use the following study method:

1. Study each chapter carefully, making sure you fully understand the information and the test objectives listed at the beginning of each chapter.

2. Complete all hands-on exercises in the chapter, referring to the chapter so that you understand the reason for each step you take. If you do not have Cisco equipment available, make sure to study the examples carefully.

3. Answer the review questions related to that chapter. (The answers are in Appendix A.)

4. Note which questions confuse you, and study those sections of the book again.

5. Before taking the exam, try your hand with the practice exams included on the companion CD. They'll give you a complete overview of what you can expect to see on the real thing.

6. Remember to use the products on the CD included with this book. Visio, EtherPeek, and the Edge Test test preparation software have all been specifically picked to help you study for and pass your exam.

To learn all the material covered in this book, you'll have to apply yourself regularly and with discipline. Try to set aside the same time period every day to study, and select a comfortable and quiet place to do so. If you work hard, you will be surprised at how quickly you learn this material. All the best!

What's on the CD?

We've worked hard to provide some really great tools to help you with your certification process. All of them should be loaded on your workstation when studying for the test.

The EdgeTest for Cisco CLSC Test Preparation Software

Provided by EdgeTek Learning Systems, this test preparation software prepares you for successfully passing the Cisco LAN Switch Certification exam. To find more test simulation software for all Cisco and NT exams, look for the exam link at www.lammle.com.

Visio

Visio Professional, combined with Visio Network Equipment, offers the most complete network documentation solution. Work with over 14,000 exact-replica, manufacturer-specific network hardware and telecom images and icons to create proposals, implementation plans, and any other documents your company uses to represent and manage its networks. Install the Visio Professional 5.0 30-day test drive and the sampling of over 100 Visio Network Equipment shapes included on the CD. To order a Visio product, obtain more information, or locate your nearest reseller, call (800) 248-4746 or visit Visio's Web site at www.visio.com for more information.

Network Utilities from AG Group

Four AG Group products appear on the CD that accompanies this book: EtherPeek, TokenPeek, NetTools, and NetSense.

EtherPeek and TokenPeek are network and protocol analysis tools designed to help you troubleshoot, optimize, plan, and configure networks. The "Peeks" work by capturing all network traffic and by providing the tools to filter, analyze, and interpret traffic patterns, data packet contents, statistics, and protocol types. (When installing EtherPeek or TokenPeek, you will be asked to enter a serial number. To obtain a demo serial number, please register online at www.aggroup.com/demos/ or call 1-800-466-2447.)

AG NetTools is a shareware IP utility suite available for Windows 95/98/NT 4.0. NetSense is a powerful software application that performs peer-to-peer packet transaction analysis of network protocols on Ethernet or Token Ring trace files. Designed specifically as a 32-bit Windows program, NetSense provides a wealth of information from packets contained in trace files captured from EtherPeek and TokenPeek. "Nuggets" of information from each packet are extracted by NetSense and displayed in several formats.

How to Contact the Authors

You can reach Todd Lammle through Globalnet System Solutions, Inc. (www.lammle.com)—his Training and Systems Integration Company in Colorado—or e-mail him at todd@lammle.com.

To contact Ward Spangenberg, you can e-mail him at wards@ins.com.

To reach Rob Padjen, send him e-mail at RobPadjen@aol.com.

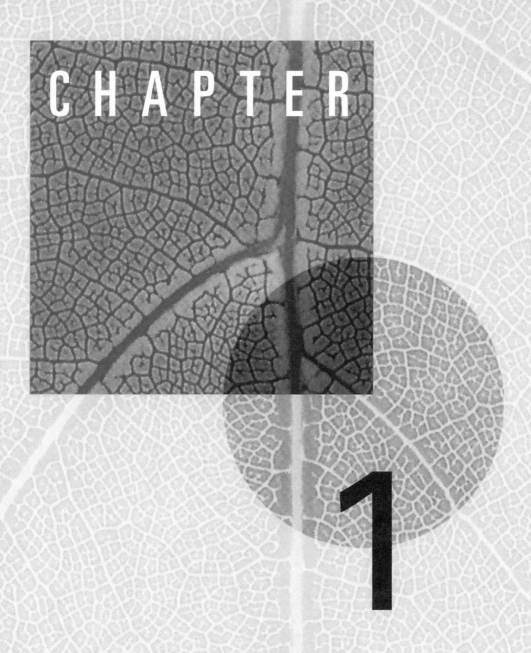

CHAPTER

1

General Switching Concepts

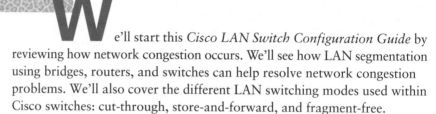

e'll start this *Cisco LAN Switch Configuration Guide* by reviewing how network congestion occurs. We'll see how LAN segmentation using bridges, routers, and switches can help resolve network congestion problems. We'll also cover the different LAN switching modes used within Cisco switches: cut-through, store-and-forward, and fragment-free.

We'll also review full- and half-duplex technologies, and we'll explain the concepts of Token Ring and how switching works within a Token Ring network.

This chapter covers the following CCNP/CLSC exam objectives:

- Describe the advantages of LAN segmentation.

- Describe LAN segmentation using bridges.

- Describe LAN segmentation using routers.

- Describe LAN segmentation using switches.

- Name and describe two switching methods.

- Describe full- and half-duplex Ethernet operation.

- Describe Token Ring switching concepts.

Network Congestion

Faced with today's combination of powerful workstations, audio and video data exchanged across the network, and network-intensive applications, 10Mbps Ethernet networks no longer offer enough bandwidth to fulfill the business requirements of the typical large business.

As more and more users are connected to the network, an Ethernet network's performance begins to lag as users fight for more bandwidth. Like too many cars entering a freeway at rush hour, this increased utilization can cause an increase in network congestion as more users try to access the same network resources. Congestion causes users to scream for more bandwidth. However, simply increasing bandwidth doesn't always solve the problem. A slow server CPU or insufficient RAM on the workstations and servers could also be the culprits and need to be considered as well.

One way to solve congestion problems and increase the networking performance of your LAN is to divide a single Ethernet segment into multiple network segments. This maximizes available bandwidth. Some of the ways to relieve network congestion are:

Physical segmentation: You can segment the network with bridges and routers, thereby breaking up the collision domains. This minimizes packet collisions by decreasing the number of workstations on the same physical segment.

Network switching technology (microsegmenting):   Like a bridge or router, switches can also provide LAN segmentation capabilities. LAN switches (for example, the Cisco Catalyst 5000) provide dedicated, point-to-point, packet-switched connections between their ports. Since this provides simultaneous switching of packets between the ports in the switch, it increases the amount of bandwidth open to each workstation.

Full-duplex Ethernet devices: Full-duplex Ethernet can provide almost twice the bandwidth of traditional Ethernet networks. However, for this method to work, the network interface cards (NIC) must be able to run in full-duplex mode.

Fast Ethernet: Using Fast Ethernet switches can provide 10 times the amount of bandwidth available from 10BaseT.

FDDI (Fiber Distributed Data Interface):   An older, dependable technology that can provide 100Mbps bandwidth. When implemented in dual rings, it can provide up to 200Mbps. It's typically used between closets, floors, or buildings in a campus environment.

Reducing the number of users per collision domain increases the bandwidth on your network segment. (A *collision domain* is the area within an Ethernet network within which frames that have collided will spread.) If you keep the traffic local to the network segment, users have more available bandwidth and enjoy a noticeably better response time than if you simply had one large backbone in place.

If you segment your network with repeaters, the network will appear like one large Ethernet network to all workstations, and basically, it *is* one large collision domain. It's a good idea instead to segment your network with bridges and routers when it grows too large. These devices use different technologies that, if used improperly, can cause some delay and reduce communication efficiency—the reason it's so important to segment your network correctly.

Segmentation with a Bridge

A bridge can segment or break up your network into smaller, more manageable pieces. But if it's placed incorrectly in your network, a bridge can cause more harm than good!

Bridges do their work at the MAC sublayer of the Data Link layer. To reduce traffic load, they create network segments that are both physically and logically separate. There are solid advantages to bridging—by segmenting a logical network into multiple physical pieces, it ensures network reliability, availability, scalability, and manageability.

As Figure 1.1 shows, bridges work by examining the MAC or hardware addresses in each frame and forwarding the frame to the other physical segments—only if necessary. These devices dynamically build a forwarding table of information in which each entry consists of a MAC address and its network segment.

FIGURE 1.1

Segmentation with a bridge

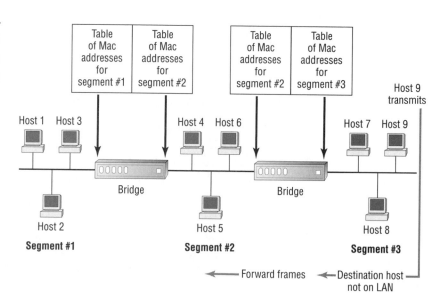

A bridge receives the entire frame being transmitted on the LAN before any processing takes place. It will then check the source and destination hardware address of the frame. The source address is put into the dynamic bridge table, and the destination hardware address is checked to see if it is on the same local segment as the source hardware address. If it is, the frame is discarded. If the destination is not on the local segment or is unknown, the bridge will forward the frame to all segments except the port it received the frame from.

Latency is the time it takes for a frame to get from the source host to the destination host. This delay can increase significantly if the frame cannot be immediately forwarded because of current activity on the destination segment. With bridges, the latency period for processing of frames can be 20–30 percent when using connection-oriented protocols and 10–20 percent when using sliding-window protocols.

A bridge will forward multicast and broadcast frames to all other segments that it is attached to. Because the addresses from these broadcasts are never seen by the bridge, and hence are not filtered, broadcast storms can result. This same problem can happen with switches, as theoretically, switch ports are bridge ports.

Spanning Tree Protocol

Redundancy—providing multiple physical paths between network nodes—can be a valuable way of achieving fault tolerance. But if a bridge, switch, or hub has more than one path to the same destination, loops can be created and routing problems can occur. The Spanning Tree Protocol (IEEE 802.1d) was developed to prevent bridging loops in a network. This protocol is executed between the devices to detect and logically block redundant paths from the network. The main function of the Spanning Tree Protocol (STP) is to allow redundant network paths to exist physically without causing loops in the network.

The Spanning Tree Algorithm (STA) implemented by the STP prevents loops by calculating a stable spanning-tree network topology. When creating fault-tolerant internetworks, a loop-free path must exist between all Ethernet nodes in the network. The STA is used to calculate a loop-free path throughout a Cisco Catalyst series switched network. Spanning tree frames called *bridge protocol data units* (BPDUs) are sent and received by all switches in the network at regular intervals. The switches participating in the spanning tree don't forward the frames; instead, they're processed to determine the spanning tree topology itself. Cisco Catalyst series switches use STP 802.1d to perform this function. The following EtherPeek trace shows a Cisco switch transmitting a frame containing STP information:

```
    Flags:          0x80  802.3
    Status:         0x00
    Packet Length:64
    Timestamp:      09:59:09.990000 02/19/1998
802.3 Header
  Destination:    01:80:c2:00:00:00
  Source:         08:00:02:0b:59:34
  LLC Length:     38
802.2 Logical Link Control (LLC) Header
  Dest. SAP:      0x42  802.1
  Source SAP:     0x42  802.1  Null LSAP
  Command:        0x03  Unnumbered Information
802.1 - Bridge Spanning Tree
  Protocol Identifier:  0
  Protocol Version ID:  0
  Message Type:         0  Configuration Message
  Flags:                %00000000
  Root Priority/ID:     0x8000  /  08:00:02:0b:59:34
  Cost Of Path To Root: 0x00000000  (0)
  Bridge Priority/ID:   0x8000  / 08:00:02:0b:59:34
  Port Priority/ID:     0x80  /  0x01
  Message Age:          0/256 seconds (exactly 0seconds)
  Maximum Age:          5120/256 seconds (exactly 20seconds)
  Hello Time:           512/256 seconds (exactly 2seconds)
  Forward Delay:        3840/256 seconds (exactly 15seconds)
  Extra bytes (Padding):
   .#..|...              02 23 00 07 7c f3 02 00
Frame Check Sequence:  0x00000000
```

Figure 1.2 shows how the STP would see a bridged environment.

In the bridged environment shown in Figure 1.2, bridge C will not forward traffic destined for the segment between D and E out interface 2. However, if bridge C were to stop hearing BPDU on interface 1(because bridge B is down), it would begin forwarding frames to interface 2 on bridge E.

F I G U R E 1.2

The Spanning Tree
Protocol in action

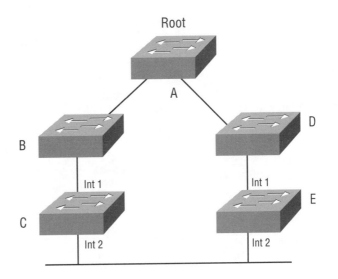

Segmentation with a Router

As you know, routers work at the Network layer and are used to route packets to destination networks. Routers, like bridges, use tables to make routing decisions. However, router tables only keep information about getting to remote networks, not to hosts, and routers use this information to route packets through an internetwork. For example, routers use IP addresses instead of hardware addresses when making routing decisions. The router keeps a routing table for each protocol on the network—a Cisco router will keep a routing table for AppleTalk, a different one for IPX, and still another for IP as shown in Figure 1.3.

Using routers offers the following benefits:

Manageability: Multiple routing protocols give the network manager who's creating an internetwork a lot of flexibility.

Increased functionality: Cisco routers provide features addressing the issues of flow, error, and congestion control, plus fragmentation, reassembly, and control over the packet's lifetime.

Multiple active paths: A router can have more than one network connection to a network. This allows redundancy and possibly more bandwidth between networks.

FIGURE 1.3

A router maintains
separate routing
tables for each
Network layer
routing protocol.

IP ROUTING TABLE	
Subnet	Interface
172.16.10.0	E0
172.16.20.0	S0
172.16.30.0	S0

IP ROUTING TABLE	
Subnet	Interface
172.16.30.0	E0
172.16.20.0	S0
172.16.10.0	S0

IPX ROUTING TABLE	
Network	Interface
117	S0
108	E0
10	S0

IPX ROUTING TABLE	
Subnet	Interface
10	S0
108	E0
117	S0

AppleTalk ROUTING TABLE	
Cable Range	Interface
2-2	E0
10-10	S0
1-1	S0

AppleTalk ROUTING TABLE	
Subnet	Interface
1-1	E0
10-10	S0
2-2	S0

To provide these advantages, routers are more complex and more software-intensive than bridges. Measured in the number of frames or packets they can process per unit, routers provide a lower level of performance. A router must examine more fields in a packet than a bridge, resulting in a 30–40 percent loss of throughput for acknowledgment-oriented protocols and a 20–30 percent loss for sliding-window protocols.

Segmentation with LAN Switches

LAN switching is a great strategy for LAN segmentation. LAN switches improve performance by employing packet switching that permits high-speed data exchanges.

Just like bridges, switches use the destination MAC address to ensure that the packet is forwarded to the right outgoing port.

There are three types of LAN switching: port configuration, frame switching, and cell switching (ATM, or asynchronous transfer mode).

- Port configuration switching allows a port to be assigned to a physical network segment under software control. It's the simplest form of switching.

- Frame switching is used to increase available bandwidth on the network. Frame switching allows multiple transmissions to occur simultaneously. This is the type of switching performed by all Catalyst switches.

- Cell switching (ATM) is similar to frame switching. ATM uses small, fixed-length cells that are switched on the network. It's the switching method used by all Cisco LightStream switches.

A LAN switch supplies you with considerably higher port density at a lower cost than standard bridges do. Since LAN switches permit fewer users per segment, the average available bandwidth per user increases. This fewer-users-per-segment trend is known as *microsegmentation*, and it lets you create dedicated segments. When you have one user per segment, each one enjoys instant access to the full available bandwidth, instead of competing for it with other users. Because of this, the collisions so common with shared medium-sized networks that use hubs just don't happen.

A LAN switch bases the forwarding of frames on the frame's Layer 2 address (Layer 2 LAN switch) or on the frame's Layer 3 address (multilayer LAN switch). LAN switches are sometimes referred to as frame switches because they generally forward Layer 2 frames; by contrast, ATM switches forward cells. As network use increases, you'll see more Token Ring and FDDI LAN switches, but Ethernet LAN switches are still the most common type.

LAN switches uniquely support some very cool new features, including these:

- Numerous, simultaneous conversations

- High-speed data exchanges

- Low latency and high frame-forwarding rates

- Dedicated communication between devices

- Full-duplex communication

- Media rate adaptation (both 10Mbps and 100Mbps hosts can work on the same network)

- Compatibility with existing 802.3-compliant network interface cards and cabling

Because of the dedicated, collision-free communication between network devices, file-transfer throughput is increased. Many conversations can occur simultaneously by forwarding or switching several packets at the same time, which expands the network capacity by the amount of supported conversations.

Switching Modes

The latency for packet switching through the switch depends on the chosen switching mode. There are three switching modes: store-and-forward, cut-through, and fragment-free.

Store-and-Forward   *Store-and-forward* switching is one of three primary types of LAN switching. With the store-and-forward switching method, the LAN switch copies the entire frame onto its onboard buffers and computes the cyclic redundancy check (CRC). Because it copies the entire frame, latency through the switch varies with frame length.

The frame is discarded if it contains a CRC error, if it's too short (less than 64 bytes including the CRC), or if it's too long (more than 1518 bytes including the CRC). If the frame doesn't contain any errors, the LAN switch looks up the destination hardware address in its forwarding or switching table and determines the outgoing interface. It then forwards the frame toward its destination. This is the mode used by the Catalyst 5000 series switches.

Cut-Through (Real-Time)   *Cut-through* switching is the other main type of LAN switching. With this method, the LAN switch copies only the destination address (the first six bytes following the preamble) onto its onboard buffers. It then looks up the hardware destination address in its switching table, determines the outgoing interface, and forwards the frame toward its destination. A cut-through switch provides reduced latency because it begins to forward the frame as soon as it reads the destination address and determines the outgoing interface.

Some switches can be configured to perform cut-through switching on a per-port basis until a user-defined error threshold is reached. At that point, they automatically change over to store-and-forward mode so they will stop forwarding the errors. When the error rate on the port falls below the threshold, the port automatically changes back to cut-through mode.

Fragment-Free Switching   Fragment-free is a modified form of cut-through switching in which the switch waits for the collision window (64 bytes) to pass before forwarding. If a packet has an error, it almost always occurs within the first 64 bytes. Fragment-free mode provides better error checking than the cut-through mode with practically no increase in latency.

Figure 1.4 shows the different points where the switching mode takes place in the frame.

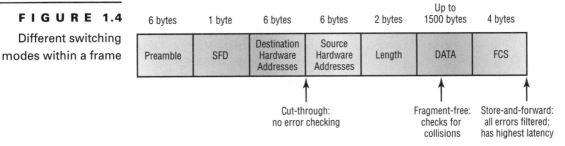

Should I Route or Should I Switch?

Many people wonder if routing is dead. Nothing could be farther from the truth. Routing is alive, and switches complement a routed network; they don't replace it. LAN switches improve response time and available bandwidth for end users with desktop computers and local servers, while allowing you to upgrade the all-important routing technology as data communication switches (pun intended) from the LAN to the WAN. Routers can help you create firewalls, create internetworks, limit broadcast and multicast packets, and enable LAN-to-WAN connections.

By running full-duplex between switches and routers, you can theoretically double bandwidth between devices. Cisco now supports full-duplex technologies in almost all of its higher-end products, and even some of its lower-end products.

Full- and Half-Duplex Ethernet

Most Cisco switches have been designed to run in either full- or half-duplex mode. Also, for the higher-end Cisco routers, Fast Ethernet with full-duplex capabilities can be added as add-on modules. This means that you can now have a full-duplex connection from every workstation to a server. Let's talk about the difference between full and half duplex.

Full-duplex Ethernet can both transmit and receive simultaneously, which theoretically doubles throughput on a network. Full-duplex Ethernet uses point-to-point connections and is typically described as *collision-free* since it doesn't share bandwidth with any other devices. Frames sent by two nodes cannot collide, because they are on physically separate transmit and receive circuits between the nodes. Half-duplex uses the same wires to transmit and receive, which means that collisions can occur.

If you have a full-duplex 10Mbps Ethernet operating bidirectionally on the same switch port, you can theoretically have 20Mbps aggregate throughput. Full-duplex can now be used in 10BaseT, 100BaseT, 100BaseFL, and ATM media, but all devices (for example, NICs) must be able to support full-duplex transmission and connect with point-to-point links between switches, not shared hubs.

Full-duplex communication can only be achieved by one of these methods:

- Connecting a host directly to a switch

- Connecting a switch to a switch

Half-Duplex Ethernet Design

Figure 1.5 shows the circuitry involved in half-duplex Ethernet. When a station is sending to another station, the transmitting circuitry is active at the transmitting station, and the receive circuitry is active at the receiving station. This uses a single cable similar to a narrow one-way bridge.

FIGURE 1.5

Half-duplex circuitry

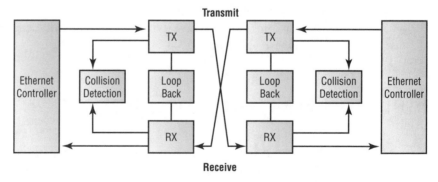

Full-Duplex Ethernet Design

Figure 1.6 shows full-duplex circuitry. Full-duplex Ethernet switch technology (FDES) provides point-to-point connections between the transmitter of the transmitting station and the receiver of the receiving station. Half-duplex standard Ethernet can usually provide 50–60 percent of the bandwidth available. In contrast, full-duplex Ethernet can theoretically provide an entire 100 percent because it transmits and receives simultaneously, and because collisions don't occur.

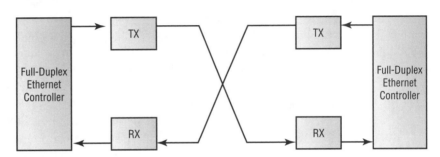

FIGURE 1.6

Full-duplex circuitry

In order to run full-duplex, you must have the following:

- Two 10/100Mbps full-duplex-capable paths
- Full-duplex NIC cards
- Loopback and collision detection disabled
- Software drivers supporting two simultaneous data paths
- Adherence to Ethernet distance standards
- 10BaseT/100BaseT: maximum length 100 meters
- 10BaseFL/100BaseFX: maximum length 2 kilometers

Token Ring Switching

Before moving on to more complex topics related to Token Ring switching, this section begins with an introduction to Token Ring and its background.

IBM created Token Ring in the 1970s, and it became popular with true-blue customers needing to migrate from a mainframe environment. It lost to Ethernet in the popularity polls because it's expensive by comparison. Depending on what you're looking for, however, Token Ring may still be a good value. It is a more resilient network, especially under heavy loads. Sometimes you actually do get what you pay for.

As it did with Ethernet, the IEEE came out with its own standard for Token Ring, named 802.5. This standard was so close to the IBM standard that the IEEE is now responsible for administrating both specifications.

At the physical layer, Token Ring runs as a star topology using shielded twisted-pair wiring (STP). Each station connects to a central hub called a MultiStation Access Unit (MSAU). Logically, it runs in a ring where each station receives signals from its nearest active upstream neighbor (NAUN) and repeats these signals to its downstream neighbors.

Token Ring uses MAC (hardware) addresses, as Ethernet does, but that's where the similarities end.

Stations can't transmit whenever they want, as Ethernet stations can. Instead, they have to wait to be given a special frame called a *token*. When a station receives a token, it does one of two things:

- It appends the data it wants to send onto the end of the frame, and then changes the token bit in the frame. Doing that alerts the receiving station that data is attached.

- If the station that gets a token doesn't need to send any data, it simply passes on the token to the next station in the ring.

The information frame circles the ring until it gets to the destination station. The destination station copies the frame and then tags the frame as being copied. The frame continues around until it reaches the originating station, which then removes it. It is important to remember that the source station is responsible for removing any frames it puts on the ring.

Typically, only one frame can be on a ring at any given time. However, by using early token release, a station can transmit a new token onto the ring after transmitting its first frame. Furthermore, collisions don't happen, because stations can't transmit unless they have a token.

The frame in a Token Ring network is different from the frames in Ethernet. Figure 1.7 shows the media access control field of the frame. The token frame uses a priority system that permits certain user-designated, high-priority stations to use the network more frequently.

Access Control Field

The bits in the frame are as follows:

P Priority bits

T Token bits

M Monitor bits

R Reservation bits

There are four fields within the Media Access Control field. The two fields
that control priority are (predictably) the priority field and the reservation
field. If a priority token is transmitted, only stations with a priority equal to
or higher than the priority of that token can claim it. The network administrator configures priority levels. After the token is claimed and changed to an
information frame, only stations with a priority rating higher than the transmitting station can reserve the token for the next pass around the network.
When the next token is generated, it includes the highest priority for the
reserving station. Stations that raise a token's priority level must reinstate the
previous lower priority level after their transmission is complete.

The frame status field is shown in Figure 1.8. The address (A) bit and the
copied (C) bit are used to indicate the status of an outstanding frame.

Frame Status Field

A	C	r	r	A	C	r	r	
0	0							Destination not found
0	1							Copied but not acknowledged
1	0							Unable to copy data from frame
1	1							Station found or frame copied to another ring by a bridge

Both bits are turned off when the sending station transmits the frame. Once the sending station receives the frame back again, the station will read this information to ensure that the data was received correctly by the destination computer; if it wasn't, the data needs to be retransmitted.

Active Monitors on Token Ring Networks

One station on a Token Ring network is always an *active monitor*. The active monitor makes sure there isn't more than one token on the ring at any given time. If a transmitting station fails, the active monitor steps in, removes the token, and then generates a new one (since the original station wouldn't be able to remove the token as it made its way back through the ring). In case the active monitor goes off line, many stations on the ring should be designated as backups, called *standby monitors*.

Unfortunately, congestion problems still occur in Token Ring LANs just like any other LAN. This is especially true in the "collapsed backbone" environments of the late 80s and early 90s, where all network traffic centered on the backbone and centralized servers. Since then, the microsegmentation technique has allowed for successful segmentation of Token Ring networks.

But before switches were designed, bridges were used to segment a Token Ring network. Token Ring bridges connect multiple rings together and forward frames between the rings connected. Bridges make the network function equally between the local ring and the extended network. Bridges copy frames destined for other rings and transmit packets from other rings destined for the local ring.

Switch-Connected LANs

To help meet the business requirement for more bandwidth, manufacturers designed higher-speed LANs as well as Token Ring switches.

With higher-speed LANs, you still have the same limitations of a shared LAN; traffic is subject to delay based on how busy the network segment is at any given time. This can be unacceptable in a multimedia environment.

Because each switch port can have its own token, you can have more control over your internetwork environment. Unlike upgrading a shared LAN to a higher-speed LAN, which requires changing all the cabling and network interface cards (NIC), using switches allows media adaptation. This means that you can upgrade only a few NICs and their wiring where needed. Token

Ring switches can be placed in the network without requiring changes to the clients or servers. You also will have better remote monitoring and management than if you used bridges, creating many physical and logical segments.

Cisco Switched Token Ring supports the following bridging technologies:

Source-Route Bridging (SRB):   Uses the routing information field (RIF) in the frame to make forwarding decisions. The Cisco switch modifies the RIF field when it is an explorer packet.

Routing Information Field: (RIF):   Contains a single bit that defines the path direction of the frame or Token (left to right or right to left). It is also defined as part of a MAC header for source-routed frames, which contains path information. This bit is used in an explorer frame to notify computers that it is on its return path.

Transparent Bridging (TB):   Uses the hardware (MAC) address to make forwarding decisions.

Source-Route Transparent Bridging (SRT):   Can use either the MAC address or the RIF field when making forwarding decisions.

Source-Route/Transparent Translational Bridging (SR/TLB):   The switch converts SRB frames to TB frames.

Source-Route Switching (SRS):   Uses the RIF field to make forwarding decisions, but unlike SRB, does not modify the RIF field.

Source-Route Bridging

IBM created source-route bridging (SRB) in the mid-1980s to connect corporate Token Rings to their IBM mainframes. This protocol maps out the entire route to a destination before any data is transmitted. It is called *source-route bridging* because the source device gets to choose the entire route to the destination device. SRB is part of the IEEE 802.5 Token Ring specification.

SRB was not designed for large internetworks. The specifications for IBM Token Ring define a maximum of 8 rings and 7 bridges. The 802.5 specification defines up to 14 rings and 13 bridges.

Types of Explorer Packets

A source device determines the best path to a destination device by sending *explorer packets*. There are three types of explorer packets:

Local explorer packets: Used to find local destination devices.

Spanning explorer packets: Used to find the best route to the final destination. Also known as *single-route* and *limited-route explorer packets*.

All-routes explorer packets: Used to find all routes to a destination host by checking all rings. Also known as *all-rings explorer packets*.

Here is how the three types of explorer packets work together to find a route to a destination device:

1. A NetBIOS or SNA device generates a local explorer packet to determine if the destination device is connected to the local ring.

2. If the destination device is not located on the local ring, the transmitting device sends either a spanning or an all-routes explorer packet. (A NetBIOS device sends a spanning explorer packet while the SNA device sends an all-routes explorer packet.)

3. The destination device responds to the explorer packets, which then return to the originating device. By examining the RIF (route information field), the source can determine the route to take to the destination. Remember that the RIF bit is used to notify computers that the packet is on its return path.

From that point forward, the source will determine the path; hence the name source-route bridging.

Configuring Cisco SRB

The syntax for creating a bridge between two Token Rings is:

```
source-bridge local-ring bridge-number target-ring
```

Below is an example of how to configure Cisco routers with SRB:

```
RouterB#conf t
Enter configuration commands, one per line. End with Ctrl-Z.
RouterB(config)#interface to0
RouterB(config-if)#source-bridge 401 5 400
RouterB(config-if)#source-bridge spanning
```

```
RouterB(config-if)#interface to1
RouterB(config-if)#source-bridge 400 5 401
RouterB(config-if)#source-bridge spanning
RouterB(config-if)#^Z
RouterB#
```

We use the `source-bridge 401 5 400` command on interface To0 to indi-cate that the local ring is 401, the target ring is 400, and the bridge number is 5. We do the inverse on interface To1. The `source-bridge spanning` com-mand indicates that we are using a manual Spanning Tree configuration. If we wanted to enable automatic Spanning Tree configuration, we would pro-ceed as follows:

```
RouterB#conf t
Enter configuration commands, one per line. End with Ctrl-Z.
RouterB(config)#bridge 10 protocol ibm
RouterB(config)#interface to0
RouterB(config-if)#source-bridge 401 5 400
RouterB(config-if)#source-bridge spanning 10
RouterB(config-if)#interface to1
RouterB(config-if)#source-bridge 400 5 401
RouterB(config-if)#source-bridge spanning 10
RouterB(config-if)#^Z
RouterB#
```

Transparent Bridging

A transparent bridge can connect two or more network segments into a single data-link LAN. It is called a *transparent* bridge because the devices on the network are unaware that the bridge is even there. The bridge simply lis-tens to frames and passes them along. It does not address, modify, or receive frames. It really is transparent to the devices on the network.

Transparent bridging is generally used with Ethernet. To be transparent to network devices, the bridge performs certain functions:

- Learning MAC addresses
- Forwarding packets
- Filtering packets

These functions allow the bridge to act transparently. Additionally, with multiple bridges, there is the possibility of an endless loop, so the bridge is required to perform a fourth function:

▪ Avoiding loops

We will discuss each of these steps in more detail.

Learning MAC Addresses

When you hook a transparent bridge to an Ethernet segment, it will actually receive all frames transmitted on that segment (remember the *MA—Multiple Access* in CSMA/CD). Now, suppose you have the bridge in Figure 1.9.

F I G U R E 1.9

A transparent bridge

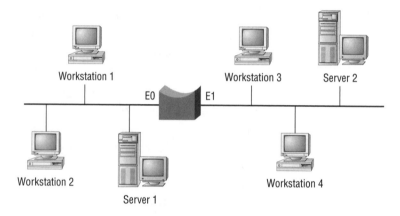

When Workstation 1 is communicating with Server 1, the bridge overhears all of this traffic on its E0 interface. It quietly notes the source MAC address of each frame received on E0 and enters those into a table as originating from E0. It does the same for all traffic received by its E1 interface. Pretty soon, the bridge will have a fairly comprehensive database of all attached devices (their MAC addresses) on each of its interfaces. The bridge updates the database each time it receives a frame to keep the database current. If the bridge does not see a frame from a device for some predetermined period of time (typically five minutes), the entry for that device is removed from the database.

In this sense, a transparent bridge can accurately be called a *learning* bridge. By simply listening to traffic, it quickly learns the location of all network devices on those segments to which it is attached. By continuously updating the database and discarding stale entries, this technique keeps the map of the network accurate.

Forwarding Packets

Suppose that in Figure 1.9, you have just turned on the bridge, so it has an empty database. It will immediately begin populating its database with MAC addresses from frames that it receives. Now, suppose that the first frame the bridge receives is the one shown in Figure 1.10.

FIGURE 1.10

WS1 ➢ S1 frame

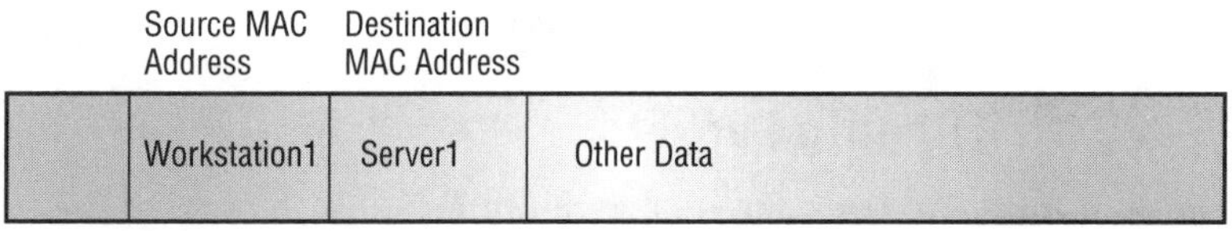

Source MAC Address	Destination MAC Address	
Workstation1	Server1	Other Data

The bridge now knows that Workstation 1 is connected to its E0 interface and makes an appropriate entry into its database. However, it still does not know where Server 1 is. The bridge will *flood* the frame—it will forward the frame out all interfaces except the one on which the frame was received. This is to ensure that Server 1 will still receive the frame addressed to it, no matter where Server 1 is. Now, we know from the above diagram that this is not necessary, but the bridge does not know that (yet). However, consider what happens next. Server 1 receives the frame from Workstation 1, and generates a reply as pictured in Figure 1.11.

FIGURE 1.11

S1 ➢ WS1 frame

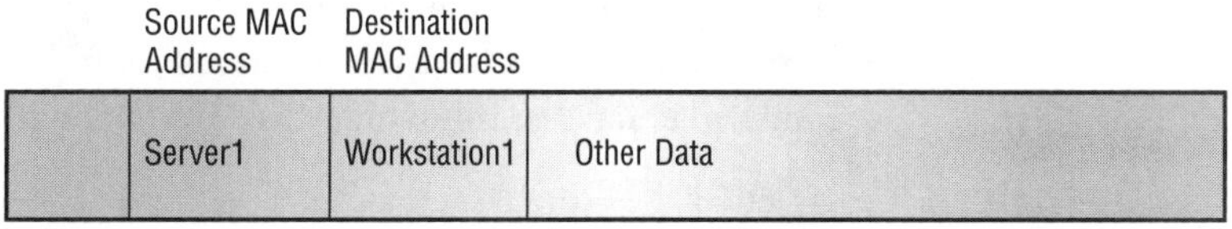

Source MAC Address	Destination MAC Address	
Server1	Workstation1	Other Data

The bridge receives this frame on its E0 interface, makes an entry for Server 1 in its database, and now knows that both of these devices are located on the same segment. At this point, the transparent bridge begins the next step: filtering.

Some frames must always be flooded by the bridge—whenever they are received, they must be forwarded to all interfaces (other than the one on which they were received). They include the following types:

- Frames destined for unknown MAC addresses

- Broadcast frames

- Multicast frames

We will discuss some of the ramifications of this requirement in the "Avoiding Loops" section.

Filtering Packets

Let's continue with our example. Now that the bridge knows the MAC address of Workstation 1 and Server 1 and also knows that they are on the same segment (the same bridge interface), it no longer needs to flood packets destined for those two machines out its other interfaces.

Suppose now that Workstation 1 sends out a packet to Server 2. If the bridge does not recognize the MAC address of Server 2, it will flood the packet. However (assuming Server 2 is running), it will immediately learn Server 2's location when it responds to Workstation 1's request. From that point forward, the bridge will filter (drop) packets between Workstation 1 and Server 1, because they are on the same segment and do not require the bridge's help to communicate. The bridge will forward frames between Workstation 1 and Server 2, because without the bridge's help, these two devices would not be able to communicate. Finally, if Workstation 2 addresses a frame to an unknown device, the bridge will flood the frame (and hopefully learn the new device's location when it responds).

The bridge has the following three options whenever it receives a frame:

- Filter

- Forward

- Flood

The MAC address database is kept in cache on the bridge to speed up the decision-making process.

Avoiding Loops

Redundant paths can be good or bad. When they work correctly, they provide fault tolerance for certain failures. However, when redundant paths do not work correctly, they can cause complete network failure. Consider the network shown in Figure 1.12.

FIGURE 1.12

Redundant bridges

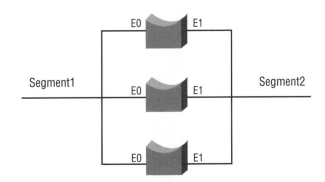

Three bridges connect Segment 1 and Segment 2. All three bridges hear all frames on each segment; all three bridges also build MAC address databases. However, what if all three bridges forward frames? Suppose that a frame on Segment 1 is destined for a device on Segment 2 and that all three bridges forward the frame. How will the destination device react when it receives three identical frames? It will probably be a bit confused.

There is, however, a worse case. Suppose that a *broadcast* is issued on Segment 1. All three bridges would pick it up and flood it to Segment 2. But now, each bridge hears two broadcasts on Segment 2 (one from each of the other two bridges). They are actually copies of the same broadcast, but since these are transparent bridges, there is no way to know that. So each bridge floods the two broadcasts it received on Segment 2 back to Segment 1. Now we have six frames on Segment 1, which becomes 12 frames on Segment 2, which becomes 24 frames on Segment 1, and so on. This is called a *broadcast storm*, and it is a real problem with topological loops and bridges.

As this example shows, a single broadcast frame can cause a broadcast storm that will consume all available bandwidth in seconds. This problem results from the transparency of the bridges. Routers tear apart and rebuild packets, and therefore can address issues such as TTL, number of hops, etc. They also handle broadcasts much differently than bridges. However, transparent bridges by definition do not modify packets. They just filter, forward, or flood. Of course, there is a solution.

The Spanning Tree Protocol, introduced earlier in this chapter, solves this problem. It allows multiple paths to exist for fault tolerance but creates a loop-free topology to reduce the risk of broadcast storms.

Cisco supports two Spanning Tree Protocols for transparent bridging. They are not compatible—they will not communicate with each other. They are as follows:

- DEC

- IEEE 802.1D

The IEEE protocol was actually derived from work done by DEC. Nevertheless, the two are not compatible.

Spanning Tree works in the following manner:

- All bridges in the Spanning Tree environment agree on a *root* bridge.

- Each bridge discovers all possible paths to the root, and then selects the lowest-cost path.

- Each bridge blocks all other interfaces to prevent loops.

Examples of bridging configurations using Spanning Tree are shown in the next sections.

Source-Route Transparent Bridging

Source-route transparent bridging (SRT) was introduced by IBM in 1990. In SRT, both SRB and transparent bridging occur within the same device. You can use SRT on Token Ring networks where some devices use SRB but others do not. SRT does not translate between two bridging domains—the SRB and transparent bridging systems do not communicate via the SRT. If the traffic arrives with SRB routing information, SRB is used. If not, transparent bridging is used. SRT does not provide Token-Ring-to-Ethernet communication.

Configuration is simply a marriage of transparent bridging and SRB. Using our earlier example, to implement SRT instead of SRB, we simply do as follows:

```
RouterB#conf t
Enter configuration commands, one per line. End with Ctrl-Z.
RouterB(config)#bridge 1 protocol ieee
RouterB(config)#interface to0
RouterB(config-if)#source-bridge 401 5 400
RouterB(config-if)#source-bridge spanning
RouterB(config-if)#bridge-group 1
RouterB(config-if)#interface to1
RouterB(config-if)#source-bridge 400 5 401
RouterB(config-if)#source-bridge spanning
RouterB(config-if)#bridge-group 1
RouterB(config-if)#^Z
RouterB#
```

Notice that as mentioned, this is simply the combination of transparent bridging and SRB commands.

Source-Route/Transparent Translational Bridging

Source-route/transparent translational bridging (SR/TLB) is used when bridging domains must be crossed. With SRT, communication from Ethernet to Token Ring is not supported. With SR/TLB, that issue can be addressed. SR/TLB is a Cisco IOS feature and not an industry standard.

When bridging between Ethernet and Token Ring, a number of issues must be addressed:

- MTU size
- Lack of support for RIF in Ethernet frames
- Different systems for MAC addresses

Configuring SR/TLB

To configure SR/TLB, you must first configure multiport SRB and transparent bridging as described earlier in this chapter. Then, you use the `source-bridge ring-group` command to configure a virtual ring, to which all SRB interfaces bridge. Finally, you use the `source-bridge transparent` command to enable bridging between the two environments. Syntax for this command is as follows:

```
Source-bridge transparent [ring-group] [psuedo-ring]
[bridge-number] [tb-group] [oui]
```

- `ring-group` is the virtual ring created by the `source-bridge ring-group` command.

- `pseudo-ring` is the ring number by which the transparent bridging domain will be known to the SRB domain.

- `bridge-number` is the SRB number of the router.

- `tb-group` is the number of the translational bridge group.

- `oui` is the organizational unit identifier. This optional parameter can be set to 90-compatible, Cisco, or standard.

Below is an example of an SR/TLB configuration:

```
RouterB#conf t
Enter configuration commands, one per line. End with Ctrl-Z.
RouterB(config)#bridge 1 protocol ieee
RouterB(config)#source-bridge ring-group 450
RouterB(config)#source-bridge transparent 450 451 5 1
RouterB(config)#interface to0
RouterB(config-if)#source-bridge 401 5 450
RouterB(config-if)#source-bridge spanning
RouterB(config-if)#interface e0
RouterB(config-if)#bridge-group 1
RouterB(config-if)#^Z
RouterB#
```

At this point, the SRB environment out of interface To0 will see the entire bridge group 1 as ring 451.

Verification

You can use several commands to verify and monitor operation of SRB. As always, `show interface` commands are useful to display interface operations. There are also several other helpful `show` and `debug` commands:

- `show rif` displays the current contents of the RIF cache.

- `debug rif` displays the routing information field data of token ring frames passing through the router.

- `show source bridge` displays the current source bridge configuration and miscellaneous statistics.

Summary

In this chapter, we covered how network congestion occurs and how network segmentation can help relieve some network congestion. This included how bridges, routers, and switches can be used to segment a network and the benefits of each.

- By segmenting your network with bridges, you can create smaller collision domains. However, bridges forward broadcasts, which can cause network congestion problems, especially in larger networks.

- By segmenting your network with routers, you essentially create both logically and physically smaller networks. You can then assign each of these networks a logical network address. Routers, by default, do not pass broadcasts.

- By segmenting your network with switches, you can add many advantages to your internetwork. These include:

  - Numerous, simultaneous conversations.

  - High-speed data exchanges.

  - Low latency and high frame-forwarding rates.

  - Dedicated communication between devices.

- Full-duplex communication.

- Media rate adaptation (both 10Mbps and 100Mbps hosts can work on the same network).

- Ability to work with existing 802.3-compliant network interface cards and cabling.

- We also covered the operation of the Spanning Tree Protocol and its benefits. We introduced this protocol and how it stops loops on the network. This was introduced when we covered LAN switching because all Cisco switches use the STP by default.

- We also talked about the three LAN switching methods:

  - Store-and-forward

  - Cut-through

  - Fragment-free

- Full- and half-duplex Ethernet operation was discussed in detail. We showed the difference between full- and half-duplex and the requirements necessary to run full-duplex.

- We finished the chapter with Token Ring Switching concepts, including transparent, source route, and translational bridging.

Review Questions

1. Which of the following is a characteristic of a Layer 2 switch?

   A. Switches forward packets based on the IPX or IP address in the frame.

   B. Switches must use a Layer 3 address in their filter tables.

   C. Switches forward packets based on the LLC address in the frame.

   D. Switches forward packets based on the MAC address in the frame.

2. How does the cut-through switching technique work?

   A. The LAN switch copies the entire frame into its onboard buffers and then looks up the destination address in its forwarding (switching) table and determines the outgoing interface.

   B. The switch waits only for the header to be received in order to check the destination address and then starts forwarding the packets.

   C. By using broadcast addresses as source addresses.

   D. By using a Class II repeater in a collision domain.

3. How do switches use store-and-forward?

   A. The switch waits only for the header to be received in order to check the destination address and then starts forwarding the packets.

   B. The LAN switch copies the entire frame into its onboard buffers and then looks up the destination address in its forwarding (switching) table and determines the outgoing interface.

   C. By using a Class II repeater in a collision domain.

   D. By using broadcast addresses as source addresses.

4. Which of the following is needed to support full-duplex Ethernet? (Choose all that apply.)

   A. Multiple paths between multiple stations on a link

   B. Full-duplex NIC cards

   C. Loopback and collision detection disabled

   D. Automatic detection of full-duplex operation by all connected stations

5. Which of the following are advantages to segmenting with routers? (Choose all that apply.)

   A. Manageability

   B. Flow control

   C. Explicit packet lifetime control

   D. Multiple active paths

6. Which of the following are advantages to using a switch to segment a LAN?

   A. Faster disk access on servers

   B. Reduced router costs

   C. More bandwidth allocated per user

   D. Flow control of segments

7. Transparent bridges operate differently on which of the following Layer 3 protocols?

   A. IPX

   B. DDP (AppleTalk)

   C. IP

   D. None of the above

8. Which of the following are functions of a transparent bridge?

   A. Avoiding loops

   B. Filtering frames

   C. Forwarding frames

   D. Learning MAC addresses

   E. All of the above

9. Which of the following are legal Spanning Tree types on Cisco routers? (Choose all that apply.)

   A. CCITT

   B. IEEE

   C. ARPA

   D. DEC

   E. IPX

10. Suppose you have a loop in your network topology. Which of the following describes what the Spanning Tree Protocol will do?

   A. Locate a point of redundancy, and then load-balance.

   B. Locate a point of redundancy, and then disable the interface until it is needed.

   C. Locate a point of redundancy, and then permanently disable the interface.

   D. Locate a point of redundancy, and then block all packets with expired TTLs.

11. Which two options will allow you to run full duplex?

   A. Connecting a shared 10BaseT hub to a switch

   B. Connecting a host directly to a switch

   C. Connecting a switch to a switch

   D. Running an MTU size of 1518

12. What type of bridging protocol makes forwarding decisions using only the MAC address?

   A. SRB

   B. RIF

   C. SR/TLB

   D. TB

13. In which of the following ways does SRB locate routes to destinations?

   A. Discoverer

   B. Explorer

   C. Voyager

   D. Flood

14. Which IEEE standard defines Token Ring?

   A. 802.1

   B. 802.1D

   C. 802.3

   D. 802.5

15. Which of the following can be addressed only with SR/TLB?

   A. IP-to-SNA communication

   B. IPX-to-SNA communication

   C. Transparent bridging

   D. Ethernet-to-Token-Ring bridging

16. Which bridge type forwards frames based on the RIF and can also modify the RIF for explorer frames?

   A. TB

   B. SRB

   C. SRT

   D. SRS

17. Which bridge type forwards frames based on the RIF but does not modify the RIF?

   A. TB

   B. SRB

   C. SRT

   D. SRS

18. Which bridging method can make forwarding decisions based on either the MAC address or information in the RIF field?

   A. TB

   B. SRB

   C. SRT

   D. SRS

19. Which of the following does LAN switching provide? (Choose all that apply.)

    A. Numerous, simultaneous conversations

    B. High-speed data exchanges

    C. High latency and low frame-forwarding rates

    D. Dedicated communication between devices

20. Which is true regarding Token Ring LANs?

    A. They are incompatible with Ethernet switches.

    B. The destination station is responsible for removing any frames it puts on the ring.

    C. The source station is responsible for removing any frames it puts on the ring.

    D. You can only have one ring per switch.

21. Which is true regarding explorer frames?

    A. Local explorer packets are used to find the best path to a remote device.

    B. Spanning explorer packets are used to find all routers to a destination host by checking all rings.

    C. The RIF bit is changed to notify computers that the packet is on its return path.

    D. Explorer packets don't use a RIF field.

22. Which is true regarding RIF?

    A. It consists of multiple bits that indicate the path direction (left to right or right to left).

    B. It is part of a MAC header for source-routed frames, which contains path information.

    C. It can only be used in Ethernet_II frames.

    D. RIF is used to make sure only one token at a time is on the ring.

23. Which is also true regarding RIF?

   A. It contains a single bit that defines the path direction (left to right or right to left).

   B. It is part of a Network header for source-routed frames, which contains path information.

   C. It is used only with SR/TLB.

   D. It is used as a keep-alive for tokens delayed by unexpected latency problems.

24. What does the command `debug rif` display?

   A. The routing information field data of Token Ring frames passing through the router

   B. The current contents of the RIF cache

   C. IP-to-frame conversions

   D. The IP header of Token Ring frames passing through the router

25. Write in the command that will set up the bridge to use source-route bridging from ring 23 to ring 34 using bridge number 5.

CHAPTER

2

Virtual LANs (VLANs)

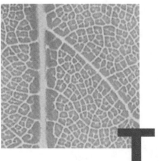

This chapter discusses virtual LANs and how they work in a Cisco switched environment. You'll learn why VLANs are used in internetworking and why switches are the core equipment used in VLANs. When you create VLANs, you are essentially creating smaller broadcast domains within a switch.

This chapter also explains the VLAN technologies and the standards used in Layer 2 switching. Finally, we will discuss Cisco's VLAN technology and architecture, which includes both Ethernet and Token Ring internetworks.

This chapter covers the following CCNP/CLSC exam objectives:

- Name seven reasons to create VLANs.

- Describe the role switches play in the creation of VLANs.

- Describe VLAN frame filtering and VLAN frame tagging.

- Describe how switches can be used with hubs.

- Name the five components of VLAN implementations.

- Describe the VLAN technologies.

- Describe Cisco's VLAN architecture.

- Describe Token Ring VLANs.

Why VLANs?

A Virtual Local Area Network (VLAN) is a logical grouping of network users and resources connected to administratively defined ports on a switch. By creating VLANs, you are able to create smaller broadcast domains within a switch by assigning different ports in the switch to different subnetworks. A VLAN is treated like its own subnet or broadcast domain. This means that frames broadcast are only switched between ports in the same VLAN.

Using virtual LANs, you're no longer confined to physical locations. VLANs can be organized by location, function, department, or even the application or protocol used, regardless of where the resources or users are located.

The seven reasons to create VLANs are:

- Simplified administration

- Reduced administration costs

- Broadcast control

- Security

- Flexibility and scalability

- Distribution of traffic

- Distribution of network services

Administration Simplification and Cost Reduction

Some organizations have "roving users," who seem to be constantly moving from floor to floor or building to building. VLANs can help maintain a group of users regardless of their physical location. When users were attached to hubs, which were then connected to routers, administrators sometimes had to reconfigure the router or routers and workstations to help facilitate users every time they moved their physical location within a company.

Now as a user moves, an administrator just has to make sure the user's new switch port is part of their existing VLAN. Network addresses do not change, so administration is easier. Administrators no longer have to worry about security and opening of resources into a network segment just because one user needs access to the resource.

Cisco has documented that at least 20 to 40 percent of the workforce changes or moves each year. Without VLANs, making these changes would be a full-time job for someone. However, with VLANs, the router configuration stays the same, which makes it easier for administrators and brings down administrative costs.

The maximum number of users that you can define per known network is 1000. However, Cisco recommends that a VLAN contain no more than 150 to 200 users.

Broadcast Control

Broadcasts occur in every protocol; but how often they occur depends upon the protocol, the application(s) running on the internetwork, and how these services are used.

Some older applications have been rewritten to reduce their bandwidth needs. However, there is a new generation of applications that are bandwidth-greedy—consuming all they can find. These are multimedia applications that use broadcasts and multicasts extensively. Faulty equipment, inadequate segmentation, and poorly designed firewalls can also add to the problems of broadcast-intensive applications.

As an administrator, you must make sure the network is properly segmented to keep problems on one segment from propagating through the internetwork. The most effective way of doing this is through switches and routers.

Since switches have become cost effective, a lot of companies are replacing the collapsed backbone with pure switched networks. This has also added a new chapter to network design, since broadcasts can propagate through the switched network. Routers, by default, send broadcasts only within the originating network, but switches forward broadcasts to all segments. This is called a *flat network* because it is one broadcast domain.

Routers, or route switch modules (RSMs), must be used in conjunction with switches to provide firewalls between networks (VLANs), which can stop broadcasts from propagating through the entire internetwork.

Security

The problem with the collapsed backbone internetwork was that security was implemented by connecting hubs together with routers. Security was then maintained at the router, but anyone connecting to the physical network could have access to the network resources on that physical LAN. Also, a user could plug a network analyzer into the hub and see all the traffic in that network. Another problem was that users could join a workgroup by just plugging their workstation into the existing hub.

By using VLANs and creating multiple broadcast groups, administrators now have control over each port and user. Users can no longer just plug their workstation into any switch port and have access to network resources. The administrator controls each port and whatever resources it is allowed to use.

Because groups can be created according to the network resources a user requires, switches can be configured to inform a network management station of any unauthorized access to network resources. If inter-VLAN communication needs to take place, restrictions on a router can also be implemented. Restrictions also can be placed on hardware addresses, protocols, and applications.

Flexibility and Scalability

Switches only read frames for filtering; they do not look at the Network layer protocol. This can cause a switch to forward all broadcasts. However, by creating VLANs, you are essentially creating broadcast domains. Broadcasts sent out from a node in one VLAN will not be forwarded to ports configured in a different VLAN. By assigning switch ports or users to VLAN groups on a switch or group of connected switches (called a *switch-fabric*), you have the flexibility to add only the users you want in the broadcast domain regardless of their physical location. This can stop broadcast storms caused by a faulty network interface card (NIC) or an application from propagating throughout the entire internetwork.

When a VLAN gets too big, you can create more VLANs to keep the broadcasts from consuming too much bandwidth. The fewer users in a VLAN, the fewer affected by broadcasts.

To understand how a VLAN looks to a switch, it's helpful to begin by first looking at a traditional collapsed backbone. Figure 2.1 shows a collapsed backbone created by connecting physical LANs to a router.

Each network is attached to the router, and each network has its own logical network number. Each node attached to a particular physical network must match that network number to be able to communicate on the internetwork. Now let's look at what a switch accomplishes. Figure 2.2 shows how switches remove the physical boundary.

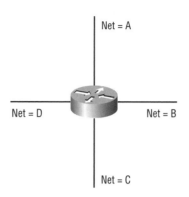

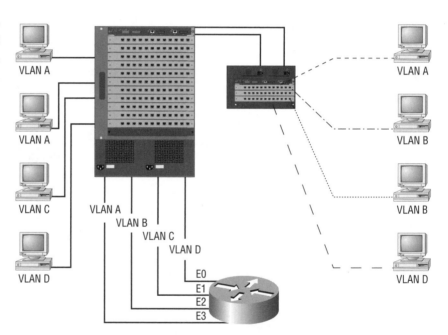

Switches create greater flexibility and scalability than routers can by themselves. You can group users into communities of interest, which are known as VLAN organizations.

Because of switches, we don't need routers anymore, right? Wrong. In Figure 2.2, notice that there are four VLANs or broadcast domains. The nodes within each VLAN can communicate with each other, but not with any other VLAN or node in another VLAN. When configured in a VLAN, the nodes think they are actually in a collapsed backbone as in Figure 2.1. What do these hosts in Figure 2.1 need to do in order to communicate to a node or host on a different network? They need to go through the router, just like when they are configured for VLAN communication as shown in Figure 2.2. Communication between VLANs, just as in physical networks, must go through the router.

Traffic Distribution

When placing bridges in your network, a general rule of thumb to follow is the 80/20 rule. This means that 80 percent of the traffic should stay on the local broadcast domain, and 20 percent or less should be forwarded through the bridge. When creating VLANs, these rules still apply. Eighty percent of the traffic flow should be local, or within the VLAN, and no more than twenty percent should flow between VLANs.

Network Service Distribution

To help keep traffic from having to traverse VLANs, servers can be *trunked*. That is, you can place a server into a switch and assign it as a member of all VLANs or just a selected few VLANs. This allows for all users to see the network services locally without creating inter-VLAN traffic.

The network administrator can assign a server to as many as 1005 VLANs. By default all VLANs are included when you create a trunk, and the administrator must actually remove VLANs from the trunk.

Also, by setting up Simple Network Management Protocol (SNMP), the administrator can use a Cisco software product called VlanDirector that can help the management and configuration of Cisco switches and VLANs.

VLAN Fundamentals

In this section, we will talk about the basic VLAN technology available with Cisco switches. Cisco's VLAN technology includes:

- VLANs across multiple backbones using Fast Ethernet, FDDI, and ATM.
- Static VLANs

- Dynamic VLAN

- Inter-Switch Link (ISL)

- Spanning-Tree Protocol

- Frame Filtering

- Frame Tagging

VLANs Across Multiple Backbones

Typically, when an administrator is talking about a fast backbone, you should be thinking Fast Ethernet, ATM, or even FDDI. Each of these is a transport protocol that can be used across a *trunked link*—a port or ports on a switch assigned to multiple VLANs.

In VLAN Trunk Protocol (VTP), all switches advertise their management domain on their trunk ports, their configuration revision number, and their known VLANs along with their individual boundaries. One or more interconnected devices that share the same VTP domain name make up a VTP domain. When configuring switches, remember that a switch can be assigned to only one VTP domain.

Within the VTP domain, its servers and clients maintain all VLANs in the switch fabric, and a VTP domain sets the boundaries of individual VLANs. A VTP's servers and clients also send information through trunks to other attached switches and receive updates from those trunks.

VTP servers maintain information in one of two ways, either in the Trivial File Transfer Protocol (TFTP) or in nonvolatile random-access memory. VTP servers will enable you to modify the VLAN information by using the VTP Management Information Base (MIB) or the command-line interface (CLI). This allows both servers and clients to be notified that they should be prepared to receive traffic on their trunk ports when VLANs are added and advertised. The VTP server also enables switches to delete VLANs and disable all ports assigned to them.

You configure a new VLAN on only one device in the management domain, because all other devices automatically learn the configured information through advertisement frames sent to a multicast address. These advertisement frames can be received by all neighboring devices but are not forwarded by normal bridging procedures. This is how all devices in the same management domain learn about any new VLANs configured in the transmitting device. Because of this, VTP is sent on all trunk connections, including ISL, 802.1Q, and LANE.

VTP defines overall configuration values and publishes the following configuration information by using multicast advertisements:

- VTP Domain Name
- VTP Configuration revision number
- VLAN IDs (ISL)
- Emulated LAN names (ATM LAN Emulation)
- 802.10 SAID values (FDDI)
- Maximum transmission unit (MTU) size for a VLAN
- Frame format
- VLAN configuration, including maximum transmission unit (MTU) size for each VLAN

VLAN Transport Protocols Across Backbones

Virtual LANs use communication protocols to communicate across trunked links. These VLAN protocols allow a single link to carry information from multiple VLANs. These protocols work with the VLAN Trunk Protocol (VTP) to automatically group VLAN trunk ports between switches. VTP is popular because it provides interoperability within the internetworking industry and is not network resource intensive. It is available for Layer 2 and Layer 3 VLANs.

VTP information can be distributed to all stations throughout the network, including servers, routers, and switches that participate as a VLAN configuration. VTP also provides auto-intelligence for configuring switches across the network.

The VLAN transport protocols include:

Fast Ethernet: Inter-Switch Link (ISL) is a VLAN transport protocol used across a Fast Ethernet trunked link.

FDDI: IEEE 802.10 is a VLAN transport protocol used across an FDDI trunked link. VLAN ID is a required field in the FDDI SAID header, which includes both a clear and a protected header. The 4-byte SAID field also allows for 4.29 billion distinct VLANs. The 802.10 SAID field is used to identify the VLAN ID.

ATM: LAN Emulation (LANE) is a VLAN transport protocol used across an ATM trunked link.

Static VLANs

This is the typical way of creating VLANs, and it is the most secure. The switch port that you assign a VLAN association always maintains that association until an administrator changes the port assignment. This type of VLAN configuration is easy to set up and monitor, working well in a network where the movement of users within the network is controlled. Using network management software to configure the ports can be helpful but is not mandatory.

To configure a static VLAN port, the administrator needs to connect to the switch either through the console cable and using the CLI (command line interface), or a Cisco product called CWSI (Cisco Works for Switched Internetworks) from an NT or Unix device. We'll learn about CWSI in Chapter 11. Let's take a look at how a static VLAN can be configured from a console port.

```
5000> (enable) set vlan 1 name Admin
Vlan 1 configuration successful
5000> (enable) set vlan 1 3/1-4
VLAN 1 modified.
VLAN    Mod/Ports
----    ----------------------
1       3/1-4
        5000> (enable)
```

This dialog creates VLAN 1 and names it Admin. The name is optional; we set it so that we'll know which department VLAN 1 represents. We then told the switch to assign ports 1 through 4 on card 3 to this VLAN.

Dynamic VLANs

Dynamic VLANs determine a node's VLAN assignment automatically. Using intelligent management software, you can enable hardware (MAC) addresses, protocols, or even applications to create dynamic VLANs.

For example, suppose MAC addresses have been entered into a centralized VLAN management application. If a node is then attached to an unassigned switch port, the VLAN management database can look up the hardware address and assign and configure the switch port to the correct VLAN. This can make management and configuration easier for the administrator. If a user moves, the switch will automatically assign them into the correct VLAN. However, more administration is needed initially to set up the database.

Cisco administrators can use the VMPS service to set up a database of MAC addresses that can be used for dynamic addressing of VLANs. VLAN Management Policy Server (VMPS) is a MAC-address-to-VLAN mapping database.

VLAN Management Policy Server (VMPS)

VMPS allows you to assign switch ports to VLANs dynamically. The hardware (MAC) address of the host is used to determine the VLAN assignment. This permits users to move their workstations or laptops without having to change VLAN assignments or configurations.

The VMPS database is stored on a TFTP host and downloaded when the switch is loaded. VMPS uses UDP to communicate and listen for client requests. When a request is received on the switch, the VMPS checks the database for a match. VMPS will shut down the switch port if no match is found. You can create an explicit deny for any MAC address on any VLAN.

Dynamic Port VLAN Membership

You can assign a dynamic (non-trunking) port to only one VLAN at a time on a Catalyst series switch. A dynamic port is isolated from its static VLAN when the link comes up. In an attempt to match the MAC address to a VLAN in the VMPS database, the source MAC address from the first packet of a new host on the dynamic port is sent to VMPS. If there is no match, VMPS will deny the request or shut down the port, depending on the VMPS secure mode setting. If there is a match, VMPS supplies the VLAN number to assign to the port.

Dynamic VLAN membership is not supported on the three-port Gigabit Ethernet module (WS-X5403).

If they are all in the same VLAN, multiple hosts—MAC addresses—can be active on a dynamic port. The port returns to an isolated state if the link goes down on a dynamic port. MAC addresses that come online through the port are checked again with VMPS before a port is assigned to a VLAN.

The following standards and limits apply to dynamic port VLAN membership:

- VMPS must be configured before you configure ports as dynamic.

- Spanning-tree PortFast is enabled automatically for any port you configure as dynamic, which prevents applications on the host from timing out and entering loops caused by incorrect configurations. If you wish, you can disable the spanning-tree PortFast mode.

- A port will connect immediately to the VLAN if you reconfigure it from static to dynamic. However, after a given period, VMPS will check the legality of the specific host on the dynamic port.

- Static secure ports cannot become dynamic ports unless you first turn off security on the static secure port.

- Static ports that are trunking cannot become dynamic ports unless you first turn off trunking on the trunk port.

The VTP management domain, the management VLAN of VMPS clients, and the VMPS server must all be the same.

Inter-Switch Link

Intel and Xpoint Technologies have designed an Inter-Switch Link (ISL) network interface card that allows you place a node, or port, in more than one VLAN at a time. This is helpful for servers that need to communicate to all or most users, like an e-mail server.

On multi-VLAN (trunk) ports, each frame is tagged as it enters the switch. The ISL cards allow servers to send and receive frames tagged with multiple VLANs so the frame can traverse multiple VLANs without going though a router, which reduces latency. This technology can also be used with probes and certain network analyzers. It also makes it easy for users to attach to servers, quickly and efficiently, without going through a router every time they need to communicate with a resource. Administrators can use the ISL technology to have fileservers be included in multiple VLANs simultaneously.

In addition, ATM LANE server cards can support up to eight emulated LANs (ELANs). LAN Emulation (covered in Chapter 3) uses a connectionless broadcast service to emulate a single LAN segment that converts packets to cells and resolves hardware addresses to ATM addresses.

Spanning-Tree Protocol

We introduced the Spanning Tree Protocol in Chapter 1. As you may recall, STP was developed by IBM to stop network loops in bridged environments. Since switches can be theoretically seen as multiport bridges, Spanning Tree is important to understand, especially in multi-VLAN organizations.

If we connect more than one switch port to a destination switch or other network device, the ensuing network loop can bring the network down. Cisco runs STP by default on their switch family, so you cannot accidentally loop your network. If the spanning-tree algorithm (STA) finds more than one connection to the same switch, it will set one link on standby. It's quite common to find multiple connections between switches as a network grows. This means the probability of a link failing or going down is higher, and the network will be disrupted as STP recalculates the topology.

By using VTP, Cisco switches can use STP for each VLAN, which means that if a link fails, only the VLAN with the connection failure would notice any instability. Because VLANs are typically smaller collision domains, recovery time would improve.

No switches, no VLANs. If you are using hubs, remember that when a signal is received on one port, it is transmitted out all ports. However, in a switch, the hardware destination is looked up in the switch filter table. The frame is then forwarded out the outgoing port only. However, if it is a broadcast, the switch will send it out all ports in that VLAN.

Switches are the core of VLANs and allow frames entry into the switch fabric for internetwork communication. Switches provide the intelligence that a hub cannot provide. Switches allow administrators to group users, ports, and logical addresses; create and maintain filtering tables (hardware addresses); and communicate with other switches and routers.

Frame Filtering

Switches build a table of known MAC (hardware) addresses and keep track of which port each node is connected to. This allows the switch to send a frame only to the destination and not to all other connected nodes.

Switches can synchronize this table with other switches, which can help locate nodes and cut down on broadcasts looking for destination hardware addresses. However, remember that frame filtering can affect latency and overall network performance.

Frame Tagging

When nodes or hosts need to communicate between VLANs, the packets need to go through a router. Since switches do not look at the packet information (Layer 2 switches), the frame is sent to the router, and the router extracts the packet out of the frame and then discards the frame. When the router determines the correct exit interface, it puts the packet back into a frame to traverse the new VLAN.

The switch needs a way of keeping track of users and frames as they travel the switch fabric and VLANs. Frame identification (frame tagging), a Cisco idea, uniquely assigns a user-defined ID to each frame. When a frame is received on a port, the switch places a unique identifier in each frame as it is forwarded through the switching fabric. This identifier defines the VLAN with which the frame is allowed to communicate.

When the frame goes from the switch to a router to be forwarded to a different VLAN, the switch will remove the identifier and then, when the frame re-enters the switch to find the new VLAN, it will add a new identifier with the VLAN information it is now traversing.

If you are using NetFlow switching hardware on your Cisco switches, this will allow devices on different VLANs to communicate after taking just the first packet through the router. This means that communication can occur from port to port on a switch, rather than port to router to port when traversing VLANs.

Switches and Hubs

Network administrators have been installing active hubs for many years. Should these be replaced with switches? It would be nice to have 100Mbps switched connections to every desktop, but that is not always cost effective. Shared hubs (10 and 100Mbps) are rather inexpensive and can work within a switched fabric. You can also leverage your existing investment in shared hubs by connecting switches to the backplane of hubs. Backplane hub connections are defined as a connection into a backbone.

You can connect a hub into a switch port and the switch will create a filter table of all hardware addresses connected to that port. You can make this port part of an existing VLAN or create a VLAN with just that one port.

However, you cannot make individual nodes connected to that hub part of different VLANs.

It is best not to overload a switch port with a large number of users connected to a hub. A good example of how to use hubs and switches together is to use the hubs to connect printers to the switches. Generally, printers do not consume a large amount of bandwidth. However, connecting many (for example) CAD users to one switch port through a hub might not be a wise choice.

By using your legacy hubs, you can migrate your network over slowly from a shared to a switched environment. Start by moving your servers to a switch port, and then find heavy network users and give them a dedicated port. This flexibility allows network managers to keep an existing environment and still build VLANs.

VLAN Standardization

The IEEE 802.1Q committee has standardized on frame tagging as the solution for VLANs. Before frame tagging, each node was placed in a filter table, and each time the switch received a frame, it looked up the address in this filter table to decide the frame's fate.

With each frame tagged as it enters the switch, the frame contains all the information it needs to traverse the switch fabric, and no table is needed.

It is important to remember that the CCNP: Cisco LAN Switch Configuration exam (640-404) covered by this book only covers Layer 2 switching, but Layer 3 and 4 switching are available now.

Token Ring VLANs

Essentially, a VLAN is a broadcast domain. There is only one type of broadcast frame in transparent bridging, and therefore, only one level of broadcast domain and one level of VLAN. However, you should know that in source routing there are two kinds of broadcast frames:

- Those restricted to a single ring.

- Those that traverse the entire bridged domain.

This means there are also two levels of VLANs in a Token Ring switched network.

The first level is the Token Ring Concentrator Relay Function (TrCRF), where the VLAN is a logical ring assigned a ring number. The logical ring contains one or more physical ports on a Token Ring switch. Source Route Switching (SRS) forwards frames within a TrCRF using the MAC address or Route Descriptor. On an RSM, you can define a logical ring (TrCRF) that does not contain any physical ports but is used only to process source-routed traffic that terminates the RIF.

The Token Ring Bridge Relay Function (TrBRF) is the second level of VLAN, the parent VLAN to which TrCRF VLANs are assigned. Here the VLAN is a logical bridge and assigned a bridge number (not a ring number) and forwards frames between groups of ports with the same ring number (TrCRF), employing SRB or SRT. In Figure 2.3 you can see the relationship between TrCRF and TrBRF VLANs.

F I G U R E   2.3

TrCRF and TrBRF
VLANs

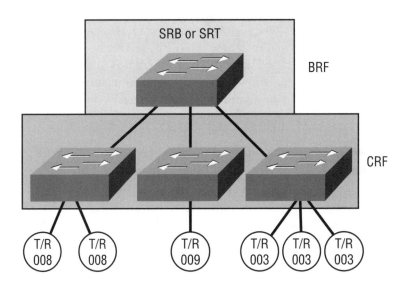

Token Ring VLAN Support on the RSM

Token Ring VLAN support on the RSM enables multiprotocol bridging and routing for Token Ring VLANs on the RSM. The RSM can function by itself, providing inter-VLAN routing. It also can be paired with a Catalyst VIP2 (Versatile Interface Processor), supplying external network connections with the identical port adapters used on Cisco 7500 series routers. The RS coupling enables routing between Catalyst VIP2 port adapters and VLANs.

Token Ring VLAN support on the RSM enhances the Catalyst 5000 switch by supplying the following functions:

- IP and IPX routing for source-routed and non–source-routed frames between Token Ring (TrBRF) VLANs and/or Ethernet VLANs and VIP2 interfaces.

- Source-route bridging (SRB) that occurs between Token Ring (TrBRF) VLANs and VIP2 interfaces.

- Source-route translational bridging (SR/TLB) that happens between Token Ring (TrBRF) VLANs and Ethernet VLANs and VIP2 interfaces.

- Source-route transparent bridging (SRT), occurring between Token Ring (TrBRF) VLANs and SRT-capable VLANs and VIP2 interfaces.

- APPN and DLSw+ are supported for Token Ring VLANs on the RSM, but RSRB is not supported on the RSM.

The Route Switch Module (RSM) is a card that plugs into a Catalyst switch and runs the Cisco IOS. The RSM is used in Token Ring networks to make it possible to route between Token Ring VLANs and Token Ring to Ethernet VLANs. The RSM interface is defined at the Token Ring Bridged Function (TrBRF) level.

You will need to create a logical ring on the RSM if you are running source-route bridging VLANs. This will allow the RSM to perform Routing Information Field (RIF) processing.

Summary

In this chapter, we named seven reasons to create VLANs:

- Simplified administration
- Reduced administration costs
- Broadcast control
- Security

- Flexibility and scalability
- Distribution of traffic
- Distribution of network services

We also described the role switches play in the creation of VLANs.

- We discussed VLAN frame filtering and VLAN frame tagging. Remember that the switch assigns a unique ID to each frame as it enters the switch.

- We learned how switches can be used with hubs. You can utilize your legacy equipment by plugging a hub into a switch port. However, remember to weigh this against overhead associated with multiple workstations plugged into one switch port.

- We named the five components of VLAN implementations: VLANs across multiple backbones using Fast Ethernet, FDDI, and ATM; Static and Dynamic VLANs; Inter-Switch Link (ISL); Spanning-Tree Protocol; and Frame Filtering.

- We described the VLAN technologies.

- We looked at Cisco's VLAN architecture.

- We described Token Ring VLANs.

Review Questions

1. Which of the following is true regarding VLANs? (Choose all that apply.)

   A. VLANs replace routers in an internetwork.

   B. VLANs are a group of ports or users in the same collision domain.

   C. VLANs are a group of ports or users in the same broadcast domain.

   D. VLANs are configured by physical location only.

2. Which is true regarding VLANs? (Choose all that apply.)

   A. They reduce administration costs

   B. They reduce server broadcasts.

   C. They make security holes.

   D. They reduce the propagation of broadcasts.

3. Which of the following is used with VLAN technology? (Choose all that apply.)

   A. Frame injection

   B. Frame filtering

   C. Frame tagging

   D. ArcNet

4. Which of the following is true regarding frame tagging? (Choose all that apply.)

   A. It is used by all Cisco switches.

   B. It is used by the Catalyst 5000 switches.

   C. It is used by all routers.

   D. It involves comparing frames with table entries.

5. Which of the following is true regarding frame filtering? (Choose all that apply.)

   A. Cisco created frame filtering specifically for use with VLANs.

   B. Frame filtering compares frames with table entries.

   C. Frame filtering places a unique identifier in the header of each frame as it traverses the switch fabric.

   D. Frame filtering decreases administration costs.

6. Which is true when installing switches? (Choose all that apply.)

   A. You must replace all shared hubs when installing switches.

   B. Switches and shared hubs can be used together.

   C. Shared hubs can participate in multiple VLANs.

   D. You must use only 100Mbps network interface cards in servers.

7. If you are using dynamic VLANs, which of the following are true?

   A. The administrator assigns VLAN by port.

   B. A VLAN configuration server can be used.

   C. It provides for automatic configuration of a new network user.

   D. It requires more configuration in the wiring closet than static VLANs.

8. If you are using static VLANs, which of the following are true?

   A. The administrator assigns VLAN by port.

   B. A VLAN configuration server can be used.

   C. It provides for automatic notification of a new network user.

   D. It requires more configuration in the wiring closet than dynamic VLANs.

9. Which VLAN transport protocol does Fast Ethernet use?

   A. ISL

   B. 802.10

   C. LANE

   D. VTP

10. Which VLAN transport protocol is used with FDDI?

   A. ISL

   B. 802.10

   C. LANE

   D. VTP

11. Which VLAN transport protocol is used with ATM?

   A. ISL

   B. 802.10

   C. LANE

   D. VTP

12. If you have multiple VLANs, which of the following is true regarding STP? (Choose all that apply.)

   A. Multiple instances of STP are allowed.

   B. Only one instance of STP per VLAN is allowed.

   C. Only one instance of STP is allowed per switch.

   D. You can have up to 64 instances of STP per VLAN.

13. If you are using FDDI, what field in the header is used as the VLAN ID and allows 4.29 billion distinct VLANs?

   A. T/RT

   B. VLAN

   C. SAID

   D. SIAD

14. Which of the following is true regarding frame tagging? (Choose all that apply.)

   A. A unique identifier is placed in each frame as it is forwarded through the switching fabric.

   B. A filtering table is developed for each switch.

   C. Frame tagging is a technique used to identify frames based on user-defined offsets.

   D. It is used on all Cisco routers and switches.

15. Which statement is true regarding 802.10 VLANs?

   A. They define multiple protocol data units.

   B. A VLAN ID is required.

   C. The header includes a clear header and a protected header.

   D. The clear header replicates the source address contained in the MAC.

16. Which of the following is true regarding 802.10?

   A. The 802.10 SAID identifies traffic as belonging to a particular VLAN.

   B. It is used with ATM and LANE.

   C. The FDDI 802.10 SAIDs are associated by the Catalyst 5000 Ethernet VLANs to create multiple broadcast domains.

   D. The 802.10 SAID field is used as a VLAN ID.

17. Which statements are true regarding VLAN trunk protocols?

   A. VTP provides auto-intelligence for configuring switches across the network.

   B. VTP provides static reporting for adding VLANs across the network.

   C. VTP information can be distributed to all stations throughout the network including servers, routers, and switches that participate as a VLAN configuration.

   D. VTP provides a manual mapping scheme going across mixed media backbones.

18. Which statement is true regarding frame tagging?

   A. A filtering table is developed for each switch.

   B. Frame tagging is a technique used to identify frames based on user-defined offsets.

   C. Frame tagging assigns a unique user ID to each frame.

   D. It is used on all Cisco routers and switches.

19. Which statements regarding 802.10 VLANs are true?

   A. The 4-byte SAID allows for 4.29 billion distinct VLANs.

   B. The 802.10 SAID identifies traffic as belonging to a particular VLAN.

   C. The 6-byte SAID allows for 4.29 billion distinct LANs.

   D. The FDDI 802.10 SAIDs are associated by the Catalyst 5000 Ethernet VLANs to create multiple broadcast domains.

20. Which VLAN technology is a standard protocol on a Catalyst 5000 switch that allows you to map trunking protocols together to create an integrated VLAN implementation across a user-defined management domain?

A. ATM

B. LANE

C. ISL

D. VTP

CHAPTER

3

ATM LAN Emulation

Asynchronous transfer mode (ATM) is only used as a backbone protocol, so we do not need to worry about our packet-based, broadcast LANs trying to communicate with the cell-based ATM networks, right? Unfortunately, nothing could be farther from the truth. What we need is a way to resolve the difference between ATM's connection-oriented, point-to-point protocol and the connectionless, broadcast domains of a LAN medium.

Cisco, a leading member and original founder of the ATM Forum LAN Emulation Sub-Working group, has implemented LAN Emulation (LANE) in its core products. Cisco designed LANE to hide ATM and look like 802.3 Ethernet and 802.5 Token Ring networks to end users on a LAN. LANE works by making the ATM network emulate a Media Access Control (MAC) broadcast network. Before LANE, a proprietary conversion device was needed to convert from LAN to ATM.

Since it is possible that upper-layer protocols expect the lower layer to use a connectionless service, LANE is used to allow an upper-layer protocol to make connections to lower-layer ATM connection-oriented services. What this means is that LANE provides a switching service that is transparent to the 802.*x* networks.

In this chapter you will learn about ATM LANE, the components that make up LAN emulation, and how LANE emulates a broadcast medium.

This chapter covers the following exam objectives:

- Define LAN Emulation.

- Describe the LAN Emulation components.

- Describe the start-up procedure of a LAN Emulation Client.

- Learn how one LEC establishes communication with another LEC.

- Discuss how internetworking is acheived in a LANE environment.

Introduction to LAN Emulation

LAN Emulation is an ATM service defined by the ATM Forum specification *LAN Emulation over ATM, ATM Forum 94-0035*. The ATM Forum sat down together and devised a specification for LAN Emulation services across ATM to include three important characteristics:

- Connectionless service between LANs

- The ability to carry multicast services

- Media Access Control driver service

LANE services must provide connectivity between all ATM devices and all LAN devices. This connectivity extends to devices that are attached ATM stations as well as attached LAN devices that are crossing the ATM network. Connectivity between ATM devices and all other LAN devices is done through emulated LANs (ELANs).

ELANs are also used to create independent broadcast domains that are similar in concept to Ethernet segments or Token Ring networks. ELANs also allow ATM to work with existing older equipment.

ELANs have some similarities to VLANs. ELAN workstations are independent of physical location, and ELANs must be connected to a router in order to communicate with each other. You can create an unlimited number of emulated LANs in an ATM network, and a router can participate in any number of these emulated LANs.

Connectivity begins at the MAC sublayer of the Data Link layer, allowing Windows upper-level NDIS/ODI driver interfaces to transmit Layer 3 protocols like TCP/IP, IPX, AppleTalk, and APPN, as well as allowing existing applications to continue operating without disturbance.

LANE provides a conversion process that allows you to take the connectionless environment of a LAN and change it into the connection-oriented world of ATM. The LANE converter receives LAN packets, places a 5-byte ATM-specific identification header on the front of the cell, and removes the checksum (frame check sequence) from the packet. It then fragments the packets into a 48-byte payload with a 5-byte header, creating a 53-byte cell. After the packet has traveled the ATM network, the ATM information is removed and the packet is reassembled and returned to the LAN environment.

The LANE 1.0 specification is basically a software interface for the Layer 3 protocols identical to existing LANs, which encapsulates user data in either

Ethernet or Token Ring frames. It doesn't actually become the media access method of Ethernet or Token Ring, but uses three servers that clients access over a number of ATM connections. FDDI can be used with LANE 1.0, but it is not really defined as Ethernet and Token Ring is. ATM devices map FDDI packets into either Ethernet or Token Ring using existing translation bridging techniques. LANE 1.0 defines operation over ATM with best-effort delivery. LANE 2.0 has added QoS or quality of service guarantees, a feature that gives ATM with LANE a benefit over existing LANs.

The ATM Protocol Model

The ATM protocol dictates how two end-devices communicate with each other across an ATM network through switches. The ATM protocol model contains three functional layers:

The ATM physical layer: Bit timing and the physical medium

The ATM layer: Generic flow control, generation of call header, multiplexing and demultiplexing

The ATM adaptation layer: Support for higher-layer services such as signaling, circuit emulation, voice and video

These layers are very similar to Layer 1 and Layer 2 of the OSI reference model, as you can see in Figure 3.1.

F I G U R E   3.1

The ATM Model compared to the OSI reference model

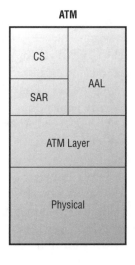
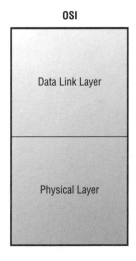

ATM Sublayers	ATM	OSI
Service Specific (SS)	CS	Data Link Layer
Common Part		
Segmentation and Reassembly	SAR / AAL	
Virtual Channel	ATM Layer	
Virtual Path		
Transmission Path	Physical	Physical Layer
Digital Section		
Regenerator Section		

The ATM Physical Layer

The ATM physical layer is in charge of sending and receiving bits on the physical level. This layer also manages ATM cell boundaries and controls the cell packaging in the correct frame type for the ATM media you use. The ATM physical layer consists of two sublayers:

- The physical medium dependent (PMD) sublayer

- The transmission convergence (TC) sublayer

The PMD sublayer sends and receives a constant flow of bits that contain associated timing information to synchronize transmission and reception. The physical medium sublayer relies on the media used for transport, and thus, ATM only works on ATM-specific media. Standards include DS-3/E3, FDDI (Fiber Distributed Data Interface), 155-Mbps local fiber, and SONET (Synchronous Optical Network)/SDH. The ATM Forum is considering proposals for twisted-pair wire.

The TC sublayer maintains several functions. It mainly extracts and inserts ATM cells within either a Plesiochronous or Synchronous (PHD or SDH) Time Division Multiplexed (TDM) frame and passes this to and from the ATM layer. The other functions it provides are listed below:

Cell delineation: It maintains ATM cell boundaries.

Header error control sequence generation and verification: It creates and checks header error control to ensure valid data.

Cell rate decoupling: It inserts or suppresses unassigned ATM cells to adapt the rate of valid ATM cells to the payload capacity of the transmission system.

Transmission frame adaptation: It packages ATM cells in appropriate frames for physical layer implementation.

Transmission frame generation and recovery: It generates and maintains the given physical-layer frame structure.

The ATM Layer

The ATM layer connects the virtual connections and carries ATM cells through the network. It accomplishes this by using information contained within the header of each ATM cell. The ATM layer is responsible for:

- Multiplexing and demultiplexing ATM cells from different virtual connections. You can identify these different connections by their VCI and VPI values.

A VCI (Virtual Circuit Identifier) can also be called a virtual channel. This is simply the identifier for the logical connection between the two ends of a connection. A VPI (Virtual Path Identifier) is the identifier for a group of VCIs that allows an ATM switch to perform operations on a group of VCs.

- Translation of VCI and VPI values at the ATM switch or cross-connect.

- Extraction and insertion of the header before or after the cell is delivered from or to the ATM adaptation layer.

- Governing the implementation of a flow-control mechanism at the UNI. User-Network Interface (UNI) is basically two ports connected by a pair of wires, typically fiber.

- Passing and accepting cells from the AAL.

ATM Adaptation Layer (AAL)

The ATM Adaptation Layer (AAL) provides the translation between the larger service data units of the upper layers of the OSI reference model and ATM cells. This function works by receiving packets from the upper-level protocols and breaking them into 48-byte segments to be dumped into the payload of an ATM cell. The AAL has two different sublayers: Segmentation and Reassembly (SAR) and the Convergence Sublayer (CS). The CS has further sublayers: the Common Part (CP) and the Service Specific (SS). Like protocols specified in the OSI Reference model, Protocol Data Units (PDUs) are used to pass information between these layers.

Specifications exist for a few different ATM adaptation layers:

AAL1 (Class A): Used for transporting telephone traffic and uncompressed video traffic. Known as Constant Bit Rate (CBR) service. Uses end-to-end timing and connection oriented. Examples are DS1, E1, nx64 Kbps emulation.

AAL2 (Class B): Does not use the CS and SAR sublayers. Multiplexes short packets from multiple sources into a single cell. Uses a Variable Bit Rate (VBR), end-to-end timing and connection-oriented. Examples are packet, video, and audio.

AAL3/4 (Class C):   Designed for network service providers, uses VBR with no timing required, but still connection-oriented. Examples are Frame Relay and X.25.

AAL5 (Class D):   Used to transfer most non-SMDS data and LAN emulation. Also uses VBR with no timing required. Connectionless service. Examples are IP and SMDS.

ATM networks can provide the transport for several different independent emulated LANs. When a device is attached to one of these emulated LANs, its physical location no longer matters to the administrator or implementation. This process allows you to connect several LANs in different locations with switches to create one large emulated LAN. This can make a big difference, since attached devices can now be moved easily between emulated LANs. Thus, an engineering group can belong to one ELAN and a design group can belong to another ELAN, without ever residing in the same location.

LANE also provides translation between multiple media environments, allowing data sharing. Token Ring or FDDI networks can share data with Ethernet networks as if they were part of the same network.

LANE Components

LANE consists of several components that interact and relate in different ways to provide network connectivity based upon the client-server model. The interaction of these components allows broadcast searching, address registration, and address caching. The LANE model is made up of the following components:

The LAN Emulation Client (LEC):   A LANE client emulates a LAN interface to higher layer protocols and applications. It proxies for users attached into ATM via a non-ATM path.

The LAN Emulation Server (LES):   Address resolution, and registration services to the LANE clients in that emulated LAN. The LES keeps a database of all LANE Servers. It also manages the stations that make up the ELAN.

The LAN Emulation Configuration Server (LECS):   Using a database, keeps track of which emulated LAN a device belongs to (each configuration server can have a different named database).

The Broadcast-and-Unknown Server (BUS):   Used for broadcasting, sequencing, and distributing multicast and broadcast packets. The BUS also handles unicast flooding.

Make careful notice that LEC and LECS are completely different terms and components!

Figure 3.2 illustrates the components of LANE and their relationships, which we will discuss in the following sections. First we'll define all the components before talking about how they work together within LANE.

FIGURE 3.2

LANE components

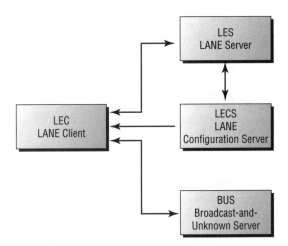

The LAN Emulation Client (LEC)

The LAN Emulation Client, or LEC, provides the emulation of the Link Layer interface that allows the operation and communication of all higher-level protocols and applications to continue. The LEC client runs in all ATM devices, which include hosts, servers, bridges, and routers. The LANE client is responsible for providing:

- Address resolution

- Data transfer

- Address caching

- Interfacing to the emulated LAN

- Driver support for higher-level services

The LEC provides both ATM-attached devices and ATM-capable systems (non-LANE systems such as Token Ring and Ethernet systems, legacy LAN hosts, and so on) the ability to coexist within an ATM emulated LAN environment.

The Address Resolution function provides address registration and resolution services. This function is used for address and route descriptor types based on the LANE specification. The architecture can support resolution for other services. LANE specifications include support for:

- MAC address registration for non-Token Ring LANs.

- MAC address and route descriptor registration for Token Ring LANs.

Each LEC can be a member of only one emulated LAN. You can assign routers to exist within different emulated LANs by using multiple clients for each emulated LAN the router belongs to. The Cisco IOS provides the functionality to route information between multiple emulated LANs.

The Data Transfer function is aptly named. It allows the transport of frames between other LECs and the BUS. If an LEC does not have a corresponding LEC address to send unicast frames to, the frames are forwarded to the BUS for distribution between the remaining LECs.

Address Caching gives each LEC a "Rolodex" of LAN addresses and their respectively assigned ATM addresses for the LANs. The information is contained within a database, with tags pointing to other existing stations using different LECs.

Another function, interfacing to the emulated LAN, requires each LEC to establish connectivity to the LECS and receive the initial configuration services. These services can include receiving the LES ATM address based upon the LANE identifier. Usually the connection to the LECS is broken for continued operation after initial configuration has been received. After receiving the LES address, the LEC then begins communication with the LES. The initial conversation with the LES allows the LEC to join the emulated LAN and to register and resolve MAC addresses. The LEC also establishes communications with the BUS for all broadcast and unicast data.

Finally, the LEC provides driver interface support. This support allows existing higher-level applications and protocols to continue operation on the emulated LAN without change.

The LANE Server (LES)

The LANE Server, or LES, is the central LANE component that provides the initial configuration data for each connecting LEC. The LES typically is located on either an ATM-integrated router or a switch. Responsibilities of the LES include:

- Configuration and support for the LEC

- Address registration for the LEC

- Database storage and response concerning ATM addresses

- Interfacing to the emulated LAN

The LES acts as traffic control for all LECs connecting to the emulated LAN, providing the address resolution, registration, and broadcast and unknown server information that guides communication among LEC. Figure 3.3 shows an example of a typical LANE design.

FIGURE 3.3

LANE components

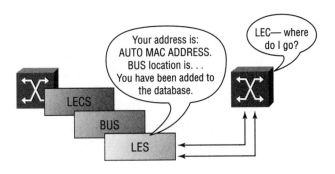

The configuration of each LEC is requested from the LES at connection. This information contains the ATM address the LEC will use, a LAN identifier, and if configured, an optional MAC address. Verification of each LEC also occurs in the initial connection, with the server checking and insuring that each LEC has permission to join the requested emulated LAN.

The LES also handles address registration. The LES maintains a database that gives any addresses needed for resolution. Registration occurs after the LEC joins the emulated LAN. Each LEC is allowed to have one registered address, so you can use the join request and no separate registrations are necessary.

The LES contains the ATM address database that responds for address resolution queries attempting to locate partner LECs. The LES responds in kind with the ATM addresses for the targeted emulated LANs. If no address can be found the request is forwarded on to other LECs on other emulated LANs.

Ultimately, the LES arranges control connections with the LEC. These connections are commonly known as either the *control direct ATM VCC* (virtual channel connection) or the *control distribute ATM VCC*. This connection handles address resolution and registration responses. The LES also establishes communication with the LECS, providing verification for LECs that are joining. The only item with which the LES does not maintain a constant connection is the BUS; instead, it provides each LEC with the ATM address of the BUS for forwarding.

LAN Emulation Configuration Server (LECS)

The LAN Emulation Configuration Server, or LECS, is an important part of emulated LAN services, providing the configuration data that is furnished upon request from the LES. These services include address registration for Integrated Local Management Interface (ILMI) support and configuration support for the LES addresses and their corresponding emulated LAN identifiers. The LECS supplies:

- Registration of LECS ATM address

- Configuration support for the LES

- An interface to the emulated LAN

The registration of an LECS ATM address uses ILMI functions connecting to the ATM network, usually based on a switch. After registration, the network can supply the LEC with the address using ILMI on the return trip. Figure 3.4 shows the relationship of the LECS to the overall design.

FIGURE 3.4

The role of the LECS component

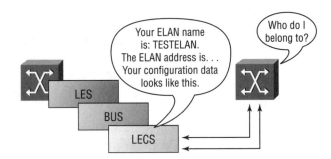

Support for configurations from the LECS ensures that the correct LES address is supplied to the LEC. Configurations can be as simple as providing a single LES address, or more complicated, providing attributes for correlation. These entries include:

- The emulated LAN name and the corresponding ATM address of a LANE server

- The LANE client MAC address and the corresponding emulated LAN name

- The LANE client ATM template and the corresponding emulated LAN name

- The default emulated LAN name

- The LEC address and the LES

- The emulated LAN name and the LES

- The ATM address prefix and the LES

- The emulated LAN type and the LES

The LECS supplies configuration data directly to the LECs. An LEC queries for configuration data and then receives the LES address. The LECS, based upon the attributes received, assigns the correct LES address for each LEC. The LES can also establish a connection with the LECS, verifying each LEC's request to join the LES.

Broadcast and Unknown Server (BUS)

The Broadcast and Unknown Server, or BUS, provides broadcast management support necessary for LANs. The BUS must supply the following services:

- Distribute multicast data to all LECs.

- Distribute unicast data.

- Interface to the emulated LAN.

The BUS must sequence and distribute multicast and broadcast data to all LECs. Broadcasting such data to all LECs can impact the overall performance of the system and network. When you need to place implementing restrictions upon the LANE systems controlling the maximum rate, the BUS will provide support for broadcast traffic. Figure 3.5 shows the BUS and the communication sequence by which it exists in LANE.

FIGURE 3.5

The role of the BUS component

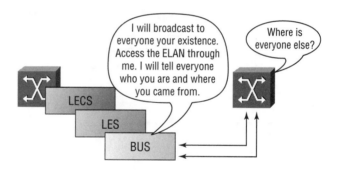

Distribution of unicast data includes the support and transmission of data to the LEC. In most cases, an LEC will be able to establish a direct connection to another LEC. When this isn't possible, the BUS receives the data and must, in turn, broadcast the data to each LEC on the ELAN in search of the correct LEC. Again, you should configure this option carefully so that the expense of network travel is not increased by unicast broadcasts to each LEC.

When interfacing to the emulated LAN, the BUS establishes a bidirectional connection, allowing forwarding of multicast and unknown destination unicast frames.

The Optional Types

Most of what LANE does is defined in detail, to allow interoperability. However, some parts are left open so that vendors can create their own specialized ATM networks. Some of these are:

LE_ARP messages: Used to allow a LEC to indicate that a particular MAC address is local. This is then redistributed to all other LECs, which then update their address caches. Once a client has joined an ELAN and built its LE_ARP cache, it can establish a VCC to the desired destination and transmit packets to that ATM address using a bidirectional point to point data direct VCC.

Intelligent BUS: Tells the LES the MAC addresses it knows about. The BUS then can forward packets received from other LECs directly to the destination LEC across a bidirectional multicast send VCC instead of a point-to-multipoint forward VCC.

Virtual LANs: LANE can be used as the basis for VLAN) service over ATM backbones. This can be accomplished through extension to the LECS and LES. Vendors can use this to overcome the limitation of early bridges and LAN switches.

LEC Communication

We have just reviewed the individual pieces that make up the LANE model; now let's examine the communication process. LANE components communicate by switched virtual circuits (SVCs). There are different types of SVCs: unidirectional, bidirectional, point-to-point, and point-to-multipoint. LANE configurations use virtual channel connections (VCCs), which can also be called virtual circuit connections.

When a client first joints an ELAN, it must build an ATM address to Ethernet MAC address table. These are the steps that occur:

1. The LEC sends an LE_ARP to the LES (a point-to-point VCC).

2. The LES forwards the LE_ARP to all clients on the ELAN (a point-to-multipoint control distribute VCC).

3. Any client that recognizes the MAC address responds.

4. The LES forwards the response (a point-to-multipoint control distribute VCC) to the LEC.

Figure 3.6 shows the path each LEC takes as it establishes a connection with the emulated LAN and another LEC. After a quick look at each step, we'll go into more detail about the internetworking and the mechanics behind what's happening.

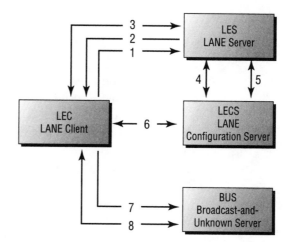

1. A query is made to the ATM switch containing the LECS, using ILMI. The query requests the ATM address of the LES for its emulated LAN. The switch contains an MIB variable containing the requested ATM address. This connection is a bidirectional, point-to-point configure direct VCC. The LEC will attempt to locate the LES using these steps:

A. Use ILMI to connect to LECS.

B. Look for a locally configured ATM address.

C. Receive a fixed address defined by the MIB variable using UNI.

D. Access PVC 0/17, a well-known permanent virtual circuit.

What is inside the query? The LEC fires off a cell with the ATM address of the LECS (locally configured). This wakes the configure direct VCC, sending an LE_CONFIGURE_REQUEST down the pipe. The query is compared to the LECS database, and if a match is found, an LE_CONFIGURE_RESPONSE is returned, providing the ATM address for the local LES server for that emulated LAN.

2. The LECS responds across the established connection, providing the ATM address and name of the LES for the LEC's emulated LAN.

3. The LEC then establishes a connection with the LES based upon the configuration data received in the previous connection. Again, the connection is a bidirectional point-to-point control direct VCC and remains up for the duration of the process. Figure 3.7 illustrates steps 1 through 3.

F I G U R E 3.7

LES-to-LEC communication, steps 1–3

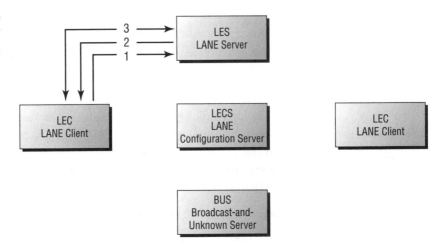

4. While the connection is established with the LEC requesting entry (a configure direct VCC) to the emulated LAN, the LES makes a bidirectional connection to the LECS asking for verification so that the requesting LEC may enter the emulated LAN. The server configuration that was received in the first connection is now verified against the LECS database, determining authenticity and allowing membership. Figure 3.8 shows the difference from step 3 to step 4.

What's going on? The LEC creates another packet—now with the correct ATM address for the LES, again causing the control direct VCC to establish a connection. The LEC fires out an LE_JOIN_REQUEST to the LES containing the LEC ATM address and the MAC address to register with the emulated LAN. The LES makes a quick check with the LECS verifying the LEC. The LES receives the data and creates a new branch for the LEC as well as issuing an LE_JOIN_RESPONSE back to the LEC. This response contains the LANE client identifier (LECID)—a unique identifier for each client. This ID is used to filter return broadcasts from the BUS.

FIGURE 3.8

LES-to-LEC communi-
cation, step 4

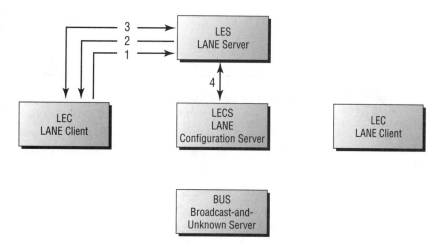

5. The LES replies to the LEC's request (through the existing configure direct VCC) by either allowing or denying membership in the emulated LAN.

6. If the LES allows the connection, the LEC is added to the point-to-multipoint control distribute VCC. Then the LEC is granted a connection using the point-to-point control VCC to the corresponding LEC or service it was searching for originally, and the higher-level protocols take over. If the LES rejects the LEC's request, the session is terminated. Figure 3.9 provides a view of what has occurred in steps 5 and 6.

7. After being given permission by the LES, the LEC must now find the ATM address for the BUS and become a member of the broadcast group.

FIGURE 3.9
LES-to-LEC communi-
cation, steps 5 and 6

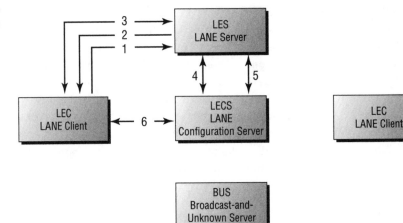

FIGURE 3.9
LES-to-LEC communi-
cation, steps 5 and 6

What is going on? The LEC must locate the BUS, so an LE_ARP_REQUEST
packet containing the MAC address 0xFFFFFFFF is sent. This packet is sent
down the control direct VCC to the LES, which understands the request for
the BUS. The LES then responds with the ATM address for the BUS.

8. Eventually the BUS is located and the LEC becomes a member of the
   emulated LAN. Figure 3.10 shows the final outcome as the emulated
   LAN is joined.

FIGURE 3.10
LES-to-LEC communi-
cation, final outcome

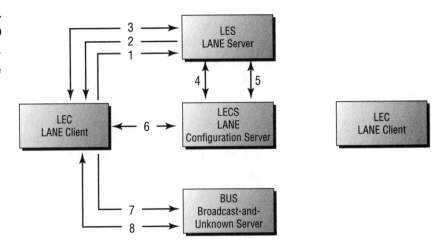

What will you get by going through this whole process? LANE provides an ATM forwarding path for unicast traffic between LECs. This forwarding path enables you to move data across the ATM network to unknown destinations.

Accomplishing this means the LEC issues an LE_ARP_REQUEST to the LES using the control direct VCC. The LES takes the request and forwards it out the control distribute VCC to all the LECs listening. At the same moment, the unicast packets are fired away to the BUS, where they are forwarded out to all endpoints. Remember, this sudden influx of unicast traffic isn't great for the network and will continue passing through until the LE_ARP_REQUEST is answered.

As the ARP request is translated and forwarded along by interfaces belonging to the emulated LAN, hopefully another LEC down the line resolves everything by replying with an LE_ARP_RESPONSE. The response is forwarded back to the LES, and the address is added to the database, relating a new MAC address to an ATM address.

Once it receives the resolution, the LEC immediately does two things. First, it requests a Data Direct VCC that will carry the unicast traffic between the LECs. (Remember, at this moment the BUS is still forwarding unicast traffic at 10 packets per second.) As soon as the Data Direct VCC becomes available, the LEC performs its second duty and generates a flush packet on the Multicast Forward VCC. After passing through the network the flush packet will return to the sending LEC, signaling that the LEC can begin communication with the located LEC. Figure 3.11 summarizes the process, showing how each connection is accomplished and where it is going.

FIGURE 3.11

Complete LES-to-LEC communication

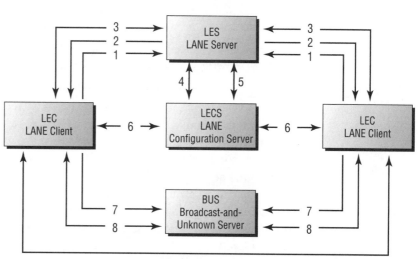

LEC-to-LEC Communication

LANE Implementation

As the following chapters show in detail, LANE can be implemented using many products offered by Cisco. All of the Cisco switches from the 1900 series through the 5000 series can handle implementation. LANE can also be implemented using the Cisco 4000, 4500, 7000, and 7500 routers.

As we have learned, all ATM switches carry out the basic task of cell relay. However, each switch is different in its makeup. They may vary in several ways:

- The collection of interfaces and services offered

- Redundancy

- Application of ATM internetworking software

- Traffic management capabilities

Besides these functional differences, the Cisco products offer a range of performance levels. If you're designing a network implementation or upgrade, you can examine the level of performance and price and quickly determine what product is needed for the job. Cisco has grouped the product lines into four specific network types, providing a level of performance for the needs of both applications and users needs. These levels begin working with the smallest implementations and gradually work up to the largest:

- Workgroup ATM switches

- Campus ATM switches

- Enterprise ATM switches

- Multiservice switches

Workgroup switches are generally the smallest. This series can include the 2820 and the 1900 series switches by Cisco, covered in Chapters 4 and 5. However, the Catalyst 5000 (Chapters 8–10) can be implemented as a workgroup switch. Workgroup switches tend to be Ethernet-oriented and provide an ATM uplink to a campus switch. These are usually located in the closet, close to the desktop user.

Campus ATM switches includes those in the LightStream 1010 family of ATM switches. Campus ATM switches are typically implemented to relieve the network of congestion across the existing backbone by providing new services like VLANs. Campus switches support a wide variety of interfaces,

often having connections to current backbone and WAN. Yet th
a price-to-performance break that makes them suitable for local backᵇᵒᵘ
installations. This type of switch also needs a higher level of management
and congestion control, allowing several switches to be tied together.

Enterprise ATM switches are the next step up from the campus ATM
switch, allowing multilevel campus ATM switches to be tied together in
enterprise installations. They provide the internetworking necessary for the
multiprotocol traffic of an enterprise network to travel. These are not used
as core backbone switches, but instead they act as single points of integration
for the varying technologies found within the enterprise. Cisco's BPX/AXIS
is designed to meet the needs of high-traffic enterprises or even public service
providers.

Multiservice Access Switches are there to provide a multitude of services
for the growing needs of blossoming networks. They can provide the services
to support the MAN, the WAN, and the campus.

Summary

This chapter has closely examined ATM LANE implementation. We
have poked around inside the ATM network to try and figure out exactly
what is going on and when. This has given you a fundamental understanding
of how ATM works. So let's review the objectives of the chapter, and see
what we learned:

- Defining LAN Emulation. We learned that as specified by the ATM
  Forum, three services must be emulated:

  - Connectionless services

  - Multicast services

  - LAN media access control driver services

- Describing the LAN Emulation components. We looked at the separate components that make up an emulated LAN. These components
  include the LEC, the LES, the LECS, and the BUS.

- The start-up procedure of a LAN Emulation Client entails the LEC
  establishing communication with the LES and the BUS.

- A LAN Emulation Client establishes communication with another LEC
  by requesting the location of another LEC to establish a direct VCC.

Review Questions

1. What is the primary function of the LAN Emulation Server (LES)?

    A. To provide the IP address for the ELAN the LEC is attempting to connect to

    B. To provide the initial configuration data for each connecting LEC

    C. To function as the director of all LEC functionality

    D. To configure all the emulated LANs on the network

2. What is the primary function of the BUS?

    A. To distribute multicast data to all LECs

    B. To distribute unicast data

    C. To interface to the emulated LAN

    D. All of the above

    E. None of the above

3. What is the primary function of the LAN Emulation Server (LES)?

    A. To supports configuration for the LES addresses and their corresponding LANE identifiers

    B. To provide address registration for the LECs

    C. To configures all the emulated LANs on the network

    D. To support the driver interface for high-level applications

4. What type of request is sent by the LEC to the BUS?

    A. uses ILMI

    B. LE_CONFIGURE_REQUEST

    C. LE_ARP_REQUEST

    D. LE_JOIN_REQUEST

5. What is the well-known PVC that the LEC uses for connections?

   A. PVC 0/18

   B. PVC 0/71

   C. PVC 0/16

   D. PVC 0/17

6. What type of connection is set up between the LEC and the LES?

   A. Bidirectional connection

   B. Point-to-point connection

   C. Bidirectional multipoint-to-point connection

   D. Broadcast connectionless

7. Which two statements are true regarding LAN emulation components?

   A. The BUS is responsible for handling both broadcasts and multicasts.

   B. The BUS registers and resolves all MAC address to ATM addresses using the LANE address resolution protocol.

   C. When a device on the ELAN has data to send to another device on the ELAN, the sender requests the ATM address of the destination from the BUS.

   D. The LES manages the stations that make up the ELAN.

8. What type of transport does ATM use?

   A. Cell

   B. Token

   C. Packet

   D. A combination of tokens and packets

9. Once an LEC has established the ATM address of another LEC (via the LES) using an LE_ARP, what type of VCC is used to contact the LEC?

  A. Point-to-multipoint control distribute VCC

  B. Point-to-point control direct VCC

  C. Point-to-point data direct VCC

  D. Multicast forward VCC

10. What media types can utilize ATM LANE?

  A. Token Ring

  B. Ethernet

  C. ATM

  D. All of the above

  E. None of the above

11. Which two of the following are not functions of the LEC?

  A. Control

  B. Data forwarding

  C. Address resolution

  D. ELAN assignment

12. How many bytes long is an ATM cell?

  A. 45

  B. 48

  C. 52

  D. 53

  E. 64

13. At what layer of the OSI model is ATM defined?

    A. Layers 2 and 3

    B. Layers 3 and 4

    C. Layers 4 and 5

    D. The Data Link Layer

    E. Layers 1 and 2

14. What is a VCI?

    A. Virtual Circuit Identifier

    B. Virtual Channel Identifier

    C. Virtual Connection Integration

    D. Both A and B

    E. Both A and C

15. What is the ATM layer accountable for?

    A. Multiplexing and demultiplexing ATM cells from different virtual connections

    B. Cell delineation

    C. Transmission frame generation and recovery

    D. Header error control

16. How many LANEs can a single LEC belong to?

    A. Any amount configured

    B. 5

    C. 1

    D. None

    E. 10

17. How does the LEC query the LECS?

   A. It sends an `LE_CONFIGURE_REQUEST` to the LES.

   B. It sends an `LE_CONFIGURE_REQUEST` to the LECS.

   C. It sends an `LE_CONFIGURE_RESPONSE` to the BUS.

   D. It sends an `LE_ARP_REQUEST` to the LES.

18. What does the address 0xFFFFFFFF do?

   A. It is a request for the location of the BUS from the LEC.

   B. It is the broadcast address.

   C. Both A and B

   D. None of the above

19. What does the LEC do when it has resolution of another LEC?

   A. Request another address for the BUS

   B. Request a data direct VCC

   C. Flushes the multicast forward VCC

   D. Both B and C

   E. Both A and B

20. What routers in the Cisco series can implement LANE?

   A. Cisco 2500, 2510 and 2511

   B. Cisco 5000 and 5500

   C. Cisco 4000 and 4500

   D. Cisco 8000 and 8001

21. What performs MAC-to-ATM address resolution?

   A. LECS

   B. LES

   C. BUS

   D. LEC

22. How are transmissions to unknown stations performed?

   A. LECS

   B. LES

   C. BUS

   D. LEC

23. When a client first joins an ELAN, it must build a table mapping ATM addresses to Ethernet MAC addresses. In which order do the following steps occur?

   A. The LEC sends an LE_ARP to LES (a point-to-point VCC).

   B. The LES forwards the response (a point-to-multipoint control distribute VCC) to the LEC.

   C. The LES forwards the LE_ARP to all clients on the ELAN (a point-to-multipoint control distribute VCC).

   D. Any client that recognizes the MAC address responds.

CHAPTER

4

Cisco Catalyst 1900
and 2820 Switches

Cisco has not *engineered* its various switches as much as it has *acquired* those switches. Cisco started by purchasing Crescendo and Kalpana, who started Ethernet switching. For ATM switches, Cisco bought LightStream, and then Grand Junction for Fast Ethernet and Granite Systems for Gigabit Ethernet. Noshoba Networks is where Cisco acquired its Token Ring switches, and it went to Stratacom for WAN switches and carrier-class ATM switches.

Cisco is slowly but surely moving all equipment to the Cisco IOS, but VLANs are not having much luck in the interoperability arena. Cisco created CiscoFusion architecture to add integration of the switches, ATM, and routing.

We will begin our examination of Cisco switching technology by reviewing Cisco's 1900 and 2820 series of workgroup switches. This chapter will include a review of each switch's hardware, architecture, and IOS (Internetwork Operating System) features.

This chapter covers the following CLSC test objectives:

- Describe the major features and benefits of the Catalyst 1900 and Catalyst 2820 switches.

- Describe the architecture and functions of the major components of the Catalyst switches.

- Describe the hardware components and functions of the Catalyst 1900 and Catalyst 2820 switches.

- Describe the architecture and operation of the Catalyst 1900 and Catalyst 2820 switches.

- Describe the following key features and applications of the Catalyst 1900 and 2820 switches:

  - Switching modes

  - Virtual LANs

  - Multicast packet filtering and registration

  - Broadcast storm control

  - Management support, CDP, and CGMP

- Trace a frame's progress through a Catalyst 1900 or Catalyst 2820 switch.

Hardware

The Catalyst 1900 and Catalyst 2820 are the base for Cisco's line of high-performance switches. They are designed to allow an easy transition from the traditional LAN to the new switched networks and are an important part of CiscoFusion, Cisco's solution for internetworking. They also provide a new degree of adaptability as well as providing a solution that won't break your budget when introducing switches to your LAN.

The Cisco line of switches includes the 1900, 2820, 3000, and 5000 series switches. Figure 4.1 shows the relative cost/flexibility breakdown of each switch.

F I G U R E   4.1

The Catalyst switch family

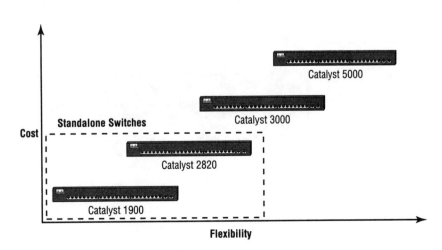

The 1900 and 2820 are the low-cost members of the Cisco switching family.

You need to remember that Cisco has updated their switches, but the CLSC course and exam only cover the 1900, 2820, 3000, and 5000 series switches.

Catalyst 1900

The Catalyst 1900 is available in two models—Catalyst 1912 and Catalyst 1924. Each model will function for small workgroups.

The Catalyst 1912 has twelve 10BaseT ports and one 15-pin AUI (Attachment Unit Interface). This AUI accepts a transceiver connection to either thick coaxial, thin coaxial, 10BaseT, or fiber-optic media, and it offers the option of either a 2-port 100BaseTX or one 100BaseTX port and one 100BaseFX port. There are no modular slots available. The switch can be configured with up to four overlapping bridge groups or 1024 ISL VLANs. The Catalyst 1912 comes with 1MB of flash memory and 2MB of DRAM.

The Catalyst 1924 has 24 10BaseT ports and one 15-pin AUI (Attachment Unit Interface). This AUI accepts a transceiver connection to either thick coaxial, thin coaxial, or fiber-optic media, and it offers the option of either a 2-port 100BaseTX or one 100BaseTX port and one 100BaseFX port. There are no modular slots available. The switch can be configured with up to four overlapping bridge groups or 1024 ISL VLANs. The Catalyst 1924 comes with 1MB of flash memory and 2MB of DRAM.

Figure 4.2 shows the front view of the Catalyst 1924.

FIGURE 4.2

Front view of the Catalyst 1924 switch

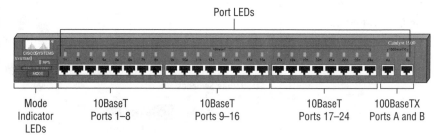

Each switch uses Cisco's 1 Gbps ClearChannel architecture. This allows the Catalyst 1900 series to have a packet-forwarding rate of 440 Mbps. The switches have a low latency switching time of 70 microseconds between the 10BaseT ports and 11 microseconds between the 100BaseT ports. Each switch supports multiple MAC addresses. The Catalyst 1924 cache supports 1024 addresses shared among all 27 ports.

The Catalyst 1900 series supports Cisco Visual Switch Manager. This product allows Web-based interfacing with the switch, providing ease of installation, administration, and management. The product also is supported by CiscoWorks. The switch can be managed in-band by either SNMP or Telnet, including a menu-driven, out-of-band management console. The switch also supports CGMP (Cisco Group Management Protocol).

The front panel of a Catalyst 1900 series switch has several LEDs that provide information about the general operating environment of the switch:

- The System LED shows you the status of the switch. If the switch is operating normally, the LED will be a bright green. If the switch has failed POST (power-on self-test), the LED color will be amber. If the LED is not lit, the switch is not powered on.

- The Redundant Power Supply (RPS) LED shows the operating status of the redundant power supply. If the LED is green, then the switch is using the RPS, and the local power supply is not operating. If the RPS LED is blinking green, this tells you that the RPS is operating, and the local power supply is plugged in. If the LED is amber, then the RPS is installed but is not operational. If the LED is not lit, the RPS is not installed.

- The Port LEDs indicate one of three modes. These LEDs will show you the Port Status (STAT), Bandwidth Utilization (UTL), or Full-Duplex Status (FDUP). To select one of the mode choices, press the MODE button until the desired LED is lit. The individual port LEDs will indicate a port's connection status.

- The Port Status Mode is lit green when a device is attached to the device. The LED will blink green when traffic is being transmitted and received. The LED will flash green-amber when a link-fault occurs. The LED will not be lit if there is no link present. Keep in mind that the default startup mode for the switch is Port Status.

- The Catalyst 1900 series also has a full-duplex mode, and the Full-Duplex Status (FDUP) Mode LED will show you when the device is being used in this mode. If the LED is not lit, the device is not using full-duplex mode.

- The Utilization Mode LED allows you to find the present and peak utilization of the switch. Peak utilization is captured during the current bandwidth interval. The bandwidth is displayed through a series of lit green LEDs and one rapidly blinking LED. The rightmost LED indicates the peak utilization during that period. Table 4.1 provides an estimate for the utilization determined by reading the LEDs.

T A B L E 4.1 Port and Bandwidth Utilization of 24-Port Catalyst 1900 and 2820 Switches	Port Status LEDs	Mbps Activity
	1 to 8 LEDs	0.1 to < 6
	9 to 16 LEDs	6 to < 120
	17 to 24 LEDs	Above 120

The rear of the Catalyst 1900 series has a fan opening, an EIA/TIA-232 port, a Reset button, a connection for a redundant power supply, and the AUI port.

The EIA/TIA-232 port or RS-232 port allows you to connect a modem or terminal to the back of the switch. Both the Catalyst 1900 and 2820 series are shipped with null modem cables, allowing a computer using a terminal program to access the switch. You can access the management console by using either a Telnet session or an ASCII terminal or by using an SNMP-compatible management station.

The Reset button is recessed in the back of the switch. You can use a paper clip or pen to push the button. The switch should only be reset when network communication has been broken or management is unable to control the switch. The reset is similar to powering your switch off and then on again.

Catalyst 2820

The Catalyst 2820 supports up to 25 10Mbps switch ports and has one AUI on the back panel to allow a 10Mbps connection to a thinnet, thicknet, or

10BaseT network. The 2820 replaces the earlier 2800 switch. The Catalyst 2820 series also offers the convenience of adding modules. Figure 4.3 shows a 2820 with two optional modules: the FDDI fiber DAS and eight-port 100BaseTX shared modules.

Eight-port 100BaseTX module

F I G U R E   4.3

Catalyst 2820 with two optional modules

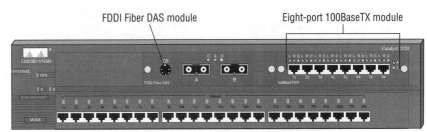

These modules can include:

- one-port 100BaseTX
- eight-port 100BaseTX (shared)
- one-port 100BaseFX
- four-port 100BaseFX (shared)
- FDDI fiber DAS
- FDDI fiber SAS
- FDDI UTP SAS (CDDI)
- ATM UTP
- ATM MMF
- ATM 155 single-mode medium-reach fiber
- ATM 155 single-mode long-reach fiber

The Catalyst 2820 comes with 1MB of flash memory and 2MB of DRAM. The 2820 series of switches come in two varieties: 2822 and 2828.

2822: 24 10BaseT ports, one AUI, two high-speed expansion slots. It can handle up to 2048 MAC addresses in its cache and can be configured with up to four overlapping bridge groups or 1024 ISL VLANs.

2828: 24 10BaseT ports, one AUI, two high-speed expansion module slots. It can handle up to 8192 MAC addresses in its cache and can be configured with up to four overlapping bridge groups or 1024 ISL VLANs.

The only difference is the size of the cache, which is not upgradable.

The 2820 switch supports an RPS (redundant power supply) and CDP (Cisco Discovery Protocol) as well as IEEE 802.1d Spanning Tree Protocol.

The Catalyst 2820 series also has an Expansion Slot Status LED, which indicates whether a module inserted in the chassis is operational. The LED will flash green when the module is progressing through POST; it will be lit amber if the module does not complete its POST correctly. The LED will not be lit if there is no module present or power is not present.

The modules available for the 2820 switch series include four 100BaseT configurations, three FDDI configurations, and two ATM modules. We will begin by looking at the options available with 100BaseT.

The 100BaseTX Modules

The 100BaseTX modules are compatible with the IEEE 802.3u standard. These modules accept RJ-45 connections and use Category 5 UTP cabling. The modules available with 100BaseTX configurations include:

100BaseTX/1: This module contains one switched 100BaseTX port. It is capable of full-duplex operation.

100baseTX/8: This module contains eight shared 100BaseTX ports. These are repeater ports and are not capable of full-duplex operation.

Figure 4.4 shows the 100BaseTX/8 module. As you can see, it has diagnostic LEDs that allow you to determine if there are any problems with the network. The LEDs determine Link Integrity, Network Activity, or Receive and Disabled. The single-port modules include a Full-Duplex LED.

FIGURE 4.4

The Catalyst 2820 series 100BaseTX/8 module

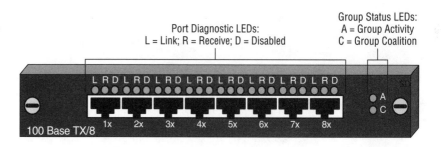

- The Link LED is used to determine whether a port is active. The LED will be lit if the switch port has passed the integrity test. If the LED is not lit, the port has failed. If the LED is blinking on and off, the port has been receiving improperly formed packets.

- The Activity LED is only available on switched modules: the 100BaseTX/1 and 100BaseFX/1. The Activity LED will be lit when the port is either transmitting or receiving data. If there is high activity on the network, the LED will be continuously lit. The LED will not be lit if there is no activity.

- The Receive LED is only available on shared modules: the 100BaseTX/8 and 100BaseFX/4. The Receive LED will be lit when the port is either transmitting or receiving data. If there is high activity on the network, the LED will be continuously lit. If there is no traffic present, the LED will not be lit.

- The Disabled LED will be lit when the port has been disabled by some action: manually through the Management console; by a network connection error; or by a secure address violation. If either a jabber error or an auto-partition error has disabled the port, the LED will blink.

- The Full-Duplex LED, which can be found only on the switched 100BaseT modules, will be lit only when the port has been configured and is operating in full-duplex mode. If the LED is not lit, the port is operating at half-duplex.

- The Group Status LEDs, which can be found only on the shared 100BaseT modules, show port activity and group collisions. If the Group Activity LED is lit, traffic is either being transmitted or received. If there is a high rate of activity, the LED will remain lit. The Group Collision LED indicates whether a packet collision has occurred. If the LED is not lit, there are no collisions.

The 100BaseFX Modules

The 100BaseFX modules are compatible with the IEEE 802.3u standard. These modules accept ST connections and use 50/125-micron or 62.5/125-micron multimode fiber cabling. Figure 4.5 shows the two modules available with 100BaseFX configurations:

100baseFX/4: This module contains four shared 100BaseFX ports. These ports are repeater ports and not capable of full duplex operation.

100BaseFX/1: This module contains one switched 100BaseFX port and is capable of full-duplex operation.

FIGURE 4.5

Catalyst 2820 series
100BaseFX4 and FX1
modules

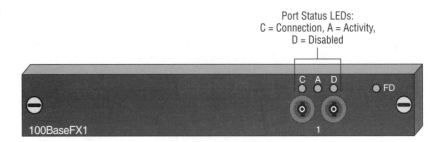

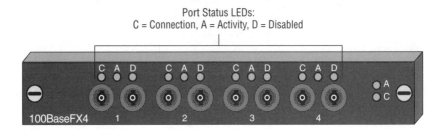

The FDDI Modules

There are three FDDI modules. They all support automatic packet recognition/translation (ApaRT), maximum transmit unit (MTU) path discovery, and IP fragmentation. These modules also are capable of detecting the proper Ethernet and FDDI format for the media. Figure 4.6 shows front views of the following modules:

Fiber DAS Module: This module provides a dual attachment station (DAS), which is compatible with the ANSI X3T12 standard. The module has two MIC connectors and accepts either 50/125 or 62.5/125-micro multimode fiber. The module also has a six-pin mini-DIN connector to connect to an optical bypass switch.

Fiber SAS Module: This module contains one MIC connection which accepts either 50/125 or 62.5/125-micro multimode fiber.

UTP SAS Module: This module has one RJ-45 connector that accepts two-pair Category 5 cabling.

The FDDI modules (Figure 4.6) have diagnostic LEDs that allow you to determine if there are any problems with the network. The LEDs are labeled Connection, Activity, and Disabled.

F I G U R E   4.6

Catalyst 2820 series
SAS and DAS FDDI
modules

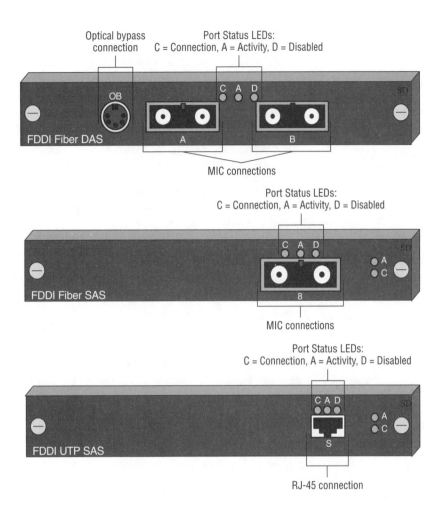

- The Connection LED shows you whether the port is properly connected to an active FDDI ring. This LED will be lit if the connection is operating.

- The Activity LED verifies by blinking if the port is transmitting or receiving data. Rapid blinking of the LED indicates a higher level of traffic activity. If the LED is not lit, there is no activity on the FDDI ring.

- The Disabled LED indicates whether the management console or a secure address violation has disabled the port.

The ATM Modules

The ATM modules include either the ATM 155 multimode fiber (MMF) module with one SC connector or the ATM 155 UTP with one RJ-45 connector. These modules provide an interface between the ATM module and an ATM switch and allow the connection of ATM-capable switches, hubs, or workstations. The ATM modules also allow connections with other ATM switches (Cisco LightStream 1010), any of the Catalyst 5000 series, or a router with an ATM interface such as the Cisco 7000 series router. The two ATM modules that are available for the Catalyst 2820 series are:

ATM 155 MMF: This module contains one SC connector port. It is capable of full-duplex operation with a transfer rate of 155.52Mbps.

ATM 155 UTP: This module contains one RJ-45 connector. It is capable of full-duplex operation with a transfer rate of 155.52Mbps.

The ATM modules also have a diagnostic LED that allows you to determine if there are any problems with the network. Its status can be either Connection, Activity, or Disabled.

The single LED will be lit solid green if there is a present connection to an operational ATM switch. The LED will then blink green as data is transmitted and received. If the LED is amber, the module is disabled. Disabling can result from an address violation or a POST failure, or the module can be disabled manually from the management console. If the LED is not lit, the module is not connected to an operating ATM network or device.

The ATM modules use store-and-forward packet relay, a LAN Emulation Client for emulated LANs, and ATM Adaptation Layer 5 for LAN emulation data transfer.

These ATM modules can be installed while the Catalyst 2820 is powered up without affecting network operation. They can be inserted into the high-speed expansion slots without tools. The switch will automatically diagnose and configure the module to the specific network as well as verify the general health of the module.

Architecture

In this section we'll examine the internals of the Catalyst 1900 and 2820 switches. This will include a look at how a frame enters the packet exchange bus and is moved through the architecture to come out another port.

ClearChannel Architecture

Cisco's ClearChannel architecture, the heart of the Catalyst 1900 and 2820 series switches, consists of the packet exchange bus (X-bus), the forwarding engine, the embedded control unit (ECU), the management interface, and the shared buffer memory and switched ports. Figure 4.7 shows a simplified model of ClearChannel architecture.

FIGURE 4.7

ClearChannel architecture

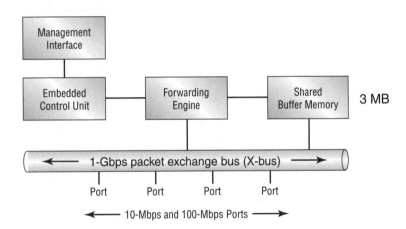

As noted earlier in this chapter, the switch uses a shared memory buffer with a 3MB capacity and a 1Gbps-packet exchange bus.

Data enters the bus based on a priority system. Transaction priority and time of arrival determine the priority. A transaction priority is determined by a combination of time of arrival, transaction priority, and port priority. Types of transactions include buffer memory requests, a packet transmission termination, etc. Port priority is based on the port origination of the packet, port 1 being the lowest and port 27 (a 100BaseT port) the highest.

ClearChannel architecture provides you with 27 switched ports using less than half (450Mbps) of the 1Gbps bandwidth.

The Forwarding Engine

Figure 4.8 shows how Cisco implements the Forwarding Engine on an ASIC, providing you with lower latency and higher throughput. The implementation of the Forwarding Engine supplies the logic necessary for packet examination, allocation of packet buffers, determining destination addresses, and statistical collection. Statistics collected include packet lengths, throughput, errors, and exceptions that can be relayed to management stations located on the network for review.

FIGURE 4.8

The forwarding engine

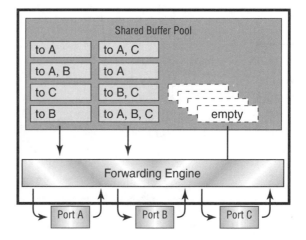

The Forwarding Engine determines whether a packet needs to be forwarded upon arrival at the bus. If the packet must be forwarded, the forwarding engine pauses and receives the bytes associated with the configured switching mode (fast forward, fragment free, or store-and-forward), then the packet is correctly forwarded to the outgoing port.

Catalyst 2820 and 1900 switches use a shared buffer implementation. Most switches have port buffers that cause head-of-line blocking of packets.

The Embedded Control Unit (ECU) is a separate subsystem that handles the components of network management. The ECU subsystem provides diagnostics, error handling, switch configuration, in-band and out-of-band management, and statistics reporting. This clear separation frees the Forwarding Engine to use its full processing power for packet forwarding, leaving the ECU to process its own operations.

The ECU consists of an embedded CPU, 512KB of DRAM, and 1MB of flash memory for firmware, configuration data, and statistics. The flash is divided into three areas: the software image (768KB), switch configuration data (192KB), and the boot sector (32KB). The ECU also contains an embedded RMON software agent that provides you with enhanced management information.

WARNING

Remember that the boot sector is write protected. If this weren't the case, the switch could crash and not be recovered. There is a diagnostic console available in the boot sector that will help you diagnose problems during a failed flash upgrade.

The shared memory buffer is made up of 3MB of DRAM. The DRAM supports 2048 packet buffers by establishing guidelines for how large each packet buffer may be. This methodology allows the switch to eliminate the problem of Head of Line blocking, a common underutilization problem associated with switches. In order to maintain control over a port's utilization of the shared buffer, a median has been established allowing no port to control more than 1.5MB of the packet buffer memory. This means that no more than half of the available memory can be controlled by any one port.

Features

In this section we'll review the package of features available with Catalyst 1900 and 2820 switches. We'll look at the best switching methodologies available for optimum packet switching. We'll also discuss VLAN implementation, multicast address filtering and registration, and broadcast storm control.

Finally, we'll address the methods you can use to manage Catalyst switches, briefly touching on CGMP and CDP—proprietary protocols used by Cisco for network management.

This section does not discuss the management interface for configuring these features. Installation and configuration of the 1900 and 2820 switches are the subjects of Chapter 5.

Switching Modes

The Catalyst 2820 and 1900 series switches support three types of switching methods: FastForward, FragmentFree, and Store-and-Forward.

FastForward (cut-through): This method provides the least amount of latency by immediately forwarding the packet after reading the destination address of the packet. Problems can arise with this type of switching because the packet is not checked for errors, which means that packets with errors are sent. Latency is measured in FastForward by timing first in, first out (FIFO). Fast Forward is typically used on ports connected to single nodes.

FragmentFree (modified cut-through): This method removes some of the problems associated with FastForward switching by eliminating collision fragments. Essentially, this method waits until the switch has determined that the frame is not fragmented before forwarding the frame, so you might want to try this method if your network is experiencing a significant number of collision fragments. Again, latency is measured by FIFO.

Store-and-Forward: This method stores the entire frame before forwarding it on to another port. Typically used for forwarding between 10Mbps and 100Mbps segments, this switching configuration is suggested for networks experiencing FCS or alignment errors. The switch controls unwanted errors, providing the most error-free methodology. Latency is measured by last-bit received to first-bit transmitted (LIFO).

The method of switching you choose is applied to the entire switch. Configuration of a specific methodology is accomplished from the System Configuration menu, as explained in Chapter 5.

VLANs

In Chapter 3 we discussed what a VLAN is, and we touched briefly on the theory used behind the configuration of a VLAN.

The Catalyst 2820 and 1900 series switches each support up to four separate VLANs. This allows you to configure four separate broadcast domains for devices plugged into ports on the switch. You'll gain two benefits from implementing VLANs between broadcast domains: it allows the control of multicast flooding within a VLAN, and traffic does not cross over to other VLANs. It is necessary to have a router present to route traffic between domains when moving between VLANs.

Each VLAN has its own bridge MIB information and can support its own implementation of the Spanning Tree Protocol (STP).

Multicast Address Filtering and Registration

Multicast Address Filtering allows the Catalyst switches to handle both IP multicasts and MAC address multicast protocols. You can combine the filtering with source port filtering to balance the server load across servers. Source port filtering is the method of filtering traffic based on the destination of the packet and the source port.

Multicast Address Registration allows you to specify which multicast addresses and their ports are allowed to receive forwarded packets. Beware, the default configuration has the switch forwarding all multicast or broadcast packets to all ports, which will flood your network. Use the switch management to specify which ports will handle which multicast traffic and disable flooding of multicasts across the network.

Broadcast Storm Control

Cisco also has included broadcast storm control. Cisco's IOS allows you to control deployment between routers and switches, thus restricting packets' transmissions to specified ports. Communication with routers is established using Cisco Group Management Protocol (CGMP).

The Catalyst 2820 and 1900 switches have a management option that allows you to set a threshold that controls the number of broadcast packets which can be received from a port before forwarding is disabled at that port. Another management option allows you to configure a packets-per-second (pps) threshold that enables the port once again to forward packets. Broadcast storm control is disabled in the initial startup of the switch; Chapter 5 shows how to enable this feature.

It is important to know that the switch does not eliminate broadcasts; it only prevents a broadcast storm from being forwarded across all ports.

Management

In this section we'll review some of the management options possible once you've deployed one of the switches. Cisco has developed both in-band and out-of-band management capabilities into all of its switches. Besides providing management tools, Cisco has allowed for statistics collection by including an RMON MIB. An implementation of RMON called SPAN allows you to place a traffic analyzer on the switch to monitor traffic across the backplane.

SNMP Management

Any SNMP or SMT-based management platform can help you manage the Catalyst 1900 and 2820 switches. You can access the menu by connecting a console or modem to the RS-232 port on the rear of the switch. If the switch has been configured with an IP address, then you can manage it with a Telnet session. Up to seven sessions can be held simultaneously. A built-in RMON MIB allows a platform that communicates via SNMP to monitor nine groups of information pertaining to the switch's operation.

CDP

Cisco Discovery Protocol (CDP) is a protocol developed and used by Cisco devices to exchange information between themselves and other devices on the network. Cisco IOS employs its CDP to form a "picture" of the surrounding network.

CDP gathers information from other devices concerning their types, configuration information, as well as the amount of interfaces and their activity within each device. The CDP packet is sent in a Sub-Network Access Protocol (SNAP) frame and is not routable. In other words, no logical Layer 3 information is contained in the header. CDP packets are broadcasted every 60 seconds by default out all active interfaces.

CGMP

Cisco Group Management Protocol provides a methodology for intelligent routing software that limits multicast flooding to only specific ports interested in receiving the traffic. CGMP is a Layer 3 enhancement that bridges the gap between Cisco's switches and the routers' IOS.

Summary

In this chapter we reviewed Catalyst 1900 and 2820 hardware, architecture, and the features that are inherent to the Cisco IOS (Internetwork Operating System) that each switch is using.

The following features, architecture, and hardware were covered in detail:

- We described the major features of the Catalyst switches, the different models, and the port density and memory requirements of each switch.

- We talked about the architecture and functions of the 1900 and 2820 series of Catalyst switches.

- We discussed the hardware components and their functions of the Catalyst 1900 and Catalyst 2820 switches.

- We described the ClearChannel architecture and Forwarding Engine of the Catalyst 1900 and Catalyst 2820 switches.

- We finished by describing switching modes, virtual LANs, multicast packet filtering and registration, broadcast storm control, CDP, and the CGMP of the Catalyst 1900 and 2820 switches.

Review Questions

1. How many switched 10BaseT Ethernet ports does the Catalyst 1912 switch support?

   A. 15 ports

   B. 16 ports

   C. 12 ports

   D. 24 ports

2. How many VLANs can the Catalyst 2820 support?

   A. 4 VLANs

   B. 8 VLANs

   C. 2 VLANs

   D. 16 VLANs

3. The Catalyst 2820 cache supports how many MAC addresses?

   A. 1024 addresses

   B. 2048 addresses

   C. 4096 addresses

   D. 8192 addresses

4. The Cisco Catalyst 1900 and 2820 switches support which three LAN switch types?

   A. FastForward

   B. FastSwitching

   C. FragmentFree

   D. Store-and-Forward

5. Which LAN switching methodology runs a CRC?

    A. Store-and-Forward

    B. FastForward

    C. First-In First-Out

    D. LIFO

6. What is the default switching method configured on startup for the Catalyst 1900?

    A. Store-and-Forward

    B. Modified Cut Through

    C. FastForward

    D. FragmentFree

7. How many 100BaseT optional modules does the Catalyst 2820 support?

    A. 2

    B. 8

    C. 6

    D. 4

8. What ATM adaptation layer does the Catalyst 2820 support?

    A. AAL 7

    B. AAL 6

    C. AAL 5

    D. AAL 3

9. What does STP stand for?

   A. Spanning Tree Process

   B. SToP processing

   C. Standard Tree Protocol

   D. Spanning Tree Protocol

10. How does the Catalyst 2820 handle Broadcast Storm Control? (Choose all that apply.)

   A. Menu Configuration

   B. Port Closure

   C. Threshold setting

   D. Spanning Tree Protocol

11. What type of AUI port is located on the rear of the Catalyst 1900 and 2820 switches?

   A. RS 231

   B. 15-pin AUI

   C. RS 235

   D. SCSI connector

12. What does the forwarding engine do? (Choose all that apply.)

   A. Examines packets

   B. Maintains switch statistics

   C. Controls STP

   D. Diagnostics and error handling

13. What does the ECU do? (Choose all that apply.)

   A. Examines packets

   B. Maintains switch statistics

   C. Controls STP

   D. Diagnostics and error handling

14. What does a blinking Link LED on a Catalyst 2820 port indicate?

   A. Activity is present on the port

   B. Improperly configured port

   C. Improperly formed packet

   D. Port is receiving traffic

15. What switching methodology is best suited for FCS errors?

   A. Store-and-Forward

   B. Modified Cut Through

   C. FastForward

   D. FragmentFree

16. Does the switch default to controlling broadcast storms?

   A. Yes

   B. No

   C. Only if the environment is Token Ring

   D. Only if a 100BaseT connection is present

17. How fast does ATM offer data transfer?

   A. 125.53 Mbps

   B. 152.55 Mbps

   C. 155.52 Mbps

   D. 412.04 Mbps

18. What type/types of Multicast protocols can the Catalyst switches support?

   A. IP Multicast

   B. ICMP

   C. CNP

   D. MAC address-based

19. What type of modules is the Receive LED available on?

   A. Shared modules

   B. 100BaseTX/8

   C. 100BaseTX/1

   D. 100BaseFX/4

20. The shared memory buffer consists of how much DRAM on a Cisco Catalyst 1900 or 2820 switch?

   A. 12MB

   B. 128MB

   C. 64MB

   D. 3MB

CHAPTER

5

Installing and Configuring the Cisco
Catalyst 1900 and 2820 Switches

his chapter will review the proper guidelines for installing and configuring a Catalyst 1900 or 2820 switch. For each switch we'll present a sample configuration exercise and review the menu steps necessary for configuring the switches in multiple type environments.

This chapter covers the following test objectives:

- Describe the POST and diagnostic messages on the Catalyst 1900 and Catalyst 2820 switches.

- Describe the cabling guidelines for the Catalyst 1900 and Catalyst 2820 switches.

- Describe the firmware upgrade procedures for the Catalyst 1900 and Catalyst 2820 switches.

- Use the command-line or menu-driven interface to configure trunks, virtual LANs, and ATM LAN Emulation.

- Use the Catalyst 1900 and Catalyst 2820 switch menus for configuration.

- Configure IP addresses and ports on the Catalyst 1900 and the Catalyst 2820 switches.

- Configure VLANs on the Catalyst 1900 and Catalyst 2820 switches.

- View the Catalyst 1900 and Catalyst 2820 switch reports and summaries.

- Use the statistics and reports to maintain the Catalyst 1900 and 2820 switches.

- Configure the ATM LANE module on the Catalyst 2820 switch.

- Place the Catalyst series switches in a network for optimal performace benefit.

Pre-Installation Checklist

The first thing to do in preparing for the installation of the switch is to review the placement of the switch. The placement of the switch must take into account several factors:

1. Insure that the cable lengths from the switch to other network equipment are within the guidelines established for Ethernet:

Ethernet Cabling Type	Maximum Number of Nodes per Segment	Maximum Distance per Segment
10Base2	30	185 m
10Base5	100	500 m
10BaseT	1024	100 m
10Base-FL	2	2000 m

2. In deciding where to place switches you must also consider the physical environment. Is the table/room/closet too hot? Too cold? What is the humidity? Is altitude a factor? Here are the environmental operating ranges of the Catalyst 1900 and 2820:

Operating Temperature	23° to 113°F (−5 to 45°C)
Storage Temperature	−13° to 158°F (−25 to 70°C)
Operating Humidity	10 to 85% (noncondensing)
Operating Altitude	Up to 9842 ft. (3000 m)

3. Insure that there is ample clearance around the switch so that air may flow freely. Check to make sure that there will be nothing to block viewing of the front LEDs or hamper air from being pulled into the switch from the rear. The physical dimensions of each switch are shown below:

Catalyst 1900

Weight	7 lbs. (3.2 kg)
Dimensions (H × W × D)	1.73 × 17.5 × 8.25 in. (4.4 × 44.5 × 21 cm)

Catalyst 2820

Weight (no modules)	13 lbs. (5.9 kg)
Dimensions (H × W × D)	3.5 × 17.5 × 12 in. (8.9 × 44.5 × 30.5 cm)

4. Check to make sure that there will be ample power for the switch. Here are the guidelines provided by Cisco:

AC Input Voltage	100 to 127/200 to 240 VAC (auto-ranging) 50 to 60 Hz
DC Input Voltage	+5V @ 6A, +12V @ 1A
Power Consumption	50W

5. Finally, check to insure that all cabling meets the Ethernet guidelines and is not placed directly next to any sources of electrical noise.

Console Port Connections

This section will review how to connect to the Catalyst 1900 and 2820 switches using the console port. The console connection allows you to connect some type of management station or modem to the back of the switch.

Locate the console port on the back of the switch. The port is an RJ-45 port labeled Console Port. A package included in the Catalyst 1900 box contains several adapters/connectors and a rollover RJ-45-to-RJ-45 null-modem cable. Follow these instructions to establish a connection and begin configuration of the Catalyst 1900 or 2820 switch.

1. Plug the RJ-45-to-RJ-45 cable into the console port on the back of the switch.

Do not connect an Ethernet cable, ISDN, or live telephone line into the console port. These things can damage the electronics of the switch.

2. Start the management console or modem and configure the properties to match the configuration below.

   - Baud rate: 9600

   - 8 data bits

   - 1 stop bit

   - No parity

   - No flow control

3. Plug the other end of the RJ-45-to-RJ-45 null-modem cable into the appropriate adapter for the modem or management console you are using.

4. Power the switch on. The screen should scroll as the switch begins POST (power on self-test). If your switch fails the POST with a fatal error, the switch will not work and the console will not be available. Your only option is to send the switch to Cisco.

5. However, if the switch has a non-fatal error during the POST, the system LED will be amber and a POST failure message will be displayed. The example message displayed below for a Catalyst 1900 switch shows ports 1x to 8x failed the POST. (The 2820 output is exactly the same).

```
Catalyst 1900 Management Console
Copyright (c) Cisco Systems, Inc.  1993-1997
All rights reserved.
Ethernet address:      00-C0-1F-3E-A4-21
PCA Number: 72-2249-03
PCA Serial Number: SAD01200021
Model Number: WS-C1924-EN
System Serial Number: FAA01200021
-------------------------------------------------
*** Power On Self Test (POST) failed ***
*** Failed Test(s): 1
*** Failed Port(s): 1 2 3 4 5 6 7 8
1 user(s) now active on Management Console.
Press any key to continue.
```

6. If the POST is successful, the Management Console Logon screen should appear as shown below:

```
Catalyst 2820 Management Console
Copyright (c) Cisco Systems, Inc.    1993-1998
All rights reserved.
Standard Edition Software
Ethernet address:       00-D0-1D-7D-D4-40
PCA Number: 99-9999-01
PCA Serial Number: ABC1234567
Model Number: WS-C2822-A
System Serial Number: ABC12345678
-----------------------------------------------
          User Interface Menu
              [M] Menus
              [I] IP Configuration
Enter Selection:
```

7. If nothing has happened after a few moments, check the connections between the switch and the modem or the management console. If the connections are in order and the terminal is configured correctly according to the guidelines above, begin the troubleshooting sequence for the switch. (See Chapter 12 for troubleshooting sequences.)

8. At this point the switch may be configured from the switch menus.

IP Configuration

This section will demonstrate how to assign an IP address to the switch for in-band management. Configuring an IP address on the switch then allows you to configure the switch from a Telnet session, an SNMP-compatible workstation, or a Web console.

Configuration on both the Catalyst 1900 and Catalyst 2820 is menu-driven from the management console. There are some key points to understand before configuration may begin:

- To access a menu, press the bracketed letter shown to the left of that command. For example, pressing **I** opens the menu for IP configuration. Choosing any command will either open a lower-level menu or take you directly to the configuration of the item chosen.

- Always press the Enter key after inputting each parameter.

- In any menu, the X key will take you back to the previous menu.

- Input is not case sensitive. The only time case sensitivity can be an issue is when descriptive strings are entered into the switch.

- The Backspace key works as expected, deleting the previous character in the string. Pressing Backspace when the cursor is over the beginning of the character string will erase the entire parameter.

A parameter will take effect immediately, but it may take up to 30 seconds before being written to memory. If the switch is rebooted during this time, the change will be lost.

After POST finishes, the Console Logon screen appears. Press the I key to enter the IP Configuration menu.

1. The IP Configuration menu will appear on the management console screen as shown below:

```
Catalyst 2820 - IP Configuration
Ethernet Address:     00-D0-1D-7D-D4-40
-------------------Settings-----------------
[I] IP address                          0.0.0.0
[S] Subnet mask                         0.0.0.0
[G] Default gateway                     0.0.0.0
[M] IP address of DNS server 1          0.0.0.0
[N] IP address of DNS server 2          0.0.0.0
[D] Domain name
[R] Use Routing Information Protocol       Enabled
---------------------- Actions ------------------------
[P] Ping
[X] Exit to previous menu
Enter Selection:
```

2. Press I again to assign an IP address to the switch. Press Enter to accept the address after you have finished typing it in.

3. Press **S** to assign the subnet mask to the switch. Press Enter to accept the address after you have finished typing it in.

4. Press **G** to assign the default gateway to the switch. Press Enter to accept the address after you have finished typing it in.

5. If the network utilizes DNS servers, they may also be assigned from this menu by pressing **M** to assign the first DNS address and **N** to assign the secondary DNS address. A domain name may also be configured for the switch. Typically, this is used in environments with DNS servers so that a name resolution can be made to the switch. To configure the domain name, press **D**, type the domain name on the command line, and press Enter.

6. Press **X** to exit the IP menu. The switch is now configured with an IP address.

Remember that the switch will take 30 seconds before it saves the configuration change to memory. The IP address, however, has already taken effect once you press Enter.

7. After waiting at least a minute (to make sure the switch has taken the configuration), you can reset the switch.

Switch Menus

Once you've completed the IP configuration, the Management Console screen shown in the previous section will reappear. This time, choose the [M] option to enter the Main menu, where you'll do all your other configuration. The menu is shown below:

```
Catalyst 1900 - Main Menu

[C] Console Settings
[S] System
[N] Network Management
```

```
[P] Port Configuration
[A] Port Addressing
[D] Port Statistics Detail
[M] Monitoring
[V] Virtual LAN
[R] Multicast Registration
[F] Firmware
[I] RS-232 Interface
[U] Usage Summaries
[H] Help


[X] Exit Management Console
```

The Main menu of the Catalyst 2820 is shown below:

```
Catalyst 2820 - Main Menu
[C] Console Settings
[S] System
[N] Network Management
[P] Port Configuration
[A] Port Addressing
[D] Port Statistics Detail
[M] Monitoring
[B] Bridge Group
[R] Multicast Registration
[F] Firmware
[I] RS-232 Interface
[U] Usage Summaries
[H] Help
[X] Exit Management Console
Enter Selection:
```

The following sections will examine each item within the configuration menus, going through the different levels to explain how each function works. Each section will have some suggestions concerning using the configuration in deployment. One thing to make note of here is that the 1900 has a VLAN option and the 2820 has a Bridge Group option instead of the VLAN option.

Console Settings Menu

The Console Settings menu can be accessed by pressing **C** from the Main menu. The settings on this menu allow you to change the switch password and implement other system security measures. The menu as it appears for both the Catalyst 1900 and the Catalyst 2820 switch is shown below:

```
Catalyst 1900 - Console Settings
------------------Settings-----------------
[P] Password intrusion threshold              3 attempt(s)
[S] Silent time upon intrusion detection      None
[T] Management Console inactivity timeout      None
[D] Default mode of status LED                Port Status
------------------Actions------------------
[M] Modify password
[X] Exit to Main Menu
Enter Selection:
```

The functions of the menu options are as follows:

[P] Password Intrusion Threshold: Controls the number of attempts at entering the correct password that will be allowed. After either the default of three attempts or the value you define, the console is disabled for the amount of time you define in the next option.

[S] Silent Time Upon Intrusion Detection: Controls the interval that must elapse after the Password Intrusion Threshold has been violated before another attempt can be made. This control is defaulted to no wait but can be any amount of time between 1 and 65,500 minutes.

[T] Management Console Inactivity Timeout: Controls the amount of time that the management console can remain inactive without timing out. After it has timed out, the user must reenter that password to activate the switch console.

[D] Default Mode of Status LED: Sets the default mode for the LED 30 seconds after setting the mode. The default mode setting is [1] Port Status. Other options available are [2] Utilization or [3] Duplex Status.

[M] Modify Password   Allows you to change the password. The password may be four to eight characters long and any character on the keyboard. Remember, though, that the password is not case sensitive. If there is an existing password the user must enter that password before a change will occur.

[X] Exit to Main Menu: Drops the user back one level to the Main menu.

System Configuration Menu

The System Configuration menu is available from the Main menu by choosing option [S]. This menu is used to set system parameters as well as switching methods and the configuration for broadcast storm control. The sample menu shown below is representative of both the Catalyst 1900 and Catalyst 2820 switches.

```
Catalyst 2820 - System Configuration
System Revision:    0    Address Capacity:    2048
System UpTime:     0day(s) 00hour(s) 11minute(s) 29second(s)
-------------------Settings------------------
[N] Name of system
[C] Contact name
[L] Location
[S] Switching mode                          FragmentFree
[U] Use of store-and-forward for multicast  Disabled
[A] Action upon address violation           Suspend
[G] Generate alert on address violation     Enabled
[I] Address aging time                      300 second(s)
[P] Network Port                            None
[H] Half duplex back pressure   (10-mbps ports) Disabled
[E] Enhanced Congestion Control (10 Mbps Ports) Disabled
-------------------Actions------------------
[R] Reset system                [F] Reset to factory defaults
-----------------Related Menus--------------
[B] Broadcast storm control             [X] Exit to Main Menu
Enter Selection:
```

The functions of the most important menu options are as follows:

[N] Name of System: Allows you to set the name of the switch. The name may be up to 255 characters long.

[C] Contact Name: Allows you to configure a name or group to contact that will be responsible for managing the switch. The Contact Name may be 255 characters long.

[L] Location: Allows you to set the location name for the switch. The Location may be 255 characters long.

[S] Switching Mode: Allows you to choose either FastForward, Fragment-Free, or store-and-forward. The default setting for the switch is FragmentFree.

[U] Use of Store-and-Forward for Multicast: Choosing option E allows the switch to use store-and-forward for multicast frames. If the option is disabled, multicast frames will follow the switch's configured switching mode. This option is disabled by default.

[A] Action upon Address Violation: Allows you to define how the switch responds to address violations. The switch can be configured to respond in one of three ways:

[S] Suspend (default):   Stops the port from forwarding any packets until a source address is received.

[D] Disable: Disables the port until you manually re-enable it.

[I] Ignore: Allows the port to continue operating without change.

[G] Generate Alert on Address Violation: Determines whether a switch changes the status of the port when an address violation occurs. This option can send an SNMP alert to a management station. By default, this option is enabled.

[I] Address Aging Time: Sets the time after which an unused dynamic address is automatically removed. If the Port Fast mode is disabled, the forward-delay parameter ages ports more quickly. The value may be set from 10 to 1,000,000 seconds. The default is 300 seconds (5 minutes).

[P] Network Port: Configures a specific port as the destination port for all packets with unknown unicast addresses. The switch does not forward unknown unicast addresses to any other ports. A secured port cannot be the network port. If you select a secure port for the network port, you are prompted to disable security for that port. The default setting is None.

[R] Reset System: Resets the switch. The running configuration will not be lost and all configured addresses will be saved.

[F] Reset with Factory Default: Returns the switch to its factory settings. All configurations will be removed.

[B] Broadcast Storm Control: Displays the Broadcast Storm Control submenu:

```
Catalyst 2820 - Broadcast Storm Control
-------------------Settings-----------------
[A] Action upon exceeding broadcast threshold   Ignore
[G] Generate alert when threshold exceeded      Disabled
[T] Broadcast threshold (BC's received / sec)   500
[R] Broadcast re-enable threshold               250
[X] Exit to previous menu
Enter Selection:
```

[A] Action upon Exceeding Broadcast Threshold: Determines the behavior the switch takes when the broadcast threshold is exceeded. The Block option drops all broadcast packets received from a port when the number exceeds the broadcast threshold. The switch begins forwarding again when the number drops below the threshold. The default setting is Ignore.

[G] Generate Alert When Threshold Exceeded: Generates SNMP alerts when the broadcast threshold is exceeded. The SNMP trap is generated every 30 seconds. The default setting is Disabled.

[T] Broadcast Threshold: Configures the broadcast threshold, a measurement of packets per second arriving at a port. If the threshold is exceeded, a switch does not forward packets received from the port and generates an SNMP alert (depending on the settings of the A and G options). The default threshold is 500 packets per second.

[R] Broadcast Re-enabled Threshold: Defines when broadcast storm control is automatically disabled. The number of broadcast packets received must drop below this threshold before forwarding begins again. The default is 250 packets per second. Enter a number between 10 and 14,400.

[X] Exit to Main Menu: Drops you back one level to the Main menu.

Port Configuration Menu

The Port Configuration menu (accessed from the Main menu by pressing **P**) allows you to display the operating status of a port or module. You can also configure port descriptions, modify a port's status, and configure STP parameters. Typical Port Configuration menus for a 10BaseT and two different 100BaseT ports are shown below.

10BaseT port configuration:

```
Port Configuration Menu (10BaseT Ports)
Catalyst 2820 - Port 1 Configuration
Built-in 10Base-T
802.1d STP State:    Blocking    Forward Transitions:    0
-------------------Settings-----------------
[D] Description/name of port
[S] Status of port                    Suspended-no-linkbeat
[F] Full duplex                       Disabled
[I] Port priority (spanning tree)     128 (80 hex)
[C] Path cost (spanning tree)         100
[H] Port fast mode (spanning tree)    Enabled
-----------------Related Menus--------------
[A] Port addressing          [V] View port statistics
[N] Next port                [G] Goto port
[P] Previous port            [X] Exit to Main Menu
Enter Selection:
```

Switched 100BaseT port configuration:

```
Port Configuration Menu (Switched 100BaseT Ports)
Catalyst 2820 - Port B1 Configuration (Right Slot)
Module Name:    100Base-TX(1 Port UTP Model), Version 0
Description:    1 Port 100Base-TX
802.1d STP State:    Blocking    Forward Transitions:    0
---------------------- Settings ------------------------
[D] Description/name of port
---------------------- Module Settings -------------------
[M] Module status                     Suspended-no-linkbeat
[I] Port priority (spanning tree)     128 (80 hex)
[C] Path cost (spanning tree)         10
[H] Port fast mode (spanning tree)    Disabled
```

```
[E] Enhanced congestion control        Disabled
[F] Full duplex / Flow control         Half duplex
--------------------- Related Menus --------------------
[A] Port addressing           [V] View port statistics
[N] Next port                 [G] Goto port
[P] Previous port             [X] Exit to Main Menu
Enter Selection:
```

Shared 100BaseT port configuration:

```
Port Configuration Menu (Shared 100BaseT Ports)
Catalyst 2820 - Port A1 Configuration (Left Slot)
Module Name:    100Base-TX(8 Port UTP Model), Version 0
Description:    8 Port 100Base-TX Class 2 Repeater
802.1d STP State:    Blocking    Forward Transitions:    0
--------------------- Settings -------------------------
[D] Description/name of port
[S] Status of port                     Suspended-no-linkbeat
--------------------- Module Settings -------------------
[M] Module status                      Suspended-no-linkbeat
[I] Port priority (spanning tree)      128 (80 hex)
[C] Path cost (spanning tree)          10
[H] Port fast mode (spanning tree)     Disabled
[E] Enhanced congestion control        Disabled
[F] Full duplex / Flow control         Half duplex
--------------------- Related Menus --------------------
[A] Port addressing           [V] View port statistics
[N] Next port                 [G] Goto port
[P] Previous port             [X] Exit to Main Menu
Enter Selection:
```

The functions of the most important menu options above are as follows:

[D] Description/Name of Port: Allows you to assign a description to an individual port. The field will accept up to 60 characters.

[S] Status of Port: Provides an indication of the current status of a port.

[V] View Port Statistics: Displays a detailed port statistics report.

[N] Next Port: Shows the Port Configuration menu for the next numbered port of the switch.

[G] Goto Port: Displays the Port Configuration menu for a specified port.

[P] Previous Port: Displays the Port Configuration menu for the port whose number is one less than the current port .

[X] Exit to Main Menu: Drops you back one level to the Main menu.

Configuring VLANs

To display the menu for configuring VLANs, select V. The Catalyst 1900 and Catalyst 2820 can be configured with up to four VLANs. The default configuration of a switch has all ports belonging to VLAN 1. The Management Domain is also contained within VLAN 1. A proper configuration will have at least one port that belongs to VLAN 1.

The 2820 creates its VLANs using bridge groups.

The opening menu for VLAN Configuration on a 1900 looks like this:

```
Catalyst 1900 - Virtual LAN Configuration
-----------------Information---------------
VTP version: 1
Configuration revision: 1
Maximum VLANs supported locally: 1005
Number of existing VLANs: 6
Configuration last modified by: 172.16.30.196 at 05-03-1999 18:35:56


-------------------Settings------------------
[N] Domain name
[V] VTP mode control Server
[F] VTP pruning mode Disabled
[O] VTP traps Enabled


-------------------Actions------------------
[L] List VLANs          [A] Add VLAN
[M] Modify VLAN         [D] Delete VLAN
```

```
[E] VLAN Membership      [S] VLAN Membership Servers
[T] Trunk Configuration [W] VTP password
[P] VTP Statistics       [X] Exit to Main Menu

Enter Selection:
```

The functions of the most important menu options are as follows:

[N] Domain Name: Allows you to assign a management domain to the switch before creating a VLAN. A Catalyst 1900 or Catalyst 2820 switch comes configured in a no-management domain state until a management domain is configured or the switch receives an advertisement for a management domain.

[V] VTP Mode Control: May be set to either Transparent or Server. A Catalyst 1900 or Catalyst 2820 switch is configured as a VTP server by default, receiving advertisements on a configured trunk port. A switch automatically changes from VTP server mode to VTP client mode when it receives an advertisement with more than 128 VLANs.

[F] VTP Pruning Mode: Controls whether to restrict the flood traffic of a VLAN to just those switches that have member ports. Each trunk is configured with its own pruning eligible list of VLANs.

[A] Add VLAN: Adds a VLAN to the allowed list for the trunk. The default configuration allows all configured VLANs on a single trunk.

[M] Modify VLAN: Allows you to modify an existing VLAN.

[D] Delete VLAN: Allows you to delete an operating VLAN. The ports assigned to the VLAN will default back to VLAN 1.

[X] Exit to Main Menu: Drops you back one level to the Main menu.

Defining a VLAN

Defining a VLAN requires setting some attributes, including the VLAN number, name, IEEE 802.10 SAID value, and MTU size.

1. First access the VLAN Configuration menu by selecting **V** from the Main menu. Then press **A** to select Add VLAN.

2. Next you must choose the type of VLAN. For Ethernet, enter **1**.

3. Press **N** to configure the VLAN Number, and enter the number of the VLAN to be added.

4. Define the VLAN name by pressing **V** and entering the name of the VLAN to be added.

5. To set the IEEE 802.10 SAID value, press **I** and enter the appropriate value. The SAID value must be within the range shown, and it cannot be the same as another IEEE 802.10 value.

6. To set the MTU size, press **M** and enter the MTU size.

7. Enable the VLAN by pressing **T** to select VLAN State, and select Enabled.

Configuring VLAN Trunks

A VLAN trunk is important because it allows a physical link between two VLAN-capable switches or a VLAN-capable switch and a VLAN-capable router. A VLAN trunk can carry the traffic of multiple VLANs. This allows you to have VLANs extend into multiple Catalyst switches.

1. Access the Virtual LAN menu by selecting **V** from the Main menu.

2. Press **T** to access the Trunk Configuration menu. Select the appropriate trunk port by choosing either **A** or **B** and press Enter.

3. To turn on trunking for the selected port, enter **T**, Select **1**, and press Enter.

Configuring VLAN Trunk Protocol

The VLAN Trunk Protocol (VTP) helps maintain the VLAN uniformity across the network as well as assisting with the alteration of VLANs. VTP allows VLAN changes to be communicated across the network to the other switches.

1. Access the Virtual LAN menu by selecting **V** from the Main menu.

2. Confirm that a management domain name has been set.

3. Then press **N** to access the Domain Name menu.

4. Confirm that the server has a VTP management domain, which ensures that VTP information can be exchanged with other VTP switches in the management domain.

5. Press Enter to view the Virtual LAN Configuration menu.

6. Open the VTP Mode Control menu by selecting **V**.

7. Choose the server mode by entering **S** at the prompt.

The switch can only learn about other VTP configured switches by receiving their advertisements across the network. There must also be at least one trunk port configured on a switch.

The Diagnostic Console

The 1900 and 2820 diagnostic console is a menu-driven interface that allows you to recover from corrupted firmware, recover a forgotten or lost password, or reset the switch and console port to their factory default settings.

To bring up the diagnostic console menu, connect a terminal with a crossover null-modem cable to the switch and start your emulation program. Unplug the power cord to reboot the switch. Then press the MODE button on the front panel while plugging in the power cord. The Diagnostic Console Logon Screen should appear as displayed below:

```
-------------------------------------------------
Cisco Systems Diagnostic Console
Copyright(c) Cisco Systems, Inc. 1997
All rights reserved.
Ethernet Address: 00-E0-3F-6D-B4-24

-------------------------------------------------
Press enter to continue.
```

Press Enter, and the Diagnostic Console menu will appear as shown below:

```
Diagnostic Console  - Systems Engineering
Operation firmware version:  6.00 Status: valid
Boot firmware version:  3.02
[C] Continue with standard system start up
[U] Upgrade operation firmware (XMODEM)
[S] System Debug Interface
Enter Selection:
```

The list below explains the Diagnostic menu options:

Operation Firmware Version: The current version of the switch firmware. The status will show either Valid or Invalid. If it is invalid, the [C] options does not appear in the menu.

Boot Firmware Version: Current version of the write-protected part of the firmware that supports the diagnostic console.

[C] Continue With Standard System Start Up: If the firmware was invalid, you can fix it with the [U] option. After the firmware is upgraded, use the [C] option to bring up the firmware as usual.

[U] Upgrade Operation Firmware: Use this option to initiate a firmware upgrade. After the upgrade, you will be prompted for a console baud rate; 9600 will be the default.

[S] System Debug Interface: Use this option to display the Diagnostic Console. This menu is displayed below:

```
Diagnostic Console  - System Debug Interface
[G] Generic I/O
[M] Memory (CPU) I/O
[F] Return system to factory defaults
[R] Reset main console RS232 interface to 9600,8,1,N
[V] View Management Console password
[P] POST diagnostic console
[X] Exit to Previous Menu
Enter Selection:
```

[G] Generic I/O: Used by Cisco personnel only.

[M] Memory (CPU) I/O: Used by Cisco personnel only.

[F] Return System to Factory Defaults: Returns the switch to its factory settings. The changes take effect the next time the switch is reset.

[R] Reset Main Console RS232 Interface to 9600, 8, 1, N: This option is used if you have lost the management console connection because of an improper modem configuration. The changes take effect the next time the switch is reset.

[V] View Management Console Password: Displays the password set for the management console. You can also change the password here. You must be physically connected to the switch to use this option.

[P] POST Diagnostic Console: Used by Cisco personnel only.

Upgrading the Switch Firmware

To upgrade Catalyst firmware, copy the new file into a temporary directory or TFTP default directory. When you upgrade, the switch will validate the new file before copying it to flash memory and resetting itself. Be sure you know the filename and the IP address of your TFTP host before proceeding.

To upgrade or replace the switch firmware, choose the [F] option from the Console main menu. This will display the firmware version currently in use and the size of the switch flash memory. (The same options work for both the 1900 and 2820 switch.)

```
Catalyst 2820 - Firmware Configuration
-----------------System Information------------
FLASH:  1024K bytes
V6.00
Upgrade status:
No upgrade currently in progress.
-------------------Settings-----------------
[S] Server:  IP address of TFTP server        0.0.0.0
[F] Filename for firmware upgrades
[A] Accept upgrade transfer from other hosts   Enabled
-------------------Actions------------------
[U] System XMODEM upgrade       [D] Download test subsystem
                                             (XMODEM)

[T] System TFTP upgrade         [X] Exit to Main Menu
Enter Selection:
```

[S], [F], [T]: Used together, these upgrade the firmware from a TFTP server. You need to first enter the name of the TFTP server and the name of the file containing the upgrade.

[A] Accept Upgrade Transfer from Other Hosts: Use this option to enable [E] or disable [D] the switch from accepting an upgrade the firmware from another host on the network.

[U] System XMODEM Upgrade: Allows an upgrade via the XMODEM protocol through the console port on the switch.

[D] Download Test Subsystem (XMODEM): Used by Cisco personnel only.

[X] Exit to Main Menu: Displays the Console Main menu.

Do not interrupt the download by turning off the switch. It could possibly corrupt the firmware. It is important to remember that the switch might not respond for several minutes during the download.

Configuring ATM LAN Emulation

This section demonstrates the steps necessary for configuring the ATM module as a trunk or non-trunk ATM module. You'll see how to configure the ATM LAN Emulation (LANE) client (LEC) from the command-line interface and verify the configuration. The Catalyst 2820 supports four types of ATM modules—the ATM 155 multimode (MM) Fiber module, the ATM 155 single-mode (SM) medium-reach (MR) Fiber module, the ATM 155 single-mode (SM) long-reach (LR) Fiber module, and the ATM 155 UTP. You can use the ATM module to connect workstations, hubs, and other switches to a range of ATM devices.

The ATM modules include the following features:

- Full-duplex operation

- 155.52 Mbps data transfer rate

- Store-and-forward packet relay

- LAN emulation client (LEC) for emulated LANs (ELANs)

- ATM Adaptation Layer 5 (AAL5) for LAN emulation (LANE) data transfer

- Multiple-ELAN support for LANE (Catalyst 2820 switch firmware version 7.02 or later with Cisco IOS 11.3 or later)

- Multiple virtual LAN (VLAN) mappings for RFC 1483 (Catalyst 2820 switch firmware version 7.02 or later with Cisco IOS 11.3 or later)

- User-Network Interface (UNI) 3.0 and 3.1 for switched virtual connections (SVCs) and permanent virtual connections (PVCs)

- Support for Catalyst 2820 switch firmware version 5.35 and version 7.02

The ATM modules support these ATM management features:

- Interim Local Management Interface (ILMI) for ATM UNI 3.0 and 3.1 Management Information Bases (MIBs)

- Operation, Administration, and Maintenance (OAM)

To access the command-line interface from the Catalyst 2820 management console, select **P** (Port Configuration) from the Catalyst 2820 Main menu. Select the port where the ATM module is installed. For slot A (interface 0), press **A** or, if the module is installed in Slot B (interface 1), press **B**.

Next you'll see the Port Configuration menu either for a Non-trunk ATM Module or for a Trunk ATM Module. Select [K] from either menu to access the command-line interface. The switch responses for both types of modules are shown:

```
Port Configuration Menu for Nontrunk ATM Module
      Catalyst 2820 - Port A Configuration (Left Slot)
      Module Name:   ATM 155 MM Fiber, Version 01
      Description:   Multimode Fiber ATM Network Status: Operational
      802.1d STP State:  Forwarding   Forward Transitions: 5
      -------------------Settings------------------
      [D] Description/name of port
```

```
------------------Module Settings-------------
[M] Module status                        Enabled
[I] Port priority (spanning tree)        128 (80 hex)
[C] Path cost (spanning tree)            10
[H] Port fast mode (spanning tree)       Enabled
-------------------Actions------------------
[R] Reset module   [F] Reset module with factory defaults
-----------------Related Menus--------------
[K] Command Line Interface     [L] ATM and LANE status
[A] Port addressing            [V] View port statistics
[N] Next port                  [G] Goto port
[P] Previous port              [X] Exit to Main Menu

Port Configuration Menu for ATM Trunk Module
         Catalyst 2820 - Port A Configuration (Left Slot)
         Module Name:  ATM 155 MM Fiber, Version 03
         Description:  Multimode Fiber  ATM Network Status: Operational
---------------------- Setting --------------------------
[D] Description/name of port
[S] Status of trunk                      Enabled
--------------------- Module Settings -------------------
[I] Port priority (spanning tree) - option 1    128 (80 hex)
[J] Port priority (spanning tree) - option 2    128 (80 hex)
[C] Path cost (spanning tree)                   10
--------------------- Actions ---------------------------
[E] Show VLAN port priorities     [Z] Show VLAN States
[M] Assign VLANs to option 1 port priority
[O] Assign VLANs to option 2 port priority
[R] Reset module       [F] Reset module with factory defaults
--------------------- Related Menus ---------------------
[K] Command Line Interface     [L] ATM and LANE status
[A] Port addressing            [V] View port statistics
[N] Next port                  [G] Goto port
[P] Previous port              [X] Exit to Main Menu
Enter Selection:
```

The ATM module does not forward any frames from the switch until the LANE clients have been defined. After configuring a LANE client with an ELAN mapped to a VLAN, you must configure the ATM module with the VLAN information. The ATM module then forwards the traffic to the appropriate ELAN.

To configure the LEC from the command-line interface:

1. To enter the privileged EXEC mode, enter the `enable` command:

```
ATM> enable
ATM#
```

2. To enter the global configuration mode enter the `configure ter-minal` command:

```
ATM# configure terminal
```

3. Enter the interface configuration mode by entering the `interface type_number.subif` command:

```
ATM(config)# interface atm0.1
ATM(config-if)#
```

4. To configure the LEC, enter the `lane client ethernet vlan_number elan_name` command:

```
ATM(config-if)# lane client ethernet 1 marketing
ATM(config-if)#
```

5. Exit the interface configuration mode and return to EXEC mode:

```
ATM(config-if)# ^Z
ATM#
```

The ATM module is now configured to transmit and receive data between the LAN and the ATM network. The next step is to verify that the configuration is operating correctly.

You can verify the ATM and LANE status by using the `show lane` command, which verifies that the LEC is operational and shows the ATM addresses of the LANE configuration.

```
ATM> show lane
    LE Client ATM1.1 ELAN name: TESTELAN Admin: up State: operational
Client ID: 2 LEC up for 6 minutes 14 seconds
Join Attempt: 2
    HW Address: 00c0.1dfc.a2fc Type: ethernet Max Frame Size: 1516
    VLANID: 1
    ATM Address: 39.000000000000000000000000.00A02DFCA2FC.00 ATM Address
    VCD rxFrames txFrames Type ATM Address
    0 0 0  configure 39.000000000000000000000000.00705C28DA23.00
    4 0 2  direct 39.000000000000000000000000.00604D38DA21.01
```

```
5 0 0   distribute 39.00000000000000000000000.00605C28DA21.01
 0 20send 39.00000000000000000000000.00605C28DA22.01
 13 0  0 forward 39.00000000000000000000000.00605C28DA22.01
 8 58 55 data 39.00000000000000000000000.00605C28DA20.01
ATM>
```

To verify that the ATM module is transmitting and receiving data across the ATM network, you can review the port statistics. The display shows the number of ATM Adaptation Layer 5 (AAL5) frames and ATM cells transmitted and received. To view port statistics on the Catalyst 2820, first press **P** from the Main menu to display the Port Configuration menu; then press **V** to choose View Port Statistics. A typical ATM statistical report is shown below:

```
Catalyst 2820 - Port B (Right Slot)
     Receive Statistics                  Transmit Statistics
------------------------------------- ---------------------

Good AAL5 frames             0  Good AAL5 frames             1
Good ATM cells               0  Good ATM cells               3
Broadcast/multicast frames   0  Broadcast/multicast frames   0
Good frames forwarded        0  Queue full discards          0
Frames filtered              0
Runt frames                  0
No buffer discards           0
Other discards               0
Errors:
CRC errors                   0
Cell HEC errors              0
Giant frames                 0
Address violations           0
Select [A] Port addressing, [C] Configure port,
       [N] Next port, [P] Previous port, [G] Goto port,
       [R] Reset port statistics, or [X] Exit to Main Menu:
```

Summary

This chapter reviewed the proper guidelines for installing and configuring the Catalyst 1900 and 2820 switches.

- We began by looking briefly at the physical connection of the console ports and the initial POST sequence.

- Next we walked through the procedure for configuring IP addresses and related values such as subnet masks and gateway addresses. These settings need to be made before further configuration can be done.

- We spent most of the chapter reviewing the configuration options available through the Main menu: the System Configuration menu, the Port Configuration menu, and the menus for configuring VLANs, VLAN trunks, and the VLAN Trunk Protocol (VTP), as well as ATM LAN emulation.

Review Questions

1. Which menu item is not found in the Main Console menu?

   A. Console Settings

   B. Bridge Group

   C. IP Configuration

   D. Port Statistics Detail

   E. Help

2. How is out-of-band management done?

   A. SNMP

   B. Telnet

   C. TFTP

   D. AUX Port

3. What is the maximum number of nodes per segment for 10BaseFL?

   A. 4

   B. 3

   C. 2

   D. 1

4. What is the optimal operating temperature range for the Catalyst 1900 and 2820 switches?

   A. −29° to 80°C

   B. 23° to 113°F

   C. −15° to 80°C

   D. 24° to 100°F

5. What is the power consumption of the Catalyst 2820 switch?

   A. 50W

   B. 23W

   C. 110W

   D. 220W

6. What is the default baud rate setting for the console port?

   A. 4800

   B. 52000

   C. 28.8

   D. 9600

7. What does POST stand for?

   A. Power On Self Test

   B. Place On Standard Transmit

   C. Power On Standard Traffic

   D. Power Off Self Test

8. How many seconds before a configuration is saved into memory?

   A. 45

   B. 23

   C. 30

   D. 50

9. What does an amber light on the System LED mean?

   A. Switch is in loopback

   B. Switch had a fatal error

   C. Switch had a non-fatal error

   D. Switch console is ready

10. How do you enter the Diagnostic Console on a Catalyst 1900 switch?

A. Press the Sys Req button on power-up.

B. Press the Console button on power-up.

C. Press the Mode button on the back panel upon power-up.

D. Press the Mode button on the front panel upon power-up.

11. How do you access the option to change the Contact name?

A. System Configuration Menu

B. IP Configuration Menu

C. VLAN Menu

D. Port Configuration

12. What is the default switching method used by the Catalyst switches?

A. FastForward

B. FragmentFree

C. Store-and-Forward

D. Fragmentless

13. What is the default setting for the Action Upon Exceeding Broadcast Threshold?

A. Disable

B. Enable

C. Ignore

D. Power Off

14. How many characters are allowed for the description/name of a port?

   A. 255

   B. 75

   C. 100

   D. 60

15. What does the Goto option do?

   A. Display a module's information.

   B. Re-configure a specific port.

   C. Display the configuration menu for a specific port.

   D. Exit to the Main menu.

16. How can you see the console password on a 1900 switch if it is lost or forgotten?

   A. From the Main menu.

   B. From the Diagnostic menu.

   C. From the back panel, press Sys Req when booting.

   D. You can't.

17. How do you access the ATM Module from the main console menu?

   A. Option P

   B. Option V

   C. Option M

   D. Option X

18. What does the show lane command do?

    A. Verifies the ATM and LANE status.

    B. Verifies VTP is working.

    C. Verifies the IP configuration of LANE.

    D. Verifies the ATM address of the LEC.

19. What types of ATM modules does the Catalyst 2820 support?

    A. The ATM 155 multimode (MM) Fiber module

    B. The ATM 155 single-mode (SM) medium-reach (MR) Fiber module

    C. The ATM 155 single-mode (SM) long-reach (LR) Fiber module

    D. The ATM 155 UTP

    E. All of the above

20. The default configuration for a VLAN allows?

    A. All configured VLANs on multiple trunks.

    B. All configured VLANs on a single trunk.

    C. All configured VLANs on a single ELAN.

    D. All configured VLANs on multiple ELANs.

Laboratory Exercises: Configuring the Catalyst 2820 Switch

These labs will give you practice installing and configuring a Catalyst 2820 switch. To complete them you will need the following equipment:

- Catalyst 2820 switch (WS-C2822 or WS-C2828)

- Catalyst 2820 100BaseTx/1 Module (WS-X2811)

- Catalyst 2820 FDDI SAS Module (WS-X2841)

- Category 5 TP cables

- Null-modem cable

- PC for terminal emulation

Install or place your Catalyst 2820 switch in a rack or on a table. Configure your PC with these emulation settings: 9600 bps, 8 data bits, 1 stop bit, and no parity. Connect a null-modem cable to the switch from your PC.

EXERCISE 5.1

System Configuration

In this first lab, you will learn how to set your Password and System Configuration. From the Main menu, set your console password first.

1. Press **C** at the Main menu to select the Console Password menu.

2. Press **M** to enter the Modify Password menu.

3. Type in a password.

4. Type it in a second time to verify your password.

5. Press **X** to exit to the Main menu.

Now set your system configuration information:

1. From the Main menu, press **S** to select the System menu.

EXERCISE 5.1 (CONTINUED)

2. Type in the following information:

   - Name of System

   - Contact Name

   - Location

   - Switching Mode

   - Action upon address violation

3. Leave the rest of the entries at their default settings.

4. Press **B** to select the Broadcast Storm Control menu. (You'll find it under the Related Menus section.)

5. Once in the Broadcast Storm Control menu, press **A** to select the Action upon Exceeding Broadcast Threshold menu and then press **I** to select Ignore.

6. Press **X** to go up one menu and then press **X** again to exit to the Main menu.

EXERCISE 5.2

VLAN Configuration

In this exercise, you will move ports from the default of VLAN 1 to new VLANs.

1. Press **V** in the Main menu to select the Virtual LAN menu.

2. Press **C** to select the Configure VLAN menu.

3. Select VLAN 2 by typing **2** as the VLAN number and pressing Return or Enter.

4. Press **V** to select the VLAN Names menu and name VLAN 2 as **VLAN2**. Press **M** to move ports 1–6 to VLAN2.

5. Press **X** to go back one menu and then press **C** to select the Configure VLAN menu.

6. Select VLAN 3 by typing **3** as the VLAN number and pressing Return or Enter.

7. Press **V** to select the VLAN Names menu and name VLAN 3 as **VLAN3**. Press **M** to move ports 7–12 to VLAN3.

EXERCISE 5.3

Network Management Configuration

In this next exercise, you will configure the 2820 switch with an IP address and then configure it to be managed by SNMP.

1. Choose **N** from the Main menu to select the Network Management menu.

2. Press **I** to select the IP Configuration menu.

3. Once in the IP Configuration menu, press **I** to access the IP Address Configuration menu.

4. Press **S** to access the Subnet Mask Configuration menu.

5. Type in your IP address. An example would be:

   - IP Address VLAN 1: **172.16.10.1**

   - IP Subnet Mask VLAN 1: **255.255.255.0**

   Remember that VLAN 1 is the default for all ports on the switch.

6. Press **X** twice to return to the Main menu.

7. Press **N** to return to the Network Management menu.

8. Press **S** to select the SNMP Management menu.

9. In the SNMP Configuration menu, press **R** to set the Read community string.

10. Set the Read community string to Public.

11. Press **W** to set the Write community string.

12. Set the Write community string to Private.

13. Press **X** to exit the menu.

14. From the Network Management menu, select the Bridge Spanning Tree menu and select VLAN 1.

15. Press **M** to change the Max age to 30 seconds.

16. Press **X** twice to return to the Main menu.

EXERCISE 5.4

Port Configuration

In this lab, you will use the Port menu to enable switch ports and configure Full-Duplex settings.

1. Choose the Port Configuration menu from the Main menu by pressing **P**.

2. Enable port 1 by using the Port Selection screen to select port 1.

3. Enable ports 2 through 4.

4. Select port A from the Port Selection screen and then press **F** for Full Duplex.

5. Press **X** twice to return to the Main menu.

EXERCISE 5.5

FDDI Port Configuration

In this lab, you will install and configure the FDDI module in the 2820 switch.

1. If the FDDI module is not installed in the switch, install it now in the correct expansion slot.

2. Select **P** from the Main menu to select the Port Configuration menu.

3. Check and make sure that the FDDI module is operational. You can use the Port Configuration screen to check the Ring Status, 802.1d STP State, and Novell SNAP frame translation.

4. Select **1** from the Port Configuration menu to view the Basic FDDI Settings.

5. Select **2** from the Basic FDDI Settings to view the Secondary FDDI settings.

6. Press **X** twice to return to the Main menu.

EXERCISE 5.6

Viewing Usage Summaries

In this lab, you will check switch reports and statistics.

1. Select **U** from the Main menu to open the Usage Summaries menu.

2. Select and view the following from the Usage Summaries screen:

   - Port Status Report

   - Exception Statistics Report

   - Utilization Statistics Report

   - Bandwidth Usage Report

3. Press **X** twice to return to the Main menu.

CHAPTER

6

The Cisco Catalyst
3000 Series Switches

An Ethernet switch, such as any of the Cisco Catalyst 3000 series, can significantly increase the throughput between Ethernet segments, because it can sustain concurrent conversations that occur in parallel. And because switched connections between segments last only as long as necessary for the packet to be processed, new connections are free to be created between other segments for subsequent packets.

Ethernet switches also are wonderful tools to apply to typical congestion problems that arise when you have too many users, as well as applications and network devices with voracious appetites. For instance, with these switches, you can allot each bandwidth-greedy device (like a server) its very own 10 or 100Mbps segment.

It's very common for throughput bottlenecks to occur at servers and between other bandwidth-challenging devices like routers, bridges, and switches in a standard Ethernet network. With the Catalyst 3000, you can address this issue by configuring full-duplex communication for each segment connected to one of its ports. Ethernet usually functions in half-duplex mode, allowing devices to either transmit or receive. Full-duplex technology, however, enables two stations to receive and transmit simultaneously. And with that kind of free flow, bandwidth capacity is multiplied from 10Mbps to 20Mbps for 10BaseT ports and increases to a staggering 200Mbps on Fast Ethernet ports!

The Catalyst 3000-series switches comply with IEEE 802.3 and are designed to increase the throughput on an Ethernet network within the range of 300 to 1000 percent! And since they're MAC-layer machines, they are versatile, protocol independent, and work in complete harmony with a variety of systems from NetWare, XNS, and AppleTalk to TCP/IP, LAT, and DECnet.

In this chapter, we'll cover the major features of the Catalyst 3000 switches, the architecture used, and the functions of their major components.

The CLSC exam objectives covered in this chapter include:

- Describe the major features of the Catalyst switches.

- Describe the architecture and functions of the major components of the Catalyst switches.

- Describe the Catalyst Stack System.

- Describe Catalyst 3000 series LAN switch products.

- Describe Catalyst 3000 series LAN switch product differences.

Hardware

There are a variety of configurations where the Catalyst 3000 series switches become stars that will lavish you with greatly enhanced network performance. Each Cisco Catalyst product affords its users the ability to design systems that are highly efficient as well as fluidly scalable. Those qualities, combined with the Catalyst 3000's reliability and its capacity for media flexibility, make these products ideal solutions for both present and future networking requirements in your Ethernet configuration.

And they're versatile too—along with the EtherChannel, the Catalyst 3000 and can be combined with other Catalyst products, giving you a myriad of options and solutions.

A unique feature of the Catalyst 3000 series is that the switches can be cabled together to form a Catalyst Stack. See "The Catalyst Stack System" later in this chapter to learn about the potential benefits of this configuration; and see Chapter 7 for hardware configuration details.

The rest of this chapter will help you discover the distinct features and beauty of working with the 3000, 3100, and 3200 Catalyst switches.

Catalyst 3000

The Catalyst 3000 switch can have sixteen 10Mbps switch ports; twenty-four 10baseT ports; and two 100BaseT, ATM or 100VG-AnyLAN ports. The standard configuration is sixteen 10BaseT ports, 8MB of DRAM, 1MB of flash memory, a console port, a SwitchProbe port, an AUI, and two optional slots. You can configure the optional slots in the switch with the following options:

- 4 port 10baseT
- 1 port 10pBaseT/F
- 2 port 100VG-AnyLAN
- 3 port 10BaseFL
- 1 port 155 Mbps ATM
- 3 port 10Base2 thinnet
- 3 port 100BaseT/ISL
- 2 port 100BaseT/ISL

Figure 6.1 shows the front and back of the 3000 switch. Notice that the back has Reset and Sys Req buttons, console and SwitchProbe ports, and switches for setting full- or half-duplex mode. We'll look at these ports in detail later in the chapter.

F I G U R E   6.1

The Cisco Catalyst 3000 switch, front (top) and back (bottom)

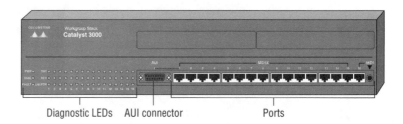

Diagnostic LEDs   AUI connector   Ports

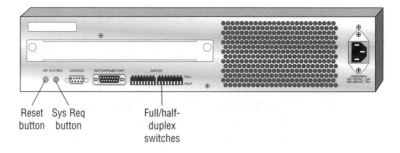

Reset   Sys Req   Full/half-
button   button   duplex
                              switches

The Catalyst 3000 switch can be configured administratively to support half- and full-duplex operation on all ports, cut-through or store-and-forward switching, VLAN support, and demand aging for hardware address tables. Demand aging is used to purge the address table when it reaches capacity.

The 3000 can support up to 1700 addresses per port and up to 10,000 addresses per switch. Also, by using the Catalyst Matrix, you can connect up to eight switches to create a stack system.

Catalyst 3100

The Catalyst 3100 provides all the features of the 3000 and more. It comes with 24 switched 10Mbps ports and a FlexSlot that can be used for WAN access or an expansion module. By using the double-wide FlexSlot with the WAN access module, you can create a Catalyst Stack with WAN support.

The WAN module has two serial ports and a BRI port for ISDN capability. The serial ports can support speeds up to E1 (2.048Mbps) and can run in either asynchronous or synchronous mode. The WAN module also has an auxiliary port that can be used for either console modem support or as a backup asynchronous line. However, no LAN support is included on the WAN module. All local packets are routed from the Cisco WAN module through the Catalyst 3100 or 3200 AXIS bus (discussed later). The WAN module supports connectivity to a single VLAN network or network segment. Figure 6.2 shows the Cisco Catalyst 3100 switch.

FIGURE 6.2

The Cisco Catalyst 3100 switch

Catalyst 3200

The Catalyst 3200 is a larger chassis than either the 3000 or 3100 switch. It can handle seven slots with one slot available for an extra-wide module. Its other features are:

- Up to twenty-one 10BaseFL ports
- Support for the double-wide WAN module
- Redundant power supplies
- 8MB of DRAM
- Fast Ethernet ISL and LANE support

It is important not to oversubscribe the 3200 switch. Refer to the user guidelines before buying any module, or ask your Cisco reseller for information about the 3200 high-speed modules and their performance. Figure 6.3 shows the Cisco Catalyst 3200 switch.

FIGURE 6.3

The Cisco Catalyst 3200 switch

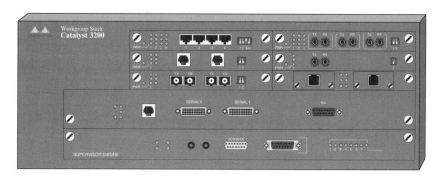

Four Main Elements

All of the Catalyst 3000 switches have four main elements. These are:

Cross-point switch matrix (AXIS bus): This is used to connect between two network segments. Each connection lasts only as long as packets are being transmitted.

AUI connector: The Attachment Unit Interface is typically used to connect by way of a transceiver (transmitter/receiver) to dissimilar physical media, such as connecting thinnet to 10BaseT or 10BaseFL.

Expansion Module: Two expansion slots are included in each 3000 Catalyst switch. You can add up to eight 10Mbps ports or two Fast Ethernet connections for connecting to servers or backbones. ATM and fiber-based LANs are also supported.

Stack Ports: The 3000 switch supports up to eight Catalyst 3000 units connected together, forming one virtual unit.

Architecture

This section discusses the architecture of the 3000 Catalyst switches, describing the AXIS bus, the LAN Module ASIC (LMA), and the Proprietary Fat Pipe ASIC (PFPA).

The 3000 switch uses the AXIS bus to facilitate frame switching. If you have a node at 10Mbps that has a destination node running 10Mbps, the switch will use the LAN Module ASIC (LMA) to perform the port switching. Any ports running above 10Mbps will use the Proprietary Fat Pipe ASIC (PFPA). Figure 6.4 shows the Catalyst 3000 architecture.

FIGURE 6.4

Catalyst 3000
Architecture

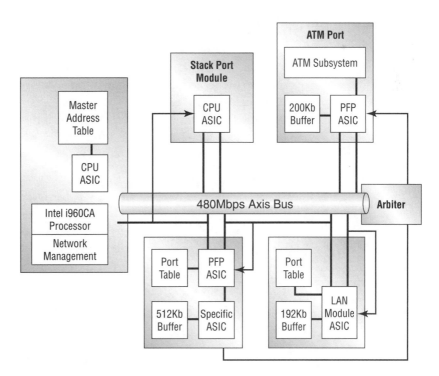

Notice in Figure 6.4 how all switching ASICs connect to the AXIS bus, and each ASIC has its own buffer to prevent congestion. 10Mbps ports have 192KB buffers, and 100Mbps ports have 512KB buffers.

AXIS Bus

The AXIS bus uses a synchronous time-division multiplexed (TDM) bus for 10Mbps-to-10Mbps traffic and asynchronous for all others. The basic purpose of the AXIS bus is to switch packets between heterogeneous LMAs and PFPAs. The central bus Arbiter allocates bandwidth for the AXIS in 52 time slots rated at 10Mbps. The AXIS bus supports simultaneous packet transfers of 10 to 170Mbps. This helps prevent packet overflow by supporting over-subscription or congestion of bandwidth.

ASIC

An Application Specific Integrated Circuit (ASIC) is a chip that is built around a general core and is usually available as a set of different cores brought together to work on the same chip. The different cores that the Catalyst 3000 switch uses are LMA, PFPA, and CPA.

LAN Module ASIC (LMA)

A switch port LAN Module ASIC will receive a packet from a LAN and request access to the destination port. The LMA at this point will put the packet onto the AXIS bus if the destination port is not busy. If it is busy, the packet is buffered in the output port. The packet will be forwarded as soon as the destination port is available. However, if the destination port is unknown, it will forward the packet to the CPU, which in turn will forward the packet as a broadcast out all ports except the receiving port.

Proprietary Fat Pipe ASIC (PFPA)

The Fat Pipe is used to connect different types of network topologies to the AXIS bus, which allows switching. Any time an expansion module is added to the 3000 switch, the module will implement a PFPA. The PFPA is used in the following modules:

StackPort: Uses a 280Mbps interface to the Matrix.

100BaseX: PFPA is the interface between the standard ASIC and AXIS bus.

ATM: PFPA is the interface between the bus and SAR.

ISL: Allows communication to the AXIS bus from ASIC ISL.

CPU ASIC (CPA)

The 3000 switch uses an Intel i960SA 16.25Mhz processor that has four main components:

CPA: The CPU ASIC gives the CPU access to address filtering, aging, and learning.

Main Memory: Used to store the system code.

Network Memory: This is where the master address is stored. When a packet is received with an unknown destination, the packet will be sent to the network memory, which tells the CPU to begin address learning.

i960SA: The CPU processor.

LAN Switching

The 3000 switch uses both cut-through and store-and-forward LAN switching techniques. Switching modes are used to determine how a frame is forwarded through the switch.

Cut-Through

Cut-through switching is faster than store-and-forward LAN switching. It does not copy the frame to its buffers, nor does it run a CRC. The switch only checks the destination hardware address in the frame and forwards the frame based on that information. The cut-through switch has the lowest latency of all LAN switching types because only the first part of the frame is read before any forwarding is done. This method enables packets to arrive at the output port 40 microseconds after entering the input port.

Store-and-Forward

Store-and-forward switching is used in the 3000 and 5000 series of Catalyst switches. It is the slowest (highest latency) but the most dependable. Every frame is copied from the wire to the buffer in the management card. The switch IOS then runs a CRC on the frame to make sure it is error free. If no error is found, it will then look in the table of hardware addresses and forward the frame based on that information. Since frames can vary in length, the latency of the store-and-forward switching method depends on frame length.

The 3000 switch can be set to full-time store-and-forward operation to ensure that every packet is checked for errors before being forwarded.

3000 Product Features

As stated earlier in the chapter, the Catalyst 3000 switches comply with IEEE 802.3 and significantly amplify throughput on Ethernet networks. They are MAC-layer devices that are versatile and protocol independent, working in complete harmony with a variety of systems, ranging from NetWare, XNS, and AppleTalk to TCP/IP, LAT, and DECnet. The following are Catalyst 3000 product features:

- Multiple simultaneous conversations

- Low latency

- Address management

- Address filtering

- On-board filtering

- Full-duplex

- Virtual LAN

- EtherChannel

- Error handling

Multiple Simultaneous Conversations

One drawback of Ethernet is that it cannot support more than one conversation at a time. The Catalyst 3000 fixes this problem by providing support for multiple simultaneous, full-duplex conversations, which improves throughput. The beauty of the Catalyst 3000 is that it creates multiple data paths that combine fast-packet switching technology with Fast Ethernet. Switched connections between segments last only as long as it is necessary for the packet to be processed. So new connections between different segments are made as needed for the next packet.

Throughput is increased in direct proportion to the number of LAN segments that are connected through the switch, just as more lanes can support a proportional increase of cars on the road.

An individual segment can be dedicated to one host or shared by up to 1700 others. You can optimize throughput, by giving high-speed servers a dedicated Catalyst 3000 port. Going back to our road analogy, think of a standard Ethernet network as a one-lane highway. Using Catalyst 3000 switches will transform your old road into an eight-lane freeway that allows multiple conversations (or trips) at the same time. Because Catalyst 3000 switches send multiple Ethernet packets simultaneously, overall network throughput is amplified.

The Catalyst 3000 will send broadcast and multicast packets on all Catalyst 3000 segments at the same time except for the port of entry. For example, Figure 6.5 shows Host 1 sending a packet to Host 2. Because it isn't necessary to send packets to all other ports, the Catalyst 3000 only connects lines 1 and 2. Another switching circuit can then connect Host 3 and Host 4 at the same time, resulting in simultaneous conversations.

F I G U R E   6.5

Multiple conversations through a Catalyst 3000 Switch

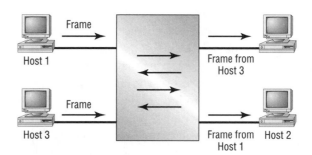

Low Latency

Network devices that use the cut-through switching method enable another great Catalyst 3000 feature—minimized latency—by initiating packet transmission immediately after looking at the first six bytes of the packet's destination address. (Remember that latency is the time required to forward a packet from one Ethernet segment to another.) Packets arrive at the output port only 40 microseconds after entering the input port. And if a packet needs to be switched to another LAN segment, its data will begin flowing out the destination port before the entire packet has been received.

Devices that use the store-and-forward method will cause much higher latency, because the entire packet must be received before it can be forwarded.

Address Management

At power-up, the Catalyst 3000 system address table does not hold any information—it's a blank sheet, you might say. As the switch begins processing packets, it records both the source and destination addresses in its table. If a Catalyst 3000 receives a packet with an unknown source or destination address, before it forwards the packet, it learns the new source address by putting its location into memory. Once the Catalyst 3000 learns the new source address, it forwards the packet to its destination address. If the destination address is not known, the packet will be sent to all of the Catalyst 3000 output ports. After the response packet comes back, its location is added to the address table. The Catalyst 3000 uses all of the learned addresses to switch subsequent packets with less processing, ultimately creating faster transmission.

The system address table holds up to 10,000 entries with 8MB of DRAM. The port address tables maintain up to 1700 active Ethernet addresses.

As discussed earlier in the chapter, demand aging allows you to define a standard based on a specific time interval or a percentage of address table capacity, ensuring that the address table contains only the most frequently used addresses. The address table can be managed by adjusting the aging interval to limit the number of addresses. Any node that has not shown activity within the aging interval you define on the network management console will be removed automatically. If older nodes reactivate or new ones become active, they are recorded with the transmission of just one packet, allowing users to connect transparently to high-volume backbone networks.

Address Filtering

The Catalyst 3000 supports MAC layer filters for source or destination addresses to be configured on a per-port basis. This feature allows you to manage the network and maintain security by designating client access to certain resources, restricting access to servers or MAC addresses, or permitting an end-user to communicate with only one server.

On-Board Buffering

The Catalyst 3000 will store a packet in one of its internal buffers if the destination port is receiving a packet from another Catalyst 3000 port or if the output segment is busy. This feature helps control network throughput when the system is near its peak load and more than one packet is sent to the same port at the same time. Each buffer is capable of holding up to 768 packets, 384 in each direction (incoming and outgoing).

Full-Duplex Communication

Catalyst 3000 allows you to select half-duplex or full-duplex communication. You can double the throughput capacity on the segment by using full-duplex because packets flow in both directions at the same time. This flexibility is a huge advantage.

Full-duplex communication also eliminates the poor performance that results from packet collisions. Packets are prevented from colliding, because each traverses its own designated path.

Virtual LAN (VLAN)

One Catalyst 3000 can be divided into VLANs, each containing its own set of ports, by activating the Catalyst VLAN feature. This will confine packet forwarding to ports belonging to the same VLAN. Again, this allows you to manage traffic or to maintain security by restricting access from one segment to another.

EtherChannel

EtherChannel is a high-bandwidth connection between two Catalyst units, forming from two to seven ports for up to 140 Mbps bandwidth in full-duplex mode. By using EtherChannel connections to a Catalyst 3000, existing Catalyst devices can access high-speed routers, servers, and backbones joined to Fast Ethernet ports. You can create a single "fat pipe" by connecting multiple 100Mbps ports.

Error Handling

Packet collisions caused by low throughput are a primary source of errors in Ethernet networks. The Catalyst 3000 reduces latency, which increases throughput, by using cut-through switching. The workstations' network interface cards (NICs) check for packet errors that the Catalyst 3000 might forward to them. So you can set the Catalyst 3000 not to duplicate this function, thereby maintaining low latency.

However, beware of slugs that can infest your network! Devices such as routers and bridges that perform store-and-forward error-checking on all frames can create delays between 51.2 and 1214 microseconds with their redundant operation. The delay is caused because the Frame Check Sequence (FCS) makes up the final 32 bits of an IEEE 802.3 packet, so these devices must receive the complete packet before forwarding it to its destination port.

Each port on the Catalyst 3000 can be set to run in one of three ways:

- In a dedicated low-latency, low-error cut-through switching mode.

- In the store-and-forward mode.

- In an automatic mode. The automatic mode monitors the number of CRC errors in the cut-through mode and automatically switches to store-and-forward if the level rises above the configured setting. It also automatically switches back to cut-through when the error level falls below the configured setting. Error handling is only used in the store-and-forward mode for connecting ports of different speeds (10Base to 100Base, for example).

Modules

The Catalyst 3000 series of switches provides optional modules that can be used to build your internetwork. These modules are:

Single Port 100BaseT Module: WS-X3001 is a single RJ-45 port 100BaseTX expansion module. DIP switches on the front panel are used to enable full-duplex communication.

Four-Port 10BaseT Module: WS-X3002 is a four-port RJ-45 10BaseT expansion module. DIP switches on the front panel are used to enable full-duplex communication.

Three-Port 10BaseF Module: WS-X3003 is a three-port ST connector 10BaseF expansion module. DIP switches on the front panel are used to enable full-duplex communication.

Single-Port 100BaseF Module: WS-X3005 is a single-port ST connector 100BaseF expansion module. DIP switches on the front panel are used to enable full-duplex communication.

ATM Expansion Module: WS-X3006A is a single-port ATM expansion module that supports speeds up to 155Mbps. To use ATM, you must have at least 8MB of RAM, and no more than two ATM modules per switch can be configured. The module performs cell-to-packet and packet-to-cell conversion.

StackPort Module: WS-X3004 is the Catalyst StackPort module used to connect multiple 3000 switches together. The module uses a SCSI-2 connector with proprietary signaling to connect up to eight switches together.

100VG-AnyLAN Module: Two modules are available, WS-X3007 with UTP and WS-X3008 with 100BaseFX transceivers.

Dual Fast Ethernet with ISL Modules: WS-X3009 and WS-X3010 provide Fast Ethernet expansion modules. WS-X3009 has dual-port SC fiber-optic connectors and the WS-X3010 has dual-port UTP connectors.

10Base2 Ethernet Module: WS-X3013 is a 10Base2 thinnet Ethernet expansion module that provides three ports.

The optional modules in a Catalyst 3000 switch cannot be hot-swapped; you need to power down the system before swapping modules.

The Catalyst Stack System

A Catalyst 3000 series Stack is not just a bunch of switches connected together; it virtually combines to form a single unit—what a concept! There are two ways of configuring Catalyst 3000s, either as single stand-alone units or as a logical combination of up to eight units. The logical combination of units is called a Catalyst Stack.

Catalyst Stacks can be configured in either of the following ways:

- Two Catalyst 3000 series switches cabled directly together in a back-to-back configuration.

- A Stack of up to eight Catalyst 3000 series switches connected together via a Catalyst Matrix.

Catalyst 3000 series switches were designed with savvy! On power-up, after first running through a prescribed set of self-diagnostics, the Catalyst 3000 runs through a stack discovery mode, which is used to find out if the switch is cabled to another Catalyst 3000. If the switch is connected to one or more others, the switches automatically combine to form a stack. If a Catalyst 3000 is not connected to another, it will function as a stand-alone.

The creation of a 3000 Catalyst Stack gives a port density of up to 192 10BaseT Ethernet ports, 16 Fast Ethernet, or 16 ATM interfaces and can provide up to 280Mbps connections between switches.

The Catalyst Matrix is a cross-point matrix switch designed for high throughput that performs a round-robin port arbitration. Each port can operate independently and in parallel.

The connections between the Catalyst 3000 switch and the matrix are a SCSI-2 cable with male connectors on both ends. Also, two modules can be placed in the matrix for full redundancy.

The Catalyst Matrix has the following features:

- Eight I/O Stack Ports using 50-pin SCSI-2 type connectors (one per port).

- 280Mbps per port (full-duplex).

- 1.12Gbps total Catalyst Matrix capacity.

- The ability to move packets between switches.

- Round-robin output port arbitration.

- Independent, parallel port operation (except for multicast).

- Replication of multicast packets.

- No processor; the device is managed by the attached Catalyst 3000 units.

- Optional redundant modules.

- Modules are hot-swappable.

- Front access to field-replaceable modules.

Stack Management Software

The 3000 Catalyst Stack is software driven. Connecting two Catalyst switches together, or three or more switches together using the Catalyst Matrix can create a stack. The stack software is responsible for the topology and configuration of the stack.

As you already know, a Catalyst 3000 switch runs a discovery mode when two or more switches are connected. It does this by sending out a heartbeat broadcast to its neighbors, which includes the stack ID, MAC address of the source box, and box number. If a new switch is inserted into the stack, the switch console will prompt the administrator to push the Sys Req button. This will download the stack parameters to all switches.

When a switch is removed from the stack or a unit fails, all other switches will reconfigure the stack. All switches send out a heartbeat every two seconds. If the neighbor units do not hear a heartbeat for five consecutive heartbeats, it will assume the unit has failed or been removed. If a unit has been removed from the stack but is still powered up, it will revert to stand alone mode.

The Catalyst 3000 must have a different password than the Catalyst Stack. If you have forgotten the password, you can delete it by depressing the Sys Req button on the back panel of the Catalyst 3000 for five seconds, releasing it, and then selecting Clear Non-Volatile RAM from the menu that appears. Also, you can only change the password from the console itself. There are no command line interface (CLI) commands available.

Software Architecture

The Catalyst 3000 switches maintain and distribute address tables throughout the stack, which enables them to learn the location of the end stations. It places the location of the end stations in an address table. This results in faster network response.

Address Tables

The 3000 switch can use two types of address tables: master and port. The master table is in DRAM and lists all the MAC addresses found on the network. This master table is consistent across a 3000 stack. The port table is stored in a buffer on each switch port and is updated by the master table. This allows the port to transmit the packet to the switch bus without using the CPU.

The tables are built just as in any other bridge. As the switch receives frames for forwarding, it remembers the port the frame is received on and then sends the frame to the system module for processing. If the source hardware address is unknown, the switch will add the port and address to the master table, which in turn will update the other switches in the stack. The port table is then updated. If the system module finds the destination hardware address in the address table, it will forward the frame out the appropriate port. If, however, the destination address is unknown, it will broadcast the frame out all active ports. When a response is received, it puts the port and the hardware address into the address table.

Summary

In this chapter we discussed the important features of the Catalyst 3000 switch, the architecture used, and the functions of the major components of the Catalyst switch.

The Cisco 3000 Catalyst switch architecture uses the AXIS bus, the LAN Module ASIC (LMA), and Proprietary Fat Pipe ASIC (PFPA). The 3000 switch uses the AXIS bus to facilitate frame switching. If you have a node at 10Mbps that has a destination node running 10Mbps, the switch will use the LAN Module ASIC (LMA) to perform the port switching. Any ports running above 10Mbps will use the Proprietary Fat Pipe ASIC.

We explored the four main elements of Catalyst 3000 switches:

- Cross-point switch matrix (AXIS Bus)
- AUI connector
- Expansion module
- Stack ports

We then discussed the Catalyst 3000 product features:

- Multiple simultaneous conversations
- Low latency
- Address management
- Address filtering
- On-board filtering
- Full-duplex operation
- Virtual LAN support
- EtherChannel
- Error Handling

We ended the chapter discussing how the Catalyst 3000 switches maintain and distribute address tables throughout the stack, which enables the switches to learn the location of the end stations.

Review Questions

1. How many switch ports are available on a single Catalyst 3000 switch?

    A. 4

    B. 8

    C. 16

    D. 24

2. How many MAC addresses can be supported in a Catalyst 3000 stack?

    A. 500

    B. 1700

    C. 24,000

    D. 10,000

3. If you have a full stack of Catalyst 3000 switches, how many 10Mbps switch ports are available?

    A. 24

    B. 192

    C. 480

    D. 280

4. How many hardware addresses are supported per port on a Catalyst 3000 switch?

    A. 500

    B. 1700

    C. 24,000

    D. 10,000

5. The input buffer on a Catalyst 3000 switch port can hold?

    A. 10 packets

    B. 200 packets

    C. 284 packets

    D. 384 packets

6. Which of the following is true regarding the Catalyst 3000 switch? (Choose all that apply.)

    A. Each switch in the stack must have different passwords.

    B. All passwords throughout the stack must be the same.

    C. You can delete a Catalyst 3000 switch password by pressing the Sys Req button at bootup.

    D. You can delete a Catalyst 3000 switch password by pressing Esc+Del at bootup.

7. Which of the following are true regarding store-and-forward LAN switching? (Choose all that apply.)

    A. The switch starts to forward the frame as soon as the header is received.

    B. The switch receives the entire frame before forwarding.

    C. Latency remains constant regardless of frame length.

    D. This is only used with the Catalyst 3000 series of switches.

8. Which of the following are true regarding store-and-forward LAN switching? (Choose all that apply.)

    A. The switch starts to forward the frame as soon as the header is received.

    B. Latency remains constant regardless of frame length.

    C. Latency varies with frame length.

    D. It's used only in the Catalyst 5000 series of switches.

9. Which LAN switching method runs a CRC on each frame?

   A. Fast-forward

   B. Fragment-free

   C. Store-and-forward

   D. Cut-through

10. If a switch receives a frame and only reads the destination hardware address before forwarding, which type of LAN switching type is being used?

   A. Fast-forward

   B. Fragment-free

   C. Store-and-forward

   D. Cut-through

11. A single Catalyst 3000 switch can support how many 100VG AnyLAN ports?

   A. 1

   B. 2

   C. 12

   D. 24

12. The Catalyst Matrix supports how many SCSI-2 ports?

   A. 1

   B. 2

   C. 4

   D. 8

13. Which of the following is used to connect different types of network topologies to the AXIS bus, which allows switching?

A. PFPA

B. ASIC

C. LANE

D. LMA

14. The serial port on the WAN module can support up to what speed?

A. 1.544Mbps

B. 128Kbps

C. 2.048Mbps

D. 4Mbps

15. How many expansion slots are included in each Catalyst 3000 switch?

A. One

B. Two

C. Four

D. Eight

16. Each Catalyst 3000 buffer can hold up to ___ packets in each direction (incoming and outgoing).

A. 10

B. 100

C. 285

D. 384

17. By default, what is the amount of latency for a packet switched through a Catalyst 3000 switch?

   A. 10 microseconds

   B. 30 microseconds

   C. 40 microseconds

   D. 50 microseconds

18. The AXIS bus uses which of the following technologies for connecting one 10Mbps port to another 10Mbps port?

   A. Synchronous TDM

   B. SONET

   C. ASIC

   D. Asynchronous TDM

19. The Catalyst 3100 comes with how many 10Mbps switch ports by default?

   A. 8

   B. 16

   C. 24

   D. 32

20. Which of the following is true regarding passwords on a 3000 switch?

   A. You can use Esc+Del to clear the password.

   B. The password must be at least five characters.

   C. You can only change the password from the console.

   D. The password for a 3000 switch must be the same as for the Catalyst Stack.

CHAPTER

7

Installing and Configuring the Cisco
Catalyst 3000 Series Switches

Chapter 6 introduced the features and architecture of the Cisco Catalyst 3000 series switches. This chapter introduces the installation and configuration of the Catalyst 3000 switches. The 3000 switch is configured entirely through a menu-driven system, which is illustrated throughout this chapter. You will learn in this chapter how to configure a switch using this menu system for IP addressing, ATM, VLANs, and port parameters. This chapter demonstrates all of the features of the 3000 switch.

The Cisco CLSC exam objectives covered in this chapter include:

- Place Catalyst series switches in a network for optimal performance benefit.

- Use the command-line or menu-driven interface to configure the Catalyst series switches and their switching modules.

- Use the command-line or menu-driven interface to configure trunks, virtual LANs, and ATM LAN Emulation.

- Perform the initial setup of a Catalyst 3000 series switch.

- Configure the switch for management.

- Configure port parameters.

- Configure VLANs and trunk links.

- Configure the ATM LANE module.

- Perform basic router module configuration.

Installing Catalyst 3000 Switches

To install and configure the Cisco Catalyst 3000 switches, you need to connect to the switch either by physically connecting a stand-alone PC to the console port or, after an initial installation, by Telnetting into the switch from a computer on the network.

Cisco describes these different approaches as in-band or out-of-band management.

- *Out-of-band* management is management "outside" of the network using a console connection. This means you're not using the same physical channels used for network traffic.

- *In-band* management is the management of the Catalyst 3000 "through" the network using Simple Network Management Protocol (SNMP) or Telnet. This means your connection is through the network cabling, and it therefore uses network software.

Connecting by the Console Port

The first thing we will learn is how to connect the console cable to the 3000 switch. Console interfacing can be established by connecting to the Console serial port on the back panel of the Catalyst 3000. Here are the three steps:

1. Connect the Catalyst 3000 to a PC or other DTE (Data Terminal Equipment) device using a straight, 25-pin-to-9-pin EIA RS-232 cable and a null-modem adapter. The male DB-9 connector on the Catalyst 3000 is configured as a DTE device.

2. Set the console configuration parameters on your PC's terminal session as shown in Table 7.1.

T A B L E 7.1 Console Configuration Default Settings	**Configuration Item**	**Setting**
	Baud rate	2400, 4800, 9600, 19.2K, 38.4K, 57.6K (default: 9600)
	Parity	None

T A B L E 7.1 *(cont.)* Console Configuration Default Settings	**Configuration Item**	**Setting**
	Data bits	8
	Stop bits	1
	Handshaking	None
	Terminal emulation	VT100
	Duplex	Full
	Soft flow control (XON/XOFF)	Off (input and output)
	Hard flow control (RTS/CTS)	Off

Establishing a Telnet Session

To connect using Telnet, you need to have the switch plugged into a live network with a valid IP address. Your workstation running the Telnet program must also be on a live network with a valid IP address. We will show you how to set an IP address on the switch later in this chapter.

Once your IP addresses are set, you can then use Telnet or an SNMP management program on your workstation to connect to the switch. This will allow you to manage and configure the switch.

Using the Catalyst 3000 Console

Once you've made the physical connection, powered up the switch, and gone through the initial diagnostics, you're ready to work with the management console application. It's a very simple menu-driven program; there are just a couple of basic things to remember before starting with it.

- You choose a menu item by using the arrow keys to highlight it and pressing Return or Enter. You'll be prompted if the program needs additional information for that item.

- Generally, new choices are saved once you select Return to Previous Menu.

- The term "More" indicates that there is more information than can be displayed on one screen. Select "More" and press Return to view the next screen of information.

- To return to the Main menu from any screen, press Ctrl+P. Don't forget that any change made to the screen you were in will not be saved in such an instance. To return to the initial Greeting screen, press Ctrl+B.

- If you are using a Catalyst VLAN, remember to set up IP, SNMP, and spanning tree values.

- The console automatically returns to the Greeting screen after five minutes of inactivity. (You can change this default time using the Main ➤ Configuration ➤ Console Configuration menu.)

- You can protect your system against unauthorized access to configuration screens by setting a password that users must enter at the initial Greeting screen. If a password is not already configured, press Return or Enter to bring up the Main menu. You may set a password using the Main ➤ Configuration ➤ Password menu.

The Main Menu

The Main menu (Figure 7.1) is used for all management operations: configuring the switch, monitoring statistics, and downloading and uploading files. In this chapter we'll focus on configuration, but we'll also look briefly at the other menus available here.

The Main menu offers the following options:

Configuration: Displays the Configuration menu, which enables you to view and set the Catalyst 3000 configuration parameters.

Statistics: Displays the Statistics menu for the Catalyst 3000. The statistics can be used to monitor switch and network performance, which is a valuable troubleshooting aid.

Download/Upload: Used to load the flash memory in the Catalyst 3000. The Download menu displays two download options: Trivial File Transfer Protocol (TFTP) and Serial Link download.

Reset: Displays the reset options available through the Catalyst 3000 switch.

FIGURE 7.1

The Catalyst 3000 management console's Main menu

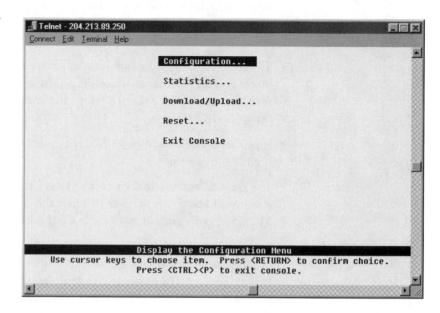

Exit Console: Highlighting this selection and pressing the Return or Enter key will return the console to the Greeting screen (on a Telnet session, this causes the session to close).

The Configuration Menu

The Configuration menu enables you to view and set the Catalyst 3000 configuration parameters. As you can see in Figure 7.2, there are quite a few items you can configure. The following sections describe each of the Configuration submenus.

Switch Information

Figure 7.3 shows the Switch Information screen, where you enter the basic ID information about the switch and its location and role in your network:

System Description: The name and model of the switch unit.

System ID: Assigned at the factory.

FIGURE 7.2

The Configuration
menu

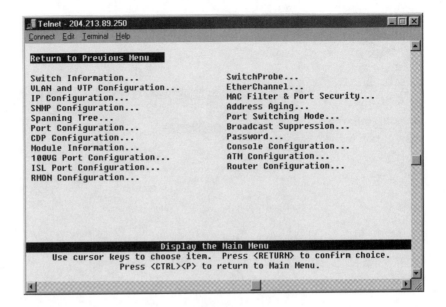

MAC Address: The hardware address of the switch.

Boot Description: The firmware revision.

Interface Description: The type of switch.

System Name: The name assigned by the administrator.

System Location: Administratively assigned; optional.

System Contact: The administratively assigned name for contact purposes.

Time of Day: The internal clock.

Enhanced Features: Indicates if advanced features are installed, for example LANE and VLANs.

DRAM Installed: The amount of RAM.

FLASH Memory Installed: The amount of flash memory.

NOTE   If the unit is part of a stack, parameters for the entire stack will be displayed.

FIGURE 7.3

The Switch Information menu

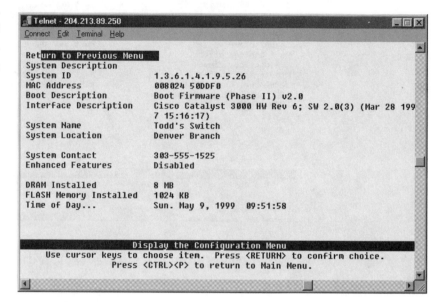

VLAN and VTP Configuration

This menu is used to set up VLANs. From the Configuration menu, choose VLAN and VTP Configuration. Figure 7.4 displays the VLAN and VTP configuration screen. It has the following options:

Local VLAN Port Configuration: Shows the current VLAN port assignments. You can change the assignment by using the cursor and then selecting Change. Only 14 ports are displayed at a time. Select the "More" option to see the other assigned ports.

VTP Administrative Configuration: Displays the domain name and the operation mode of the domain—server, client, or transparent. In server mode, changes can only be made from the local device. In Client mode, you can only make changes from remote devices, and the transparent mode passes VTP packets.

VTP VLAN Configuration: Shows each VLAN administratively assigned and allows you to edit the assignments.

Local Preferred VLANs Configuration: Shows all configured VLANs.

Reassign Ports in Local VLAN: Used for moving a fully configured stack into an existing VTP administrative domain.

F I G U R E   7.4

The VLAN and VTP Configuration menu

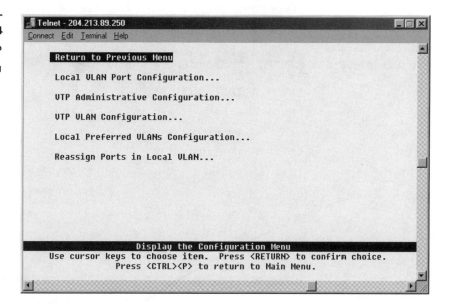

IP Configuration

Use the IP Configuration menu, shown in Figure 7.5, to configure the IP address and related information for the switch.

As an administrator, you must know the values of these options before trying to configure your switch.

Interface MAC Address: This is the hardware address of the switch, assigned by the manufacturer.

IP Address: Shows the configured IP Address. The default is 0.0.0.0.

Default Gateway: Shows the current default gateway assigned. The default is 0.0.0.0.

Subnet Mask: Shows the currently assigned mask.

IP State: Can be IP Disabled, BootP When Needed, or BootP Always.

IP Packet Type: Shows the media used.

Send PING: Can be used to Ping a device from the switch console.

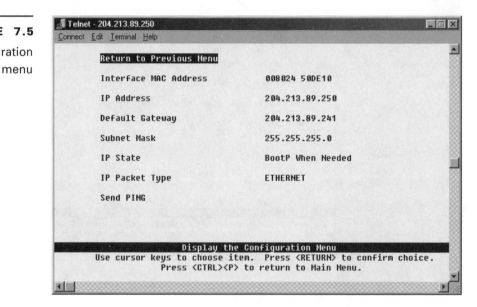

FIGURE 7.5

The IP Configuration menu

SNMP Configuration

SNMP can be configured through the SNMP Configuration screen as displayed in Figure 7.6.

Send Authentication Traps: Can be set to either Yes or No and indicate whether SNMP should send trap messages.

Community Strings: Can be set with either Read or Read/Write permissions. The default is Read for public and Read/Write for private. This is shown in Figure 7.7. Notice that the public community string is read-only and the MISAdmin community string is read/write.

Trap Receivers: Used to tell the switch where to send trap messages.

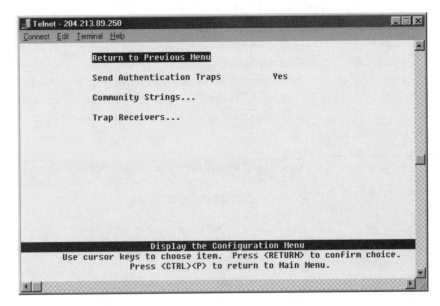

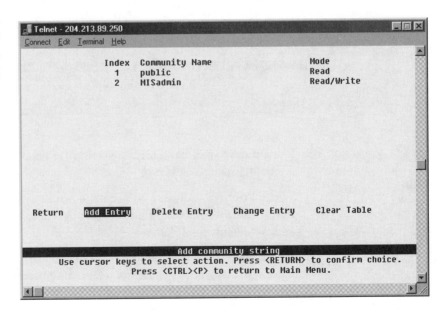

Spanning Tree

As introduced in Chapter 2, the Spanning Tree Protocol (STP) was developed to stop network loops in bridged environments. STP is a bridge-to-bridge link management protocol that allows multiple paths to the same location without loops occurring in the network. To use STP with Catalyst 3000 switches, you must assign a port cost and a port priority to each network segment. Figure 7.8 shows the Spanning Tree menu.

FIGURE 7.8

The Spanning Tree menu

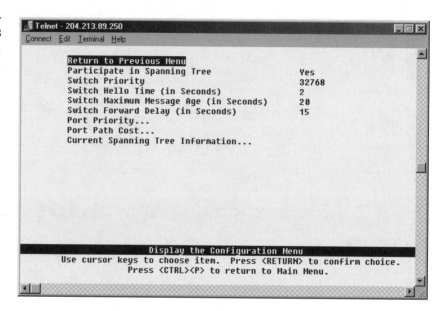

Participate in Spanning Tree: Selecting Yes enables STP when the screen is exited. The default is No.

Switch Priority: Allows you to enter a priority value for the switch. The lowest value is the switch that becomes the root. The range is 0 – 65,535 and the default is 32,768.

Switch Hello Time (in Seconds): Allows you to enter a value for the configuration messages when the switch is configured with the lowest switch priority or root. It can't be lower than 1 or higher than the lower of 10 or (Switch Maximum Message Age/2 – 1). The upper range limit that appears reflects the value currently selected for Switch Maximum Message Age. The default is 2.

Switch Maximum Message Age (in Seconds):   Used when the switch is configured as the root and sets the maximum message age. The minimum cannot be less than 6 or twice the Switch Hello value plus 1. The maximum cannot be more than the lower of 40 or (2 × (Switch Forward Delay – 1)). The default is 20.

Switch Forward Delay (in Seconds):   The time a switch waits between transitions from listening to learning and from learning to forwarding. It can't be less than 4 or (2 × (Switch Maximum Message Age/2 +1)), and cannot be higher than 30. Default is 15.

Port Priority: A user-selected value for choosing the topology path to the root.

Port Path Cost: A user-selected value that shows the value of the port in the path to the root.

Current Spanning Tree Information: Shows the switch's current spanning tree information.

Port Configuration

The Port Configuration screen (Figure 7.9) allows you to enable or disable individual ports on the switch. For each port, the screen shows the following information.

Port: The port number.

Type: The interface type.

Link: Used to indicate if a valid link is connected.

MDI/MDIX: The setting for 10BaseT.

Speed: The speed of the port.

Mode: Displays the LAN Switching type. A-CT is Auto/Cut-Through. F-FS is Store and Forward and F-CT is Cut-through.

Duplex: Displays whether the port is using full- or half-duplex communication. (This can be configured from the Port configuration screen option.)

Enable/disable: The status of the port and the only configurable part of this menu.

```
Telnet - 204.213.89.250                                                  _ □ ×
Connect  Edit  Terminal  Help

  Port    Type     Link   MDI/MDIX   Speed   Mode   Duplex   Enabled/Disabled
   1      AUI      up       MDIX      10     A-CT    Half        Enabled
   2      10BaseT  down     MDIX      10     A-CT    Half        Enabled
   3      10BaseT  --       MDIX      10     A-CT    Half        Disabled
   4      10BaseT  down     MDIX      10     F-SF    Half        Enabled
   5      10BaseT  down     MDIX      10     F-CT    Half        Enabled
   6      10BaseT  down     MDIX      10     A-CT    Half        Enabled
   7      10BaseT  down     MDIX      10     A-CT    Half        Enabled
   8      10BaseT  down     MDIX      10     A-CT    Half        Enabled
   9      10BaseT  down     MDIX      10     A-CT    Half        Enabled
  10      10BaseT  down     MDIX      10     A-CT    Half        Enabled
  11      10BaseT  down     MDIX      10     A-CT    Half        Enabled
  12      10BaseT  down     MDIX      10     A-CT    Half        Enabled
  13      10BaseT  down     MDIX      10     A-CT    Half        Enabled
  14      10BaseT  down     MDIX      10     A-CT    Half        Enabled
  Return      More         Change

                         Return to previous menu
      Use cursor keys to choose item.  Press <RETURN> to confirm choice.
              Press <CTRL><P> to return to Main Menu.
```

CDP Configuration

Cisco Discovery Protocol is used to gather information about neighbor routers. It can gather information from all Cisco devices that run the IOS. Figure 7.10 shows the CDP Configuration screen.

Port: The port on which the switch receives the CDP information.

Enabled/Disabled: Turns on or off CDP on a port.

Transition Frequency Time: The default interval for update packets sent to neighbor devices. The default is 60.

Default TTL Value: Shows the default CDP packet time-to-live (or *holdtime*) of 180 seconds. After this time, the switch will discard any information from a device if it has not heard an update in three time periods.

FIGURE 7.10

CDP Configuration

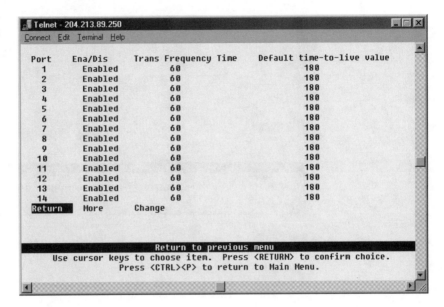

Module Information

The Module Information screen displays the modules currently installed in the switch. Figure 7.11 shows the module information screen. You can't change anything here.

100VG Port Configuration

The 3000 Catalyst switch can support 100VG-AnyLan. By default, the 100VG ports are enabled and do not need configuring.

The menu items are as follows:

Port: Refers to the port on the 100VG modules. The only ports available on a 3000 switch are 17, 19, 21, or 23.

F I G U R E   7.11

The Module
Information screen

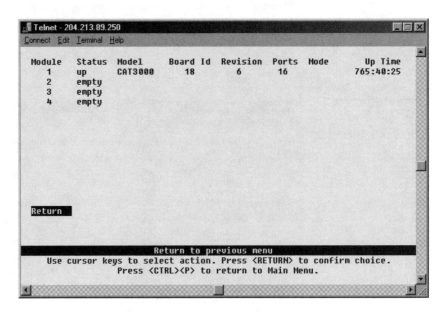

Type: Refers to the type of transceiver installed in the 100VG module. Possible options are:

UTP: Unshielded twisted pair.

STP: Shielded twisted pair.

F27:   Recessed 100VG Fiber-Optic.

VG-Empty: Means that no transceiver installed.

VG-New: A new transceiver installed after the software was created.

Link: Details whether the port has been trained.

ISL Port Configuration

Inter-Switch Link (ISL) can be used to trunk ports on a Catalyst 3000 switch. You want to trunk ports when you need a host in more than one VLAN at the same time; for example, in a server. The ISL menu is used to configure the ISL trunking mode for each ISL port.

The ISL screen displays four menu headings:

Port: Shows the participating ISL ports on the switch.

State: Gives the state of the port, either trunk or static.

Note: A diagnostic message about the trunking states.

Trunking Mode: Gives the status of the port—On, Off, Auto, or Desirable.

RMON Configuration

The 3000 Catalyst switch can be used to communicate with a Remote Monitoring device (RMON). Figure 7.12 shows the RMON configuration.

F I G U R E 7.12

RMON Configuration

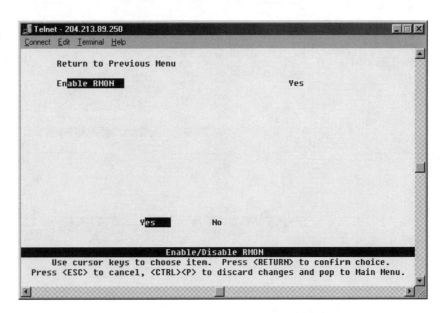

Enable RMON allows you to either enable the switch to communicate with a RMON or not. You must reboot the switch to make the change effective. This works with the SNMP configuration in that you can set the community string for the RMON in the SNMP configuration.

SwitchProbe

The SwitchProbe menu is used to select ports to be used for monitoring with an analyzer. Figure 7.13 shows the SwitchProbe options.

SwitchProbe Port Number: Used to enter the number of the port you want to monitor with a network analyzer. The default is 0 for all ports, which means monitoring is disabled.

Traffic to Probe: Configures either receive or transmit traffic. Half-Duplex always monitors both transmit and receive, while full-duplex can monitor either.

FIGURE 7.13

SwitchProbe options

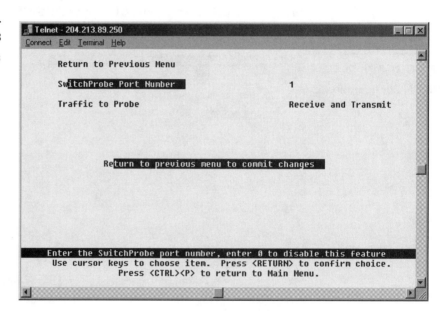

EtherChannel

EtherChannel is used to combine multiple FastEthernet links between Cisco switches. Choosing EtherChannel from the Configuration menu displays the screen shown in Figure 7.14, where you can set (or simply view) configuration options:

EtherChannel Configuration: Used to get into the EtherChannel Configuration screen, which has the following options:

EtherChannel: Lists the different Ethernet Channel setups.

Ports: Refers to ports configured for EtherChannel.

Add Entry: Allows you to select the ports used in EtherChannel.

Delete Entry: After prompting to confirm your selection, deletes the selected EtherChannel.

Change Entry: Prompts you to reenter the port numbers in the selected EtherChannel.

Clear Table: MSDeletes all EtherChannel information.

Running EtherChannel Information: Shows you the existing configured EtherChannel information.

F I G U R E   7.14

The EtherChannel menu

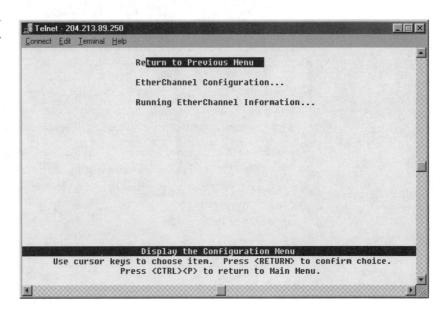

MAC Filter and Port Security

You can access the Filter menu by selecting the MAC Filter and Port Security option. Figure 7.15 shows the Mac Filter and Port Security screen.

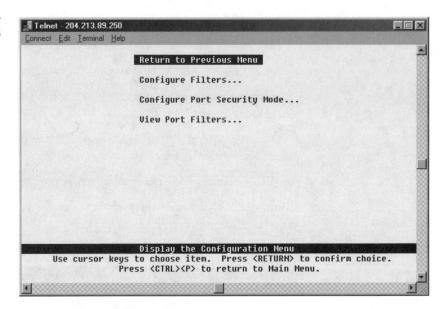

FIGURE 7.15

MAC Filter and Port Security

Configure Filters: Displays the options shown in Figure 7.16. You can block using source or destination hardware addresses. You also can force a packet with a hardware destination address to go out only certain ports.

Configure Port Security Mode: Establishes secure address levels for specific ports. Figure 7.17 shows the Configure Port Security Mode screen. Press Return or Enter after highlighting Change to configure a port. You can configure port security by source, destination, or both source and destination hardware address.

View Port Filters: Displays the ports using MAC address filter and port security functions.

F I G U R E 7.16

MAC Filter Options

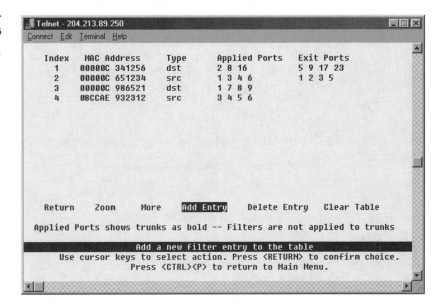

F I G U R E 7.17

Configure Port
Security Mode

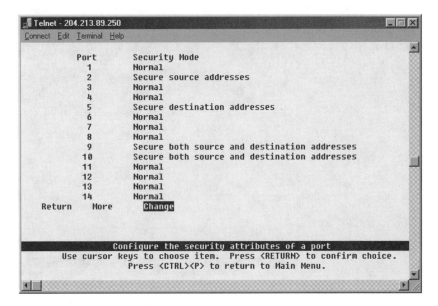

Learn and Lock   The Learn and Lock feature lets you control and monitor switch port access, which can provide security. It is also known as MAC Address Port Security because it uses Ethernet or Fast Ethernet MAC addresses to block access to a switch port. When a MAC address that has been listed in the filter is detected, the port is immediately disabled and an SNMP trap is sent to the SNMP Manager.

Learn and Lock Variable: Used to enable or disable Learn and Lock.

Static Address Learning: Displays the options:

Port: Refers to the switch port

MAC Address: The hardware address

Status: Enabled or disabled

Time Left: The remaining time that the port will be disabled

Address Aging

The aging tables are used to flush out older MAC or hardware addresses from the switch filter tables. Figure 7.18 shows the Address Aging menu.

F I G U R E   7.18

The Aging menu

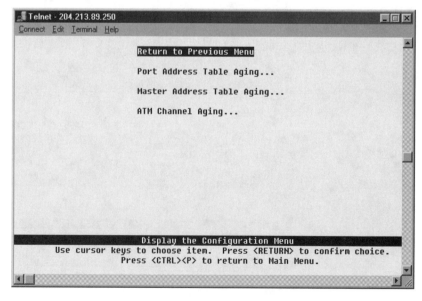

Port Address Table Aging: Displays the switch ports, aging time, and Demand Aging Level, which sets the threshold of address table capacity.

Master Address Table Aging: Used to set the threshold for unused MAC addresses. The aging time that can be set is 0 to 9999 minutes; the default is 15 minutes.

ATM Channel Aging: Used to remove less-frequently-used ATM modules. This sets the Virtual Circuit Identifier age and Virtual Circuit demand level for virtual circuits.

Port Switching Mode

The Port Switching Mode screen is used to set the LAN Switching modes on the 3000 switch. Figure 7.19 shows the Port Switching menu.

FIGURE 7.19

The Port Switching Mode menu

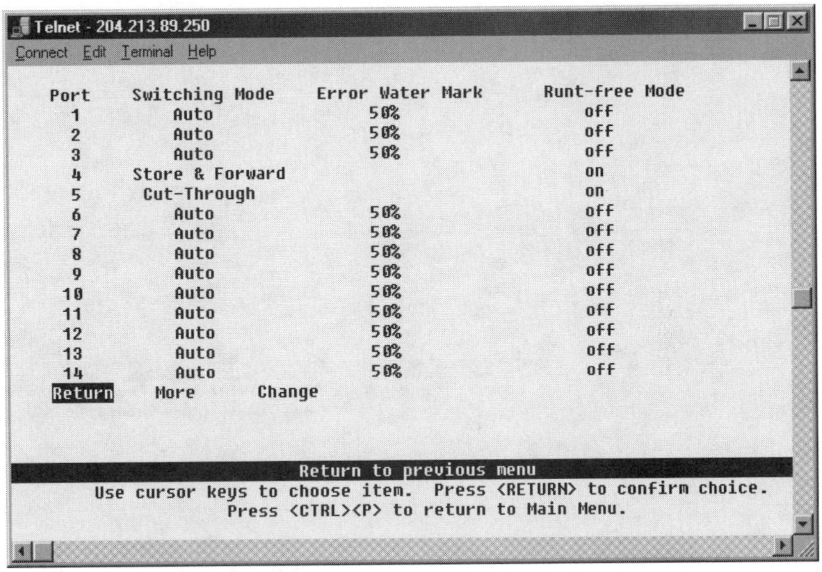

You can choose from Auto, Cut-Through, and Store and Forward. In Auto mode, the port runs cut-through unless the Error Water Mark threshold is exceeded, in which case the switch will automatically convert to store-and-forward until the error threshold drops.

The Runtless mode, if turned On, will discard any packets less than 64 bytes. If this mode is turned Off, the switch will forward the packet.

Broadcast Suppression

The Catalyst 3000 can be configured to suppress broadcast packets on individual ports. The value you configure is the percentage of the total number of packets that can be sent as broadcasts. If the broadcasts sent from a configured port exceed the configured percentage, broadcasts are suppressed until the broadcast level drops below the configured threshold. The Broadcast Suppression menu is shown in Figure 7.20.

F I G U R E 7.20

Broadcast Suppression

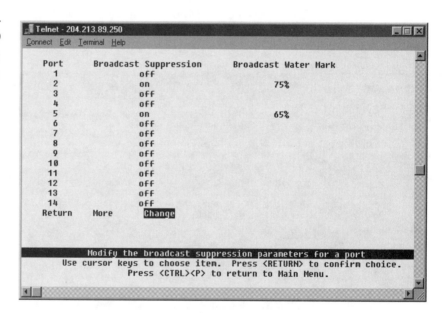

Port: Refers to the ports available for broadcast suppression.

Broadcast Suppression: Indicates the ports with broadcast suppression enabled.

Broadcast Water Mark: A user-defined percentage.

Password

To set a password for managing the 3000 switch, use the Password menu as shown in Figure 7.21.

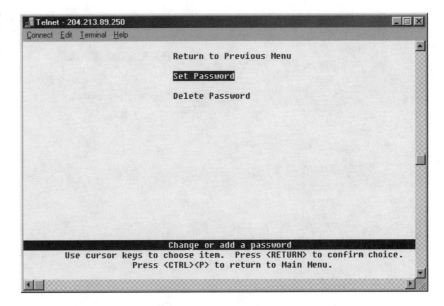

Set Password: Allows you to set a password for the management console.

Delete Password: Allows you to delete a password from the switch.

If a password is already set, you must enter the present password before you can change or delete it.

If the Catalyst 3000 is part of a Catalyst Stack, each individual unit must have a different password than the Stack. If you have lost your password, press the SYS REQ button on the back panel of the switch for 1 second, release it, and then select Clear Nonvolatile RAM from the menu that is displayed.

Console Configuration

The Console Configuration screen allows you to configure the console for modem and Telnet. The menu is displayed in Figure 7.22.

FIGURE 7.22

The Console Configuration menu

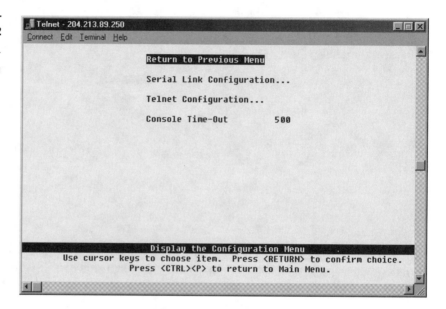

Serial Link Configuration You can choose Serial Link Configuration to configure the switch, allowing a modem to be connected to the console port. The Serial Link Configuration screen offers the following options:

Hardware Flow Control: Used to enable or disable the RTS/CTS handshaking and is disabled by default.

Software Flow Control: Used to enable the XON and XOFF characters, which are 11 and 13 hex, respectively. By default, it is disabled.

Autobaud upon Break: Enables the autobaud feature, which is used to detect the baud rate of incoming communications and set the console's baud rate to match. Pressing the Return key sends a Break character, which triggers the autobaud detection. This option is turned on by default.

Console Baud Rate Default: 9600

To connect and login to the switch through a modem, use the settings shown below:

1. Wait for a Connection should be set to 45 seconds.

2. Pause Between Calls should be set to 6 seconds.

3. Make sure that Autobaud Detect is On.

4. Set Drop DTR (Data Terminal Ready) between Calls to Yes.

5. Set Send CR between Calls to Yes.

6. Set Send Init If CD High to Yes.

Configuring Telnet Parameters   The Telnet Configuration menu (Figure 7.23) allows administrators to enter the following Telnet session parameters:

Number of Telnet Sessions Allowed: Allows configuration of from 1 to 5 connections.

Disallow New Telnet Session: Can be only Yes or No.

Terminate All Active Telnet Sessions: Used to immediately terminate any connected hosts.

Telnet Sessions: Displays any active Telnet session on the switch.

FIGURE 7.23

Telnet Configuration

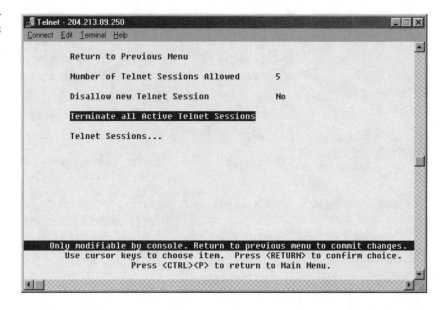

Console Timeout   The Console Timeout configuration sets the value of the console timeout when no activity occurs on the console. The range is from 0 to 1440 minutes. Figure 7.24 shows the configuration screen.

FIGURE 7.24

The Console Timeout
Screen

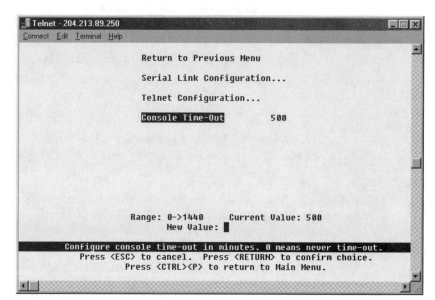

FIGURE 7.24

The Console Timeout Screen

ATM Configuration

Asynchronous Transfer Mode (ATM) can be used with the Catalyst family of switches, including the 3000 series. Local Area Network Emulation (LANE) is used on the switch to emulate a network broadcast environment like Ethernet. See Chapter 3 for more information on ATM and LANE. The Catalyst 3000 uses the WS-X3006A ATM module for ATM support.

The ATM Configuration menu provides three options:

Operation Mode: Can be set to either client or server.

Configuration Type: Sets the address for registration to the ATM switch.

ATM SNAP Prefix: Sets the ATM prefix, LECS ESI address, and a selector byte value of FF to form the ATM address for the LECS.

Router Configuration

There are some configurable parameters on the 3000 switch for a router module. The parameters that can be configured are the bootup process, router reset, flow control, and access. This can only be done if a router module is present.

The configuration screen of the router module configuration has only one option:

Enter a port number: The port number associated with the router module.

The Statistics Menu

Accessible from the Main menu, the Statistics menu (Figure 7.25) displays the options for showing switch statistics.

FIGURE 7.25

The Statistics menu

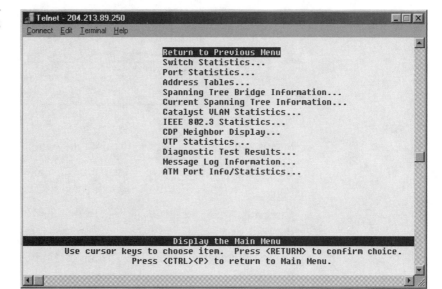

```
Telnet - 204.213.89.250
Connect  Edit  Terminal  Help

                        Return to Previous Menu
                        Switch Statistics...
                        Port Statistics...
                        Address Tables...
                        Spanning Tree Bridge Information...
                        Current Spanning Tree Information...
                        Catalyst VLAN Statistics...
                        IEEE 802.3 Statistics...
                        CDP Neighbor Display...
                        UTP Statistics...
                        Diagnostic Test Results...
                        Message Log Information...
                        ATM Port Info/Statistics...




                        Display the Main Menu
        Use cursor keys to choose item.  Press <RETURN> to confirm choice.
                 Press <CTRL><P> to return to Main Menu.
```

The Cisco CLSC course only covers the first two options in the Statistics menu.

Switch Statistics

This screen displays statistics and information about stations connected to the 3000 switch. Figure 7.26 illustrates a typical Switch Statistics screen; the parameters are explained below.

FIGURE 7.26

The Switch
Statistics menu

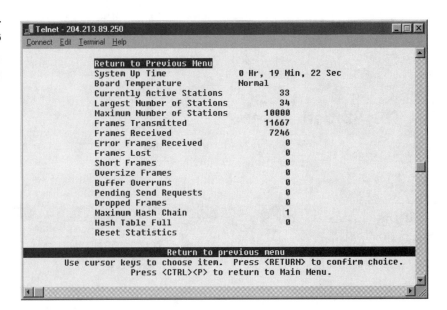

System Up Time: Refers to the time the switch has been powered up.

Board Temperature: Typically reads Normal. However, if it indicates High, the temperature of the switch is over 122 degrees.

Currently Active Stations: Refers to the number of MAC addresses in the address table.

Largest Number of Stations: The largest number of MAC addresses mapped to a port since the last power-up.

Maximum Number of Stations: The number of MAC addresses that can be supported simultaneously. The default is 10,000 for 4MB DRAM and 20,000 for 8MB DRAM.

Frames Transmitted: The number of frames transmitted since power-up.

Frames Received: The number of frames received since power-up.

Error Frames Received: The number of errors received since power-up.

Frames Lost: The number of frames lost due to buffer overruns since power-up.

Short Frames: The number of short frames (runts) since power-up.

Oversize Frames: The number of large frames since power-up.

Buffer Overruns: The number of frames dropped since power-up.

Pending Send Requests: The number of software-transmitted packets that are waiting for queues to hardware.

Dropped Frames: The number of frames dropped because the CPU's processing capacity was exceeded.

Maximum Hash Chain: The largest number of MAC addresses that have hashed to the same location in the lookup tables.

Hash Table Full: The number of times the hash table has reached capacity.

Reset Statistics: Clears the statistics on the screen.

Port Statistics

This screen gives details on a port-by-port basis. Figure 7.27 shows the details for Port 1.

Local Frames Received: The number of frames not forwarded.

Frames Switched by Hardware: The number of frames forwarded to another MAC address.

All Forwarded Frames: The number of broadcast, multicast, and unicast frames forwarded.

Number of Learned Stations: The number of stations whose frames were sent to the CPU for processing because the MAC address was not in the filter table.

Frames Delivered for Learning: The number frames that were sent to the CPU for processing because the MAC address is not in the filter table.

FIGURE 7.27

Port Statistics for Port 1

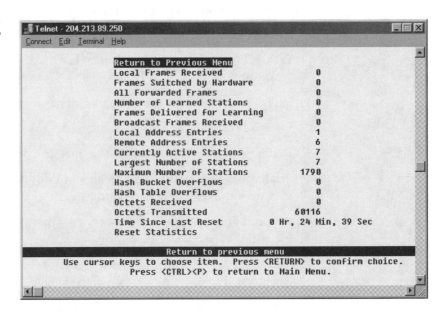

Broadcast Frames Received: The number of broadcast frames received on this port.

Local Address Entries: The MAC addresses on the segment attached to this port.

Remote Address Entries: The number of MAC addresses on this port that are attached to another segment.

Currently Active Stations: The total number of MAC addresses associated with this port.

Largest Number of Stations: The number of active MAC addresses since the last reboot.

Maximum Number of Stations: Lists the maximum number of MAC addresses supported on this port.

Hash Bucket Overflows: Used by technical support for troubleshooting.

Hash Table Overflows: Used by technical support for troubleshooting.

Octets Received: Used by technical support for troubleshooting.

Octets Transmitted: Used by technical support for troubleshooting.

Time Since Last Reset: The amount of time in hours, minutes, and seconds since the port traffic counters were reset.

Reset Statistics: Resets the counters for the port.

The Download/Upload Menu

The Download/Upload menu is used to download or upload the flash memory, which stores the Cisco IOS. The two options are through a direct console connection using the Serial Link menu or by Telnetting and using the TFTP Download/Upload options as shown in Figure 7.28.

FIGURE 7.28

Download/Upload options

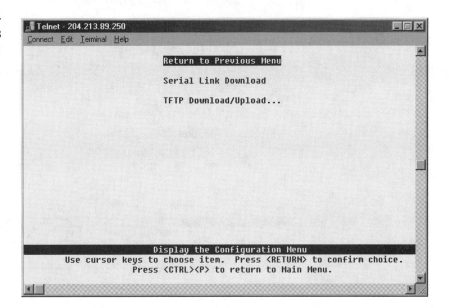

Serial Link Download

To download a new IOS into the Catalyst 3000 switch using the console, choose the Serial Link Download option.

This is a straightforward way to download the flash, but you must make sure that if you have a Catalyst Stack, all switches have the same software version. If there are different versions in the stack, the stack will not boot.

Because of this, it is important to download each switch individually before connecting them into a stack, instead of downloading the flash memory to a switch that's part of a stack.

TFTP Download/Upload

This option is used to put a new version of software into the 3000 switch via TFTP (Trivial File Transfer Protocol). TFTP is not a normal part of the 3000 software because it is only used to upload or download software, which should happen very rarely. The TFTP Download screen is shown below in Figure 7.29.

FIGURE 7.29

TFTP Download/ Upload

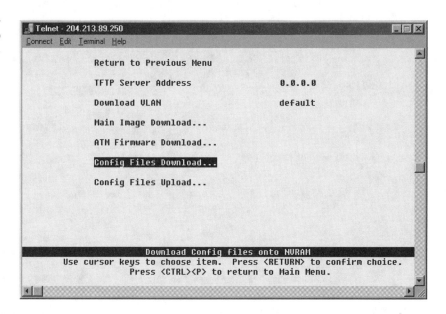

TFTP Server Address: The address of the TFTP host.

Download VLAN: Lets you select the VLAN through which the TFTP server is to be accessed.

Main Image Download: Used to download the main system image.

ATM Firmware Download: Used to download firmware to an ATM card.

Config Files Download: Copies the switch configuration from a TFTP host to NVRAM.

Config Files Upload: Copies the switch configuration to a TFTP host.

Upload Procedures   To upload new versions of software using TFTP, the file needs to be on a TFTP host like a Unix workstation or server. You need to know the default TFTP directly on the TFTP host and the IP address of the device that holds the software. Make sure that you can Ping from the switch to the TFTP host before attempting a download. This will ensure IP connectivity.

The Reset Menu

The Reset screen, as shown in Figure 7.30, displays the reset options available with the Catalyst 3000.

Number of Resets Since Diagnostics: This displays the number of resets since diagnostics were last run.

Reset Switch With Diagnostics: This resets the hardware, runs diagnostics, clears all counters, and starts the switch.

Reset Switch Without Diagnostics: This resets the hardware, clears all counters, and starts the switch.

Reset Port Address Table: This resets the address table and traffic counters for a particular port.

Clear Non-Volatile RAM: This erases all user-configured parameters.

Reset ATM Module Reset: Resets the ATM module in a specified slot.

Power-On Diagnostics: Enables or disables power-on diagnostics.

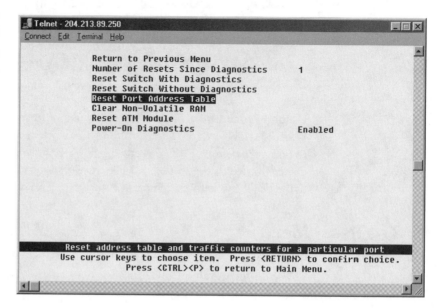

Summary

In this chapter, we covered the installation of the Catalyst 3000 switch through the menu system.

- We learned how to use the menu-driven interface to configure the 3000 Catalyst switches.

- We used the menu-driven interface to configure trunks, virtual LANs, and ATM LAN Emulation.

- By using the menu-driven Catalyst system, we were able to perform an initial setup of a Catalyst 3000 series switch.

- We covered how to configure the 3000 switch with SNMP and other switch management.

- We demonstrated and talked about many different ways to configure port parameters on the 3000 switch.

- The 3000 series Catalyst switch can support ATM LANE. We talked about how to configure the ATM LANE module.

- While traversing through the menu system, we learned how to perform basic router module configuration.

Review Questions

1. Which LAN switching mode monitors for errors and changes from cut-through to store-and-forward if the error threshold is reached?

    A. Cut-through

    B. Store-and-forward

    C. Auto

    D. Runt-free

2. Which menu allows you to set the duplex mode?

    A. Configuration

    B. Module

    C. Switch

    D. Port

3. Which of the following is true about CDP?

    A. It allows you to change configurations on remote switches.

    B. It discovers local and remote Cisco devices.

    C. It discovers directly connected Cisco devices only.

    D. It discovers remote Cisco devices only.

4. Which of the following are examples of in-band management? (Choose all that apply.)

    A. Console

    B. Telnet

    C. Async

    D. SNMP

5. Which of the following is an example of out-of-band management?

   A. Console

   B. Telnet

   C. MIB

   D. SNMP

6. Which of the following is true of passwords on a Catalyst 3000?

   A. You can only change the password from in-band management.

   B. The Catalyst 3000 must have a different password than the Catalyst Stack.

   C. The Catalyst 3000 must have the same password as the Catalyst Stack.

   D. It doesn't matter if the passwords in the stack are the same.

7. If you lose your password on a 3000 Catalyst switch, what should you do?

   A. Press Esc+Del to clear, and then select Clear Nonvolatile RAM from the menu that is displayed.

   B. Press Ctrl+Break; then press Clear Nonvolatile RAM from the menu that is displayed.

   C. Press the SYS REQ button on the back panel of the switch for 1 second, release it, and select Clear Nonvolatile RAM from the menu that is displayed.

   D. Press the SYS REQ button on the front panel of the switch for 1 second, release it, and select Clear Nonvolatile RAM from the menu that is displayed.

8. Which menu lets you send a Ping?

   A. Configuration

   B. Diagnostic

   C. IP Configuration

   D. Console

9. How is the SwitchProbe used?

   A. It allows you to monitor applications.

   B. It allows you to block ports in the switch.

   C. It allows you to monitor traffic.

   D. It allows you to change duplex on a port.

10. Which menu allows you to physically connect more than one port to another switch and combine the bandwidth?

   A. IP configuration

   B. Console

   C. EtherChannel

   D. VLAN/VTP

11. Which is true regarding VLANs? (Choose all that apply.)

   A. They can be created by protocol.

   B. They create smaller broadcast domains.

   C. They create smaller collision domains.

   D. They can't be used on a 3000.

12. Which menu will give you the length of time the switch has been up?

   A. Configuration

   B. Statistics

   C. Switch/Stack Information

   D. Console

13. Which menu will give you the number of frames dropped?

   A. Configuration

   B. Statistics

   C. Switch/Stack info

   D. Console

14. What is the maximum time the console timeout can be set for?

  A. 1000 seconds

  B. 1410 seconds

  C. 1440 seconds

  D. 1540 seconds

15. How many simultaneous Telnet sessions are allowed in a Catalyst 3000 switch by default?

  A. 1

  B. 2

  C. 5

  D. 10

16. Which menu allows you to set the time and date?

  A. Configuration

  B. Switch/Stack Information

  C. Console

  D. IP Configuration

17. From which menu can you reach the VLAN Configuration menu?

  A. Switch Information

  B. VTP Configuration

  C. Statistics

  D. Download

18. Which menu can be used to download new software to flash memory?

   A. Configuration

   B. Statistics

   C. Download

   D. Reset

19. Which menu can be used to enable viewing and setting Catalyst 3000 parameters?

   A. Configuration

   B. Statistics

   C. Download

   D. Reset

20. Which menu can be used to monitor switch and network performance?

   A. Configuration

   B. Statistics

   C. Download

   D. Reset

Laboratory Exercises

In these exercises, you will learn how to configure the Catalyst 3000 switch using the menu-driven interface. Connect a console cable to your switch and start your emulation program on your terminal.

EXERCISE 7.1

Logging in

In this first lab exercise, you will power up the switch, log in, and change the console baud rate.

1. Make sure your 3000 switch has no network connections.

2. Power up the switch. The switch will then run through its power-up diagnostic self-test sequence.

3. After the self-test is complete, the Cisco Catalyst Manager is displayed. Press Return (or Enter).

4. Enter a password if one is set.

5. From the Main menu, choose Configuration. You can do this by using your cursor control keys to highlight the option and then press Return (Enter).

6. From the Configuration menu, choose Console Configuration.

7. Select Serial Link Configuration.

8. From the Serial Link Configuration screen, select the Console Baud Rate and press Return (Enter).

9. The default is 9600. You can change the baud rate to as high as 57600. Highlight your choice and press Return (Enter).

10. Follow the instructions displayed at the bottom of the screen so your console and switch baud rates are identical. If not, you will lose the connection.

11. Return to the Configuration menu.

EXERCISE 7.2

Setting a Console Password

In this exercise, you will set a console password. It is imperative that you do not set the switch password the same as the Catalyst stack. They *must* be different.

1. From the Configuration menu, choose the Password option.

2. From the Password menu, select Set Password.

3. Enter the old password if set.

4. Enter a new password.

5. Confirm your password by typing it in again.

6. Return to the Configuration menu.

EXERCISE 7.3

Configure Port Switching

In this lab, you will set your LAN switch types and Water Mark percentage.

1. From the Configuration menu, select the Port Switching Mode option.

2. In the Port Switching Mode screen, change the switching mode of a port by selecting Change at the bottom of the screen.

3. Enter a port number to change.

4. Select Auto.

5. For the Error Water Mark percentage, type **50**. This will set your percentage of errors the port will allow before automatically switching from cut-through to store-and-forward.

6. Choose a different port and then choose Cut-through. The port will now only perform cut-through LAN switching. Leave the default of Runt-Free switching on.

7. Choose another port and choose Store and Forward. The port will now exclusively perform store-and-forward. Leave the Runt-Free switching at the default of Off.

8. Return to the Configuration menu.

EXERCISE 7.4

VLANs and VTP Configuration

In this lab you will set up the VLAN and VTP configuration on a 3000 switch. An ISL module is required to perform this lab.

1. From the Main Configuration menu, select the VLAN and VTP Configuration option.

2. From the VLAN and VTP Configuration menu, choose VTP Administration Configuration. Use this menu to configure domain names and IDs for your VLANs.

3. Create a new VLAN named Sales and another named Marketing.

4. Return to the VLAN and VTP Configuration screen.

5. Choose the Local VLAN Port Configuration option.

6. Select Change to change the port assignments on the switch.

7. Use the cursor keys to highlight the VLAN to which you want to assign the port and press Return (Enter).

8. Put four ports into the Sales VLAN and four ports into the Marketing VLAN.

9. Return to the Configuration menu.

EXERCISE 7.5

IP Configuration

In this lab, you will add IP information to your 3000 switch.

1. From the Configuration screen, select the IP Configuration option.

2. Select the Sales VLAN.

3. Enter the IP address, subnet mask, and default gateway.

4. Select IP State.

5. Set the IP state to BootP When Needed and press Return (Enter).

6. Set the IP Packet Type to Ethernet.

7. Set these options for all configured VLANs.

8. Return to the Configuration screen.

EXERCISE 7.6

Spanning Tree Configuration

In this lab, you will change the spanning tree options for your two VLANs.

1. From the Configuration screen, choose the Spanning Tree Configuration option.

2. You will see a list of VLANs with spanning tree information for each VLAN.

3. Change the port priority of the Sales VLAN.

4. Change the port fast mode of the Marketing VLAN.

5. Return to the Configuration menu.

EXERCISE 7.7

CDP Information

In this lab you will view and change the CDP information on the 3000 switch.

1. From the Configuration menu, choose CDP Configuration.

2. Select the Change option.

3. Enter a port number.

4. Highlight Enable/Disable to enable CDP on the port.

5. Return to the Configuration menu.

CHAPTER

8

The Cisco Catalyst 5000 System

The previous chapters in this book have addressed the 1900, 2820, and 3000 versions of the Catalyst product line. While excellent switches, they are ill suited to the demands of the data center and are inflexible compared to Cisco's 5000 and 5500 products. The 5000 series offers significant features for complex networks, including greater port density, greater flexibility in the media it supports, internal routing (with the RSM module), network monitoring and analysis (with the NAM module), redundancy via dual Supervisor engines (in the 5500 series), and ATM integration (in the 5500 switch). These features position the 5000/5500 series products at the core and distribution layers of network design, and they lend themselves to placement in wiring closets or the access layer of the network.

The Catalyst 5000 system includes two distinct components. The hardware component includes the various chassis, line cards, Supervisor modules, and integrated circuits within the system. Software interoperates with the various hardware components to provide configuration and system flexibility. This chapter and the following chapters will present the Catalyst 5000/5500 product line. There will be many similarities with the other Catalyst products as presented in this book; however, a thorough understanding of the 5000/5500 product will greatly assist administrators as their needs for network complexity increase. In addition, the 5000 product provides a foundation for new products within the Catalyst product line.

As presented in previous chapters, the primary function of Catalyst switches is to provide Layer 2 services in the wiring closet and network core. During the product's evolution this scope has expanded to include Layer 3 functionality and media independence, including ATM, Token Ring, and FDDI, in addition to Ethernet. With NetFlow and the RSM module, the product continues to evolve. With the release of the Catalyst 5500, Cisco further enhanced the product by integrating the LS1010 backplane and feature cards into what had been a frame-only product. The LS1010 provides cell-based ATM services and adds a 5Gbps backplane to the chassis. The 5002 and smaller switches in the line are useful towards the access layer and in workgroups, and in some ways they compete with the 1900 series switches. Cisco continues to add more systems to the product line as well—integrating new features while responding to user needs for greater backplane capacity or lower price points. As of this writing, Cisco has released the 2900, 6500, and 8500 series switches, in addition to the 4003 and new components for the 5500 series switches. Variances in other platforms are usually the result of Cisco's acquisition of other companies and their technologies. Most of the 5000 series commands and processes are being continued in the product line with the newer platforms.

While it is possible to install and maintain the Catalyst system with a limited understanding of the internal components, it is very beneficial to comprehend the entire system and the myriad features that are available to network designers and administrators. Many administrators are surprised at the number of default services available within the product.

This chapter will cover the following exam objectives:

- Describe the hardware features and functions of the modules in the Catalyst 5000 series switches.

- Describe the hardware features and functions of the Supervisor engine.

- Describe the hardware features, functions, and benefits of the Catalyst modules in the Catalyst 5000 series switches.

- Describe the architecture and functions of the following components of the Catalyst 5000 series switch:

  - Processors: NMP, MCP, and LCP

  - Logic units: LTL, CBL, Arbiter, and EARL

  - ASICS: SAINT, SAGE, SAMBA, and Phoenix

- Trace a frame's progress through a Catalyst 5000 series switch.

- Describe the Catalyst 5000 series switch product evolution.

- Describe the Catalyst 5000 product features.

- Describe the Catalyst 5002 product features.

- Describe the Catalyst 5500 product features.

Catalyst Hardware

The impressive functionality of the Catalyst switch is made possible by the specialized hardware contained within the system. This hardware includes the Application Specific Integrated Circuits (ASICs), which permit processing at wire speeds and the wide variety of physical interfaces available in the platform. This section will address the physical framework of the Catalyst 5000 chassis and the various components. While there are many similarities between the 5000/5500 product line and other products within the Catalyst series, the 5000 is significantly different from the 3000 series product and incorporates the foundation for most development within Cisco for new products. As Cisco develops and acquires new technologies, it is likely that the 5000 will remain a foundation platform from which changes will be deployed. An interesting note is that the Catalyst 5000 technology was actually created by another firm—Catalyst. Following Cisco's acquisition of the product, it was modified for better integration with the Internetwork Operating System (IOS) and other Cisco products.

The Catalyst Chassis

The Cisco Catalyst switching technology is available in a wide variety of form factors to provide the needed port density in various installations. Table 8.1 describes the different chassis in the 5000 product line, in addition to the 2900, 4000, 6500, and 8500 product lines. The focus of this chapter will remain limited to the 5000 and 5500 platforms.

T A B L E 8.1 The Cisco Catalyst Chassis	Chassis	Features
	1900	The 1900 series product is quite limited in configuration and performance; however, it offers a very low cost per port compared to the more advanced switches in the Cisco Catalyst product line. Given its limitations, it is suited for the wiring closet, or access layer, of the network for terminating workstations.
	2820	The 2820 product is similar to the 1900 series; however, modules are available for ATM and FDDI. The 2820 is ideally suited for access services.

T A B L E 8.1 *(cont.)* The Cisco Catalyst Chassis	**Chassis**	**Features**
	2900	The 2900 series uses a fixed configuration and the Supervisor I engine from the Catalyst 5000 product. Although it's more expensive, many companies choose this product for workgroup deployment. This is one of many switches included in the current Cisco product line but not covered by the Cisco 640-404 exam and not presented in a formal manner in this book. It is included in this table for comparison with current (as of this writing) offerings. Fortunately, the use of the Supervisor I engine results in a switch that is similar to the 5000.
	3000	The 3000 product line differs significantly from the 5000 product; however, Cisco has incorporated a number of features that make the 3000 a good choice for certain deployments. Incorporation of WAN links (with the serial module), stackability, and Catalyst features such as ISL provide many services needed by administrators for remote locations. The 3000 platform may be well-suited to smaller installations where WAN connectivity is required, compared to the 5000/5500.
	3900	Not covered by the Cisco 640-404 exam, and not discussed in this book. The 3900 product is a fixed-configuration Token Ring switch. As an access layer switch, it is designed to interconnect with a core Token Ring switch. The 5000/5500 is designed to address this role.
	4000	The 4000 series includes the 4003 and 4912 models. They are positioned for the wiring closet and server farm installations. This is a newer switch within Cisco's Catalyst product offerings. Not covered by the Cisco 640-404 exam, and not discussed in this book.
	5000	The Catalyst 5000 provides five slots, a 1.2Gbps backplane, and optional redundant power supplies. It will be presented in greater detail in this chapter.

T A B L E 8.1 *(cont.)*	Chassis	Features
The Cisco Catalyst Chassis	5500	The Catalyst 5500 provides 13 slots for interface cards (although slot 13 is unavailable for frame switching) and is the largest of the 5000/5500 series switches. Fully populated, the switch weighs 176 pounds. It provides a 3.6Gbps backplane in crossbar configuration (three 1.2Gbps backplanes) for frame switching and a 5Gbps backplane for ATM cell switching. In addition, the platform provides for optional redundant Supervisor engines and optional redundant power supplies, and it includes dual backplane clocks.
	5502	The 5502 is a two-slot, two-power-supply modular switch. It is well suited for the smaller network or the access layer.
	5505	The 5505 is a five-slot Catalyst 5500 series switch capable of redundant Supervisor engines. It is frequently used in the distribution layer of the network, where the port density of the 5500 is unnecessary. It should be noted that the cost differential between the 5505, 5509, and 5500 chassis is very small, and administrators should review the cost differences before ordering to protect against "forklift upgrades" in the future.
	5509	The 5509 is a nine-slot Catalyst 5500 series switch capable of redundant Supervisor engines. The release of the 5509 included provisions for greater gigabit port density in the 5500 series.
	6500	The 6500 product line builds upon the 5500 series and provides additional gigabit performance. It was released in early 1999. Not covered by the Cisco 640-404 exam, and not discussed further in this book.
	8500	The 8540 is designed for ATM and Gigabit Ethernet services in the network core, in addition to future voice services. It is well suited to the data center and network core. Not covered by the Cisco 640-404 exam, and not discussed further in this book.

The Catalyst 5500 chassis requires a 20 Amp connection for its power supply (U.S. models). Administrators should verify the availability of correct facilities before installation. In addition, a fully populated 5500 generates a significant amount of heat and uses nine 5" fans for cooling. These fans are unfiltered, and clean, low-dust equipment rooms are highly recommended.

The Catalyst 5500 Backplane

The Cisco Catalyst 5500 provides the services of both the Catalyst 5000 frame switch and the LS1010 ATM cell switch. This is a significant difference between the 5500 platform and the other versions of the 5000 and 5500 series, and we'll take a closer look at the 5500 backplane in this section. The limitations of backplane capacity and the positions of the modules within the switch should be carefully considered by the administrator. Note that the redundant Supervisor engine must be installed in slot 2.

The 5500 chassis provides a 3.6Gbps backplane for frame switching. This backplane consists of three separate 1.2Gbps backplanes accessible from the various module slots. These backplanes are interconnected via the Phoenix ASIC, which is described in greater detail later in this chapter. Table 8.2 documents the backplane interface options. Each letter (A, B, C) represents one of the three separate 1.2Gbps backplanes.

	Slot	Backplane and Use
T A B L E 8.2 The 5500 Backplane	1	Supervisor Engine II or III (primary), A, B, C backplanes
	2	Redundant Supervisor module or A, B, C backplanes
	3	A, B, C backplane
	4	A, B, C backplane
	5	A, B, C backplane
	6	B backplane

T A B L E 8.2 *(cont.)*	Slot	Backplane and Use
The 5500 Backplane	7	B backplane
	8	B backplane
	9	LS1010 module or B backplane
	10	LS1010 module or C backplane
	11	LS1010 module or C backplane
	12	LS1010 module or C backplane
	13	ATM Switching Engine (ASP module only)

Note that slot 13 is not available for frame-based services and is reserved for the ASP module exclusively. Administrators should carefully plan the installation of line modules in the 5500 chassis to avoid unnecessary over-subscription of the chassis.

LS1010 Modules   In addition to the ATM Switch Processor (ASP), the Catalyst 5500 supports four ATM line cards from the LS1010 (LightStream) platform. The LS1010 is available as a separate product from Cisco; however, most installations take advantage of the Catalyst framework and the benefits of the dual-function 5500 chassis.

ATM LANE installations may take advantage of this integration and use the switching capacity of the LS1010. However, some ATM deployments incorporate voice and video services as well. These links usually aggregate to a core ATM switch. The 8540 is one of the switches used for this service.

The Catalyst ATM modules (LS1010), including the ATM Switch Processor (ASP), do not connect to the Supervisor engine or frame line modules in the 5500 via the backplane. Connect the cell backplane and frame backplane with external cabling.

The Supervisor Engine

The Supervisor Engine in the Catalyst switch is the software responsible for almost all switching functions. Within the Catalyst 5000/5500 product there are three versions of the Supervisor, as outlined in Table 8.3. The original Catalyst engine, the Supervisor I is limited in features compared to the later versions. When cost is not the deciding factor, the Supervisor III is always recommended in the Catalyst 5500 platform. The Supervisor III greatly increases the performance of the product line and, when combined with the 5500, provides full access to the backplane of the system. In addition, the Supervisor III provides external flash memory services for configuration and image files and other services.

T A B L E   8.3:   The Supervisor Engine Versions

Item	Supervisor I	Supervisor II	Supervisor III
Backplane access and limitations	Cannot be used in the 5500	Support for only 1.2Gbps backplane, even in the 5500	Support for 3.6Gbps backplane
Applications and deployments	Most useful in wiring closet applications	Useful in wiring closet and backbone applications	Useful in wiring closet and backbone applications
Additonal Features		Support for the Net-Flow Feature Card (NFFC)	Support for the Net-Flow Feature Card (NFFC)
Fast EtherChannel support	No	Yes	Yes
Performance		Two to three times the original Supervisor performance	Ten times the NMP performance of the original Supervisor engine

The Supervisor Engine Module

Cisco's Supervisor modules are installed in the first slot of the Catalyst 5000/5500 chassis. The 5500/5505/5509 configurations support a redundant Supervisor engine when using the Supervisor II or III.

In addition to managing the Catalyst switch, the Supervisor modules provide network administrators with diagnostic tools via their LED status lights. Table 8.4 documents the various indications of the Supervisor LEDs on the Catalyst 5000/5500 module.

T A B L E 8.4:   The Supervisor Engine Module LEDs

Function	Red	Orange	Green	Off
System Status	Indicates the failure of a system test or an installed redundant power supply that is not active.	Displayed during system bootup or if a module is disabled.	Indicates successful diagnostic tests.	
Fan	Indicates failure of the system fan.		Indicates proper operation of the system fan.	
PS1	Indicates non-operation or failure of the power supply in the left bay.		Indicates proper operation of the power supply in the left bay.	Indicates that no power supply is installed in the left bay or that the power supply is turned off.
PS2	Indicates non-operation or failure of the power supply in the right bay.		Indicates proper operation of the power supply in the right bay.	Indicates that no power supply is installed in the right bay or that the power supply is turned off.

T A B L E 8.4:   The Supervisor Engine Module LEDs *(Continued)*

Function	Red	Orange	Green	Off
Link		If flashing, indicates a bad link and a disabled port. If solid, indicates that the port was disabled in software.	Indicates proper operation and connection of the port.	Indicates that there is no link on port.
100Mbps			Indicates that the port is connected at 100Mbps.	

Note that the Supervisor also provides information about the load on the switch. Many administrators use this for a quick diagnostic review of utilization. The LEDs display switch load in increments of 10 percent.

The face of the Supervisor module also includes a Reset button that is best accessed with a thin, nonmetallic point. This will reset the Supervisor module and will disrupt the forwarding of packets through the switch.

WARNING   Do not use a pencil, pen, or metal paper clip to access the Reset button. While problems are unlikely, these items may break, leave residue, or cause an electrical short.

The Supervisor also contains the console port, which is used for out-of-band connectivity. The console port and its use are described in greater detail in Chapter 11.

Memory on the Supervisor module is similar to the memory on Cisco's router products. The Catalyst system contains flash memory, main memory (DRAM), EPROM, and NVRAM. Flash memory is used for the storage of software images, which may be populated via a TFTP server. The run-time software is stored in DRAM, or main memory. Erasable programmable read-only memory is located on the backplane of the Catalyst 5500. By contrast, the Catalyst 5000 and 5002 switch products locate the EPROM on the Supervisor. The EPROM memory records information regarding each module, including serial numbers, part numbers, controller types, and version- and module-specific information. The 256KB of NVRAM (on the Supervisor II) is used to store configuration information. By default, the Supervisor II and III engines ship with 32MB of main memory and 8MB of flash. The Supervisor IIG and Supervisor III engines come with 512KB of NVRAM by default. As shown in the following output, the startup sequence of the Catalyst 5500 will report the amount of main memory, NVRAM, and flash available on the Supervisor. In this example, the Supervisor III has 32MB of main memory, 16MB of flash memory, and 512KB of NVRAM.

```
System Bootstrap, Version 3.1(2)
Copyright (c) 1994-1997 by cisco Systems, Inc.
Presto processor with 32768 Kbytes of main memory


Autoboot executing command: "boot bootflash:cat5000-sup3.4-5-1.bin"


CCCCCCCCCCCCCCCCCCCCCCCCCCCCCCCCCCCCCCCCCCCCCCCCCCCCCCCCCCCCCCCCCCCC
CCCCCCCCCCCCCCCCCCCCCCCCCCCCCCCCCCCCCCC

Uncompressing file:
####################################################################
####################################################################
####################################################################
####################################################################
####################################################################
####################################################################
####################################################################
####################################################################
####################################################################
####################################################################
####################################################################
####################################################################
###################


System Power On Diagnostics
NVRAM Size ..................512 KB
ID Prom Test ................Passed
DPRAM Size ..................16KB
DPRAM Data 0x55 Test .........Passed
```

```
DPRAM Data 0xaa Test ..........Passed
DPRAM Address Test ...........Passed
Clearing DPRAM ...............Done
System DRAM Memory Size .......32MB
DRAM Data 0x55 Test ..........Passed
DRAM Data 0xaa Test ..........Passed
DRAM Address Test  ...........Passed
Clearing DRAM ................Done
EARLII ......................Present
EARLII RAM Test ..............Passed
EARL Serial Prom Test ........Passed
Level2 Cache .................Present
Level2 Cache test.............Passed
Boot image: bootflash:cat5000-sup3.4-5-1.bin
Downloading epld sram device please wait ...
Programming successful for Altera 10K50 SRAM EPLD

Running System Diagnostics from this Supervisor (Module 1)
This may take up to 2 minutes....please wait


IP address for Catalyst not configured
BOOTP will commence after the ports are online
Ports are coming online ...
```

Additional information is available regarding the memory configuration of the switch, as shown in the example below. This Cisco Catalyst 5505 is configured with 8MB flash memory and 16MB DRAM. Of the available 256KB NVRAM, 107KB is in use. Note that the show flash and show version commands provided this information.

```
Switch_A> (enable) show flash
File           Version  Sector  Size    Built

c5000 nmp      3.2(1b)  02-11   1571059  05/04/98 22:37:19
      epld     3 .2     30       72920   05/04/98 22:37:23
      lcp atm  3.2(1)   12-15    23822   05/04/98 15:29:01
      lcp tr   3.2      12-15    29016   05/04/98 15:30:46
      lcp c5ip 3.2      12-15    23744   05/04/98 15:33:40
      lcp 64k  3.2      12-15    57046   05/04/98 15:32:12
      atm/fddi 3.2      12-15    24507   05/04/98 15:27:10
      lcp 360  3.2(1)   12-15   123108   05/04/98 15:37:04
```

```
                lcp       3.2      12-15    27561   05/04/98 15:25:48
                smcp      3.2      12-15    34155   05/04/98 15:22:38
                mcp       3.2      12-15    26378   05/04/98 15:24:20

        Switch_A> (enable) show version
        WS-C5505 Software, Version Mcp
        SW: 3.2(1) NmpSW: 3.2(1b)
        Copyright (c) 1995-1998 by Cisco Systems
        NMP S/W compiled on May  4 1998, 15:20:25
        MCP S/W compiled on May 04 1998, 15:22:38

        System Bootstrap Version: 3.1(2)

        Hardware Version: 1.0  Model: WS-C5505  Serial #: 066519061

        Module Ports Model       Serial #   Hw    Fw      Fw1     Sw
        ------ ----- ----------- ---------- ----- ------- ------- --
        1      2     WS-X5506    009038746  2.3   3.1(2)  2.4(1)  3.2(1b)
        2      24    WS-X5224    009624720  1.4   3.1(1)          3.2(1)
        3      48    WS-X5012    010124939  2.3   2.3(2)          3.2(1)
        4      48    WS-X5012    010127058  2.3   2.3(2)          3.2(1)

               DRAM                    FLASH                NVRAM
        Module Total  Used  Free   Total  Used  Free  Total Used
        Free

        1      16384K 7846K 8538K  8192K  3840K 4352K 256K  107K
        149K

        Uptime is 171 days, 8 hours, 23 minutes
```

Redundant Supervisor Modules

Two Supervisor II engines (or the Supervisor III) may be installed in the Catalyst chassis for redundancy. The primary Supervisor is always installed in the first slot of the chassis, while the redundant Supervisor is installed in slot 2. In single-Supervisor installations, the second slot may contain a line module. Redundant Supervisor modules are only available in the 5500 Catalyst series.

The Catalyst switch operates from a single Supervisor engine, which places one Supervisor engine in standby mode when two Supervisors are installed. The standby Supervisor obtains its configuration from the primary Supervisor during initialization.

The standby Supervisor's ports, both console and network, are disabled while it is in standby mode. They become active upon failover to the standby Supervisor. This process can take from 30 seconds to over 3 minutes. The failover process is automatic upon failure; however, the administrator may initiate failover by using the `reset` command. In enable mode, the administrator would specify `reset 1` to activate the standby Supervisor in slot 2, for example.

It is recommended that administrators avoid using the network ports in the Supervisor module if the need for redundancy is anticipated. This avoids the problems caused in failover and the loss of connectivity on the failed Supervisor ports.

Catalyst Modules

The Catalyst 5000 and 5500 series switches are quite versatile and provide the administrator with a wide array of configuration options. Cards are available for 10/100/1000Mbps Ethernet, Token Ring, FDDI, and ATM, in addition to the NetFlow, NetAnalysis, and Route/Switch Module (RSM). Each card provides different features, such as ISL, Fast EtherChannel, and Layer 3 switching, or extended RMON functions. The Catalyst modules are capable of hot-swapping. Varied pin lengths that signal the backplane to pause frame flow during the removal and insertion process provide this service. This reduces the possibility of dropped frames. Electrically, the chassis supports removal of the modules, including the Supervisor. Unless you've implemented redundancy as discussed in the previous section, however, removing the Supervisor module will cause the switch to fail. And, as noted above, the redundant Supervisor function is not activated instantaneously, and the delay is likely to cause dropped connections. Proper change control and diagnostic procedures should always precede online insertion or removal of a module, and complete shutdown of the chassis is always preferred.

The modules within the 5000/5500 product are designed for future growth within the product line. This permits incorporation of legacy line cards within new chassis (with some limitations) and some inventory protection. In addition, the modules within the 5000/5500 product are the primary reason that corporations and administrators select the product. Few switches are as flexible in today's increasingly complex networks. While other vendors may excel in specific product areas—ATM, for example—few vendors can offer the routing performance and other network topology integration along with their primary offering at the same level as Cisco.

Ethernet Modules

The Catalyst 5000/5500 Ethernet modules allow full and half-duplex operations at wire speeds, providing administrators with a wide array of options using Ethernet. Support is provided for 10/100/1000Mbps Ethernet. The Ethernet ports make use of the SAINT ASIC, described later in this chapter.

It is important to note that most Ethernet modules also support ISL, or Inter-Switch Link encapsulation. This feature provides an efficient trunking mechanism for multiple VLANs. Administrators should note that ISL is proprietary to Cisco—the 802.1q protocol is the equivalent open standard. For all Cisco installations, ISL may provide additional features for administrators, including load balancing of different spanning trees. Careful consideration should be given when selecting a standard. Note that although ISL is proprietary, many other vendors, including Intel, offer ISL-aware adapters.

Ethernet services are available on fiber and copper media, and port densities as high as 48 ports per module (RJ-21) may be obtained. (RJ-21 connectors are also referred to as telco data bus connectors.)

Token Ring Modules

While the use of Token Ring is waning in most data centers, the Catalyst provides support for these networks. In addition, the Catalyst can switch between Token Ring and Ethernet topologies to provide a migration path for companies that are converting to Ethernet.

The Token Ring modules on the Catalyst switch provide a dedicated ring on each port. This permits micro-segmentation of a single ring without Layer 3 considerations.

The Token Ring ports are processed via the SAGE ASIC, described later in this chapter.

FDDI Modules

The Catalyst line supports FDDI and CDDI interfaces, which historically have provided backbone services. While many installations of the Catalyst system ultimately use Fast and gigabit Ethernet for the backbone, the FDDI/CDDI offerings provide a migration and implementation path. Given the many benefits of FDDI, some administrators opt to retain their FDDI backbones while connecting servers via Ethernet and Fast Ethernet to the Catalyst system. As with the Token Ring module, the FDDI/CDDI ports use the SAGE ASIC.

Administrators should consider the issues of bandwidth limitation and expense when evaluating the FDDI modules. In addition, the Catalyst system incurs a high level of overhead in translating FDDI frames into Ethernet—a process that occurs even between two FDDI ports.

ATM Modules

The Catalyst system provides two forms of ATM feature cards. The Cisco LS1010 product is provided in the last five slots of the 5500 chassis and provides a 5Gbps backplane for cell switching.

In addition, Cisco provides an ATM LANE module in the frame portion of the Catalyst system. This module also uses the SAGE ASIC. This module and the ATM LANE service are described in greater detail in Chapter 9.

The Catalyst Route Switching Module

The Route Switching Module (RSM) provides Cisco 7500 series routing functions in the Catalyst switch. This brings Layer 3 awareness to the platform and provides administrators with needed routing functions while avoiding the expense and facilities requirements of an external router.

The RSM contains its own PCMCIA slots for flash memory and separate console and auxiliary ports. The RSM is covered in greater detail in Chapter 11.

The RSM CPU Halt LED is lit during normal operation. A failure is indicated when the LED is off. This differs from the other router route processors.

Catalyst Processors and Logic Units

The Catalyst processors, in concert with the ASICs, provide the intelligence behind the frame switching process. The processors, along with their supporting systems, are presented in this section.

Network Management Processor (NMP)

The network management processor, or NMP, controls the system hardware in addition to the configuration and diagnostic functions. In addition, the NMP is responsible for network management and the Spanning Tree protocol. In the Catalyst system, each VLAN has a separate spanning tree construct.

The results of the various diagnostic functions in the Catalyst may be viewed with the show test command.

```
Switch_A> (enable) show test
Environmental Status (. = Pass, F = Fail, U = Unknown)
  PS (3.3V):   .    PS (12V): .    PS
(24V):   .    PS1: .    PS2: .
  Temperature: .   Fan:      .   Clock(A/B): A   Chassis-Ser-EEPROM: .


Module 1 : 2-port 100BaseFX MM Supervisor
Network Management Processor (NMP) Status: (. = Pass, F = Fail, U = Unknown)
  ROM:  .   Flash-EEPROM: .   Ser-EEPROM: .   NVRAM: .   MCP Comm: .

  EARL Status :
        NewLearnTest:            .
        IndexLearnTest:          .
        DontForwardTest:         .
        MonitorTest              .
        DontLearn:               .
        FlushPacket:             .
        ConditionalLearn:        .
        EarlLearnDiscard:        .
        EarlTrapTest:            .


  LCP Diag Status for Module 1  (. = Pass, F = Fail, N = N/A)
  CPU       : .   Sprom    : .   Bootcsum : .   Archsum  : N
  RAM       : .   LTL      : .   CBL      : .   DPRAM    : .   SAMBA : .
  Saints    : .   Pkt Bufs : .   Repeater : N   FLASH    : N
```

```
MII Status:
Ports 1  2
-----------
      N  N


SAINT/SAGE Status :
Ports 1  2  3
--------------
      .  .  .


Packet Buffer Status :
Ports 1  2  3
--------------
      .  .  .


Loopback Status [Reported by Module 1] :
Ports  1  2  3
--------------
       .  .  .


Channel Status :
Ports  1  2
-----------
       .  .
```

In the previous example the switch has experienced no faults, and it contains two power supplies—both of which are functioning. This 5505 chassis' Supervisor engine is also configured with the two-port 100Base FX MM module. The Supervisor modules are available with a wide array of uplink options.

Master Communication Processor (MCP)

The MCP uses the serial management bus to communicate between the NMP on the Supervisor module, and the line module communication processors (LCPs) on the individual line cards in the chassis. The serial management bus operates outside of the data backplane at 761Kbps.

The MCP includes an 8051 processor, 32KB EPROM, 64KB of SRAM for code, and 32KB of SRAM for data. In addition, 32KB is allocated for I/O space. The 8051 processor contains a built-in universal asynchronous receiver and transmitter (UART).

The MCP also handles the testing and configuration of local ports, the control of local ports, the downloading of run-time code, and the diagnostics of onboard chips including memory, ASICs, and the local target logic (LTL) and color blocking logic (CBL).

Cisco documentation uses both the terms *Master Communication Processor* and *Management Control Processor* to define MCP.

Arbiter

The Catalyst system uses a two-tier method of arbitration to control the switching process. The local bus arbiter, located on each module, assigns priorities for queuing and handles all traffic on all ports of the module. This process then uses the central bus arbiter, located on the Supervisor module, to obtain permission to transmit frames to the switching engine. The central bus arbiter uses a round-robin process, with special handling for high-priority frames, to service all modules and all ports. The priority levels are configured by the administrator and provide flexibility for switching of time-sensitive traffic, including voice and video, in addition to server ports.

Collectively, the arbiter system is referred to as the ARB.

Line Module Communication Processor (LCP)

The LCP is located on each line module and is responsible for communication with the MCP on the Supervisor engine. The LCP is an 8051 processor, and communication over the management bus uses the serial communication protocol (SCP). During module initialization, the LCP boots from local ROM and prepares an information package called "resetack," which includes the boot-up diagnostics and module information. This package is sent to the MCP, which forwards the parameters to the NMP.

Local Target Logic (LTL)

The LTL works with the EARL (discussed later in this chapter) to determine the destination port or ports for each frame. This function accommodates differences in unicast, multicast, and broadcast forwarding. The LTL uses index values provided by the EARL to select one, many, or all ports on the line module for receipt of the frame.

Color Blocking Logic (CBL)

Cisco uses the concept of colors to help administrators visualize different VLANs. The color blocking logic, CBL, works by blocking traffic from entering or leaving a port that is not part of the VLAN. In addition, the CBL participates in the spanning tree process to block ports and prevent bridging loops. Recall that each port is associated with a single VLAN (assuming a nontrunk port). Each incoming frame is tagged with an identifier for the VLAN, noting its color within the switch. A frame tagged from the green VLAN would thus be blocked from exiting a red VLAN port.

Encoded Address Recognition Logic (EARL)

No kingdom would be complete without an EARL, and building on the apparent pun, the Catalyst 5000 is no different. In switching, however, EARL refers to the Encoded Address Recognition Logic. This chip works with the bus arbitration system to control access to the data-switching bus. EARL also controls the destination ports of packet transfers.

More specifically, the EARL monitors frame flow and compiles the list of MAC addresses as related to port numbers and VLAN ID. In addition, it determines the destination port of frames and maintains the timer for aging entries out of the forwarding table. By default, entries are discarded after 300 seconds, although the administrator can change this value. Valid parameters are limited between 1 and 20 minutes. The EARL can maintain a table of up to 128,000 addresses. As such, the EARL handles forwarding and filtering decisions within the switch.

Administrators do not troubleshoot the EARL per se. Rather, issues with MAC address and port mappings controlled by EARL are a part of the diagnostic process. Understanding the significant function of the EARL in the Catalyst line, and its role in all switching, can assist in hardware-related debugging.

Note that the EARL is replaced when adding the Netflow feature card (NFFC, NFFC II) with the NFFC daughterboard.

The Catalyst Switching Bus

The Catalyst switching bus provides 1.2Gbps throughput on the 5000 platform with the Supervisor 1 engine. This bus is 48 bits wide and operates at 25MHz. The Supervisor engine is responsible for controlling access to the switching bus, which is handled by a bus access arbitration scheme. All line cards and the Supervisor are connected to the switching bus.

The switching bus is used for transferring data only, with the exception of added VLAN and checksum information. The management of the switch uses the separate management bus.

In the 5500 platform, three separate 1.2Gbps backplanes are available for data transfer, with the Catalyst Switching Bus and the Phoenix ASICs handling interbus packet flow. To access all three backplanes, the Supervisor III engine is required.

Frame Forwarding in the Catalyst

The Catalyst system processes frames by store-and-forward switching. This differs from the alternative cut-through switching and provides additional control and management of the forwarding process. Cut-through switching is not an option in the Catalyst 5000/5500. The Catalyst avoids the traditional latency of store-and-forward switches by sending all frames to every port and then purging those destinations that are inappropriate. While it is still subject to variable latency, this provides a good compromise between speed and accurate frame propagation.

Administrators need to understand the frame-forwarding process in order to analyze problems and locate bottlenecks in the system. In addition, an understanding of the frame flow within the switch will provide administrators with a better appreciation for the complexities within the Catalyst architecture.

When a frame enters a port, it is placed into the receive buffer by the port's DMA controller. For this example, the frame will be Ethernet. The checksum of the frame is verified, and a 12-byte header denoting the ingress (inbound) port and VLAN number is added. The Ethernet MIB and RMON counters are also incremented to provide proper accounting of the data flow. Once the frame is stored in the frame buffer, a request is made to access the switching bus for frame forwarding. Note that this request is made via the management bus.

The bus arbiter receives the request on the management bus from the SAINT ASIC for permission to transmit the frame over the switching bus. The Supervisor is responsible for granting access to each line module, and the individual line module is responsible for granting access to an individual port. Permission is granted for a single frame only.

Once the bus arbiter grants access to the switching bus, the SAINT ASIC transmits the contents of the buffer. The frame is transmitted to all ports in the switch and stored in each individual port's input buffer. This is an important concept in the Catalyst system—as each port receives every frame, there are no rebroadcast issues for broadcast or multicast frames. In addition, there is no delay in receiving the frame at the destination port.

At this point, the switch has acted more like a hub than a switch. The frame has been forwarded to all ports, regardless of VLAN considerations and MAC layer addresses. Clearly, the transmitted frame cannot be forwarded out all ports on the switch—that would defeat the benefits of VLANs and switching.

It is at this point in the switching process that the EARL instructs each port to forward or drop the frame. This is coordinated with the LTL and CBL functions, and it depends on the VLAN, source port, MAC table, and nature of the frame—broadcast, unicast, or multicast. The EARL does not command the forwarding of frames on individual ports. Rather, the EARL commands all ports to drop the frame except those that should forward the frame.

Figure 8.1 provides a visual representation of the frame flow within the Catalyst. Note again that this example is for an Ethernet-to-Ethernet flow— a flow to FDDI or another media might require additional processing and frame conversion.

FIGURE 8.1

The Catalyst 5000 frame flow

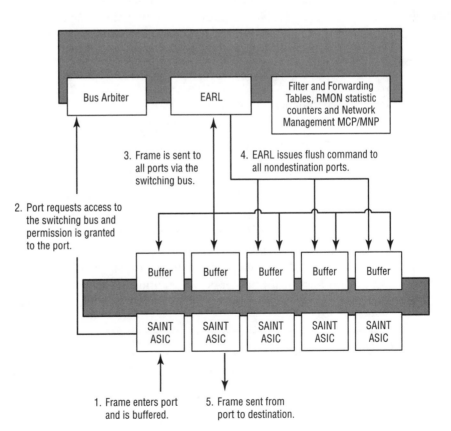

Catalyst 5000/5500 ASICs

In addition to the Catalyst processors, there are four significant components, known as Application Specific Integrated Circuits or ASICs, in the Catalyst 5500 system that manage the switching functions. They're called the SAMBA, SAINT, SAGE, and Phoenix. These ASICs provide high-speed, hardware-based processing used in switching processes.

A clear understanding of these components is useful in overall troubleshooting and administration of the Catalyst system. This is especially true when evaluating different switches and options, such as the different Supervisor engines and the RSM and NetFlow (NFFC II) features. It is also beneficial when isolating hardware problems.

The Catalyst system uses a management bus to direct the switching process, while the actual data packets use a separate 1.2Gbps backplane. The management bus operates at 761Kbps. These buses interconnect various cards within the chassis for Ethernet, Token Ring, FDDI, and in some cases ATM. Note that this description of the Catalyst system is based on the original Catalsyt 5000 and the Supervisor I. The 5500 and Supervisor III provide access to three 1.2Gbps backplanes, which are interconnected via the Phoenix ASICs.

SAMBA

The Synergy Advanced Multipurpose Bus Arbiter (SAMBA) ASIC is located on line modules and the Supervisor modules. On the line cards, this chip is responsible for broadcast suppression based on thresholds established by the administrator. This ASIC also maintains statistics on packets.

The SAMBA operates in either master or slave mode. Master mode is used on the Supervisor engine and slave mode is used on the line cards. The master is capable of addressing up to 13 line modules, while the slave is capable of serving up to 48 individual ports.

In the master/slave model, the slave SAMBA must wait for permission from the master before granting access to the port. This process is described in greater detail in the arbitration section of this chapter.

 Cisco's SAMBA should not be confused with the SAMBA utility for providing SMB (Windows NT) services on Unix platforms.

SAINT

The SAINT (Synergy Advanced Interface and Network Termination) handles Ethernet switching on the Catalyst 5000 platform, and it also handles ISL encapsulation. Each Ethernet port has an independent 192KB buffer for inbound and outbound packets, which is divided to provide 168KB to outbound traffic and 24KB for inbound frames.

The ISL functionality is covered earlier in this chapter. The buffer arrangement controlled by the SAINT has proven itself in hundreds of networks and rarely presents a troubleshooting issue—however, administrators must always consider buffer overflows and underpins as a factor. Again, capturing the appropriate counters with the show commands will provide the administrator with troubleshooting tools.

SAGE

The SAGE (Synergy Advanced Gate-Array Engine) is similar to the SAINT, except that it is used for non-Ethernet applications, including FDDI, ATM LANE, Token Ring, and the Network Management Processor on the Supervisor engine.

Phoenix

The Phoenix ASIC provides both a technical and economical expansion of the Catalyst line. First, the gate array is responsible for interconnecting the three 1.2Gbps backplanes in the Catalyst 5500 chassis to create a crossbar fabric that bridges traffic between backplanes at gigabit speeds. Second, the architecture permits the use of legacy modules, providing administrators with investment protection when upgrading from the Catalyst 5000. While the chassis needs replacement in such circumstances, some companies choose to defer trade-in or replacement of specific modules because of cost concerns.

The Phoenix ASIC includes a 384KB buffer to address congestion and is treated as a port by the bus arbiter and EARL modules.

Catalyst Software

The Cisco Catalyst uses an operating system similar to the Cisco IOS (Internetwork Operating System) routers. The switch platform differs from the router in some minor, but significant, ways. For example, administrators frequently forget to use the set command word to configure the Catalyst switch. In addition, there is no configuration mode on the Catalyst. Commands are entered from enable mode and are effective immediately.

You can display a list of the commands available in enable mode with the ? command. The ? or help commands provide the administrator with available commands and syntax needed to operate the switch. It is recommended that administrators use the ? command following any change in version, as commands are added, removed, and/or changed frequently.

```
Switch_A> (enable) ?
Commands:
```

clear	Clear, use 'clear help' for more info
configure	Configure system from terminal/network
disable	Disable privileged mode
disconnect	Disconnect user session
download	Download code to a processor
enable	Enable privileged mode
help	Show this message
history	Show contents of history substitution buffer
ping	Send echo packets to hosts
quit	Exit from the Admin session
reconfirm	Reconfirm VMPS
reset	Reset system or module
session	Tunnel to ATM or Router module
set	Set, use 'set help' for more info
show	Show, use 'show help' for more info
slip	Attach/detach Serial Line IP interface
switch	Switch to standby <clock|supervisor>
telnet	Telnet to a remote host

```
test              Test, use 'test help' for more info
upload            Upload code from a processor
wait              Wait for x seconds
write             Write system configuration to
                  terminal/network
```

You can also display the subcommands for any command. For example, the show subcommands are provided with the show ? command. Please note that this is a partial list. A complete list is shown in Chapter 10.

```
Switch_A> (enable) show ?
Show commands:
```

```
show alias        Show aliases for commands
show arp          Show ARP table
show bridge       Show bridge information
show cam          Show CAM table
show cdp          Show Cisco Discovery Protocol Information
```

A Sample Configuration File

A sample configuration file for the Catalyst is provided below. Administrators should note the various options available for port and VLAN features, in addition to the TACACS+ and switch management features. TACACS+ is a security and authentication service that uses MD5 encryption. Many large organizations use TACACS+ to avoid creating multiple accounts on all network devices. TACACS+ can also augment an audit trail process. TACACS stands for Terminal Access Controller Access Control System.

The SC0 interface is the in-band interface of the Supervisor module, while the SL0 interface is used for out-of-band SLIP connections. Management will be covered in greater detail in Chapter 11. Note that TACACS+, in addition to other Catalyst services like Telnet, NTP, and SNMP, requires that the SC0 interface be configured for TCP/IP.

This configuration is very close to the default configuration of the switch. For demonstration purposes, a VTP domain has been defined as VTP1 and an IP address has been placed on the SC0 interface. VTP will be covered in Chapter 11.

```
Switch_A> (enable) show config
.....
.........
.........
.........
.........
..

begin
set password $1$FMFQ$HfRA5UOI675hrz4h6W47
set enablepass $1$FMFQ$HfRA5UOI675hrz4h6W47
set prompt Switch_A>
set length 24 default
set logout 0
set banner motd ^C^C
!
#system
set system baud  9600
set system modem disable
set system name
set system location
set system contact
!
#snmp
set snmp community read-only       public
set snmp community read-write      private
set snmp community read-write-all secret
set snmp rmon disable
set snmp trap disable module
set snmp trap disable chassis
set snmp trap disable bridge
set snmp trap disable repeater
set snmp trap disable vtp
set snmp trap disable auth
set snmp trap disable ippermit
set snmp trap disable vmps
!
```

```
#ip
set interface sc0 1 10.1.1.10 255.255.255.0 10.1.1.255
set interface sl0 0.0.0.0 0.0.0.0
set arp agingtime 1200
set ip redirect   enable
set ip unreachable   enable
set ip fragmentation enable
set ip route 0.0.0.0          10.1.1.1   0
set ip alias default          0.0.0.0
!
#Command alias
!
#vmps
set vmps server retry 3
set vmps server reconfirminterval 60
set vmps tftpserver 0.0.0.0 vmps-config-database.1
set vmps state disable


!
#dns
set ip dns disable
!
#tacacs+
set tacacs attempts 3
set tacacs directedrequest disable
set tacacs timeout 5
set authentication login tacacs disable
set authentication login local enable
set authentication enable tacacs disable
set authentication enable local enable
!
#bridge
set bridge ipx snaptoether   8023raw
set bridge ipx 8022toether   8023
set bridge ipx 8023rawtofddi snap
!
#vtp
set vtp domain VTP1
set vtp mode server
set vtp v2 disable
set vtp pruneeligible 2-1000
```

```
clear vtp pruneeligible 1001-1005
set vlan 1 name default type ethernet mtu 1500 said 100001
state active
set vlan 1002 name fddi-default type fddi mtu 1500 said
101002 state active
set vlan 1004 name fddinet-default type fddinet mtu 1500
said 101004 state active bridge 0x0 stp ieee
set vlan 1005 name trnet-default type trbrf mtu 1500 said
101005 state active bridge 0x0 stp ieee
set vlan 1003 name token-ring-default type trcrf mtu 1500
said 101003 state active parent 0 ring 0x0 mode srb
aremaxhop 7 stemaxhop 7
!
#spantree
#uplinkfast groups
set spantree uplinkfast disable
#vlan 1
set spantree enable      1
set spantree fwddelay 15    1
set spantree hello    2    1
set spantree maxage    20    1
set spantree priority 32768 1
#vlan 1003
set spantree enable      1003
set spantree fwddelay 4     1003
set spantree hello    2     1003
set spantree maxage    10    1003
set spantree priority 32768 1003
set spantree portstate 1003 auto 0
set spantree portcost 1003 80
set spantree portpri  1003 4
set spantree portfast 1003 disable
#vlan 1005
set spantree enable      1005
set spantree fwddelay 15    1005
set spantree hello    2    1005
set spantree maxage    20    1005
set spantree priority 32768 1005
set spantree multicast-address 1005 ieee
!
#cgmp
```

```
set cgmp disable
set cgmp leave disable
!
#syslog
set logging console enable
set logging server disable
set logging level cdp 2 default
set logging level cgmp 2 default
set logging level disl 5 default
set logging level dvlan 2 default
set logging level earl 2 default
set logging level fddi 2 default
set logging level ip 2 default
set logging level pruning 2 default
set logging level snmp 2 default
set logging level spantree 2 default
set logging level sys 5 default
set logging level tac 2 default
set logging level tcp 2 default
set logging level telnet 2 default
set logging level tftp 2 default
set logging level vtp 2 default
set logging level vmps 2 default
set logging level kernel 2 default
set logging level filesys 2 default
set logging level drip 2 default
set logging level pagp 5 default
!
#ntp
set ntp broadcastclient disable
set ntp broadcastdelay 3000
set ntp client disable
clear timezone
set summertime disable
!
#permit list
set ip permit disable
!
#drip
set tokenring reduction enable
set tokenring distrib-crf disable
```

```
!
#module 1 : 2-port 100BaseFX MM Supervisor
set module name    1
set vlan 1     1/1-2
set port channel 1/1-2 off
set port channel 1/1-2 auto
set port enable     1/1-2
set port level      1/1-2  normal
set port duplex     1/1-2  half
set port trap       1/1-2  disable
set port name       1/1-2
set port security   1/1-2  disable
set port broadcast  1/1-2  100%
set port membership 1/1-2  static
set cdp enable    1/1-2
set cdp interval 1/1-2 60
set trunk 1/1   auto 1-1005
set trunk 1/2   auto 1-1005
set spantree portfast     1/1-2 disable
set spantree portcost     1/1-2 19
set spantree portpri      1/1-2 32
set spantree portvlanpri 1/1   0
set spantree portvlanpri 1/2   0
set spantree portvlancost 1/1   cost 18
set spantree portvlancost 1/2   cost 18
!
#module 2 : 24-port 10/100BaseTX Ethernet
set module name    2
set module enable  2
set vlan 1     2/1-24
set port enable     2/1-24
set port level      2/1-24  normal
set port speed      2/3-24  auto
set port speed      2/1-2  100
set port duplex     2/1-2  full
set port trap       2/1-24  disable
set port name       2/1-24
set port security   2/1-24  disable
set port broadcast  2/1-24  0
set port membership 2/1-24  static
```

```
set cdp enable    2/1-24
set cdp interval 2/1-24 60
set spantree portfast    2/1-24 disable
set spantree portcost    2/9  100
set spantree portcost    2/10 100
set spantree portcost    2/11 100
set spantree portcost    2/12 100
set spantree portcost    2/15 100
set spantree portcost    2/16 100
set spantree portcost    2/17 100
set spantree portcost    2/18 100
set spantree portcost    2/19 100
set spantree portcost    2/21 100
set spantree portcost    2/1-8,2/13-14,2/20,2/22-24 19
set spantree portpri     2/1-24 32
!
#module 3 : 48-port 10BaseT Ethernet
set module name    3
set module enable  3
set vlan 1    3/1-48
set port enable    3/1-48
set port level     3/1-48  normal
set port duplex    3/1-48  half
set port trap      3/1-48  disable
set port name      3/1-48
set port security  3/1-48  disable
set port broadcast 3/1-48  0
set port membership 3/1-48  static
set cdp enable    3/1-48
set cdp interval 3/1-48 60
set spantree portfast    3/1-48 disable
set spantree portcost    3/1-48 100
set spantree portpri     3/1-48 32
!
#module 4 : 48-port 10BaseT Ethernet
set module name    4
set module enable  4
set vlan 1    4/1-48
set port enable    4/1-48
set port level     4/1-48  normal
```

```
set port duplex      4/1-48  half
set port trap        4/1-48  disable
set port name        4/1-48
set port security    4/1-48  disable
set port broadcast   4/1-48  0
set port membership 4/1-48   static
set cdp enable    4/1-48
set cdp interval 4/1-48 60
set spantree portfast     4/1-48 disable
set spantree portcost     4/1-48 100
set spantree portpri      4/1-48 32
!
#module 5 empty
!
#switch port analyzer
set span disable
!
#cam
set cam agingtime 1,1003,1005 300
end
```

Summary

This chapter reviewed the hardware and software components of the Cisco Catalyst 5000 switch. Specifically, this chapter looked at:

- The Catalyst chassis
- The Supervisor module(s)
- The line modules
- The ASICs
- The physical media supported by the Catalyst system
- The relationship between software and hardware components
- The Catalyst backplanes
- The flow of frames within the Catalyst system
- The diagnostic LEDs on the Catalyst system

In addition, this chapter described aspects of the switching platform and the relationship between real-world networking issues and the theoretical context of this chapter. Troubleshooting processes are greatly augmented through an understanding of the LEDs on the Supervisor engine, for example. Troubleshooting is also enhanced by understanding the general relationships of systems. TCP/IP problems are sometimes resolved by understanding the ARP process, much in the same manner as frame forwarding relies on the MAC address and VLAN information. Also, administrators occasionally need to justify the more expensive options within the 5000/5500 product line compared to other switches, both Cisco and non-Cisco. And sometimes that justification includes different components within the product itself. After reading this chapter, administrators should be able to justify the purchase of the Supervisor III engine in a 5500 chassis, as an example.

Review Questions

1. Which of the following elements are required for redundancy in the Supervisor engine? Where more than one option exists, select the minimum version or least number of elements to meet the requirement.

   A. Two Supervisor modules

   B. Two Supervisor II modules

   C. Two Supervisor III modules

   D. The NetFlow Feature Card (NFFC)

   E. A 5500 series switch

   F. A Cisco 7500 series router

2. In the 5500 chassis, the Supervisor engine module may be installed in

   A. Slot 13

   B. Slot 1

   C. Any open slot

   D. The Supervisor does not require a slot, as it is a backplane component.

3. In the 5500 chassis, the ASP module must be installed in

   A. Slot 1

   B. Slot 2

   C. Any C backplane slot

   D. Slot 13

4. Switching is a _____ process.

   A. Layer 1

   B. Layer 2

   C. Layer 3

   D. Layer 4

5. The administrator notices a CPU Halt LED indication on the RSM module in a 5500 switch. The correct action by the administrator would be to:

   A. Reboot the switch with a power cycle on both power supplies

   B. Reset the active Supervisor module

   C. Remove and reseat the RSM module

   D. Connect to the local console and issue the `reset rsm` command

   E. Take no action

6. The administrator notes that the Supervisor engine module's PS2 Status LED is red. This indicates which of the following problems or conditions?

   A. The RSM module is overloaded.

   B. A redundant power supply is installed but not turned on.

   C. All diagnostic tests passed.

   D. The Supervisor module is fully operational and the power is on.

7. The following modules may be hot-swapped in the Catalyst system:

   A. Fan trays

   B. Redundant power supplies

   C. Switching modules

   D. The Catalyst 5000 Supervisor module

8. The Catalyst 5000 supports which of the following topologies?

   A. FDDI

   B. Ethernet

   C. Fast Ethernet

   D. Token Ring

   E. All of the above

9. Order the following steps, documenting the process by which an Ethernet frame is processed within the Catalyst switch.

   A. EARL commands the dropping of the frame on nondestination ports.

   B. The frame enters the switch, and the port's DMA buffer stores it in the port's receive buffer.

   C. The frame is transmitted to all ports via the high-speed switching bus.

   D. The frame is received by all ports in the switch.

   E. The port is granted bus access by the central bus arbiter.

   F. Permission to transmit the frame on the high-speed switching backplane is requested by the SAINT ASIC.

   G. The EARL, along with the LTL and CBL functions, selects the destination ports.

10. In order to process frames at Layer 3 the Catalyst system, including external components, must include:

    A. A Supervisor III engine

    B. Redundant Supervisor engines

    C. An RSM module, or a connection from each VLAN to a router, via either ISL/802.1q or direct connections to a port in each VLAN

    D. It is not possible to process Layer 3 in the Catalyst system.

11. The Catalyst 5500 has

    A. 5 slots

    B. 9 slots

    C. 13 slots

    D. A fixed configuration of 8 frame modules and five ATM modules

12. Which ASIC provides a gigabit bridge between the backplanes in the Catalyst 5500?

A. SAGE

B. SAINT

C. Phoenix

D. EARL

E. There is only one backplane in the Catalyst 5500.

13. Which component of the Catalyst system maintains the MAC address table for forwarding decisions?

A. EARL

B. Phoenix

C. SAGE

D. The MAC Address Handling Processor

E. The Catalyst does not process MAC addresses.

14. The network designer is installing a new Catalyst 5500 switch with Ethernet modules and the Supervisor III engine. The administrator will need to trunk with a non-Cisco switch. Which of the following options is the most efficient and addresses the problem?

A. ISL

B. 802.1d

C. 802.1q

D. A single connection between each VLAN on each switch

E. Trunking must be established between Cisco products.

15. The Catalyst 5000 is

   A. A cut-through switch

   B. Available for Ethernet only

   C. Ideal for wiring closets only

   D. Capable of processing frames and cells across its 3.2Gbps backplane

   E. A store-and-forward switch

16. Configuration information is stored in which of the following components?

   A. 8MB flash memory

   B. 256KB NVRAM

   C. EPROM

   D. In NVRAM on each line module

   E. The configuration must be loaded from a TFTP server and is not stored on the Catalyst.

17. When installing the NetFlow feature, the administrator must

   A. Replace the EARL with the NetFlow card and add the appropriate software license

   B. Upgrade to version 11.3 of the IOS

   C. Install the RSM module

   D. Collapse the network into a single subnet

18. In the Catalyst 5500, any advanced line module, with the redundant software option, can provide redundancy in the event of failure in the Supervisor engine.

   A. True

   B. False

19. Which of the following describes the differences between the Catalyst 5000 and Catalyst 5500?

  A. The Catalyst 5000 supports redundant Supervisor engines.

  B. The Catalyst 5000 provides a 3.6Gbps backplane.

  C. The Catalyst 5500 supports redundant Supervisor engines.

  D. The Catalyst 5500 supports a 3.6Gbps backplane.

  E. The Catalyst 5500 provides LS1010 functionality.

20. The NMP in the Catalyst 5000:

  A. Uses the system software to govern the general control of the hardware.

  B. Stores the MAC address table.

  C. Is the ASIC that handles the Phoenix function in the Catalyst 5000.

  D. The NMP is not part of the Catalyst 5000.

CHAPTER

9

Catalyst 5000/5500 Advanced
Features

The Cisco Catalyst 5000/5500 series of switches provide substantial flexibility and performance suited for deployment in the data center and network core, in addition to providing a wide array of features and functions. Some of the more advanced features in the product line include the virtual LAN architecture and support for ATM LANE and FDDI.

Some topics addressed in this chapter were introduced in Chapter 2. This chapter revisits them in the context of the 5000 product line. In addition, this chapter will focus on specific elements of the Catalyst 5000/5500 series, including support for ATM LANE, ATM cell switching (5500), and FDDI support, and will address the following exam objectives:

- Name seven reasons to create VLANs.

- Describe the role switches play in the creation of VLANs.

- Describe VLAN frame filtering and VLAN frame tagging.

- Describe how switches can be used with hubs.

- Name the five components of VLAN implementations.

- Describe static and dynamic VLANs.

- Describe the VLAN technologies.

- Describe Token Ring VLANs.

- Describe Token Ring switching concepts.

- Describe Cisco's VLAN architecture.

- Describe the major features and functions of the Catalyst 5000 FDDI/CDDI module.

- Describe IEEE 802.10 VLANs.

- Configure the Catalyst 5000 FDDI/CDDI module.

- List the features of the Catalyst 5000 LANE module.

- Define LAN Emulation.

- Describe how one LEC establishes communication with another LEC.

- Describe the start-up procedure of a LAN Emulation client.

- Describe the LAN Emulation components.

- Outline the performance ratings for the ATM bus and the switching bus.

- Describe how to access the CLI for the LANE module.

- Describe the Simple Server Redundancy Protocol (SSRP).

- Explain ATM address structure.

- Describe how ATM addresses are automatically assigned.

- Describe the rules for assigning ATM components to interfaces.

- Configure LANE components on a Catalyst 5000 switch.

- Configure the ATM LANE module.

- Use the switch LEDs to isolate problems.

- Describe the switch hardware status.

- Describe demand nodes and resource nodes.

- Describe configuration rules for demand nodes and resource nodes.

- Describe local resources and remote resources.

- Describe configuration rules for local resources and remote resources.

- Name five applications for the Catalyst 5000 series switches.

- Use the command-line or menu-driven interface to configure the Catalyst series switches and their switching modules.

- Use the command-line or menu-driven interface to configure trunks, virtual LANs, and ATM LAN Emulation.

VLANs

As discussed at greater length in Chapter 2, virtual LANs add substantially to the functionality of switching products. At their most basic level, VLANs allow segmentation of the ports within the chassis, based on the needs of the users. These divisions usually align with subnets at Layer 3.

VLANs define the broadcast domain, or the scope of ports to which a broadcast packet will be sent. This is different from the collision domain, as switches can isolate each end node in the network onto its own collision domain. Stated another way, VLANs logically segment the physical structure so that broadcast frames are switched only between ports within the same logical grouping.

There are seven primary reasons for administrators to use VLAN technology, as outlined:

- Moves, additions, and changes are simplified.

- Administrative costs are reduced.

- Broadcast packets are controlled.

- Network security may be enhanced via more restrictive policies.

- Microsegmentation of the network is possible, and scalability of the network increases.

- Traffic loads may be distributed.

- Servers may be moved into physically secured locations.

According to Cisco, up to 40 percent of the workforce is physically moved every year as part of reorganizations within corporations. Other sources place this figure above 100 percent, accounting for multiple moves of some individuals within the year.

By implementing VLANs on all switches in the enterprise, with sufficient high-bandwidth interconnections, you can grant a workgroup member non-routed access to workgroup services even if they are separated physically from the workgroup. As the VLAN is mapped to network addresses, the movement of a workstation within the VLAN does not require a change in network address, either. This simplification can reduce costs at the workstation and network levels of the organization, although the initial costs associated with the purchase of VLAN-aware switches may offset these savings for some time.

While removing the physical boundaries that previously restricted the size of a subnet or workgroup, VLAN technology also permits the segmentation of workgroups into smaller elements, which may facilitate tighter security policies.

Switches may be combined with hubs within the network. While this limits the overall benefits of switches, such a design can be a compromise between the performance advantages of switches and the higher per-port costs. When hubs are used with switches, the collision domain is reduced to the area extending from each switch port. Rather than providing each workstation with a separate interface, the switch/hub network may provide a group of twenty or more devices with a single switch port. This microsegmentation may provide needed benefits without incurring the costs of per-port switching.

Within the Catalyst 5000/5500 products, some installations are performed with a hybrid of switches and hubs. This has the advantage of reducing the initial cost of the switches, yet the servers and other high utilization devices may be connected directly to the switch. The cost reduction comes in the form of fewer switches and fewer ports. Many installations place a Catalyst 5509 in the core with a single Supervisor engine and one or two line cards. This design permits VLAN isolation, Fast Ethernet and other connections, and a foundation for additional switch services. As the budget expands and bandwidth demands increase, additional ports may be purchased, and ultimately, the entire network will be migrated to switching. This approach is best coupled with bandwidth analysis—using the port counters on the Catalyst can hint at problem areas where further attention is required. Regardless, reducing the number of users per collision domain can only serve to increase user performance.

VLAN Configuration

Perhaps the most significant consideration in VLAN configuration is the fact that each port must be part of one, and only one, VLAN—unless you're using a trunking port and protocol, such as ISL (Inter Switch Link), 802.1q, or 802.10.

Within these restrictions, administrators have a wide range of methods available for assigning VLANs, including the command-line interface (CLI), the VlanDirector application in CiscoWorks, or dynamic VLAN configuration using a VLAN configuration server (VMPS, which is presented in Chapter 11). In addition, servers may be configured with ISL-aware interfaces, which place the server in multiple VLANs without violating VLAN design considerations or requiring local routing. While ISL is described in greater detail in Chapter 2, the ISL-aware adapter option is an important consideration in all Cisco networks. ISL is a proprietary protocol that, when added to a server, can greatly reduce the port costs and cabling requirements to multihome a server.

Most Catalyst 5000/5500 installations utilize trunk connections, or connections that carry more than one VLAN. Cisco routers and switches, including the Catalyst series, often support trunking and, depending on the version of software code, more than one trunking protocol. The previous paragraph introduced the concept of homing a server to the switch via ISL. However, most installations only use ISL and trunking between switches. This limits the efficiency of the switch. For example, without trunking, each VLAN would require a physical connection to every other switch. In a three-switch network with four VLANs, this would require at least eight connections and 16 ports. In addition, each connection would be isolated, which usually results in wasted bandwidth. With trunk ports, the minimum number of ports would be four with two connections. And with Cisco's Fast Ether-Channel support, each trunk could provide more than 100Mbps of bandwidth. The command for configuring Fast EtherChannel is `set port channel 4/1-2 on`, which would create a two-port channel connection on module 4, ports 1 and 2. While this requires four connections and eight ports, this is still more efficient than single connections for each VLAN between each switch.

With or without trunking, interconnected switches must adhere to bridging rules. This often requires the use of the Spanning Tree Protocol to prevent bridging loops.

Spanning Tree

The Spanning Tree Protocol was introduced in Chapter 1 and discussed further in Chapter 2. Here's a quick recap of the basic concept.

Spanning trees are used to prevent the potential loops and broadcast storms that can occur when bridges are interconnected into a loop. As the bridge, or switch, cannot identify a frame that has been forwarded previously, there is no mechanism for removing a frame as it passes the interface numerous times. Without a method of removing these frames, the bridges continuously forward them—consuming bandwidth and adding overhead to the network.

Spanning trees prune the network to provide only one path for any packet. Administrators could accomplish this by not designing the network topology to avoid any redundant links; however, this would be very limiting and not very fault-tolerant. The spanning tree protocol (STP) and the spanning tree algorithm (STA) operate to locate a point in the network where the link may be placed in blocking mode. Upon failure of another section in the network, the spanning tree restores the pruned connection to provide full connectivity while preventing loops and the problems associated with them.

In VLAN configurations, a separate STP is used for each VLAN. The STP states are initially set by the configuration of the switch, and then modified by the STP. These states are described in Table 9.1.

T A B L E 9.1 The Spanning Tree Protocol States	**State**	**Description**
	Blocking	Bridge Protocol Data Units (BPDU) received, frames not forwarded
	Listening	Frames received but not forwarded
	Learning	MAC addresses learned but frames not forwarded
	Forwarding	MAC addresses learned and frames forwarded
	Disabled	BPDUs ignored and frames not forwarded

Administrators should keep the spanning tree concepts in mind when designing networks. Without spanning tree, redundancy is not available, and bridge failures can require a significant amount of time for recovery. Users are likely to be impacted as a result of the failure. This downtime will be substantially greater than the time required for spanning tree to restore a blocked link. In addition, you should carefully consider the network architecture when adding redundant links. While the details are beyond the scope of this chapter, the root bridge should be manually configured, and other spanning tree considerations, including the impact of Layer 2 bridging and spanning tree blocking on Layer 3 processes and ports, should be taken into account. In addition, forwarding mode should be manually configured on all switch ports connected to servers. This configuration option should be enabled for any workstation or server connection. This will reduce downtime on spanning tree calculations and, as the ports have no potential loop, there will be no impact on the network.

Catalyst 5000 Support for Spanning Tree

The status of the spanning tree or trees can be displayed on the Catalyst 5000/5500 with the show spantree command. This command provides diagnostic information regarding the costs and priority of each port, in addition to its status.

In the following sample output, spanning tree is enabled and using the IEEE Spanning Tree Protocol. This is the default protocol and is recommended unless there is sufficient reason to change to DEC. The output also reports that the root bridge is different from the local bridge—bridge and switch being synonymous in this context. Many administrators find that the automatic features of spanning tree are sufficient to address their concerns, however, the root and path costs may be adjusted from their defaults to address situations where more control is required. For example, the port cost for a VLAN may be adjusted with the set spantree portvlanpri command.

```
Switch_A> (enable) show spantree


VLAN 1
Spanning tree enabled
Spanning tree type          ieee

Designated Root             00-50-f0-8b-38-00
Designated Root Priority    32768
Designated Root Cost        29
Designated Root Port        2/1
Root Max Age   20 sec    Hello Time 2  sec   Forward Delay 15 sec


Bridge ID MAC ADDR          00-50-f0-8b-40-00
Bridge ID Priority          32768
Bridge Max Age 20 sec    Hello Time 2  sec   Forward Delay 15 sec

Port     Vlan  Port-State      Cost   Priority  Fast-Start
 1/1      1    blocking         19      32       disabled
 1/2      1    blocking         19      32       disabled
 2/1      1    forwarding       19      32       disabled
 2/2      1    forwarding       19      32       disabled
 2/3      1    not-connected    19      32       disabled
```

```
2/4     1    not-connected    19    32    disabled
2/5     1    not-connected    19    32    disabled
2/6     1    not-connected    19    32    disabled
2/7     1    not-connected    19    32    disabled
2/8     1    not-connected    19    32    disabled
2/9     1    not-connected    19    32    disabled
2/10    1    not-connected    19    32    disabled
2/11    1    not-connected    19    32    disabled
2/12    1    not-connected    19    32    disabled
```

On the router, spanning tree is also a component if bridging is enabled. In this example, the router is configured for IRB (Integrated Routing and Bridging) and BVI (Bridge Virtual Interface). If the administrator chooses to use these features on the router it is recommended that the spanning tree be manually weighted to prevent blocking of parallel paths.

```
Router_A#sh span


 Bridge group 1 is executing the IEEE compatible Spanning Tree protocol
   Bridge Identifier has priority 32768, address 00d0.06f2.14a0
   Configured hello time 2, max age 20, forward delay 15
   We are the root of the spanning tree
   Topology change flag not set, detected flag not set
   Times:  hold 1, topology change 35, notification 2
           hello 2, max age 20, forward delay 15
   Timers: hello 0, topology change 0, notification 0
   bridge aging time 300


Port 3 (FastEthernet5/0/0) of Bridge group 1 is disabled
   Port path cost 10, Port priority 128
   Designated root has priority 32768, address 00d0.06f2.14a0
   Designated bridge has priority 32768, address 00d0.06f2.14a0
   Designated port is 3, path cost 0
   Timers: message age 0, forward delay 0, hold 0
   BPDU: sent 0, received 0

Port 4 (FastEthernet8/0/0) of Bridge group 1 is disabled
   Port path cost 10, Port priority 128
   Designated root has priority 32768, address 00d0.06f2.14a0
   Designated bridge has priority 32768, address 00d0.06f2.14a0
   Designated port is 4, path cost 0
   Timers: message age 0, forward delay 0, hold 0
   BPDU: sent 0, received 0
```

Token Ring VLANs

For network designers and administrators, the issue of Token Ring versus Ethernet designs has occupied many hours in the conference room. These debates have been for good reason, as the costs associated with Token Ring are quite high and vendor support for Token Ring has been waning for years. On the other hand, Token Ring may be well suited in financial and mainframe shops, and continued use may be cheaper in conversion and capital costs than the conversion to Ethernet at the desktop. Unless there are substantial cost and technology reasons for maintaining Token Ring, however, most environments would be better off with Ethernet or Fast Ethernet and switches.

Should the enterprise require Token Ring, there are two different methodologies for connecting the Token Ring station to the switch.

Classical Token Ring is very similar to traditional Token Ring installations. The network card is attached in half-duplex to a concentrator or to the switch. In this configuration, the switch is a concentrator and the ring contains only the switch and the end node. This configuration provides a great deal of bandwidth to the end node; however, the cost is also quite high. A hybrid implementation of TKP would place the traditional concentrator or MAU between the switch and a number of end nodes. This would reduce the costs per port and could also provide microsegmentation benefits and greater bandwidth for key users. In addition, the absence of collisions in Token Ring provides some benefits, although full-duplex Ethernet has also addressed this limitation.

Dedicated Token Ring, or DTR, is a full-duplex implementation of Token Ring that was specified in IEEE draft P802.5r. The full-duplex feature makes use of Transmit Immediate, or TXI. Under this protocol either station may transmit at any time.

The most significant issue with DTR is cost and implementation. Each end node must be configured with a new Token Ring NIC in order to use full-duplex Token Ring, and the switch ports and availability are sometimes limited. The return on investment, from an accounting perspective, is usually measured in years, and the cost difference between DTR and full-duplex 100Mbps Ethernet is significant. Finally, note that Token Ring can only provide 32Mbps to the end node, in contrast to the 200Mbps in full-duplex Ethernet, and the overhead of the Ethernet-to-Token-Ring translation in the Catalyst switch is also greater than with Ethernet-only solutions.

Catalyst 5000 Support for Token Ring

With switched Token Ring, the individual ports are logically connected as a single ring within the VLAN, and the group is referred to as a concentrator relay function (CRF). Both source route translational bridging and source route bridging are supported. Table 9.2 provides a reference to the various bridging types available in the Catalyst 5000 switches, including the Token Ring options.

TABLE 9.2 Bridging Modes	Bridging Mode	Description
	Transparent Bridging (TB)	Frames are forwarded based on the destination MAC address. This is the standard bridging method used in Ethernet.
	Source Route Bridging (SRB)	Frames are forwarded based on the routing information field (RIF) in the frame. As with Token Ring bridges, the RIF is modified by the switch. SRB is only available in Token Ring. The IBM variant of the spanning tree protocol is usually used, and explorer packets—either spanning tree explorer (STE) or all routes explorer (ARE)—are used to find the route.
	Source route transparent bridging (SRT)	This is a hybrid between SRB and TB. Frames are forwarded based on either the RIF information or the destination MAC address. This is used in Token Ring and can benefit Novell IPX installations.
	Source route/transparent translational bridging (SR/TLB)	SR/TLB is used to move between Token Ring and Ethernet. The RIF information is removed or added and the source and destination MAC addresses are modified as necessary.
	Source route switching (SRS)	In SRS, the RIF field is used for forwarding decisions, however, the switch does not modify the RIF.

The Token Ring IEEE specification has contained reservation and priority bits since inception. These bits represent the values shown in Table 9.3.

T A B L E 9.3 IEEE Token Ring Priority Bits	Value	Assignment
	0–3	User defined
	4	Bridge transmit priority
	5	Multimedia, non-real time
	6	Multimedia, real time
	7	Critical MAC frames

Switches will typically combine priority bits 0 to 4 as low priority, and transmission will occur at priority 4. The multimedia priority bits will go into a high-priority queue and will use frame priority. The critical MAC frames use a separate queue from the other frames.

Token Ring frames can be forwarded by ISL links. The ISL header is added to the entire Token Ring frame, including any RIF (Routing Information Field) information and the CRC. This information is stripped off at the end of the ISL link. Servers on Token Ring should be connected with TR-ISL (Token Ring – ISL) NICs to integrate into the VLAN environment.

Application of Catalyst Switches in Token Ring Environments

While Token Ring provides a collisionless network medium, it is still prone to the negatives of shared media. This can result in unpredictable traffic patterns, congestion, and other issues, or the ring can operate uniformly and without problems. Since most networks eventually experience a problem of some sort as user demands increase, this next section will focus on the application of the Catalyst switch, and specifically the 5000/5500 platform in the Token Ring environment.

This chapter has already addressed a number of benefits that switches can bring to Token Ring environments. However, that presentation focused on somewhat detailed features of the switch and the options available.

From a network design perspective, most small networks are comprised of a single ring. As the number of nodes increases, the performance of the ring decreases. Microsegmentation design theory would employ a switch at the center of the network and interlink numerous Token Ring MAUs (concentrators) into that center. The result would be N rings, which would reduce the number of users per ring by a factor of N. This would provide no benefit from a broadcast perspective; however, it would also not require modifications to IP addresses and other workstation-specific settings.

Medium-size and larger Token Ring environments are usually designed around bridges and routers. This employs a backbone model and, in an all Token Ring network, it is possible for a number of rings to collapse into a single backbone operating at the same speed. When networks adhered to the 80/20 rule, with 80 percent of the traffic remaining local, this was acceptable. Today, the 80/20 rule is usually 20/80, and as a result the backbone at 16Mbps cannot hope to handle more than a few 16Mbps user rings. In addition, the bridges and routers interconnecting these rings can also overload and suffer from congestion.

The Catalyst 5000/5500 can resolve these issues by migrating the backbone to Fast Ethernet or ATM, and SRB, SRS, or SRT bridging can be used to maintain legacy ring numbering. In addition, with TR-ISL and ISL on Ethernet, servers can be connected at higher speeds without incurring a routing penalty. In very large Token Ring networks, or Token Ring environments with redundancy requirements, traditional dual-ring backbones can be serviced with two Catalyst switches. The Catalyst also manages ARE (all-routes explorer) packets, which are used to locate and populate the routing information field in Token Ring. Managing these packets reduces the impact and degradation of the network they have traditionally caused. Combining a Catalyst switch with a Cisco router and a CIP module (Channel Interface Processor) can greatly enhance the network performance and scalability without modification to the end nodes.

FDDI

The Fiber Distributed Data Interface (FDDI) and its copper implementation, Copper Distributed Data Interface (CDDI), have a proven track record in data networks as a backbone technology. Defined by an ANSI standard as a 100Mbps, counter-rotating, token-passing, dual-ring system, FDDI is commonly found in larger networks as an interconnection medium for Ethernet segments. FDDI also provides a wide network diameter for larger campuses, transmitting up to 30km. The dual-ring architecture also provides protection against fiber cuts and breaks. The CDDI implementation, while more limited, is well suited to server-farm installations. CDDI's most significant limitation is distance—fiber is capable of providing significantly greater network diameters.

While FDDI provides many positive benefits in network design, its features are still limited compared to those of newer architectures available today. FDDI can be very expensive to implement and maintain, and industry support for FDDI appears to be waning. In addition, latency in FDDI is much higher than in other protocols, especially when the required conversions to and from Ethernet are considered. Lastly, the maximum throughput of FDDI is still limited to 100Mbps. While this provided substantial backbone bandwidth in 10Mbps Ethernet networks, newer networks typically require greater backbone performance.

Implementing FDDI with Catalyst 5000 Switches

The Catalyst 5000 FDDI/CDDI module is available in CDDI Category 5 UTP, using an RJ-45 connector, or in FDDI with multimode or single-mode fiber. The multimode termination uses a MIC connector, and ST connectors terminate the single-mode installation.

The Catalyst 5000 platform is capable of translational bridging between Ethernet and FDDI at 850,000 packets per second (pps).

The FDDI Module   The Catalyst FDDI module is used to interconnect FDDI devices with the Catalyst system, frequently in legacy FDDI backbones for interconnections with Ethernet and Fast Ethernet servers.

Management and administration of the FDDI module is provided via the Supervisor console port, Telnet, or CiscoView. The module also supports

CDP, or Cisco Discovery Protocol, and the MIB II, FDDI MIB and Cisco private MIB. Flash memory may also be updated on the FDDI module.

By default all FDDI ports are enabled, and IPX frame translations are configured automatically. In addition, IP fragmentation and ICMP unreachable messages are enabled. The module also sets a number of timers used in the FDDI environment, including the Link Error Rate Alarm and Cutoff values.

The FDDI Module LEDs   As with other modules, the FDDI module provides administrators with diagnostic information in the form of LEDs on the module card. Table 9.4 explains what each LED means.

T A B L E 9.4:   The FDDI Module LEDs

Function	Red	Orange	Green	Off
Status	If a test fails, except for an individual port failure, the LED appears red.	The FDDI module LED is orange when running self-diagnostics, booting or when the module is disabled.	Indicates that all tests passed.	
RingOp			The ring is operational.	The ring is not operational.
Thru			The A and B ports are connected to the primary and secondary rings.	The A and B ports are not connected to the primary and secondary rings.
Wrap A			The A port is connected to the ring, but the B port is isolated.	The ring is not wrapped at this interface.

T A B L E 9.4: The FDDI Module LEDs *(Continued)*

Function	Red	Orange	Green	Off
Wrap B			The B port is connected to the ring, but the A port is isolated.	The ring is not wrapped at this interface.
A Port Status		Connection failure or dual-homed condition.	The A port is connected to the ring.	No receive signal detected.
B Port Status		Connection failure or dual-homed condition.	The B port is connected to the ring.	No receive signal detected.
In			Indicates that the optical bypass interface is active and in thru mode.	

The FDDI module must be reset when installing or removing an optical bypass switch.

APaRT   The Automated Packet Recognition and Translation (APaRT) engine associates MAC addresses with Layer 2 frame types and provides the conversion between FDDI and Ethernet framing. This is required, as FDDI cannot support all Ethernet frame types.

APaRT is enabled by default; however, the function results in degraded performance. Disabling APaRT can provide increased throughput of up to 10,000pps. When APaRT is disabled, only the default IPX translations are used, and fddicheck (discussed in the next section) is disabled. In addition, all traffic on the FDDI ring is translated and forwarded to the Catalyst backplane. As a general rule, APaRT should only be disabled when FDDI performance needs enhancement and IP is the only protocol. To disable APaRT, use the `set bridge apart disable` command. Use the `show bridge` command to show the status of the APaRT function. The following command-line dialogs demonstrate the commands and output used in APaRT and `fddicheck`.

```
Switch_A> (enable) set bridge ?
Commands:
```

set bridge apart	Dis/Enable default translation on FDDI
set bridge fddicheck	Dis/Enable FDDI to learn new addresses
set bridge help	Show this message
set bridge ipx	Set default IPX translation

```
Switch_A> (enable) set bridge apart ?
Usage: set bridge apart <enable|disable>

Switch_A> (enable) show bridge
APaRT Enabled
FDDICHECK Disabled
IP fragmentation Enabled
Default IPX translations:
    FDDI SNAP  to Ethernet     8023raw
    FDDI 802.2 to Ethernet     8023
    Ethernet 802.3 Raw to FDDI snap
```

fddicheck   The `fddicheck` function prevents an FDDI interface from learning the MAC address of a device that was already learned via an Ethernet interface. Certain situations may prevent the proper operation of the FDDI ring, especially with older FDDI equipment. Many administrators consider `fddicheck` to be a solution to a single vendor's problem with their legacy FDDI NICs. In the real world, using FDDI on numerous networks, the service has never been needed.

The `fddicheck` function is disabled by default, and Cisco recommends that it remain disabled. However, this service may be necessary if the switch exhibits symptoms of lost connectivity. Should an administrator need the fddicheck service, APaRT must also be enabled. A further performance penalty is also incurred when using both services. This performance penalty is the result of fddicheck examining the MAC address of each FDDI packet and comparing it to the CAM table.

Administrators should use the show cam command to determine if Ethernet MAC addresses are registered on the FDDI side. If this is found, fddicheck may be useful. In addition, poor FDDI performance may be an indication that fddicheck is needed. The technical description of the fddicheck process is greatly assisted by understanding the token-passing scheme in FDDI. On Ethernet, the frame may be sent whenever the station detects available time on the wire. Collisions (half-duplex) are sensed by voltage errors on the physical media.

FDDI uses a token-passing method to grant access to the media. This prevents collisions, as the sending station must wait until a token is received. Consider a frame sent from an Ethernet interface destined for an FDDI ring. The Catalyst receives the Ethernet frame in accordance with the Ethernet specifications and waits for a token for access to the FDDI ring. Upon receipt of the token, the Catalyst transmits the frame along with a void frame as part of the FDDI specification.

The token process implies that no other stations will transmit onto the ring until the original frame is removed. The Catalyst will remove any frames from the ring that appear before receipt of its void frame—such frames are illegal under the FDDI specification.

The function of fddicheck results when a void is received before the originally sent frame completes its travel around the ring. If an FDDI NIC sent a frame out without the token, and included a void frame after the transmission (again within the FDDI specification), the Catalyst would react by no longer waiting for its frame—which it is responsible for removing from the ring. In FDDI, frames are removed from the ring by their sending station.

Upon receipt of the void frame, the Catalyst begins listening for new frames. In the scenario presented in the previous paragraph, a FDDI NIC placed a frame onto the ring without obtaining the token. As this frame would be followed by a void, and the Catalyst will stop looking for its frame following a void, the Catalyst would respond by treating its own frame as a new frame from another source. This would cause two problems—first, the CAM would be updated with the MAC address and it would indicate that the Ethernet device was actually on the FDDI ring. Second, the frame would not be removed properly from the ring.

fddicheck operates by checking the CAM (MAC address) table to determine the source of the frame; it will use this information to discard frames with Ethernet interface source addresses. This action prevents the bridge (switch) from confusion regarding the source port of the frame. In addition, by monitoring the void frames, the Catalyst can remove incorrect frames from the ring. This prevents endless circulation of frames sent without the token.

FDDI and 802.10 Trunking   While VLANs provide many benefits within the confines of a single switch, their value increases significantly when more than one switch is interconnected in the same set of VLANs. This permits workgroups to share the same resources without routing, even if they need to be in facilities located several miles apart.

Larger VLANs (those spanning numerous switches) may benefit from VTP, discussed in Chapter 11.

FDDI may be used as a trunking medium in VLAN networks by incorporating the 802.10 protocol. This protocol was originally developed to provide Layer 2 security; however, use of the Security Association Identifier, or SAID, permits assignment of a VLAN ID. SAID provides for 4.29 billion VLANs.

The 802.10 encapsulation consists of a MAC header followed by a clear header. The clear header is not encrypted and consists of the 802.10 LSAP. (LSAPs are defined by the IEEE and occupy the LLC portion of the frame, comprising the destination service access point, source service access point, and control byte), the SAID, and an optional Management Defined Field, or MDF. The standard provides for a protected header to follow the MDF, with data and a checksum, referred to as the Integrity Check Value, or ICV. In VLAN trunking, only the IEEE 802.2 LSAP or 802.10 and the SAID value are used before the data block.

To configure 802.10, the administrator must define the relationship between the FDDI VLAN and the Ethernet VLAN. The first VLAN, or default VLAN, is defined automatically.

It is important to note that 802.10 VLAN packets are valid MAC frames and may cross non-802.10 devices within the network. Also, VLAN IDs and SAID values are independent of each other—except when related in the switch table.

To set up an FDDI 802.10 trunk, the administrator first creates the Ethernet VLAN with the command

`set vlan [vlan number]`

The administrator also defines the FDDI VLAN, by issuing the command.

`set vlan [vlan number] type fddi`

The command

`set vlan [ethernet vlan number] translation [fddi vlan number]`

establishes the relationship between the Ethernet and FDDI VLANs. Trunking must also be enabled on the FDDI interface; use the command

`set trunk [module/port] on`

The `show trunk` and `show vlan trunk` commands are helpful in verifying the configuration and troubleshooting.

It's a good idea to document and maintain a numbering scheme for VLAN numbers and their FDDI SAID values. In addition, while the MTU on the FDDI interface may be set larger than the default 1500 bytes, there is little reason to do so, as all traffic is translationally bridged to Ethernet to access the backplane. Note that the Catalyst will assign an SAID value to VLANs automatically if one is not specified.

ATM LANE

For many years, the integration of data, voice, and video has been presented as the future of networking. This future is often described as including the deployment of Asynchronous Transfer Mode, or ATM. ATM is a cell-based service that provides the predictability and low delay needed in voice and video networks, while maintaining the capability of serving traditional data. LAN emulation, or LANE, provides a method for placing frame-based networks on ATM systems. This supports Ethernet and Token-Ring installations and hides the internal workings of ATM from legacy systems. Chapter 3 discussed ATM LAN emulation at length. Here we'll quickly review the basic concepts before looking at how the Catalyst 5000 switches support LANE.

One of the primary services needed in LANE is broadcast support. Unlike Ethernet, ATM uses only point-to-point connections. This factor greatly impacts traditional Ethernet processes. For example, Ethernet sends messages to an all-FFs address in the MAC address. This is received by all stations on the wire (or in the VLAN), and the network drivers are responsible for determining if the datagram is necessary. Since ATM LANE establishes a point-to-point connection between each station, broadcasts would require a point-to-point connection from each station to every other station. This would consume a significant number of virtual circuits and would be very inefficient. The LANE specification defined by the ATM Forum solves this problem by placing two servers on the network: a LAN Emulation Server (LES) and a Broadcast and Unknown Server (BUS). The BUS is responsible for handling broadcasts and multicasts; the LES is responsible for registering all resources in the LANE environment.

Administrators familiar with frame-based switching frequently use the term *VLAN*, or *virtual LAN*, to describe the logical grouping of ports in a community of switches. ATM LANE introduces a new term, *ELAN*, or *emulated LAN*, to describe this function. While the overall impact of VLANs and ELANs is the same, it's important to understand the difference between these concepts and use the terms correctly.

LANE Components

As you saw in Chapter 3, LAN emulation incorporates four distinct components to provide transparency to the traditional LAN structure. This section briefly reviews those components and their interaction. Transparency is required for the broadcast and multicast issues discussed previously and also consideration of Ethernet's inability to interoperate with ATM devices without some process or protocol. The original Ethernet specification never accounted for the cell-based ATM environments of today's LANs and WANs.

The LAN Emulation Client (LEC)

The LAN Emulation Client, or LEC, is responsible for data forwarding, address resolution, control functions, and the mapping of MAC addresses to ATM addresses. The mapped addresses are also registered with the LES.

LECs are devices that implement the LANE protocol, and they may be ATM-equipped workstations, routers, or switches. It is common for an LEC to be a single element on a switch serving numerous Ethernet or Token Ring ports. To the ATM network, it appears that the single ATM LEC is requesting data—in actuality, the LEC is simply a proxy for the individual requests from the legacy nodes.

The LAN Emulation Server (LES)

The LES, or LAN Emulation Server, is unique to each ELAN. The LES is responsible for managing the ELAN and providing transparency to the LECs. As a key component in LANE, the LES registers and resolves MAC addresses into ATM addresses.

Given the interdependency of the LES and BUS services, most references use the term LES/BUS pair to denote the server providing these services.

The Broadcast and Unknown Server (BUS)

Broadcasts and multicasts are quite common in the traditional LAN environment. As all stations, even in Ethernet-switched installations, receive all frames destined for a MAC address containing all ones, this process works quite well and serves many upper-layer protocols, including the address resolution protocol, for example.

However, ATM requires that a point-to-point virtual circuit serve all connections. This requirement precludes the traditional media-sharing capabilities of Ethernet and Token Ring. To resolve this function, the ATM Forum LAN Emulation committee included a BUS. Each ELAN must have its own BUS, which is responsible for resolving all broadcasts and packets that are addressed for unknown, or unregistered, stations. Under the original LANE 1.0 specification without SSRP (a protocol we'll look at shortly), only one BUS is permitted per ELAN.

The LAN Emulation Configuration Server (LECS)

While the LECS, or LAN Emulation Configuration Server, is not required in LANE, administrators frequently find that configuration is greatly simplified when it is employed.

The LECS is similar to DHCP servers in the IP world. The workstation queries a server for all information that is needed to participate in the network. With DHCP, this is limited to IP address, default gateway, and DNS/WINS servers, depending on implementation. In ATM, the LECS provides the address information for the LES and BUS.

Simple Server Redundancy Protocol   Given the initial limitations of the LANE specification, administrators quickly identified that a single LES/BUS pair would represent a single point of failure in the network. To address this limitation, Cisco introduced SSRP, or Simple Server Redundancy Protocol, in the 11.2 release of the IOS. This feature adds a slight measure of fault tolerance in all Cisco LANE implementations.

When configured with the Catalyst 5000/5500 ATM release 3.1 or higher, SSRP provides redundancy by allowing backup LECS and LES/BUS servers for an ELAN. The feature is always enabled with Cisco LANE.

The Catalyst LANE Module

The physical LANE module for the Catalyst 5000/5500 is available in three versions of 155Mbps SONET/SDH OC-3. These include multimode, single-mode, and unshielded twisted pair interfaces. While two interfaces of each type are available, only one may be active at any time. This provides for link failure or the loss of ILMI (Integrated Local Management Interface) signaling. The Catalyst 5000 supports a maximum of three LANE modules and up to 256 LANE clients. In addition, the module supports permanent and switched virtual circuits (SVCs). SVC support is provided with the Q.2931 signaling protocol.

Some references note that ILMI also stands for *Interim Local Management Interface*. The "interim" reference historically referred to the short anticipated life span of the protocol.

The ATM configuration is contained within the LANE module, not the Supervisor.

Integrated Local Management Interface cells provide for automatic configuration between ATM systems. This is accomplished using SNMP and MIB command structures, and uses a Virtual Path Identifier (VPI) of 0 and a Virtual Circuit Identifier (VCI) of 16, or VP/VC 0/16. Many telecommunications providers and administrators will use the VP/VC shorthand to document VPI/VCI pairs—as with other acronyms, any shortcut is appreciated.

Note that the ILMI SNMP functions include both manager and agent functions. This is different from the unidirectional relationship normally associated with SNMP.

ILMI can provide sufficient information for the ATM end station to find an LECS. In addition, ILMI provides the ATM NSAP (network service access point) prefix information to the end station. This prefix is configured on the local ATM switch and is 13 bytes long. It's combined with the MAC address (6 bytes) of the end node, called an end system identifier, and a one-byte selector to create the 20-byte ATM address.

The LANE module includes functionality for the LEC, LES/BUS, and LECS functions, while supporting up to 256 LANE clients. The multimode fiber module uses an SC connector and is documented in Table 9.5.

T A B L E 9.5	**Function**	**Parameter**
The Multimode LANE module	SAR (Segmentation and Reassembly)	Capable of reassembling 512 packets simultaneously
	Virtual circuits	Support for up to 4,096 virtual circuits

T A B L E 9.5 (cont.) The Multimode LANE module	Function	Parameter
	ATM Adaptation Layer	AAL5
	Optical source	LED
	Maximum distance between devices	2 km
	Wavelength	1,270 nm to 1,380 nm
	Receiver sensitivity	–32.5 dBm to –14 dBm
	Transmitter output	–19 dBm to –14 dBm

The single-mode module is similar to the multimode module; however, it is recommended in larger campus installations where distance is a significant factor. The differences between the single-mode and multimode modules are outlined in Table 9.6.

T A B L E 9.6 The Single-Mode LANE Module	Function	Parameter
	Maximum distance between devices	10 km
	Optical source	Laser
	Transmitter output	–14 dBm to –8 dBm
	Receiver sensitivity	–32.5 dBm to –8 dBm
	Wavelength	1,261 to 1,360 nm

The UTP version of the LANE module is similar to the fiber modules, however, it is limited to very short distances and uses Category 5 cabling with an RJ-45 connector.

The ATM configuration is stored within the LANE module, not within the NVRAM on the Supervisor module, and is not displayed by the show config command.

The LANE module includes LEDs to indicate the status and functionality of the unit. The LEDs are interpreted as shown in Table 9.7.

T A B L E 9.7: The LANE Module LEDs

Function	Red	Orange	Green
Status	One or more diagnostic tests failed.	The module is disabled in software or the system is booting.	All diagnostic tests passed.
TX—Transmit			Port is transmitting a cell.
RX—Receive			Port is receiving a cell.
Link			The link is active.

Always check Cisco's online Web site, www.cisco.com, for additional modules and features. In particular, the Catalyst 5000 switches support an emerging technology called MPOA, or multiprotocol over ATM. While it's beyond the scope of this chapter, many administrators will wish to include MPOA in their ATM installations.

Network Management on the LANE module   The LANE module in the Catalyst 5000/5500 is configured via the command-line interface, or CLI. This interface is accessed through the Supervisor module console or administration port. However, the Supervisor maintains no configuration information regarding the LANE module.

The LANE module also supports SNMP, or Simple Network Management Protocol, and the following MIBs:

- MIB II

- LANE MIB

- ILMI MIB

- AToM MIB

Segmentation and Reassembly

Frame-based networks require a minimum frame size. For example, Ethernet requires a minimum size of 64 bytes. This is substantially greater than the 48 bytes of data permitted in an ATM cell—which is only 53 bytes with the header information.

In order to handle the frame-based data in a cell-based network, a process must occur to segment or reassemble the data into the needed medium. This is handled in SAR, or segmentation and reassembly, and is associated with the adaptation layer of the ATM model. SAR is one area where original ATM switches failed to provide the performance availed by the bandwidth of the pipe. To address the 155Mbps OC-3 on the Catalyst LANE module, Cisco installed two LSI ATMizers to provide low-latency and wire-speed performance. Each ATMizer operates independently; one is used for receive and one for transmit. The LANE module is capable of addressing 4096 virtual circuits, however, the default is 1024. This provides sufficient capability for most installations.

The LANE module SAR engine is capable of traffic shaping via a single-rate queue, as well. This can provide more appropriate use of WAN links, which cannot typically handle the bursts associated with LANs. The SAR process is not only responsible for breaking frames into cells, but also padding cells to result in even 48-byte (payload) increments.

Connecting in an ATM Network

It is essential for administrators to understand the initial startup and connection sequences for ATM LANE. This not only provides a basis for troubleshooting, but also helps you to evaluate proper placement of the LES/BUS and LECS modules.

Although it's not required, most LANE environments make use of the LECS to provide configuration information to the end-node. This connection, using a configuration direct VCC, queries for an LECS in the following order:

1. Use the address for the LECS that has been preconfigured on the local LEC.

2. Use ILMI to locate the LECS.

3. Use the LECS well-known address. This address is 47:00:79:00:00:00:00:00:00:00:00:00:00:00:A0:3E:00:01:00 and is specified by the ATM Forum.

After contacting the LECS, the client has sufficient information to contact the LES, including some operating information for the ELAN. The LEC-to-LES connection is established with a join command on a bidirectional control direct VCC. The LES is responsible for registering the LEC and permitting it to join the ELAN.

The LEC is now responsible for locating the BUS. This is accomplished via LE-ARP, or LAN Emulation Address Resolution Protocol. The LES will respond to this request with the address of the BUS. The LEC then registers and joins the BUS.

Figure 9.1 illustrates the initial startup sequence of ATM LANE.

Figure 9.1 illustrates the initial connection sequence with separate elements for the LECS, LES, and BUS. These resources are usually contained within a single physical device. Check with the Cisco Web site for current information regarding the location requirements of these services. The diagram is intended to illustrate the flow of messages within the ATM environment. The workstation representing the LEC could also be any LEC device, including a Catalyst with an ATM LANE module representing numerous frame-based devices.

FIGURE 9.1

The Initial ATM LANE sequence

Phase 1: The LEC queries the LECS.

Configuration Direct VCC
Initial query to obtain LES address

LEC

LECS

Phase 2: The LEC joins the ELAN.

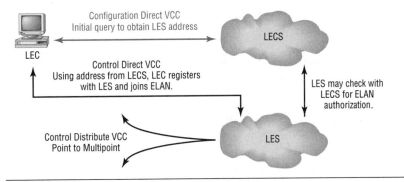

Configuration Direct VCC
Initial query to obtain LES address

LEC

LECS

Control Direct VCC
Using address from LECS, LEC registers
with LES and joins ELAN.

LES may check with
LECS for ELAN
authorization.

Control Distribute VCC
Point to Multipoint

LES

Phase 3: The LEC connects to the BUS.

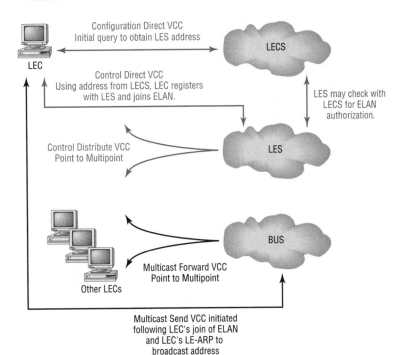

Configuration Direct VCC
Initial query to obtain LES address

LEC

LECS

Control Direct VCC
Using address from LECS, LEC registers
with LES and joins ELAN.

LES may check with
LECS for ELAN
authorization.

Control Distribute VCC
Point to Multipoint

LES

BUS

Multicast Forward VCC
Point to Multipoint

Other LECs

Multicast Send VCC initiated
following LEC's join of ELAN
and LEC's LE-ARP to
broadcast address

When a client needs to send data to an unknown resource, the LES and BUS cooperate to provide the correct information. The LEC will send an LE-ARP request to the LES for the destination station, and, prior to receiving a response, also send the initial data cells to the BUS, which will forward the data cells to the destination and all other stations. Once the destination client receives the LE-ARP request from the LES, it responds and the address information is forwarded to the source. The source then sends a "flush" message to the BUS, instructing it to stop sending any unsent cells and to discard them. The source will establish a direct connection with the destination and the remaining data will be sent.

ATM Network Design

Planning the design of an ATM network involves many of the same criteria as in designing frame-based networks. Issues of cost, corporate or business units, security, bandwidth, and technical limitations must all be considered.

A single ELAN network design is the simplest to understand and implement, and is recommended for lab installations to assist in comprehension of ATM LANE and potential issues in larger networks. Such a network may incorporate multiple LECs, with a single LECS and LES/BUS.

More advanced ATM LANE implementations may contain a single LECS serving multiple ELANs. Different switches in the network may be configured as LES/BUS pairs for an individual ELAN—recommended for removing a single point of failure, or with all ELANs served by LES/BUS pairs on a single switch in the data center. Note that ELANs cannot communicate with each other without a Layer 3 device, either a router or the RSM module in the Catalyst. All multiple ELAN designs must include a router. It is also possible for the router to serve as the LECS and LES/BUS.

LANE Configuration

When configuring the LANE module, it is important to remember that the ATM LANE configuration is not stored or modified in the Supervisor engine. As a result, the administrator must connect to the ATM LANE module in order to continue.

First, connect to the ATM LANE module and enter configuration mode. In this example, the ATM LANE module is in slot 4.

```
Switch_A> session 4
```

Second, the administrator must enter enable mode and configure the ATM interface on the LANE module:

```
ATM_LANE>en
ATM_LANE#conf t
ATM_LANE (config)#int atm 0
ATM_LANE (config-if)#mtu 1500
ATM_LANE (config-if)#lane config auto-config-atm-address
ATM_LANE (config-if)#no shutdown
```

Third, the ATM addresses of the LEC, LES, BUS, and LECS should be obtained and recorded. Note that this assumes that the LANE module is connected to the LS-1010 ASP via an LS-1010 line card or an external ATM switch.

```
ATM_LANE#show lane default-atm-address
```

While it may be necessary to configure the LS-1010 during this process, our example will focus on the LANE module. Thus, the fourth step is to start the LES and BUS:

```
ATM_LANE (config)#int atm 0.1
ATM_LANE (config-subif)#lane server-bus ethernet elan1
```

Each connection will require an LEC, which is the fifth step:

```
ATM_LANE (config-subif)#lane client ethernet 1 elan1
```

If an LECS is desired, the sixth step would be to configure the LECS database and start the LECS:

```
ATM_LANE (config)#lane database lecs_db
ATM_LANE (lane-config-database)#name elan1 server-atm-
address [server1-address]
ATM_LANE (config-if)#lane config lecs_db
```

The server1-address value is supplied by the show lane default-atm-address output in step 3. The LECS database may be named differently from the convention shown here. Many administrators prefer the easily understood convention shown. Please note that the commands to enter and leave different command modes were omitted for space considerations and clarity of the actual LANE commands. Please use the prompts to indicate changes.

Also note that this sample only configured interface ATM 0.1 and its physical interface.

Remember to issue a `write memory` command to save the configuration.

Catalyst Networks

This chapter has focused on the more advanced features of the Catalyst 5000/5500 platform, and with the exception of VLANs, it is possible for many networks to evolve without ever needing FDDI or ATM services. However, there are concepts that relate to all networks, and these concepts are applicable to advanced networks as well.

Most modern networks relate well to the client/server model. This model reflects the relationship between clients, workstations and other user interfaces, and servers, or those resources that supply clients with services. Servers should include printers and other shared devices.

In networking, the client is sometimes referred to as a demand node. This reflects the fact that these devices frequently request the information—a demand for networking purposes. Resource nodes are synonymous with servers, as they respond to demands. In the network, routers, servers and mainframes all serve as resource nodes.

Recall that switches can provide a number of services, however, one of their most basic functions is the control of the collision domain. VLANs, including those connected via ATM and FDDI, still benefit from Ethernet stations sitting on single switch ports. Performance within the network increases because the desktop is no longer burdened with collisions (full-duplex), and integration into other media augments this increased performance.

The previous chapter presented the Catalyst 5000/5500 structure, including the location and use of buffers. It would be wrong to assume that buffers are incapable of overflowing—surpassing their ability to handle incoming traffic. Buffer overflows can be resolved by identifying the packet flow within the network. Usually resources, or resource nodes, are more prone to congestion and buffer problems.

To address these problems, administrators should increase the size of the switch buffers and the size of the links to resource nodes, including servers. In addition, aggregating links can greatly address this issue. The Catalyst

5000/5500 products support Fast EtherChannel, a bonding process th.. .a.. link up to four Fast Ethernet connections. This results in a full-duplex 800Mbps connection between switches, which may also suffer from congestion and buffer overflows.

The Catalyst switch also supports a higher priority setting on a per-port basis. By increasing this setting, servers can be given more access to the Catalyst backplane. The commands for this configuration are included in the following chapter. Lastly, a packet retry process can address buffer overflow.

While the Catalyst 5000/5500 can service Token Ring, Ethernet, FDDI, and ATM connections, the overriding goal of the switch is to improve network performance. In addition, the switch can improve performance and scalability by clustering servers, providing 10/100Mbps service to workgroups and Fast Ethernet to the desktop. The Catalyst can also serve in the backbone, providing an aggregation point for the various workgroups. As a result, poor network response problems, high collision rates, and broadcasts can all be addressed within a design that includes switches.

Summary

This chapter has covered a great deal of material in a fairly brief and concise manner. Readers should come away with a solid foundation for the Catalyst FDDI and ATM LANE options, in addition to the core concepts behind VLAN and ELAN services.

Administrators should understand the services provided through VLANs, including reduced administration costs and geographic independence for users. They should also understand the use of trunking ports and protocols, including FDDI 802.10 and ATM LANE. ISL and 802.1Q, two additional trunking protocols, are covered in Chapter 2.

This chapter also addressed the benefits and limitations of VLAN and ELAN configurations.

We saw how Token Ring can be integrated into the Catalyst system, along with the various bridging options, and we reviewed the positives and negatives associated with continued use of Token Ring.

FDDI and CDDI, two historical backbone topologies, were described in the Catalyst context, along with the migration paths that Cisco provides for continued use of these technologies.

The chapter discussed ATM LANE, a transparent method for connecting legacy LAN technologies to ATM, with specific consideration paid to the Catalyst implementation and the various services available, including the LECS, LES/BUS, and LEC. This chapter also included SSRP and the LANE connection sequence, and it covered the configuration of the LANE module and the ATM LANE services—LEC, LES, BUS, and LECS.

The hardware and diagnostic functionality of the Catalyst modules were reviewed with specific attention paid to the LEDs, which provide administrators with general information that helps in diagnostic sessions to isolate problems.

Review Questions

1. Static VLAN implementations usually are defined:

A. By physical port

B. By MAC address

C. By the LECS

D. In the MAC/CAM table

2. Which of the following are required in ATM LANE?

A. LEC

B. LECS

C. LES

D. BUS

E. Optical fiber

3. When designing a multiple-ELAN network, the administrator must include which of the following?

A. DHCP

B. Router or RSM

C. Multiple switches

D. None of the above

4. The Catalyst LANE module provides which of the following?

A. SONET/SDH at 100Mbps

B. 100Mbps Ethernet

C. SONET/SDH at 155Mbps

D. The LANE module contains no physical ports, but connects to the Catalyst backplane.

5. The 802.10 protocol is available with which of the following physical media?

   A. Fast Ethernet

   B. Token Ring

   C. FDDI

   D. ATM

   E. All of the above

6. When using `fddicheck`, what other condition or conditions must be met?

   A. APaRT must be enabled.

   B. APaRT must be disabled.

   C. The Catalyst ATM LANE module must be installed.

   D. All VLANs must be numbered above 1023.

   E. All SAID values must be numbered above 1023.

7. Within the 802.10 protocol, VLAN information is available only in which of the following?

   A. VLAN information is not available through 802.10.

   B. The SAYS field in the Clear Header

   C. The SAID field in the Encrypted Header

   D. The SAID field in the Clear Header

   E. The LMI on VLAN 1023

8. The ILMI is used to provide the following services:

   A. Discover ATM addresses.

   B. Locate the LECS.

   C. Locate the LES/BUS.

   D. Encapsulate all cells for VP/VC information and calculation of the HEC.

9. A network with three VLANs and seven Catalyst switches will contain how many spanning trees, assuming a full-mesh network and a requirement for use of spanning tree?

A. 1

B. 3

C. 7

D. 21

E. Not enough information is provided.

10. ELANs incorporate which of the following:

A. A logical grouping of devices, akin to a VLAN

B. An independent broadcast domain

C. LECs and LES/BUS services

D. All of the above

11. Which of the following is true regarding the segmentation and reassembly (SAR) function?

A. SAR is serviced in the ATM layer

B. SAR is serviced in the SONET layer

C. SAR is serviced in the adaptation layer

D. SAR converts FDDI frames to Ethernet

E. All of the above

12. In order to address the limitations of bursty traffic on WAN links, the Catalyst system:

A. Performs SAR at wire speed in both directions

B. Uses APaRT to control traffic flow

C. Uses the ISL and SAID protocols to control port buffering

D. Uses a single-rate queue

E. Provides traffic shaping as part of EIGRP

13. The LANE module supports which of the following MIBs?

    A. ILMI MIB

    B. FDDI MIB

    C. LMI MIB

    D. Bridge MIB

    E. LECS MIB

14. The Catalyst LANE module can be configured to provide which of the following services?

    A. LEC

    B. LECS

    C. LES

    D. BUS

    E. All of the above

    F. None of the above

15. The Catalyst 5000 supports which two of the following:

    A. A single LANE module

    B. Dual LANE modules in a redundant configuration

    C. Three LANE modules

    D. A single FDDI module

    E. A single Supervisor engine

16. Which of the following is specified in LANE?

    A. SR/TLB

    B. Proxy ARP

    C. LES

    D. ISL

    E. 802.10

17. Which of the following services the mapping/resolution of ATM and MAC addresses?

    A. LECS

    B. LEC

    C. LES

    D. LE-ARP server

    E. BUS

18. In FDDI, the longest distance between two devices is accommodated via:

    A. CDDI

    B. ATM over FDDI using 802.10

    C. FDDI and multimode fiber

    D. FDDI and single-mode fiber

    E. CDDI and FDDI offer the same distance limitations.

19. When creating FDDI VLANs, the administrator must define SAID values.

    A. True

    B. False

20. In the initial configuration, which of the following are true?

    A. APaRT and fddicheck are disabled.

    B. fddicheck is enabled but APaRT is disabled.

    C. APaRT is enabled but fddicheck is disabled.

    D. The Catalyst 5000 FDDI module provides FDDI translational switching/bridging.

    E. 802.10 is enabled.

    F. ISL is enabled.

21. The SAID field provides for how many VLANs?

   A. 4.29 billion

   B. 65,535

   C. 1024

   D. The SAID field does not define VLANs.

22. Virtual LANs provide for:

   A. Control over broadcast frames

   B. Higher administration costs

   C. Transparency in ATM LANE networks

   D. Population of the RIF field

23. The RIF field is part of the Ethernet frame in Catalyst switching.

   A. True

   B. False

24. Spanning trees perform which of the following functions:

   A. Forwarding of Token Ring frames based on the RIF header

   B. Blocking of redundant paths in switched networks

   C. Integration of VLANs within the enterprise

   D. Protection against bridging loops by tagging each broadcast frame with a TTL bit

   E. Multicast control

25. A packet contains a RIF field. Which of the following is likely to be true?

    A. The frame is being bridged with TB.

    B. The frame is being bridged with SRB or SRS.

    C. The cell is being converted into a frame in the SAR process.

    D. The cell is on a Token Ring segment.

    E. The frame is being routed via EIGRP or OSPF.

26. Which of the following would be included as a demand node?

    A. A router

    B. A server

    C. A mainframe

    D. A workstation

    E. A switch

27. A server is a resource node.

    A. True

    B. False

28. Token Ring servers attached to the Catalyst should be attached using which of the following to provide the greatest performance?

    A. Token Ring servers should not be connected to the Catalyst switch.

    B. Connected via TR-ISL adapters.

    C. Connected with a shared MAU.

    D. Configured for TRB, RSRB, and SRB.

29. The ATM LANE module is installed in slot 3 and the Supervisor III engine is installed in slot one. Which of the following commands would be needed to configure LANE?

    A. `set vtp domain LANE`

    B. `set trunk 3/1 on`

    C. `session 3`

    D. `set session 3`

    E. `set system lane LECS`

30. To address congestion in a Token Ring backbone, a network designer could use the Catalyst 5000/5500 with which of the following to address the problem?

    A. Fast Ethernet

    B. ATM

    C. Either of the above

    D. None of the above

    E. High speed Token Ring, enabled with TR-ISL cards and the `set ring speed 155` command

CHAPTER

10

Installing and Configuring the
Catalyst 5000 System

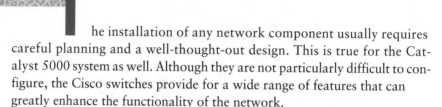

The installation of any network component usually requires careful planning and a well-thought-out design. This is true for the Catalyst 5000 system as well. Although they are not particularly difficult to configure, the Cisco switches provide for a wide range of features that can greatly enhance the functionality of the network.

Historically, networks were designed around the 80/20 rule—80 percent of the traffic should remain local to the subnet and no more than 20 percent should depart the subnet for other networks. Ironically, however, another "80/20" rule frequently seems to be in effect. The installation of a network—including Catalyst switches, VLANs, and other features—seems to require at least 80 percent of the time spent administering the network, while the remaining 20 percent of the administrator's time is sufficient to address maintenance.

In reality, this ratio is only applicable to well-designed networks. A poorly designed network will always require substantial amounts of time to research and resolve problems that arise. The best network designs frequently allow for considerations well beyond the traditional scope of a network architect or administrator. The administrator often needs to work with company management to resolve business questions regarding applications and costs, in addition to IT-based concerns, including scalability and resolution of long-term historical problems.

To that end, this chapter will cover the general issues that face administrators during network upgrades and new deployments, in addition to the following exam objectives regarding the installation and configuration of the Catalyst system:

- Establish a serial connection.

- Use the Catalyst 5000 switch CLI to:

  - Prepare network connections

- Enter privileged mode

- Set system information

- Configure interface types

- Describe the rules for assigning ATM components to interfaces

- Explain ATM address structure

- Describe how ATM addresses are automatically assigned

- Discuss how internetworking is acheived in a LANE environment.

- Configure port parameters

- Configure VLANs and trunk links

Installing the Catalyst System

Every network installation is unique. While each installation presents similar issues of business needs, facility limitations, and budget constraints, it is clear that the administrator must contend with unique circumstances every time a new network is installed.

In general, anyone planning the installation of Catalyst 5000 switches needs to consider the issues listed below. Note that these are simply the high-level issues regarding switch installation only; there are also issues such as network addressing and redundancy to consider. While the installation of the Catalyst 5000/5500 system is fairly simple, reviewing this list during the inception phase of a network project will help the administrator keep in mind all the various factors that are involved, including those beyond the switch itself.

- Cooling

- Power

- Rack space

- Cable type required

- Existing cabling

- New cabling

- Distance limitations

- Number of nodes serviced

- Budget

- Schedule

- Additional equipment

- Training

- Documentation

Installation and Startup

In most cases, the Catalyst 5000/5500 switch will be physically installed in a rack and placed at or near the core of the network.

Once a specific model of Catalyst has been selected and ordered, administrators will need to verify that sufficient facilities are provided. This may include additional cooling or dual power circuits to provide independent power to redundant power supplies. Again, the list in the previous section provides a guideline for the types of issues novice administrators should consider.

The status LEDs and other diagnostic indicators of the Catalyst 5000 system were documented in Chapter 8. However, it is important to note that the Catalyst performs a diagnostic on system startup. This diagnostic process is essentially a POST for the switch. The Catalyst diagnostic process tests the backplane and module connectors, in addition to the on-board ASICs, including the SAINT and EARL systems. All ports are also placed in loop-back mode for testing and then reset.

Connecting to the Supervisor Module

The Supervisor module is truly the brain of the Catalyst system. Administrators will need to configure the Catalyst with a basic configuration before they can do further management or define nondefault services. This process begins with the out-of-band serial port.

Serial Out-of-Band

The Catalyst Supervisor module includes an asynchronous DCE DB-25 connector (the Supervisor III uses an RJ-45 connector), which is used for out-of-band connectivity and the initial configuration of the switch. Out-of-band connectivity may include a terminal, terminal server, or modem.

By default, the console port is configured for:

- 9600 baud

- 8 data bits

- No parity

- 1 stop bit

When connecting a terminal, or a PC using terminal emulation, use a straight-through cable. A null-modem cable is needed for connections using a modem or other DCE device.

Initially the switch is configured with no password and no IP address information. As such, only an Enter or Return character is needed to obtain access to the console port. In addition, the switch will initiate BOOTP and RARP requests to locate a remote configuration and attempt to load it. These requests will occur whenever the SC0 interface is set to an IP address of 0.0.0.0 or when the configuration is cleared with the `clear config all` command.

Note that the SC0 interface is also used for file transfers via the TFTP protocol.

Consult the documentation that ships with the Catalyst switch if the initial startup sequence is unsuccessful. Note that sometimes more than one Enter character is needed to obtain the system prompt.

It is possible to administer the Catalyst switch using SLIP, or serial line IP. This connection uses the SL0 interface. Some administrators configure the SL0 interface for remote locations. To configure the SL0 interface, use the command

`set interface sl0 slip_address destination_address`

Use the `slip attach` command to set the port. When using a directly connected terminal, some administrators may choose to use the Kermit protocol to transfer files. When using SLIP, or the in-band Telnet connection, TFTP may be used.

WARNING Local console connections are not available when the SLIP connection is enabled. Resetting the switch may be necessary if the SLIP connection is lost while SLIP is enabled. Via Telnet, use the command `slip detach` or `reset system` to regain access to the console port. An alternative to SLIP would be the installation of a terminal server, which may be warranted for remote sites with no technical support nearby.

In-Band Management

Once the switch is configured with basic information, including an IP address, it is possible to Telnet to the system to make configuration changes. This occurs via the SC0 interface, which is initially placed in VLAN 1. An IP address, subnet mask, default gateway, and broadcast value must all be set from their default values of 0.0.0.0 as well. These commands are discussed further in a later section of this chapter—they are included here simply to demonstrate the commands usually needed upon initial installation and configuration of the in-band management system.

To configure the SC0 interface, use the command

```
set interface sc0 [vlan_number] ip_address
[netmask[broadcast]]
```

For example, to set the SC0 interface to VLAN 1 using IP address 10.1.1.10 on a subnet, type

```
set interface sc0 1 10.1.1.10 255.255.255.0 10.1.1.255
```

This command could be shortened to omit the VLAN number and broadcast address.

It may be necessary to issue the equivalent of the `no shutdown` command on the interface. On the Catalyst, this command to enable the interface is

```
set interface sc0 up
```

It may also be necessary to establish a default route, which is configured with the command

```
set ip route default gateway [metric]
```

This would be needed to reach switch on a different subnet from the management or Telnet console. The show ip route command should be used to verify routes, and additional routes may be established with the command

```
set ip route destination gateway [metric]
```

Moving the SC0 interface from VLAN 1 to another VLAN is not recommended. Most administrators use VLAN 1 for administration and management, while allocating other VLANs for user traffic. This design is highly recommended.

Default Configuration / SNMP

An understanding of the default switch configuration will greatly assist administrators in identifying the changes required during initial installation and subsequent troubleshooting. In addition, security risks can be assessed and addressed as warranted.

For example, SNMP, or Simple Network Management Protocol, is used to administer and configure various network devices, including Catalyst switches. As such, access to the SNMP interface on a network device can be very powerful and could permit a hacker with the ability to disrupt or deny services. Sometimes such attacks are not intentional, or hacking efforts, but simply the result of users exploring with SNMP tools on the production network.

By default the Catalyst is configured with the following SNMP community strings. These strings function as passwords in SNMP, although they are not secure. As such, it is highly recommended that access lists or other filters protect critical network devices.

Table 10.1 documents the default SNMP community strings.

T A B L E 10.1	**SNMP Community String**	**Default Value**
The Default Catalyst SNMP Community Strings	read-only	public
	read-write	private
	read-write-all	secret

To view the current SNMP configuration, use the show snmp command, as shown here.

```
Switch_A> (enable) show snmp
RMON:                   Disabled
Extended RMON:          Extended RMON module is not present
Extended RMON Netflow:  Disabled
Extended RMON Vlanmode: Disabled
Extended RMON Vlanagent: Disabled
Traps Enabled:
Port,Module,Chassis,Bridge,Repeater,Vtp,Auth,ippermit, config
Port Traps Enabled: 1/1-2

Community-Access    Community-String
----------------    --------------------
read-only           public
read-write          private
read-write-all      secret


Trap-Rec-Address                Trap-Rec-Community

10.10.1.254                     public
10.20.1.254                     public
```

Changes to the SNMP configuration are made with the set snmp community command. Table 10.2 demonstrates the applicable commands.

T A B L E 10.2 The SNMP Command Syntax	**SNMP String**	**Command**
	read-only	`set snmp community read-only` *community-string*
	read-write	`set snmp community read-write` *community-string*
	read-write-all	`set snmp community read-write-all` *community-string*

For example,

```
set snmp community read-only buster
```

would change the read-only community string to `buster` and would subsequently prevent SNMP management consoles from discovering the switch using the default `public` community string. Some administrators are unfamiliar with the read-write-all SNMP option. On the Catalyst switch this community string controls access to the community strings themselves; that is, changes to the community string are only permitted with the read-write-all value. Note that by using enable mode via the CLI, the administrator can change any of these values directly—the SNMP strings only impact SNMP processes. The read-only community string permits read access to all objects in the management information bases, or MIBs. Read-write access permits browsing and changing all MIB objects except the community strings.

By default, SNMP traps are not enabled on the Catalyst system. To configure the switch to provide this beneficial service, use the `set snmp trap` command as follows.

```
set snmp trap 10.10.1.254    public
```

In addition to its SNMP support, the Catalyst supports RMON in hardware. An additional license is available for software support as well. Information regarding a system's RMON configuration is also available from the `show snmp` command, as shown above.

Many networks also benefit from a syslog server, which records error messages from systems and is typically placed in a central location in well designed networks. The Catalyst can record system events to a host running syslogd (originally used for Unix systems) or the equivalent service. Syslog services are also available for Windows systems. Table 10.3 describes the syslog severity levels. Severity levels may be used to filter or organize messages from the reporting system.

T A B L E 10.3	Value	Definition
Syslog/Debug Severity Levels	0	emergency
	1	alerts
	2	critical
	3	errors
	4	warnings
	5	notifications
	6	informational
	7	debugging

Used together, syslog, SNMP, and RMON provide powerful tools for the network administrator and can assist in more advanced installations.

Fiber Module Installations

Fiber optics permit substantially greater distances between devices compared to copper media. In a large campus or a small MAN installation, fiber optics may be the most economical way to interconnect network devices. In addition, gigabit Ethernet and newer high-speed technologies are likely to surpass the capacity of copper cable, adding to the benefits garnered by fiber installations.

An important consideration in fiber-optic installations is the loss of signal strength. Most administrators are satisfied with the distance limitations documented in Table 10.4. However, knowledge of the limitations and the formulas used to calculate power budgets and power margins can provide added assurance that an installation will be successful. As with any cable installation, the use of professional installers trained and equipped with the latest technologies can greatly reduce the potential of problems caused by faulty physical layer media.

T A B L E 10.4 Distance Limitations with Fiber and Copper Media	Connector	Maximum Distance
	CDDI, Ethernet, Fast Ethernet (CAT 5)	100 meters
	Token-Ring (CAT 5, 16Mps)	200 meters
	FDDI (Multimode), ATM (Multimode), Ethernet (Multimode, Full Duplex)	2,000 meters
	Fast Ethernet (Single-Mode, Full Duplex)	10,000 meters
	FDDI (Single-Mode)	30,000 meters

Multimode optical fiber uses light-emitting diodes (LEDs), in contrast to single-mode fibers, where lasers are used. Multimode installations may also use injection laser diodes (ILDs). LEDs offer the benefit of low cost and high reliability, while ILDs are more generally more efficient. As such, most installations use LEDs.

Fiber-optic installations provide the benefit of greater distance and security, in addition to reduced effects from external interference. However, these benefits frequently come at greater costs and added complexity in the installation process. Fiber installations are more sensitive to installation errors and the effects of attenuation, scattering losses, absorption losses, connection losses, and bending losses.

There are two basic formulas used in calculating the losses experienced with multimode fiber. These formulas frequently present a worst-case scenario. As such, their results are usually conservative.

The maximum amount of transmitted power possible is referred to as the power budget, or PB value. The formula for the PB value is

$$PB = PT - PR$$

where PT is the minimum transmitter power and PR is the receiver's minimum sensitivity.

The power margin, or PM value, is calculated from the PB value and subtracts link loss (LL) factors from the cable. Attenuation, splices, and connectors all account for part of the link loss. The formula for the power margin is

$$PM = PB - LL$$

A link should operate correctly if the PM value is positive. Table 10.5 documents the estimated link loss values that are suggested by Cisco. However, where possible, an optical tester should be used.

Professional cable and fiber installers are well trained for the wide variety of considerations that govern installations. They have equipment for pulling cables while maintaining proper tension and minimum radius turns, and they have testing tools for certifying cable installations. Working with a knowledgeable cable installer is strongly recommended and frequently will reduce the long-term costs of the installation.

T A B L E 10.5 Approximate LED Link Loss Values	Element	Link Loss Value (Estimated)
	Fiber attenuation	1 dB per kilometer
	Splice	0.5 dB per splice
	Connectors	0.5 dB per connector
	Clock recovery module	1.0 dB
	High order mode losses	0.5 dB

A large amount of information is available from a variety of sources regarding attenuation and power budgets, in addition to fiber and copper installations. Much of this information was developed from the former Bell Labs (BellCore), in addition to AT&T and ANSI. Readers interested in additional information are recommended to consult these sources available via the Internet or in most large libraries.

Configuring the Catalyst System

The configuration of the Catalyst system resembles the setup process used for Cisco routers. After entering privileged mode, or enable mode, the administrator enters commands to define various parameters within the system. This process can be augmented with other programs or can be entered line by line within the software.

The following sections present the Catalyst IOS commands to provide administrators with an overview of the commands needed both for the CLSC exam and for real-world installations. As always, review of the documentation and hands-on experience with real switches greatly assists in the learning process.

Many administrators use a simple text editor to enter the configuration commands offline and then paste this input into a Telnet session with the router or switch. This process is best used for simple command sequences, such as access-list entry; however, it can be used for other commands as well.

Cisco Command Conventions

Within Cisco documentation, a standard methodology of presenting material is used to facilitate understanding of the various examples, commands, and explanations. These conventions are similar to those used by Sybex in the presentation of material in this text.

Table 10.6 documents the various terms and conventions used by Cisco in their technical documentation.

T A B L E 10.6 Cisco Command Conventions	**Command or Term**	**Cisco Convention**	**Sybex Equivalent**
	Commands or keywords	**Boldface** type	Screen font
	User-level command prompt in console screens	Console>	Same as Cisco, plus screen font

T A B L E 10.6 *(cont.)* Cisco Command Conventions	**Command or Term**	**Cisco Convention**	**Sybex Equivalent**
	Privileged level command prompt (also referred to as enable mode) in console screens	Console> (enable)	Same as Cisco, plus screen font
	Command arguments in syntax displays	*Italic* type	Same as Cisco, plus screen font
	Optional parameters in syntax displays	Square brackets []	Same as Cisco, plus screen font
	Required keyword alternatives in syntax displays	Separated by vertical bars: |	Same as Cisco, plus screen font
	Sample console screens	Presented in screen font	Same as Cisco
	User-entered data in console screens	Presented in **bold screen** font	Same as Cisco
	Passwords and other characters that are not presented on-screen	Presented in greater-than, less-than brackets <>	Same as Cisco

The Catalyst IOS Command Set

Unlike the router IOS, the Catalyst 5000/5500 uses `set` commands to define the switch settings. As such, there is no `configure terminal` command or mode. Chapter 8 provided a default listing of the root commands and the show commands. The remainder of this section presents a detailed view of the most significant commands.

Set Interface

```
set interface <sc0|sl0> <up|down>
set interface sc0 [vlan] [ip_addr [netmask [broadcast]]]
set interface sl0 <slip_addr> <dest_addr>
```

Usage   The `set interface` command is used to define an IP address and other configuration parameters for the SC0 and SL0 interfaces. The SC0 interface is usually configured and provides an in-band Telnet interface, in addition to SNMP. The SL0 interface, as discussed previously, is used for SLIP connections.

Example

Switch_A> (enable) **set interface sc0 10.1.1.10 255.255.255.0**

In this example, the SC0 interface will be assigned an IP address of 10.1.1.10 and a network mask of 255.255.255.0. The broadcast address will automatically be assigned as 10.1.1.255, and the virtual connection will remain bound to VLAN1.

Set IP Route

set ip route *<destination>* *<gateway>* *[metric][primary]*

Usage   The `set ip route` command is used to assign a default gateway or any static routes to the switch. The `destination` and `gateway` parameters are IP aliases or IP addresses in dot notation: a.b.c.d.

Example

Switch_A> (enable) **set ip route 0.0.0.0 10.1.1.1**

Here, the default route for the switch has been configured for the router at 10.1.1.1.

Set VLAN

set vlan *<vlan_num>* *<mod/ports...>*

set vlan *<vlan_num>* [name *<name>*] [type *<type>*] [state *<state>*] [said *<said>*] [mtu *<mtu>*] [ring *<hex_ring_number>*] [decring *<decimal_ring_number>*]
   [bridge *<bridge_number>*] [parent *<vlan_num>*]
   [mode *<bridge_mode>*] [stp *<stp_type>*]
   [translation *<vlan_num>*] [backupcrf *<off|on>*]
   [aremaxhop *<hopcount>*] [stemaxhop *<hopcount>*]

Usage The set vlan command provides multiple purposes. In most installations, the command is used to create VLANs and assign ports to particular VLANs. The parameters are as follows:

mod/port	The switch module and the port number within that module; for example, 1/1, 2/1-12,3/1-2,4/1-12
name	May be any length from 1 to 32 characters
state	May be either active or suspend
type	May be ethernet, fddi, fddinet, trcrf, or trbrf
said	May be any value from 1 to 4294967294
mtu	May be any value from 576 to 18190
hex_ring_number	May be any value from 0x1 to 0xfff, hex
decimal_ring_number	May be any value from 1 to 4095
bridge_number	May be any value from 0x1 to 0xf
parent	May be any value from 2 to 1005
mode	May be either srt or srb
stp	May be ieee, ibm, auto
translation	May be any value from 1 to 1005
hopcount	May be any value from 1 to 13

Example

```
Switch_A> (enable) set vlan 3 name Marketing
Switch_A> (enable) set vlan 3 3/1-4
```

In this example, the administrator has created VLAN 3 with the name Marketing, and ports 3/1-4 have been bound to the VLAN. Note that the 3/1–4 shorthand is available on some commands as an alternative to specifying each port individually (3/1, 3/2, 3/3, 3/4).

Set Port

```
set port broadcast
set port channel
set port disable
set port duplex
set port enable
set port flowcontrol
set port filter
set port help
set port level
set port membership
set port name
set port negotiation
set port protocol
set port security
set port speed
set port trap
```

Usage   The set port command defines characteristics of the port, including the broadcast traffic limit, full- or half-duplex operation, flow control, Token Ring filtering, priority level, VLAN membership, protocol membership, security, transmission speed, and trapping. The set port help or set port ? command displays a summary of all the set port options. The command is usually used to define the port speed and duplex.

Example

```
Switch_A> (enable) set port speed 3/1 100
Switch_A> (enable) set port duplex 3/1 full
```

Port 3/1 has been configured for 100 Mbps, full duplex, in this example.

Set Trunk

```
set trunk <mod_num/port_num>
  [on|off|desirable|auto|nonegotiate] [vlans] [trunk_type]
```

Usage The set trunk command is used to establish a trunk between two switches or a switch and router. While ports can remain in auto mode (the default), at least one side of the connection must be set to on or desirable. As such, most administrators configure both sides of the trunk manually to avoid future problems that may arise when a trunk link cable is moved to another port.

vlans	May be any number from 1 to 1005; for example, 2-10,1005
trunk_type	May be isl, dot1q, dot10, lane, or negotiate

An ISL link requires the use of a Fast Ethernet port, although a token ring specification, TR-ISL, has been developed. FDDI uses the 802.10, or dot10, specification, as reviewed in Chapter 9.

Example

```
Switch_A> (enable) set trunk 1/1 on isl

Port(s) 1/1 trunk mode set to on.
Port(s) 1/1 trunk type set to isl.
```

Port 1/1 has been manually configured for trunking using the ISL protocol.

Set Spantree

```
set spantree disable
set spantree enable
set spantree fwddelay
set spantree hello
set spantree help
set spantree maxage
set spantree portcost
set spantree portfast
```

```
set spantree portpri
set spantree portstate
set spantree portvlancost
set spantree portvlanpri
set spantree priority
set spantree root
set spantree uplinkfast
set spantree multicast-address
set spantree backbonefast
```

Usage   Aside from the `set spantree enable` command, which is configured by default, many administrators avoid manual configuration of the spanning tree process through weightings of ports and the root bridge priority. However, manual configuration of spanning tree may be required for more advanced configurations, including those that use BVI (Bridge Group Virtual Interface), backup interfaces, or HSRP (Hot Standby Router Protocol). In the example below, port 1/2 has been configured for a lower port cost for VLANs 4 and 5. This will configure the tree to prefer this trunk for VLAN 4 and 5 traffic compared to an unconfigured trunk. Note the manner in which the switch verifies the configuration. Note that VLANs 1–3 and 6–1005 have not been changed with the command in this example. The switch reports the default path cost value of 19 as a result.

Example

```
Switch_A>(enable) set spantree portvlancost 1/2 cost 10 4-5


Port 1/2 VLANs 1-3,6-1005 have path cost 19.
Port 1/2 VLANs 4-5 have path cost 10.
```

A View of Your System: The show Commands

The show commands provide a good indication of the services available on the switch. You can display a list of all the available show commands by entering **show ?** Chapter 12 includes detailed coverage of the show commands that are most relevant for troubleshooting and diagnostics; the more important of the other show commands are discussed next.

Show VLAN

```
show vlan [trunk]
show vlan <vlan> [notrunk]
```

Usage The show vlan command is used to display the current status of known VLANs and the ports assigned to those VLANs. While this command is useful in researching port and VLAN mismatches, most administrators use the show port command for this function. The show vlan command is particularly useful in initial static VLAN configurations. For example, in the display below, all ports have been configured for VLAN 1, which is also the default configuration. This is probably not optimal, as four other nondefault VLANs have been configured.

Example

```
Switch_A> (enable) show vlan
```

VLAN	Name	Status	IfIndex	Mod/Ports, Vlans
1	default	active	5	1/1-2
	2/1-12			
	6/1-24			
2	Marketing_VLAN	active	48	
3	Sales_VLAN	active	49	
4	Exec_VLAN	active	50	
5	Ops_VLAN	active	51	
1002	fddi-default	active	6	
1003	trcrf-default	active	9	
1004	fddinet-default	active	7	
1005	trbrf-default	active	8	

VLAN	Type	SAID	MTU	Parent	RingNo	BrdgNo	Stp	BrdgMode	Trans1	Trans2
1	enet	100001	1500	-	-	-	-	-	0	0
2	enet	100002	1500	-	-	-	-	-	0	0
3	enet	100003	1500	-	-	-	-	-	0	0
4	enet	100004	1500	-	-	-	-	-	0	0
5	enet	100005	1500	-	-	-	-	-	0	0
1002	fddi	101002	1500	-	-	-	-	-	0	0
1003	trcrf	101003	4472	1005	0xccc	-	-	srb	0	0

```
1004 fdnet 101004    1500   -      -     0x0   ieee -     0    0
1005 trbrf 101005    4472   -      -     0xf   ibm  -     0    0


VLAN AREHops STEHops Backup CRF
1003 7       7       off
```

Show Trunk

```
show trunk [detail]
show trunk [mod_num] [detail]
show trunk [mod_num/port_num] [detail]
```

Usage The show trunk command is very useful in verifying the configuration and status of trunk ports. In addition, the command greatly assists in the troubleshooting process. In the example below, the details regarding three trunk ports have been presented. Note that port 4/1 connects to the RSM module, which is a half-duplex, Fast EtherChannel trunk.

Example

```
Switch_A> (enable) show trunk detail

Port    Mode        Encapsulation  Status     Native vlan
2/1     on          isl            trunking   1
2/5     on          isl            trunking   1
4/1     on          isl            trunking   1


Port    Peer-Port   Mode         Encapsulation  Status
2/1     2/12        auto         n-isl          trunking
2/5     2/11        auto         n-isl          trunking


Port    Vlans allowed on trunk
2/1     1-1005
2/5     1-1005
4/1     1-1005


Port    Vlans allowed and active in management domain
2/1     1-5,1003,1005
2/5     1-5,1003,1005
4/1     1
```

```
Port      Vlans in spanning tree forwarding state and not pruned
2/1       1
2/5       1-5,1003,1005
4/1       1
```

Show Port

```
show port
show port <mod_num>
show port <mod_num/port_num>
show port broadcast
show port cdp
show port capabilities
show port channel
show port counters
show port fddi
show port flowcontrol
show port filter
show port help
show port ifindex
show port mac
show port negotiation
show port protocol
show port security
show port spantree
show port status
show port trap
show port trunk
```

Usage The show port command provides a great deal of information regarding the configuration and automatic settings of each port on the Catalyst system. The example below specifically identifies port 2/1, which is not connected. While troubleshooting is covered in greater detail in Chapter 12, this is a good example of a troubleshooting step. The indicated status of not-connect should tell the administrator to start researching the physical layer.

Example

Switch_A> (enable) **show port 2/1**

Port	Name	Status	Vlan	Level	Duplex	Speed	Type
2/1		notconnect	1	normal	auto	auto	10/100BaseTX

Port	Security	Secure-Src-Addr	Last-Src-Addr	Shutdown	Trap	IfIndex
2/1	disabled			No	disabled	10

Port	Broadcast-Limit	Broadcast-Drop
2/1	-	0

Port	Send FlowControl admin	oper	Receive FlowControl admin	oper	RxPause	TxPause	Unsupported opcodes
2/1	off	off	on	on	0	0	0

Port	Status	Channel mode	Channel status	Neighbor device	Neighbor port
2/1	notconnect	auto	not channel		

Port	Align-Err	FCS-Err	Xmit-Err	Rcv-Err	UnderSize
2/1	0	0	0	0	0

Port	Single-Col	Multi-Coll	Late-Coll	Excess-Col	Carri-Sen	Runts	Giants
2/1	0	0	0	0	0	0	0

Last-Time-Cleared
Tue Jun 1 1999, 15:06:41

Show Spantree

show spantree *[vlan]* *[active]*
show spantree *<mod_num/port_num>*
show spantree backbonefast
show spantree blockedports *[vlan]*
show spantree portstate *<trcrf>*

```
show spantree portvlancost <mod_num/port_num>
show spantree statistics [vlan]
show spantree statistics <trcrf> <trbrf>
show spantree summary
show spantree uplinkfast
```

Usage The concepts behind Layer 2 loops and the need for spanning tree have been discussed throughout this book. The show spantree command provides information regarding the spanning tree protocol in use, in addition to the MAC address of the designated root and the status of each individual link.

Example

```
Switch_A> (enable) show spantree


VLAN 1
Spanning tree enabled
Spanning tree type          ieee


Designated Root             00-50-f0-3b-38-00
Designated Root Priority    0
Designated Root Cost        38
Designated Root Port        1/1
Root Max Age   20 sec    Hello Time 2  sec
 Forward Delay 15 sec


Bridge ID MAC ADDR          00-50-f0-3b-40-00
Bridge ID Priority          20
Bridge Max Age 20 sec  Hello Time 2 sec
 Forward Delay 15 sec


Port    Vlan   Port-State      Cost   Priority  Fast-Start


1/1      1     forwarding       19        32    disabled
1/2      1     forwarding       19        32    disabled
```

Basic Configuration Commands

During the initial setup of the switch, most administrators choose to define passwords, enter system information, and set the system date and time. In addition, the IP address and configuration for the SC0 interface are usually configured during the initial setup phase.

Configuring System Information   The Catalyst provides for the documentation of administrative information within the switch. This information includes a:

- System contact
- System location
- System name
- System prompt

This information is most helpful in identifying the switch that is being accessed remotely and the administrator responsible for maintenance of that switch. The commands to configure these settings are as follows:

System Contact

```
set system contact contact_string
set system contact Joe Administrator x.60842
```

System Location

```
set system location location_string
set system location Bldg. 7, Sydney Campus
```

System Name

```
set system name name_string
set system name Switch_A
```

System Prompt

```
set prompt prompt_string
set prompt Switch_A
```

The system clock and passwords for both console and enable modes may be configured as well.

System Clock

```
set time day_of_week mm/dd/yy hh:mm:ss
set time Monday 05/05/99 12:00:00
```

Consult the Cisco Web site at www.cisco.com for the latest information regarding year 2000 (Y2K) and other date compliance issues.

Password

```
set password
```

The system will prompt for the old password and verification of the new password. The display looks like this:

```
Enter old password:
Enter new password:
Retype new password:

Password changed.
```

Enable Password

```
set enablepass
```

The system will prompt for the old enable password and for verification of the new enable password. A password of zero characters is permitted; however, this is not recommended from a security perspective.

Port Configuration

In addition to providing the initial configuration information needed for management of the switch, most administrators also configure the ports when installing the Catalyst 5000 switch.

By default, the Ethernet and Token Ring ports are configured for automatic speed detection. This usually results in the port configuring itself for the fastest available speed from the remote device. In addition, all Ethernet ports are configured, by default, for half-duplex operation. All ports are assigned normal priority, but high priority is also an option.

While the use of automatic speed and/or duplex detection is convenient, it is not recommended. Most administrators prefer the control that results from manual configuration, and there are fewer configuration mismatches.

The port duplex default is different for 10/100 cards. For Ethernet ports on 10 Mbps modules and 100 Mbps modules, it is half-duplex. On the 10/100 module the default is auto.

Manual configuration of both the port speed and duplex settings is highly recommended, as is avoiding 10Mbps full duplex. This recommendation is shared by the authors of this book and by Cisco's TAC, based on years of real-world configuration and troubleshooting. Support for 10Mbps full duplex is inconsistent between vendors, and under most circumstances there is little reason not to use 100Mbps full duplex. In addition, some NICs fail to handle the full-duplex notification correctly, in both 10Mbps and 100Mbps configurations. This can lead to problems, usually indicated by poor performance and a high number of port errors.

To set the name of the port, use the command

```
set port name module_number/port_number [name_string]
```

This command may be useful for router and server connections, as it can augment troubleshooting without having to refer to formal documentation. To have value, the name of the port must be changed whenever the physical cable is moved. This occurs rarely with server and router connections by their nature. For example, `set port name 1/1 Router_A` could indicate that port 1/1 is the router connection for the switch.

The priority level of the port is used when two ports request access to the data bus concurrently. A high priority may be applicable for server and router ports. The command syntax is

```
set port level module_number/port_number normal|high
```

The port speed and duplex functions are configured with two separate commands. To set the port speed for Ethernet, use

```
set port speed module_number/port_number 10|100|auto
```

and for Token Ring, use

```
set port speed module_number/port_number 4|16|auto
```

The Ethernet duplex mode is configured with this command:

```
set port duplex module_number/port_number full|half|auto
```

To check the configuration of a port, use the `show port` command.

Once the configuration is complete, the administrator may wish to back up the configuration to an external device. This service is available with TFTP from the SC0 interface. The commands to use are `write network` or `write host filename`.

The following is an abbreviated configuration for a sample switch in the network. Note that the complete Catalyst configuration is very long, and includes a great deal of duplicate information. This configuration establishes a system name and location value, in addition to enabling the SC0 interface. In addition, the `timezone` and `summertime` modes have been enabled, and two VLANs are in use. In addition, port 1/1 has been configured as an ISL trunk to another switch—likely another Catalyst configured as a core switch. Observe that this switch has a number of 10 Mbps ports, which are likely used for workstations.

```
set system name  Switch_A
set system location Sybex
set system contact Administrator

set password $1$T9v2$594FCWzxEReFKfr3d3L2i1
set enablepass $1$zAMC$P2U6ZgCXoj7XcWnfHNuZR1

set interface sc0 1 10.1.1.10 255.255.255.0 10.1.1.255
set interface sc0 up
set ip route 0.0.0.0        10.1.1.1      1

set timezone Pacific -8 0
set summertime enable Pacific
```

```
set trunk 1/1  on isl 1-1005
set vlan 1    1/2
set vlan 2    2/1-24

set port speed 1/2 100
set port duplex 1/2 full
set port speed 2/1-24 10
set port duplex 2/1-24 half
```

Advanced Configuration

Many installations of the Catalyst system incorporate only Ethernet. Even including the Fast Ethernet and Gigabit Ethernet variations, such configurations are fairly straightforward and are quickly implemented. (Even simple installations should incorporate careful planning and documentation, however.) The commands described in the previous sections are sufficient to configure most Catalyst switches for small and medium sized networks. Administrators may wish to consider VMPS and other options in larger networks. VMPS is defined and described in Chapter 11. Please note that gigabit and fast Ethernet configurations do not differ substantially from the configuration of 10Mbps Ethernet.

In fact, unless there are substantial arguments in favor of the more complex FDDI or ATM systems, few installations require anything more than Ethernet in its various flavors. Performance, price, and familiarity frequently accompany decisions against the introduction of FDDI and ATM, whereas voice and video integration often support ATM. FDDI is usually supported as a migration phase between legacy backbones and future Ethernet switched cores.

Sometimes, however, a new network installation does require incorporation of FDDI or ATM. There may be a need for technical interconnectivity to legacy systems—an FDDI backbone, as discussed previously, for example—or it may be done for perceived future-proofing, as may be the case for ATM LANE.

This section discusses some of the issues that present themselves when configuring and installing FDDI or ATM LANE, along with the related configuration commands.

FDDI

Chapter 9 addressed many of the considerations involved in installing FDDI in a Catalyst 5000 system. In particular, you learned how the 802.10 protocol allows FDDI to be used as a trunking medium for VLANs and how to configure that use. One issue, the chapter noted, is that the conversion between FDDI and Ethernet invariably introduces delays. Chapter 9 also showed how to enable (or disable) APaRT and fddicheck, tools that help perform the conversion.

To create an FDDI VLAN, use the

```
set vlan vlan_number type fddi [mtu mtu] said said
```

command. For example, in order to configure VLAN 2 to SAID 702, the administrator would use this command:

```
set vlan 2 type fddi said 702
```

Where possible, the network design should include a policy whereby the SAID value and the VLAN number are the same or numbered in a manner that allows easy identification of the relationship. This can greatly assist in locating misconfigured switches.

A port must be mapped to a VLAN, unless it is configured for trunking (802.10). As such, the administrator should use the set vlan command to place an FDDI port onto a VLAN as they would for an Ethernet port. The full command syntax is

```
set vlan vlan_number module_number/port_number
```

The show vlan command should be used to display and troubleshoot any VLAN issues.

It is possible to associate a FDDI VLAN with an Ethernet VLAN by using mapping to create a translation. The command is

```
set vlan ethernet_vlan_number translation fddi_vlan_number
```

Note that the transposed command (placing the FDDI VLAN first and the Ethernet VLAN second) will result in the same translation.

To configure an FDDI port for trunking, use the set trunk command. The syntax is

```
set trunk module_number/port_number [on|off] [vlan_range]
```

Unlike Ethernet, FDDI ports do not support the desirable or auto configuration options.

ATM LANE

ATM LAN emulation was the subject of Chapter 3, and Chapter 9 reviewed the most important concepts in the context of the Catalyst 5000 series support for LANE. This section looks more specifically at the addressing and configuration issues involved.

It is highly recommended that readers review the earlier discussions of ATM LANE before continuing. A thorough understanding of the LANE components—LECS, LES, BUS and LEC—is important in using and comprehending this material.

There are a number of rules within ATM LANE addressing that administrators must bear in mind when designing and troubleshooting Catalyst systems. These rules include:

- Each LEC must have a MAC layer address.

- Every LANE component within the network—the LECS, the LES, the BUS, and the LEC—must have a unique ATM address.

- All LECs on the same ATM interface have the same MAC address. This address is automatically assigned.

- The MAC address is used as the end-system identifier (ESI) part of the ATM address.

- LEC MAC addresses (or the ESI) are not unique; however, all ATM addresses are unique.

ATM Addressing Within ATM LANE, there are a number of rules for assigning LANE components to interfaces. Most administrators familiar with VLANs will find these rules quite logical, as most of them are common to other network types. For example, in frame-based networks all devices on a port must be part of the same network. In ELANs, this rule is also true.

In addition, the LAN Emulation Configuration Server (LECS) is always assigned to a major interface, while a LEC and LES within the same ELAN can be assigned to the same subinterface.

A *subinterface* is a logical assignment on a physical interface. A *major interface* is the physical interface of the device. For example, a router's major interface might be ATM 1/0, and the subinterface would be ATM 1/0.55. Administrators typically associate the subinterface number with the VCI value or ELAN number.

LECs or LESs from different ELANs cannot be assigned to the same subinterface. In addition, a LEC and LES from different ELANs cannot be assigned to the same subinterface.

Augmenting the various rules for LANE implementation, a number of addressing structures have been defined. The ATM Forum has defined three addressing formats in the UNI 3.0/3.1 specification.

ATM addresses are always 20 octets in length; however, their composition depends on the authority that assigned the address. The assigning authority is identified by the first octet of the address, called the Authority and Format Identifier, or AFI.

Table 10.7 documents the three AFI definitions.

T A B L E 10.7 ATM Addressing AFI Codes	AFI	Authority
	39	The International Organization for Standardization, ISO, defines the Data Country Code (DCC) that follows. This is the ISO NSAP DCC format.
	45	The address is E.164, and the Initial Domain Identifier (IDI) follows. This addressing is preferred for public WAN links, and the IDI is composed of a 4-bit address type, a 4-bit country code, and a 60-bit address. This is defined as ITU-TSS E.164.
	47	An ICD, International Code Designator, assigned by the British Standards Institute. The prefix is defined as ISO NSAP ICD.

The thirteen octets at the beginning of the ATM address are called the prefix, followed by the ESI, or end system identifier. The ESI is a standard MAC layer address of six octets. The network selector, or NSEL, is one octet.

Some networks have addresses defined without formal authority. This is acceptable for private networks, within the general constraints described in RFC 1918. This states that as long as the addresses are only used internally and will never interconnect with an outside network, an administrator may choose to use private IP address space. The same concept applies to the 13 octets of the ATM prefix for local significance. RFC 1918 does not refer to ATM addressing.

RFC 1918 provides for private IP addresses that will never be assigned on the Internet. These include 10.0.0.0/8, 172.16.0.0/12, and 192.168.0.0/16.

In the Catalyst system, the ATM LANE services may be manually or automatically assigned. Unless there are compelling arguments in favor of manual addressing, most networks will operate perfectly with automatic addressing.

In automatic addressing, each LANE module is assigned a pool of 16 MAC addresses. As the prefix field of the ATM address is defined by the switch, all LANE components share the same ATM prefix. Following the prefix is the ESI, defined as shown in Table 10.8.

T A B L E 10.8 Automatically Assigned ESI Values in ATM LANE on the Catalyst System	**ESI**	**Service**
	First ESI in pool	Assigned to each LEC on the interface
	Second ESI in pool	Assigned to every LES on the interface
	Third ESI in pool	Assigned to every BUS on the interface
	Fourth ESI in pool	Assigned to the LECS

In addition to the ESI, the selector field is also automatically defined. In such cases, the LANE component is assigned a selector octet value equal to the subinterface number. The LECS is assigned a selector field of zero.

A wide variety of design considerations and "rules-of-thumb" have evolved regarding the number of nodes on a segment and the percentage of broadcast traffic within a segment. For Ethernet, these rules usually define 30% sustained utilization and 10% of traffic from broadcasts. A better recommendation in most networks is using broadcasts per second as the criterion. Most workstations (Pentium 90 class) can sustain up to 100 broadcasts per second with minimal impact on the processor. This measurement is much more useful than one based on percentage. With ATM LANE, however, you need to consider another factor in addition to packets-per-second capacity: the capacity of the broadcast and unknown server (BUS), measured in packets per second (pps). Be sure to consult with the vendor of the BUS service to determine the pps capability of the system.

ATM LANE Configuration Commands The ATM LANE module is configured separately from the Supervisor engine. As such, configuration of ATM LANE requires use of the `session module-number` command. The module number is equal to the slot position in the chassis.

As with Cisco routers, the command structure is based on the Cisco IOS, and you enter configuration mode by issuing the `configure terminal` command. When you're finished, exit configuration mode with the end command word, and save the information to NVRAM with the `write memory` command.

LANE configurations are defined on a subinterface basis. These commands, along with the commands presented previously, are documented in Table 10.9. These commands are presented in this form to provide a baseline for administrators to identify those settings that may be configured in LANE installations. Note that Chapter 11 provides a breakdown of the specific commands needed for each component of ATM LANE.

T A B L E 10.9: ATM LANE Configuration Commands

Command	Usage
session *module-number*	Establishes a connection with the ATM LANE module.
configure terminal	Enters terminal configuration mode.
show lane default-atm-address	Shows LANE addresses and verifies connectivity to the LS1010 module or other ATM switch.
interface atm 0.*subinterface-number*	Specifies the subinterface for the ELAN.
lane config auto-config-atm-address	Instructs LANE to compute the ATM address for the LECS automatically.
lane server-bus ethernet *elan-name*	Starts LES/BUS services for the ELAN.
lane client ethernet *vlan-number* *elan-name*	Enables LEC services for the ELAN. This is optional, but recommended. The maximum length of the ELAN name is 32 characters.
lane database *database-name*	Creates a LECS database. This is also restricted to 32 characters.
name *elan-name* server-atm-address *atm-address* [restricted]	Associates the LES to the ELAN. The restricted command restricts LECs from joining the ELAN without permission.
default-name *elan-name*	Defines the default ELAN name.
client-atm-address *atm-address* name *elan-name*	Defines an LEC to a restricted membership ELAN.
end	Exit configuration mode.
write memory	Save configuration to NVRAM.
show lane config	Reports the current LANE configuration.

Note that the LECS database may be configured for a default ELAN or for unrestricted and restricted ELANs. The `client-atm-address atm-address name elan-name` command binds the LEC to the ELAN.

The Catalyst 5500 supports the Cisco LS1010 ATM processor and line modules, permitting ATM cell switching within the chassis. The ASP, or LS1010 switching engine, must be installed in the 13th slot of the chassis, while the line cards occupy slots 9 through 12. The ASP can be configured with a LECS address, and the address must be saved permanently. The command `atm lecs-address atm-address` is used. The `atm-address` value must include all 20 octets of the LECS address.

As in the rest of this book, the focus of this section has been on the CLSC exam material, and it is by no means intended to substitute for actual "hands-on" experience. Unlike most other installations and configurations, ATM LANE is difficult to document in text formats. As such, this section is intended to provide an overview of the issues confronted by administrators. As many new features are being added, it is further recommended that readers use Cisco's Web site to understand the most current services.

Summary

While this chapter focused primarily on the configuration of the Catalyst 5000 series switches and the ATM LANE and FDDI modules, it also served to address some of the configuration and installation issues confronting network architects and administrators in modern networks.

In addition, it is hoped that readers appreciate the wide range of features provided within the platform. The Catalyst can be installed and used as a basic Ethernet switch with virtually no configuration. However, coupled with knowledge and planning, the system can be converted into a versatile tool capable of addressing many network needs.

This chapter also addressed the following:

- Initial configuration settings usually defined by administrators
- The hardware installation of the switch
- Configuration issues and commands for ATM LANE and FDDI
- Power budgets for multimode LEDs
- Specific commands useful in configuring the Catalyst 5000/5500 switch

Review Questions

1. Which of the following commands could be used to save the configuration of the switch to a TFTP server?

   A. `write network`

   B. `write host filename`

   C. `save config`

   D. `copy config tftp host filename`

   E. `copy floppy`

2. Unique ATM addresses are required for which of these ATM LANE components?

   A. LEC

   B. LECS

   C. LES

   D. BUS

   E. All of the above

   F. None of the above

3. Which of the following ATM LANE components does not use a unique MAC address?

   A. LECS

   B. LES

   C. BUS

   D. LEC

   E. All of the above

4. Which of the following ATM prefixes would be recommended for public WAN connections?

    A. 45.00.00.00.00.00.00.00.00.00.00.00.00

    B. 39.00.00.00.00.00.00.00.00.00.00.00.00

    C. 47.00.00.00.00.00.00.00.00.00.00.00.00

    D. 08:00:06:22:11:99

    E. WAN connections do not make use of ATM prefixes.

5. Which of the following would need to be configured for a SLIP account?

    A. SC0

    B. SL0

    C. VLAN1

    D. SLIP is not available on the Catalyst system.

    E. SLIP is only available with the RSM module.

6. Which of the following commands is used to change the enable password?

    A. `set password`

    B. `set enable password`

    C. `set enablepass`

    D. `set password enable`

    E. `set system password enable`

7. After calculating the power margin, the result is negative. This probably means that:

    A. The link will work.

    B. The link will not work.

    C. The calculation is incorrect.

    D. Not enough information is provided.

8. To use BOOTP or RARP, which of the following must be true?

   A. The `set bootp enable` command must be used.

   B. The Supervisor engine must have pin 4 enabled.

   C. The sl0 interface must be set to 0.0.0.0.

   D. The sc0 interface must be set to 0.0.0.0.

   E. The sl0 interface must be set to 255.255.255.255.

9. A 10/100 port on the Catalyst is set to which of the following by default?

   A. 10Mbps

   B. 100Mbps

   C. Auto

   D. Full duplex

10. Which of the following commands would be used to configure port 5 on module 2 to 100Mbps full duplex?

   A. `set port speed 5/2 100`
       `set port duplex 5/2 full`

   B. `set port 5/2 speed 100`
       `set port 5/2 duplex full`

   C. `set port speed 5/2 full`
       `set port duplex 5/2 100`

   D. `set port 5/2 100 full`

   E. `set port speed 2/5 100`
       `set port duplex 2/5 full`

11. A Token Ring port is set to 16Mbps by default.

   A. True

   B. False

12. Which of the following commands is used to set the port priority level?

    A. `set port priority 3/3 high`

    B. `set port 3/3 priority high`

    C. `set port priority high 3/3`

    D. `set port level 3/3 high`

    E. `set port level 3/3 100`

13. Which of the following transfer protocols are permitted with the Catalyst system?

    A. DNS

    B. Kermit

    C. TFTP

    D. Zmodem

    E. 1K-Xmodem

14. To configure the port name on the FDDI interface to FDDI_Int, an administrator would use:

    A. `set port name 4/1 FDDI_Int`

    B. `set port fddi 4/1 name FDDI_Int`

    C. `set port 4/1 name FDDI_Int`

    D. `set port name 4/1 "FDDI_Int"`

    E. A name cannot be assigned to an interface.

15. Which commands could be used to create a FDDI VLAN?

    A. `set vlan 2 type fddi mtu 1500 said 610`

    B. `set vlan 2 type fddi said 610`

    C. `set fddi vlan 2 said 610`

    D. `set vlan fddi said 610 2`

    E. `set link vlan 2 fddi type 610`

16. The FDDI module on the Catalyst supports ISL, 802.10, and 802.1q.

    A. True

    B. False

17. Which of the following is required for ISL?

    A. The NetFlow Feature Card, version 2 (NFFC-2)

    B. Redundant Supervisor modules

    C. Connections via the Ethernet ports on the Supervisor module

    D. A Fast Ethernet port

    E. A crossover cable connecting two Token Ring ports on different switches

18. To view information regarding ATM LANE on the Catalyst switch, the administrator should use which of the following commands?

    A. `show atm config`

    B. `show lane`

    C. `show lane config`

    D. `show atm lane system`

    E. `set atm`

19. Which of the following is true regarding Fast EtherChannel?

    A. It creates a single spanning tree for two or more links.

    B. It bonds two modules to increase bandwidth.

    C. It can link two switches at up to 800Mbps full duplex.

    D. It is used to connect to the ESCON Channel Interface Processor on an IBM mainframe.

    E. It can run over Token Ring, although the service is called Fast TokenChannel.

20. The command `set interface` is used for which of the following?

   A. Defining routing protocols on the Catalyst switch

   B. Defining static routes on the Catalyst switch

   C. Defining the subnet mask on the SC0 interface

   D. Defining the enable and console passwords

   E. There isn't a `set interface` command. The command is `set system interface`.

Laboratory Exercises

The following laboratory exercises are intended simply to provide some hands-on practice with basic processes to familiarize users with the CLI and the configuration of the switch systems.

EXERCISE 10.1

Configuring Global Settings

This lab exercise addresses the configuring of the global system settings. The initial configuration of the Catalyst should include setting a general profile of switch information. This lab will provide a foundation for these settings. To complete this lab, the administrator should set the time and date on the switch to May 15, 1999 at 5:00 p.m. In addition, the switch name should be set to Lab Switch, and the prompt should read Catalyst switch. The password and enable passwords should also be set.

Solution: The following steps address the commands necessary to configure the basic global system settings.

1. Connect to the CLI.

2. Enter the following set commands:

```
set system name Lab switch
set time 05/15/99 17:00:00
set prompt Catalyst switch
set password
set enablepass
```

EXERCISE 10.2

Configuring the IP Address and Gateway

Configure the SC0 interface of the switch with an IP address of 192.168.1.10, and a natural network mask. Configure the default gateway as 192.168.1.1. Test and verify the configuration.

Solution: The following commands are used to configure and test the configuration of the SC0 interface. Note that the natural mask for a Class C IP address is /24, or 255.255.255.0.

1. Connect to the CLI.

2. Enter the following set commands:

```
set interface sc0 192.168.1.10 255.255.255.0
set ip route default 192.168.1.1
```

3. To verify the configuration, enter

```
show interface
show ip route
ping 192.168.1.1
```

Port Configuration

Configure the ports on the Catalyst to the following.

- Ports 2/1 and 2/2 to full-duplex 100Mbps

- Ports 3/1 through 3/9 to full-duplex 100Mbps

- Ports 3/10 through 3/22 to half-duplex 10Mbps

- Port 3/23 to full-duplex 100Mbps

- Port 3/24 to mirror (SPAN) port 3/23

Solution: Use the following steps to configure the ports on the Catalyst switch.

1. Connect to the CLI.

EXERCISE 10.3 (CONTINUED)

2. Enter the following commands:

```
set port speed 2/1-2 100
set port duplex 2/1-2 full
set port enable 2/1-2
set port speed 3/1-9 100
set port duplex 3/1-9 full
set port speed 3/10-22 10
set port duplex 3/10-22 half
set port speed 3/23 100
set port duplex 3/23 full
set span 3/23 3/24
set port enable 3/1-24
show port
show span
```

EXERCISE 10.4

LANE Configuration

Configure and verify the LES/BUS and the LEC for an ELAN. The associated VLAN should be number 3, and the ELAN name should be Admin_ELAN.

Use the following steps to configure and verify the LES/BUS and LEC configurations.

1. Connect to the CLI.

2. Connect to the ATM LANE module.

3. Enter the following commands:

```
interface atm 0.1
lane server-bus ethernet admin_elan
lane client ethernet 3 admin_elan
ctrl-z
show lane server
show lane client
```

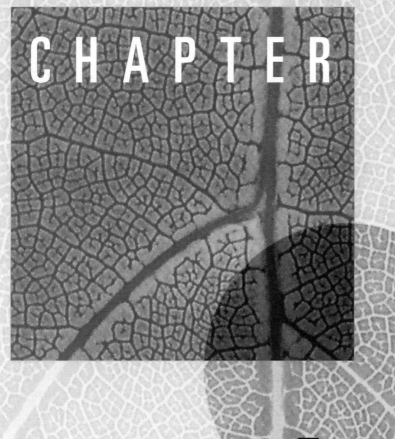

CHAPTER

11

Managing the Catalyst 5000 Switch

he techniques for Catalyst 5000/5500 switch administration will be familiar to administrators experienced with managing and troubleshooting Cisco router systems. Catalyst switches are powerful tools, capable of operating—at least in limited fashion—with little administration. Conversely, the switch may be highly controlled and monitored to enhance the functionality and services provided.

This chapter covers one very broad Cisco exam objective:

- Describe the different ways of managing the Catalyst 5000 series switch, including:

  - Out-of-band management

  - In-band management

  - RMON

  - SPAN

  - CWSI

As with most Cisco products, the Catalyst line provides for a wide variety of management options. Administrators can work with formalized management platforms, including CiscoWorks for Switched Internetworks (CWSI) and HP OpenView, or use the command-line interface (CLI), which is available via a locally connected console or Telnet session. Earlier chapters in this book discussed these applications in the context of installation and configuration. This chapter addresses the use of these applications for switch management, including monitoring and troubleshooting Catalyst switches.

Out-of-Band Management

Most administrators use out-of-band management for the initial configuration of the switch and for backup management at remote locations. The out-of-band connection is also helpful in isolating components that have degraded or failed in the WAN or LAN. Administrators use the CLI in out-of-band connections.

Chapter 10 outlined the use of the SL0 interface for SLIP connections, which are one form of out-of-band connectivity. Administrators can also use terminal servers and directly attached modems for out-of-band services.

As of this writing, the Supervisor III engine included an AUX port; however, this port is not supported. Modems should be connected via the console port. Refer to the latest documentation for additional information.

By far, the most common way to perform out-of-band administration is from a local console. From the local console, administrators can configure the switch with an IP address and set other options. See Chapter 10 for information about the commands for configuring Catalyst switches from a local console.

All out-of-band connectivity options use the console port on the active Supervisor module. This port uses an EIA/TIA-232 DCE connector on the Supervisor I and II; an RJ-45 jack is used on the Supervisor III. The console port terminal settings default to 9600, N, 8, 1. This means that the port speed is 9600 baud and it uses no parity, 8 bits, and 1 stop bit. (Most administrators find a 9600 baud connection acceptable for the CLI, so this setup may allow you to make good use of older equipment.) When the console port is used with a modem, the switch will automatically place the modem in auto-answer mode.

Although you can use other modems, a modem that is 100 percent Hayes compatible is highly recommended. Most modems are 100 percent Hayes compatible.

Administrators must perform some switch configuration via the out-of-band services in order to use the in-band options.

In-Band Management

In-band management uses existing network services to reach the Supervisor engine. In the Catalyst system, in-band connections use IP and may be over Ethernet, Token Ring, FDDI, or ATM LANE. The SC0 interface is configured with an IP address for in-band connectivity and usually bonded to VLAN 1, which is highly recommended.

Most switched networks use a single VLAN for administration, which is distributed to all switches. Although user VLANs may not appear on all switches in the network, an administration VLAN that appears on all switches greatly simplifies troubleshooting. In many cases, network problems caused by user activity will not affect the administration VLAN to the point where in-band connectivity is unavailable.

In addition to providing Telnet access to the CLI, the Catalyst switch also serves as a Telnet server and an SNMP-manageable device. The Telnet service on the Catalyst switch not only receives incoming Telnet sessions, but also permits up to eight outbound sessions.

SNMP communicates with an SNMP management station and provides traps, or alerts of significant events, in addition to configuration information. When configured correctly, SNMP traps can alert the administrator to problems, even before users start making calls to the help desk. For example, traps can alert the administrator to power-supply failures or module errors. RMON (remote monitoring) and RMON2 are part of SNMP and augment SNMP by providing additional features. RMON is discussed later in this chapter.

Management Tools

The CLI in the Catalyst system provides complete access to the configuration of the switch and can be sufficient for all management services in most networks, especially smaller environments. However, once the network surpasses five or more sites, network management tools usually provide sufficient benefits to offset their costs.

Most large networks take advantage of one of the many network management products available for UNIX and Windows NT systems. These products are particularly useful for networks that participate in operations that run continuously (7 days a week, 24 hours a day) to provide a means for visualizing the network and displaying real-time problems.

In smaller networks, management tools can provide a bridge between the operations staff and design teams. Operations supported by a single administrator may also use management products; however, the time required for configuring and automating the services of these products might not be worth their benefits.

The newest network management tools provide HTTP-based reports that display information about network availability and performance. Network users can access these reports, which may be a powerful means of marketing the network and the service provided. Users typically remember when the network was slow or unavailable, but don't consider the times when it was running smoothly. Recording the network's availability and performance and reporting this information to the users accentuates the positive performance of the network and can help offset users' negative feelings.

Network management products include HP OpenView, Sun Domain Manager (different versions are called SunNet Manager), and NetView. In addition, Cisco offers CWSI, which provides specialized tools for managing Cisco products via SNMP and RMON.

CWSI is a powerful SNMP tool in networks where Cisco switches are installed; however, it is only one portion of the Ethernet and Fast Ethernet strategy for traffic monitoring. Cisco augments network management software with embedded RMON software on its switches and routers. Switches are also provided with port mirroring, or the Switched Port Analyzer (SPAN), to present traffic to external protocol analyzers and RMON probes. Cisco offers the Cisco SwitchProbe product for monitoring networks.

The following sections discuss RMON, SPAN (and ESPAN), CWSI, and the Cisco Discovery Protocol.

Remote Monitoring (RMON)

Modern network devices allow administrators to see many details about how a network is functioning. SNMP and RMON help make these details visible to administrators. RMON is particularly useful in baselining and troubleshooting switched environments.

Catalyst 5000 switches offer an optional, software-based, embedded RMON agent. This agent operates with the corresponding management information base (MIB) on the network management station to provide more information than that provided by SNMP.

The RMON services are defined in RFC 1757, which specifies nine groups of services. The embedded RMON service on Catalyst 5000 switches supports four of these groups:

Port utilization and error statistics group   Includes collisions, broadcasts, bandwidth utilization, and malformed packets (including fragments and oversized frames).

Historical statistics group   Includes statistics from a historical perspective. This information permits some forms of trend analysis; however, additional tools are available for this function. Concord Network Health is one example of a powerful historical trend-analysis tool.

Alarm notification group   Permits the administrator to set thresholds regarding a variety of network issues. Once the switch passes one of these thresholds, an alarm is sent to the network management station. The administrator may use this information to proactively address problems. Many administrators set thresholds for CRC errors and broadcasts.

Event logging group   Provides a log of issues in real-time. This is provided in the form of SNMP traps.

The Catalyst 5000 also supports the Token Ring statistics and history RMON group (defined in RFC 1513), as well as the ProbeConfig RMON2 group (defined in RFC 2021).

Additional monitoring capabilities are available through the SPAN feature, which is also referred to as *port mirroring*. Cisco's SwitchProbe product can provide access to the other five service groups of RMON, in addition to the RMON2 (an enhanced version of RMON) groups. The SPAN capability and Cisco's SwitchProbe product are discussed in the next section. The Network Access Module (NAM) is also available as an internal line card for RMON monitoring.

Administrators should also consider using the Cisco Resource Manager application (CRM) to inventory and manage devices. CRM is targeted for enterprise implementations.

Switched Port Analyzer (SPAN) and Enhanced Switch Port Analyzer (ESPAN)

Most administrators use the SPAN feature to configure the switch to provide port mirroring, which permits the use of protocol analyzers in a switched environment. ESPAN is an upgraded version of the SPAN feature. Administrators can monitor traffic from Ethernet, Fast Ethernet, and FDDI networks on a Fast Ethernet port. When configured, ESPAN redirects VLAN or port traffic to another port; this redirected traffic would normally be blocked from ports other than the destination port.

An Ethernet port should not be used to mirror traffic from Fast Ethernet or FDDI sources. Unless mirroring will include only 10Mbps Ethernet, protocol analyzers should be configured with 100Mbps NICs and the appropriate level of hardware to prevent dropped frames. In addition, Token Ring ports must be used to monitor other Token Ring ports.

Cisco's SwitchProbe product works in concert with the SPAN/ESPAN ports. The SwitchProbe product differs from similar probes in that it provides inter-switch link (ISL) VLAN trunking awareness. In networks using ISL, this feature is useful for monitoring traffic on the trunk.

ISL is a proprietary trunking technology owned by Cisco, which other vendors have licensed. Administrators should examine the limitations and benefits of selecting ISL before deploying this technology. The "open" 802.1q standard offers many of the benefits of ISL. In addition to being proprietary, ISL incurs greater overhead than 802.1q; however, ISL also offers the benefit of automatic load balancing across spanning trees and parallel trunks. Using ISL in a network often requires an all-Cisco solution, similar to the requirements for using the EIGRP routing protocol.

As mentioned in the previous section, the SwitchProbe product adds to the embedded RMON service by providing the other five service groups, so all nine RMON groups specified by RFC 1757 are included. The use of external probes also reduces the impact of RMON on the local processor. Information from the probe may be accessed with the TrafficDirector application (part of CWSI, which is discussed in the next section). The Fast Ethernet SwitchProbe product provides RMON2 statistics on all seven layers of the OSI model.

CiscoWorks for Switched Internetworks (CWSI)

CWSI can augment HP OpenView, SunNet Manager (different versions are called Sun Domain Manager), or NetView/AIX or run as a stand-alone application on Windows NT or Unix (including Solaris, HP-Unix, and AIX) systems. CWSI includes a number of tools for installing network components and monitoring and troubleshooting networks. Table 11.1 lists the major components of CWSI.

Depending on the version and license, some of the applications listed in Table 11.1 may not be available in all installations of CWSI.

T A B L E 11.1 Major Components of CWSI	**Application**	**Description**
	CiscoView	This is a graphical application that provides virtual chassis viewing, configuration tools, performance monitoring, and minor troubleshooting functions.
	VlanDirector	This is a graphical administration tool for adding users, assigning ports, and changing associations.
	TrafficDirector	This application provides a united view of the switched network, including trunk links and switch ports.

TABLE 11.1 *(cont.)*	**Application**	**Description**
Major Components of CWSI	AtmDirector	In ATM networks, this tool facilitates installation and administration.
	User Tracking	Cisco switches permit VLAN assignments based on dynamic parameters, including the MAC layer address. User Tracking defines these dynamic VLANs and tracks stations within the network.

CiscoView, TrafficDirector, and VlanDirector are three applications in CWSI that greatly facilitate the management of Catalyst 5000 switches. The AtmDirector application is useful in ATM deployments. User Tracking can be useful in large, frame-based networks. The following sections provide more details on the CiscoView, VlanDirector, and TrafficDirector applications.

CiscoView

CiscoView provides a graphical, virtual view of Cisco devices configured with an IP address. Through this application, the administrator can obtain configuration information, real-time status, and statistics regarding the Cisco products in the network. In addition, CiscoView provides detailed views of the switch and its components, and it can manage multiple switches at the same time.

The CiscoView application is included as part of CiscoWorks; however, it can operate as a separate application on Unix systems and may be integrated with other SNMP management suites.

TrafficDirector

The TrafficDirector application provides traffic management services, including the detection of errors in the network and the addition of new workstations on the switch. By detecting added workstations, the application helps the administrator better understand the utilization of the network and new requirements. Administrators also can use TrafficDirector to configure alarms and thresholds.

As with other RMON utilities, TrafficDirector can graphically present data for reports. Administrators can access the internal RMON resources and external Cisco SwitchProbe monitors with this application.

One of the most powerful features of TrafficDirector is its ability to use the RMON probe as a packet-capture tool. This negates the need to send a separate protocol analyzer to a remote site and frequently provides sufficient information for administrators to diagnose problems.

VlanDirector

Switching is most useful when combined with VLANs. VlanDirector is an application that benefits from the Cisco Discovery Protocol (CDP) discussed in the next section.

VlanDirector provides VLAN management and port configuration tools. Its drag-and-drop feature greatly simplifies moves, additions, and changes and further reduces costs. Changes made with VlanDirector are effective immediately. (Without VlanDirector, the administrator uses the CLI to configure ports.)

In addition, VlanDirector provides a logical representation of the topology. The CDP information shared between Cisco devices augments this representation.

Cisco Discovery Protocol (CDP)

CDP is an incredibly powerful troubleshooting tool that is available from the CLI. In addition, the CWSI management applications and other CDP-aware applications can use the CDP information and present it to the administrator on a management station.

CDP is available on all Cisco routers and switches, and the protocol operates between Cisco devices on media that support the Subnetwork Access Protocol (SNAP). Use of SNAP permits network layer independence and allows CDP packets to traverse LAN segments and frame-relay clouds. The protocol has been available since router IOS (Internetwork Operating System) 10.3, and it is significant to note that CDP packets are sent as a multicast and are not forwarded by the router or switch.

The following is an example of the CDP report on a Catalyst 5505 switch with three neighbors.

```
Switch_A> (enable) show cdp neighbor detail
Device-ID: Router_A.domain.com
Device Addresses:
  IP Address: 10.1.1.1
Holdtime: 142 sec
Capabilities: ROUTER
Version:
  Cisco Internetwork Operating System Software
  IOS (tm) 4500 Software (C4500-J-M), Version 11.2(15a)P, P RELEASE SOFTWARE (fc1)
  Copyright (c) 1986-1998 by cisco Systems, Inc.
Platform: cisco 4700
Port-ID (Port on Device): FastEthernet0
Port (Our Port): 2/1
_____

Device-ID: Router_B.domain.com
Device Addresses:
  IP Address: 10.1.2.1
Holdtime: 130 sec
Capabilities: ROUTER
Version:
  Cisco Internetwork Operating System Software
  IOS (tm) 4500 Software (C4500-J-M), Version 11.2(15a)P, P RELEASE SOFTWARE (fc1)
  Copyright (c) 1986-1998 by cisco Systems, Inc.
Platform: cisco 4700
Port-ID (Port on Device): FastEthernet0
Port (Our Port): 2/2
_____

Device-ID: Router_C.domain.com
Device Addresses:
  IP Address: 10.10.1.1
Holdtime: 177 sec
Capabilities: ROUTER SR_BRIDGE
Version:
  Cisco Internetwork Operating System Software
  IOS (tm) C2600 Software (C2600-JS-M), Version 12.0(2a), RELEASE SOFTWARE (fc1)
  Copyright (c) 1986-1999 by cisco Systems, Inc.
Platform: cisco 2612
Port-ID (Port on Device): Ethernet1/0
Port (Our Port): 2/17
Packet 3 captured at 02/22/1999 09:08:57 AM; Packet size is 302(0x12e)bytes
      Relative time: 000:00:01.473
      Delta time: 0.042.868
Ethernet Protocol
      Address: 00-00-0C-1B-63-97 --->01-00-0C-CC-CC-CC
      Length: 288
```

```
Logical Link Control
        SSAP Address: 0xAA, CR bit = 0 (Command)
        DSAP Address: 0xAA, IG bit = 0 (Individual address)
        Unnumbered frame: UI
SubNetwork Access Protocol
        Organization code: 0x00000c
        Type: Custom Defined
```

A CDP datagram decodes with the EtherPeek analyzer software as follows. Note the MAC layer multicast address and the SNAP header.

```
Flags:           0x80   802.3
  Status:        0x00
  Packet Length:339
  Timestamp:     16:40:23.689000 03/16/1999
```

802.3 Header

Destination:	01:00:0c:cc:cc:cc
Source:	00:00:0c:17:b6:f2
LLC Length:	321

802.2 Logical Link Control (LLC) Header

Dest. SAP:	0xaa	*SNAP*
Source SAP:	0xaa	*SNAP*
Command:	0x03	*Unnumbered Information*
Protocol:	00-00-0c-20-00	

Packet Data:

```
.´_'....Router_A   01 b4 9e 27 00 01 00 0c 52 6f 75 74 65 72 5f 41
...6............   00 02 00 36 00 00 00 03 01 01 cc 00 04 0a 02 01
...ªª...._7.....   01 02 08 aa aa 03 00 00 00 81 37 00 0a 00 00 00
.....¶...ªª...._   0b 00 00 0c 17 b6 f2 02 08 aa aa 03 00 00 00 80
>....o....Ethern   9b 00 03 00 02 6f 00 03 00 0d 45 74 68 65 72 6e
et1..........√C    65 74 31 00 04 00 08 00 00 00 01 00 05 00 d0 43
isco Internetwor   69 73 63 6f 20 49 6e 74 65 72 6e 65 74 77 6f 72
k Operating Syst   6b 20 4f 70 65 72 61 74 69 6e 67 20 53 79 73 74
em Software .IOS   65 6d 20 53 6f 66 74 77 61 72 65 20 0a 49 4f 53
 (tm) 4000 Softw   20 28 74 6d 29 20 34 30 30 30 20 53 6f 66 74 77
are (XX-J-M), Ve   61 72 65 20 28 58 58 2d 4a 2d 4d 29 2c 20 56 65
rsion 11.0(17),    72 73 69 6f 6e 20 31 31 2e 30 28 31 37 29 2c 20
RELEASE SOFTWARE   52 45 4c 45 41 53 45 20 53 4f 46 54 57 41 52 45
 (fc1).Copyright   20 28 66 63 31 29 0a 43 6f 70 79 72 69 67 68 74
 (c) 1986-1997 b   20 28 63 29 20 31 39 38 36 2d 31 39 39 37 20 62
y cisco Systems,   79 20 63 69 73 63 6f 20 53 79 73 74 65 6d 73 2c
 Inc..Compiled T   20 49 6e 63 2e 0a 43 6f 6d 70 69 6c 65 64 20 54
hu 04-Sep-97 14:   68 75 20 30 34 2d 53 65 70 2d 39 37 20 31 34 3a
44 by richv....c   34 34 20 62 79 20 72 69 63 68 76 00 06 00 0e 63
isco 4000          69 73 63 6f 20 34 30 30 30
```

Frame Check Sequence: 0x00000000

Special Catalyst 5000/5500 Switch Features

Basic Catalyst 5000/5500 switch management tasks require only a few commands and modules. However, other features are available for scaling to enterprise deployments and augmenting the usefulness of the switch. These features include the route switch module (RSM), VLAN Management Policy Server (VMPS), and VLAN Trunk Protocol (VTP). In addition, administrators can use commands to manage the Catalyst 5000/5500 switch's flash file system.

The Route Switch Module (RSM)

As explained in previous chapters, VLANs are isolated at Layer 2 and usually encompass the diameter of a subnet. Thus, packets that need to leave the local VLAN require a router, or Layer 3 process, to travel to the remote VLAN. Stated another way, two VLANs may reside within the same chassis, but packet flow from one VLAN to another within that chassis is not possible without routing.

Although it is possible for the switch to connect to a router interface on each VLAN, or to a trunk port on a single router interface for multiple VLANs, it is not necessary in networks that use Catalyst 5000 series switches. Instead, administrators can use the RSM, which is a Cisco 7500 series router on a single-slot card. This router is capable of connecting to the backplane at 400Mbps (half-duplex).

RSM Configuration

Configuration of the RSM is primarily defined by the needs of the network. For our example, assume that there are no WAN connectivity needs and the network is comprised of three VLANs within two switches. Figure 11.1 illustrates the sample network.

In this example, the West_Switch contains an RSM in slot four. Both switches contain a Supervisor III engine and a population of 10Mbps and 100Mbps Ethernet ports for servers and workstations. A single 100Mbps port is used to connect the switches.

F I G U R E   11.1

A sample RSM
network

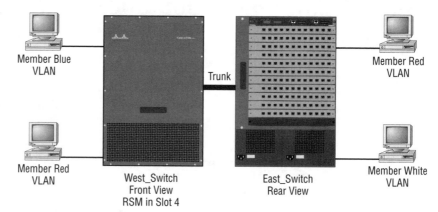

F I G U R E   11.1

A sample RSM
network

The switches are configured with port 1/1 on the Supervisor interconnected for trunking. All remaining ports for both switches are configured on a card basis: card 5 for the blue VLAN, card 6 for the red VLAN, and card 7 for the white VLAN. The following commands are used to configure the switches for the VLANs used in this example:

```
set vlan 2 name Blue_VLAN
set vlan 3 name Red_VLAN
set vlan 4 name White_VLAN
set vlan 2 5/1-24
set vlan 3 6/1-24
set vlan 4 7/1-24
set trunk 1/1 on isl
```

Although this example is intended for the West_Switch, the East_Switch could share all of these commands.

The default configuration of the Catalyst switch for trunking is auto. However, at least one end of the connection must be configured as on or desirable for the link to be established.

The Catalyst switch will automatically trunk two connected ports once one of those ports is configured for trunking. The following shows the options available with the `set trunk` command.

```
West_Switch> (enable) set trunk ?

Usage: set trunk <mod_num/port_num>
[on|off|desirable|auto|nonegotiate] [vlans]
[trunk_type]
        (vlans = 1..1005
         An example of vlans is 2-10,1005)
        (trunk_type = isl,dot1q,dot10,lane,negotiate)
```

In this example, port 1/1 is configured for trunking using ISL. Because version 4.5 supports automatic ISL trunking, the corresponding port on the East_Switch would automatically connect via ISL.

A number of protocols cover the trunking process; these protocols depend on the Catalyst software version. Following the release of 4.2, both ISL and 802.1q are supported for automatic configuration using the Dynamic Trunking Protocol (DTP). ISL was supported with the Dynamic Inter-Switch Link (DISL) protocol in release 4.1, but 802.1q links required manual configuration on both sides of the trunk. Before release 4.1, 802.1q was not supported.

If the administrator intends to use trunking on a specific port, the `desirable` keyword may be better for configuration than the default `auto` keyword. The `desirable` keyword will establish a trunk with a port set to `on`, `auto`, or `desirable`. The default `auto` keyword will connect only to a neighbor port set to `on` or `desirable`. Complete manual configuration with the `on` keyword is also available.

The administrator performs the RSM configuration on the RSM module, not on the Supervisor engine. This requires the use of the `session` command to connect to the RSM from the Supervisor CLI. The RSM configuration resides in the RSM module and is not stored in the Supervisor configuration.

In our example, the RSM is in the West_Switch, slot 4. The following shows the entire configuration for this example.

This example is a very simple configuration that demonstrates the RSM at its most basic level. This simple network could use the HSRP (Hot Standby Router Protocol) and a second RSM in the East_Switch as well as VTP (discussed later in this chapter) to transport the VLAN configurations. Consider these possibilities when reviewing this material.

```
West_Switch> (enable) session 4

Trying Router-4...
Connected to Router-4.
Escape character is '^]'.

West_Rtr>en
West_Rtr#wr t

Building configuration...

Current configuration:
!
version 11.3
service timestamps debug uptime
service timestamps log uptime
service password-encryption
!
hostname West_Rtr
!
interface Vlan2
 description Blue VLAN
 ip address 10.1.2.1 255.255.255.0
```

```
!
interface Vlan3
 description Red VLAN
 ip address 10.1.3.1 255.255.255.0
!
interface Vlan4
 description White VLAN
 ip address 10.1.4.1 255.255.255.0
!
router eigrp 10
 network 10.0.0.0
!
ip classless
!
line con 0
line aux 0
line vty 0 4

 login
!
end
```

Once it's configured with a password and IP address, administrators can Telnet to the RSM directly without using the Supervisor CLI.

RSM Interface Processing

Some administrators find the behavior of the RSM somewhat confusing with regard to the interfaces. Unlike the router, the RSM has no physical interfaces and appears to virtually connect to all VLANs via its trunk port. This is accurate; however, the RSM will not maintain an interface for which there is no physical connection. The following output was recorded following the disconnection of the switch's trunk port. The trunk port was the only physical link to VLANs two through five.

```
West_Rtr#1999 May 25 17:16:37 Pacific -07:00 %DTP-5-NONTRUNKPORTON:Port 1/1 has become
non-trunk
1999 May 25 17:16:37 Pacific -07:00 %PAGP-5-PORTFROMSTP:Port 1/1 left bridge port 1/1
1999 May 25 17:16:37 Pacific -07:00 %DTP-5-NONTRUNKPORTON:Port 1/2 has become
non-trunk
1999 May 25 17:16:38 Pacific -07:00 %PAGP-5-PORTFROMSTP:Port 1/2 left bridge port 1/2


02:22:29: %LINEPROTO-5-UPDOWN: Line protocol on Interface Vlan2, changed state to down
02:22:29: %LINEPROTO-5-UPDOWN: Line protocol on Interface Vlan3, changed state to down
02:22:29: %LINEPROTO-5-UPDOWN: Line protocol on Interface Vlan4, changed state to down
02:22:29: %LINEPROTO-5-UPDOWN: Line protocol on Interface Vlan5, changed state to down
02:22:30: %LINK-3-UPDOWN: Interface Vlan2, changed state to down
02:22:30: %STANDBY-6-STATECHANGE: Standby: 2: Vlan2 state Active      -> Init
02:22:30: %LINK-3-UPDOWN: Interface Vlan3, changed state to down
02:22:30: %STANDBY-6-STATECHANGE: Standby: 3: Vlan3 state Active      -> Init
02:22:30: %LINK-3-UPDOWN: Interface Vlan4, changed state to down
02:22:30: %STANDBY-6-STATECHANGE: Standby: 4: Vlan4 state Active      -> Init
02:22:31: %LINK-3-UPDOWN: Interface Vlan5, changed state to down
02:22:31: %STANDBY-6-STATECHANGE: Standby: 5: Vlan5 state Active      -> Init
```

This response by the RSM is understandable; however, it can be confusing to some administrators. A Cisco router will not maintain an interface in up/up mode if the interface is not connected at Layer 1. While the RSM connection to the Catalyst 5000/5500 can include all VLANs, which results in all VLANs having a "physical" connection, the RSM does not consider this an interface for the purpose of maintaining an up/up status. Ignoring the trunk between the RSM and switch as an interface will greatly assist in troubleshooting when the RSM reports an interface as "down." In such circumstances, administrators should check all trunk ports and any local VLAN ports on the switch with the RSM.

The interfaces on the RSM will not place themselves in the up/up mode until the VLAN is in use with a terminated connection. A trunk port connected to another switch can provide this connectivity for all VLANs.

The VLAN Management Policy Server (VMPS)

Originally, VLANs were configured with each physical port locked to a single VLAN. When a user changed location, the ports were manually configured to match the IP subnet that related to the user's workgroup and configuration settings. This greatly reduced the efficiency of VLANs. Granted, administrators no longer needed to rewire the patch panel, but the process still required additional steps beyond the relocation of the workstation.

The VMPS was designed to provide the dynamic capabilities of VLANs and simplify the process for accommodating moves, additions, and changes. In addition to simplifying administrative functions, the VMPS process can also augment a security policy within the corporation. By restricting the MAC addresses that may attach to the switch, data security departments can prevent unauthorized machines from attaching to the network. This can be useful when the security policy includes configuring workstations to prevent users from installing software that could compromise the environment.

The following shows the default VMPS configuration for the Catalyst 5500 switch. Note that VMPS is disabled and no IP address is defined for the VMPS TFTP server. The default filename, vmps-config-database.1, is included in the initial configuration file, however.

```
!
#vmps
set vmps server retry 3
set vmps server reconfirminterval 60
set vmps tftpserver 0.0.0.0 vmps-config-database.1
set vmps state disable
```

The VMPS process uses TFTP and requires the configuration of a TFTP server. This server and the database are downloaded to populate the switch with the information needed to associate an end-station MAC address with a VLAN. The download vmps command is used to populate the switch.

The significant parameters of the VMPS configuration file are shown in Table 11.2.

TABLE 11.2 The VMPS Configuration File Commands	Command	Function
	vmps domain <domain-name>	The VMPS domain is configured both on the switch and in the TFTP configuration file to define the relationship between resources.

TABLE 11.2 (cont.)	**Command**	**Function**
The VMPS Configuration File Commands	`vmps fallback <vlan-name>`	In the event a workstation is placed on the switch and the MAC address is not defined in the VMPS database, the switch will place the device on this default VLAN. This is a security concern where end-node control is a priority. Failure to use this setting will prevent a workstation from connecting to the network.
	`vmps mode (open|secure)`	Secure mode restricts the physical ports to which a defined resource may attach. An open configuration permits attachment at any port.
	`address <mac address>` `vlan-name <vlan>`	This line associates the MAC address of the station with the VLAN. Note that the entire file is parsed line by line, so each address command must reside on a separate line.

The VLAN Trunk Protocol (VTP)

Management of the various VLANs in the Catalyst 5000/5500 system would be very difficult if the administrator needed to configure every VLAN manually on every switch. Such a process would be time-consuming, difficult for remote locations, and prone to errors introduced by the administrator.

The VTP allows a single Catalyst 5000 series switch to integrate VLAN changes and update all other switches in the network automatically. The central switch is referred to as the *VTP server*, and the recipient switches are *clients*. All switches using VTP and sharing the same VLAN information are clustered into a VTP domain.

VTP updates are sent periodically from each trunk port on the switch. This means that a trunk link between each switch in the VTP domain is required for VTP operation.

VTP is configured on the Catalyst switch with the set keyword. As shown below, the set vtp command has a number of options, including domain configuration, the mode of the participating switch, password restrictions, and selection of VTP version two.

```
Switch_A> (enable) set vtp ?


Usage: set vtp [domain <name>] [mode <mode>] [passwd
    <passwd>][pruning <enable|disable>] [v2 <enable|disable>
        (mode = client|server|transparent
         Use passwd '0' to clear vtp password)
Usage: set vtp pruneeligible <vlans>
        (vlans = 2..1000
         An example of vlans is 2-10,1000)
```

The VTP pruning function blocks flooded traffic from crossing trunks for which there are no recipients. This function blocks broadcasts, multicasts, and other non-unicast traffic. The service operates by examining the memberships in each VLAN on a per-port basis. If a switch contains no members of a VLAN, the upstream switch will block non-unicast packets from traversing the link. This makes the trunk more efficient. To activate the service, use the set vtp pruning enable command.

VTP pruning is different from CGMP (Cisco Group Management Protocol), which is used to control IP multicast groups. VTP pruning is also different from the broadcast and multicast suppression feature of the Catalyst 5000 series.

In the following example, the VTP domain is set to Test and the switch is designated with server status. Eight VLANs are being distributed via VTP.

```
Switch_A> (enable) set vtp domain Test

VTP domain Test modified
Switch_A> (enable) set vtp mode server
```

```
VTP domain Test modified
Switch_A> (enable) show vtp

Domain Name    Domain Index VTP Version Local Mode  Password

Test           1            2            server      -

Vlan-count Max-vlan-storage Config Revision Notifications

8          1023             6               disabled

Last Updater   V2 Mode   Pruning  PruneEligible on Vlans

10.1.1.12      enabled   disabled 2-1000

Switch_A> (enable) show vlan

VLAN Name               Status    IfIndex Mod/Ports, Vlans
1    default            active    5       1/1-2
                                          2/2-12
                                          6/1-24
3    Sample_VLAN        active    49
4    Other_VLAN         active    50
5    Game_VLAN          active    51
1002 fddi-default       active    6
1003 trcrf-default      active    9
1004 fddinet-default    active    7
1005 trbrf-default      active    8       1003


VLAN Type  SAID   MTU  Parent RingNo BrdgNo Stp BrdgMode Trans1 Trans2
1    enet  100001 1500 -      -      -      -   -        0      0
3    enet  100003 1500 -      -      -      -   -        0      0
4    enet  100004 1500 -      -      -      -   -        0      0
5    enet  100005 1500 -      -      -      -   -        0      0
1002 fddi  101002 1500 -      -      -      -   -        0      0
1003 trcrf 101003 4472 1005   0xccc  -      -   srb      0      0
1004 fdnet 101004 1500 -      -      0x0    ieee -       0      0
1005 trbrf 101005 4472 -      -      0xf    ibm  -       0      0


VLAN AREHops STEHops Backup CRF
1003 7       7       off
```

The Catalyst Flash File System

The Catalyst 5000 switch uses flash memory to store configuration ....u switching module images. The Supervisor I and II modules are restricted to internal flash memory. Because the Supervisor III engine is typically used in enterprise-wide installations, the Supervisor III module contains internal flash memory and two PCMCIA slots for external flash memory cards. Using external flash memory provides several advantages:

- It permits downloading of new configuration files without deleting or overwriting older versions.

- Separate image files are needed for non-Supervisor modules, which may require additional space within the flash file system.

- It is possible to distribute images and configuration files to remote sites via flash memory, greatly reducing WAN link use.

Most of the commands to manage the flash file system are similar to DOS commands. For example, the dir command lists the contents of the flash memory.

```
Switch_A> (enable) dir

-#- -length- -----date/time------ name
  1  3429271 Jan 10 2000 18:26:51 cat5000-sup3.4-5-1.bin
```

Table 11.3 shows some other flash file system commands.

T A B L E 11.3	Command	Function
Flash File System Commands	download <ip address of server> <filename>	Used to obtain a file from a TFTP server.
	copy tftp flash	On the Supervisor III engine, serves the same function as the download command.
	copy config flash copy config tftp	Used to copy the running configuration file.
	upload <ip address of server> <filename>	Used to place a file on a TFTP server.

TABLE 11.3 (cont.) Flash File System Commands	**Command**	**Function**
	pwd	Used to display the flash device currently accessed. The name bootflash: refers to the onboard flash member, and slot0 and slot1 are the PCMCIA slots.
	cd	Used to change flash devices.
	undelete	Used to restore deleted files. The dir deleted command provides a listing of all eligible files.
	squeeze	Used to permanently remove deleted files from flash memory. The delete command marks the sectors as available but does not remove the file from the flash device.
	format	Used to prepare the flash device for use. The spare subcommand may be used to create spare sectors. These sectors may be used when other sectors fail.
	verify	Used to compare the checksum of a file with the file written to flash memory. This may be useful to confirm that a file is not corrupted.

Summary

Administrators have a wide variety of options for managing Catalyst 5000/5500 switches, ranging from the inexpensive CLI to complete RMON and SNMP network management utilities. The Catalyst system provides for in-band and out-of-band connectivity and may be augmented with external protocol analyzers and RMON probes. SPAN and ESPAN ports are an option for troubleshooting switched networks.

This chapter began with a discussion of out-of-band management and in-band management. Out-of-band management is commonly used for the initial configuration of the switch and for backup management at remote locations. Typically, administrators perform out-of-band management from a local console or terminal. In-band management uses network services to reach the Supervisor engine. In-band connections use IP.

The chapter also covered switch-management tools, including RMON, SPAN (and ESPAN), CWSI, and CDP. RMON (remote monitoring) is a baselining and troubleshooting tool for switched environments. Catalyst 5000 series switches offer an embedded RMON agent. The SPAN (Switched Port Analyzer) feature, also called port mirroring, provides additional monitoring capabilities. ESPAN (Enhanced Switch Port Analyzer) is an upgraded version of SPAN. Cisco's SwitchProbe product provides access to additional RMON information. Cisco offers CWSI (CiscoWorks for Switched Internetworks) to provide specialized switch-management tools, including the Cisco-View, TrafficDirector, and VlanDirector applications. CDP (Cisco Discovery Protocol) is a powerful troubleshooting tool that is available from the CLI. In addition, CDP-aware applications can use and display CDP information.

The final sections in this chapter described special switch features, including RSM, VMPS, and VTP, as well as the Catalyst 5000 flash file system. RSM (route switch module) is a Cisco 7500 series router on a single-slot card that can route packet flow from one VLAN to another. VMPS (VLAN Management Policy Server) simplifies VLAN administrative functions. VTP (VLAN Trunk Protocol) allows a Catalyst 5000 switch to integrate VLAN changes and automatically update the other switches in the network. The flash file system stores operating images for the Catalyst system.

Review Questions

1. The Catalyst 5000 switch support for Telnet includes which of the following?

   A. Secure, encrypted Telnet

   B. A Telnet client

   C. A Telnet server

   D. Support for up to eight outbound Telnet sessions

   E. Telnet is not supported; only SNMP is permitted

2. The TrafficDirector application performs which of the following functions?

   A. Serves as the BUS in ATM LANE

   B. Provides QoS services

   C. Graphically displays traffic levels

   D. Performs TCP and UDP filtering services

   E. Provides access-list functions within the switch environment

3. CDP packets are forwarded through all Cisco devices.

   A. True

   B. False

4. The VlanDirector application offers which of the following services?

   A. All nine groups of RMON

   B. Customization of CDP packet information

   C. Mapping of ATM LANE ELANs into VLAN trunking

   D. Management of VLANs that is not possible from the CLI

   E. Graphical administration of VLANs, including the ability to drag ports onto different VLANs

5. Which of the following is not true regarding the embedded RMON agent on the Catalyst 5000 switch?

   A. Supports the analysis group of RFC 1757

   B. Supports the statistics group of RFC 1757

   C. Supports the alarm group of RFC 1757

   D. Supports the event group of RFC 1757

   E. Supports the history group of RFC 1757

6. Which of the following is true regarding the Fast Ethernet Switch-Probe product?

   A. Modifies all ISL trunks into 802.1q compliance

   B. Provides Telnet into the Catalyst switch

   C. Is the only way to obtain RMON services on the Catalyst platform

   D. Collects statistics on all seven layers of the OSI model, per the RMON2 specification

7. The Catalyst 5000 switch may be managed from which of the following?

   A. A directly connected console using the CLI

   B. A directly connected console using the CDP

   C. A modem connection configured for PPP protocol and CHAP

   D. An X Window application served by the Supervisor engine

8. CiscoView does which of the following?

   A. Provides a graphical view of Cisco devices via NetBIOS

   B. Defines the relationship between ports and VLANs

   C. Provides a graphical view of Cisco devices configured with an IP address

   D. Captures FDDI frames for protocol analysis

9. TrafficDirector provides which of the following services?

    A. Packet capture from the internal RMON agent

    B. Packet capture from the Cisco SwitchProbe product

    C. Broadcast suppression

    D. ISL RMON monitoring

10. By default, the console port on the Supervisor engine is configured for which port speed?

    A. 1200 baud

    B. 2400 baud

    C. 4800 baud

    D. 9600 baud

    E. The port is auto-sensing

11. When managing the route switch module in slot 3, the administrator would use which of the following commands?

    A. `configure rsm3`

    B. `set rsm ip route 0.0.0.0 10.1.1.1`

    C. `session 3`

    D. `session rsm`

    E. `get rsm config`

12. VMPS provides which of the following services?

    A. Dynamic routing between VLANs

    B. RMON2

    C. Layer 4 switching

    D. Dynamic VLAN membership

    E. Static VLAN configuration

13. The VTP process requires which of the following?

    A. A trunk link

    B. Two or more trunk links

    C. An RSM in at least one switch

    D. An external router

    E. An external TFTP server

14. Which of the following protocols would provide the greatest assistance to an administrator when initially troubleshooting?

    A. CDP

    B. VMPS

    C. VTP

    D. ISL

    E. 802.1q

15. In order to reduce the impact of changes to VLAN configurations, the administrator should configure which of the following services?

    A. ISL

    B. VTP

    C. RSM

    D. RMON

    E. 802.10

16. Which of the following would be reasons to use an external RMON probe with the Catalyst 5000 switch?

    A. Lower cost

    B. Reduced processor overhead

    C. An additional physical port

    D. Greater statistical information

    E. Fault tolerance

17. Which command would be used to prepare the flash PCMCIA device for files?

    A. `squeeze`

    B. `format`

    C. `dir`

    D. `delete`

    E. `verify`

18. Which of the following is a service available within VTP?

    A. Flash system management

    B. Fast convergence of spanning tree

    C. Broadcast suppression based on percentage of port utilization

    D. High-speed routing

    E. Bandwidth management

19. User Tracking is a CWSI application for dynamic VLAN configuration. What service may be used at the CLI with a TFTP server to provide dynamic VLAN port assignment?

    A. SNMP

    B. RMON

    C. MIB

    D. VMPS

    E. NTP

20. Most of the VLAN interfaces on the RSM suddenly report down/ down. What area should the administrator check?

   A. Failure of the routing protocol

   B. Failure of a trunk port

   C. Failure of the TFTP server providing the VMPS database

   D. Failure of the 1/1 interface on the Supervisor engine

   E. Failure of the ATM LANE module

CHAPTER

12

Troubleshooting Cisco Switches

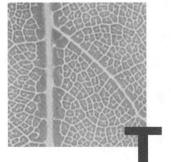

Troubleshooting is a skill that takes time and experience to fully develop. To be successful in diagnosing and repairing network failures, it's essential to have a good set of troubleshooting tools.

This chapter reviews the guidelines for troubleshooting the Catalyst series switches. We do not attempt here to solve every problem that you might encounter when configuring or deploying a switch. Our goal is instead to provide you with a diagnostic route to follow when you encounter a problem.

Given the complexities of technology today, troubleshooting can be difficult and may seem overwhelming to those new in the field. This chapter emphasizes the importance of following a specific set of steps when you try to diagnose and solve network problems, making this task more manageable. Learning these troubleshooting skills and understanding the diagnostic information available to you is imperative to your successful career.

This chapter covers the following CCNP: CLSC test objectives:

- Describe the approach for troubleshooting Catalyst switches.

- Describe the physical-layer problem areas.

- Use the show commands to troubleshoot problems.

- Troubleshoot network interfaces and connections.

- Describe the network test equipment.

- Describe the switch hardware status.

- Maintain Catalyst series switches and perform basic troubleshooting.

An Approach to Troubleshooting

When a network failure occurs, time is of the essence. When a production network goes down, the company's bottom-line is affected—network failures cost money. For example, a company employing a call-center network would rely heavily on this technology. The network must be available for its employees to take phone orders, answer inquiries, or perform other business transactions that generate income. A failure in this environment needs to be diagnosed and repaired quickly—there's no time to spare. The longer the network is down, the more money the company loses.

To minimize monetary and productivity losses, network failures must be resolved as quickly as possible. Troubleshooting ability is an integral part of getting the problem solved. However, intimate knowledge of a network also facilitates rapid resolution. Armed with a few troubleshooting skills and intimate knowledge of the network, you can solve most problems with relative ease and speed, thus saving money.

What if you're new on the job and you don't have an intimate knowledge of the network? You can probably get up to speed quickly enough, right?

Although that may have been the case in the past, today's complex networks make the task more difficult. Networks now consist of routing, dial-up, switching, video, WAN (ISDN, Frame Relay, ATM, and others), LAN, and VLAN technologies. Different protocols are used for each of these technologies, as well as different applications supported by the network. (At least the seven-layer OSI model is used to maintain a common template when designing new technologies and protocols.) It would take you a long time to master all of the technologies implemented in the network and to be able to solve network problems, based on your knowledge of the network alone.

The troubleshooting approach involves walking into a firestorm. There are managers (possibly yours) and users screaming, and the Catalyst switches have rolled over and died.

So, how do you approach a switch problem? How do you develop that plan of attack? The best troubleshooters either have years of experience, have learned everything there is to know about the switch problem, and are now getting ready to expound upon the solution, or they are like you and I and approach each problem with a set plan of attack. In most cases, these plans are developed based on your own experiences or knowledge. The troubleshooting approach taught here will provide you with a plan for attacking those problems that you haven't yet experienced or don't know how to deal with.

Developing a troubleshooting approach for switches involves creating a flow process ending with a solution. This process uses questions and responses to work through to a solution. Once you determine there is a problem with a switch, a rough outline of the process might look like the following:

1. Determine the problem. What behavior is the switch demonstrating? Are the ATM module LEDs red? Are ports 4/1–24 inactive? Find out what the symptoms are. Ask the users what they were doing before the network went down. What does the Network Manager Station report? Query as many angles as possible and narrow down the problem's scope.

2. After discovering what has happened, begin to investigate what may have caused the problem by collecting facts from the switch. This information may involve interrogating the switch using CLI commands like show or debug. A clearer definition of the problem can help develop a solution quickly.

3. Now create the attack plan based on the information you've collected from the switch. The plan should limit changes to the switch in a controlled manner. One solution may seem obvious, but if too many changes are made at once, your "solution" may create new problems.

4. Now it's time to implement the attack plan, taking the steps you've just outlined. The steps created in the attack plan must be defined and carried out in sequence to provide a clearer picture of what happened that caused the problem and also to help create a solution to address the problem if it arises again.

5. Gather new data that results from changing the configuration of the switch. This again may mean using the CLI commands show and debug. The collected data can be used to narrow the attack plan. If a solution was found and the switch is fixed, you are the hero. If the problem has narrowed and the data points to a specific module or physical connection, you can begin again at step one, eventually find the solution, and save the day.

The five steps above can be graphically represented by the flow diagram found in Figure 12.1. Each of the main steps can be divided into further steps to provide more detail. In some cases, however, a solution may immediately become evident while you are collecting data regarding the initial problem situation.

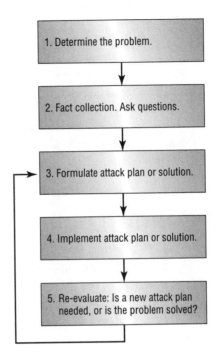

The Problem-Solving Checklist

The easiest way to solve network problems is to be able to compare current configurations against previous configurations. This sounds easy, but it requires effort to get a system established and to keep a historical baseline of your network. A *historical baseline* is simply a record of network settings and configurations kept over time. This baseline makes it easy to locate changes or differences between a current configuration and a previous one.

Baselines provide the following type of information:

- Network topology

- Router configurations

- Network and routing protocols

- Traffic levels and network events

- Applications

- Changes made to network configurations
- Historical information that documents previous troubleshooting sessions

In addition to having all of this data available to you, it is helpful to have a checklist that you can refer to when you troubleshoot. Every administrator knows their network and the types of changes that have been made on it. Every network is vastly different from every other one; so to say that this is the ultimate checklist that everyone should use when resolving network problems is unreasonable.

Troubleshooting Tools

This section examines the wide selection of troubleshooting tools that can be used when you experience a network problem. We'll look at using the switch diagnostic commands in the Cisco IOS, as well as Cisco's network management platforms. We will also look quickly at some third-party troubleshooting tools that may be encountered in the field.

Cisco engineers realized that no network would remain completely operational for years to come. So when the designers sat down and began to develop the IOS, they added multiple methods of collecting information about how the network was operating. You can compare these to the various scopes that repair shops use to test your car's operating systems. These methods or commands include:

- show
- debug
- ping
- trace

Using the show Commands

The show command is one of the most powerful utilities provided to the troubleshooter. It can provide information in the Cisco IOS about virtually everything that's happening with the switch. The command is universal across both switched and routed environments and should be one of the first steps you use to collect data concerning problems with a switch. Here is a list of all show commands available on a Cisco Catalyst switch and their descriptions:

```
Switch_A> (enable) sh ?
Show commands:
-------------------------------------------------------------------
show alias              Show aliases for commands
show arp                Show ARP table
show authentication     Show authentication information
show boot               Show booting environment variables
show bridge             Show bridge information
show cam                Show CAM table
show cdp                Show Cisco Discovery ProtocolInformat
show cgmp               Show CGMP info
show config             Show system configuration
show drip               Show DRiP Information
show dvlan              Show dynamic vlan statistics
show fddi               Show FDDI module entries
show fddicam            Show FDDI module CAM table
show flash              Show file information on flash device
show help               Show this message
show igmp               Show IGMP information
show imagemib           Show image mib information
show interface          Show network interfaces
show ip                 Show IP Information
show log                Show log information
show logging            Show system logging information
--More-
show mac                Show MAC information
show microcode          Show microcode versions
show module             Show module information
show multicast          Show multicast information
show mls                Show multilayer switching information
show netstat            Show network statistics
show ntp                Show ntp statistics
show port               Show port information
show protocolfilter     Show protocolfilter information
show rif                Show Routing Information Field (RIF)
show rsmautostate       Show RSM derived interface state
show snmp               Show SNMP information
show span               Show switch port analyzer information
show spantree           Show spantree information
```

show standbyports	Show state of standby ports feature.
show station	Show Tokenring Station info
show summertime	Show state of summertime information
show system	Show system information
show tacacs	Show TACACS information
show test	Show results of diagnostic tests
show time	Show time of day
show timezone	Show the current timezone offset
show tokenring	Show tokenring information
--More--	
show top	Show TopN report
show trunk	Show trunk ports
show users	Show active Admin sessions
show version	Show version information
show vlan	Show Virtual LAN information
show vmps	Show VMPS information
show vtp	Show VTP Information

Notice that we had screenfuls of information! Here is a closer look at a few of the show commands.

Command

show log *[mod_num]*

Usage   Displays system and module error logs.

Sample Output

```
Switch_A> (enable) sh log
Network Management Processor (ACTIVE NMP) Log:
  Reset count:   3
  Re-boot History:Jun 01 1999 15:52:21 0, May 26 1999 10:57:49
                  Jan 14 2000 16: 9:54 0

  Bootrom Checksum Failures:0 UART Failures: 0
  Flash Checksum Failures:0   Flash Program Failures:0
  Power Supply 1 Failures:2   Power Supply 2 Failures:2
  Swapped to CLKA:         0  Swapped to CLKB:
  Swapped to Processor 1: 0   Swapped to Processor 2:0
  DRAM Failures:0
  Exceptions: 0
  Last software reset by user: 6/1/1999,15:51:45
```

```
  MCP Exceptions/Hang: 0
Heap Memory Log:
Corrupted Block = none
NVRAM log:
--More--
Module 2 Log:
  Reset Count:    3
  Reset History: Tue Jun 1 1999, 15:53:10
                 Wed May 26 1999, 10:58:38
                 Fri Jan 14 2000, 16:10:43

Module 3 Log:
  Reset Count:    3
  Reset History: Tue Jun 1 1999, 15:53:33
                 Wed May 26 1999, 10:59:01
                 Fri Jan 14 2000, 16:11:06

Switch_A> (enable) sh log 3
Module 3 Log:
  Reset Count:    3
  Reset History: Tue Jun 1 1999, 15:53:33
                 Wed May 26 1999, 10:59:01
                 Fri Jan 14 2000, 16:11:06
```

Command

```
show logging
```

Usage Displays the system message log configuration.

Sample Output

```
Switch_A> (enable) sh logging ?
Usage: show logging [noalias]
       show logging buffer [-][number_of_messages]
       (number_of_messages: 1..1023, default: -20)
Switch_A> (enable) sh logging
Logging buffer size:   500
timestamp option: enabled
Logging history size: 1
Logging console:     enabled
```

```
Logging server:       disabled
server facility:      LOCAL7
server severity:      warnings(4)
Current Logging Session:enabled
```

```
Facility     Default Severity       Current Session Severity
-------------          -----------------------   -------------
cdp             2                        2
mcast           2                        2
dtp             5                        5
dvlan           2                        2
earl            2                        2
fddi            2                        2
ip              2                        2
pruning         2                        2
snmp            2                        2
spantree        2                        2
--More--
sys             5                        5
tac             2                        2
tcp             2                        2
telnet          2                        2
tftp            2                        2
vtp             2                        2
vmps            2                        2
kernel          2                        2
filesys         2                        2
drip            2                        2
pagp            5                        5
mgmt            5                        5
mls             5                        5
protfilt        2                        2
security        2                        2


0(emergencies)    1(alerts)         2(critical)
3(errors)         4(warnings)       5(notifications)
6(information)    7(debugging)
```

Command

```
show vtp statistics
```

Usage Displays VTP statistics.

Sample Output

```
Switch_A> (enable) sh vtp stat
VTP statistics:
summary advts received       2163
subset  advts received       2
request advts received       0
summary advts transmitted    0
subset  advts transmitted    0
request advts transmitted    0
No of config revision errors 0
No of config digest errors   0


(Output truncated for brevity)
```

Command

```
show netstat [tcp | udp | ip | icmp | routes | stats |
interfaces]
```

Usage Shows currently active network connections and network statistics for the TCP/IP stack.

Sample Output

```
Switch_A> (enable) sh netstat
Active Internet connections (including servers)
Proto Recv-Q Send-Q Local Address     Foreign Address    (state)
tcp     0    128  10.1.1.10.23       10.1.1.22.11000   ESTABLISHED
tcp     0      0  127.0.0.2.10000    127.0.0.4.1025    ESTABLISHED
tcp     0      0  127.0.0.2.7161     127.0.0.4.1024    ESTABLISHED
tcp     0      0  127.0.0.2.1024     127.0.0.4.10000   ESTABLISHED
tcp     0      0  *.10000                   *.*        LISTEN
tcp     0      0  *.7161                    *.*        LISTEN
tcp     0      0  *.23                      *.*        LISTEN
udp     0      0  *.*                       *.*
udp     0      0  *.161                     *.*
```

```
Switch_A> (enable) sh netstat ?
Usage: netstat [tcp|udp|ip|icmp|routes|stats|interfaces]
Commands
----------------------------------------------------------
show netstat            Show active network connections
show netstat stats      Show TCP, UDP, IP, ICMP statistics
show netstat tcp        Show TCP statistics
show netstat udp        Show UDP statistics
show netstat ip         Show IP statistics
show netstat icmp       Show ICMP statistics
show netstat interface  Show interface statistics
show netstat routes     Show IP routing table
Switch_A> (enable) sh netstat tcp:
    5657 packets sent
        3120 data packets (22847 bytes)
        10 data packets (44 bytes) retransmitted
        2442 ack-only packets (2383 delayed)
        0 URG only packets
        0 window probe packets
        10 window update packets
        75 control packets
    15251 packets received
        3134 acks (for 22892 bytes)
        11187 duplicate acks
        0 acks for unsent data
        3560 packets (150744 bytes) received in-sequence
        7 completely duplicate packets (0 bytes)
        4 packets with some dup. data (4 bytes duped)
        5 out-of-order packets (176 bytes)
        0 packets (0 bytes) of data after window
        0 window probes
        0 window update packets
        0 packets received after close
        0 discarded for bad checksums
        0 discarded for bad header offset fields
--More--
0 discarded because packet too short
    36 connection requests
    6 connection accepts
    38 connections established (including accepts)
    38 connections closed (including 0 drops)
    1 embryonic connection dropped
```

```
                    3131 segments updated rtt (of 3171 attempts)
                    18 retransmit timeouts
                        0 connections dropped by rexmit timeout
                    0 persist timeouts
                    18635 keepalive timeouts
                        11177 keepalive probes sent
                        1 connection dropped by keepalive
Switch_A> (enable) sh netstat tcp udp:
                    0 incomplete headers
                    0 bad data length fields
                    0 bad checksums
                    0 socket overflows
                    125 no such ports
```

Command

```
show module [mod_num]
```

Usage   Shows module information.

Sample Output

```
Switch_A> (enable) sh module
Module-Name   Ports   Module-Type      Model      Serial-Num Status
--- ------------------ ----- -------------------- ---------
1               2      100BaseFX  MMF Supervi WS-X5530014037817 ok
2               12     100BaseFX MM Ethernet WS-X5201R 013928340 ok
3               1      Network Analysis/RMON WS-X5380  012435726 ok


Mod MAC-Address(es)                            Hw     Fw         Sw
--- --------------------------------------- ------ ---------- --
1   00-50-f0-1b-38-00 to 00-50-f0-1b-3b-ff 3.2    3.1.2   4.5(1)
2   00-60-83-f3-e7-f8 to 00-60-83-f3-e8-03 3.0    4.3(1)  4.5(1)
3   00-60-09-ff-b4-d0                       1.1    4.3.2   4.3(1a)


Mod Sub-Type Sub-Model Sub-Serial Sub-Hw
--- -------- --------- ---------- ------
1   NFFC II  WS-F5531  0013218660 1.0
1   uplink   WS-U5533  0013871414 1.0
Switch_A> (enable) sh module ?
Usage: show module [mod_num]
Switch_A> (enable) sh mod 3
```

```
Module-Name  Ports Module-Type        Model    Serial-Num Status
--- ------------------ ----- -------------------- -
3          1     Network Analysis/RMON WS-X5380  012435726  ok

Mod MAC-Address(es)                    Hw     Fw         Sw
--- ------------------------------------- ------ ---------- --
3   00-60-09-ff-b4-d0                  1.1    4.3.2      4.3(1a)
Switch_A> (enable) sh port
Port  Name           Status    Vlan     Level  Duplex Speed Type
----- ------------------ ---------- ---------- ------ ------ -
1/1        connected    trunk    normal   full   100 100BaseFX MM
1/2        connected    trunk    normal   full   100 100BaseFX MM
2/1        connected    1        high     full   100 100BaseFX MM
2/2        connected    1        high     full   100 100BaseFX MM
2/3        notconnect   1        normal   half   100 100BaseFX MM
2/4        notconnect   1        normal   half   100 100BaseFX MM
2/5        notconnect   1        normal   half   100 100BaseFX MM
2/6        notconnect   1        normal   half   100 100BaseFX MM
2/7        notconnect   1        normal   half   100 100BaseFX MM
2/8        notconnect   1        normal   half   100 100BaseFX MM
2/9        notconnect   1        normal   half   100 100BaseFX MM
2/10       notconnect   1        normal   half   100 100BaseFX MM
2/11       notconnect   1        normal   half   100 100BaseFX MM
2/12       notconnect   1        normal   half   100 100BaseFX MM
3/1        -            -        normal   full    - Network Anal

Port Security Secure-Src-Addr Last-Src-Addr Shutdown Trap IfIndex
----- -------- ----------------- ----------------- --------
1/1  disabled                                     No  disabled 3
1/2  disabled                                     No  disabled 4
2/1  disabled                                     No  disabled 10
2/2  disabled                                     No  disabled 11
2/3  disabled                                     No  disabled 12
2/4  disabled                                     No  disabled 13
2/5  disabled                                     No  disabled 14
2/6  disabled                                     No  disabled 15
2/7  disabled                                     No  disabled 16
2/8  disabled                                     No  disabled 17
2/9  disabled                                     No  disabled 18
2/10 disabled                                     No  disabled 19
2/11 disabled                                     No  disabled 20
2/12 disabled                                     No  disabled 21
```

```
Port   Trap      IfIndex
-----  --------  -------
3/1    disabled  22
```

```
Port      Broadcast-Limit Broadcast-Drop
--------  --------------- ---------------
1/1                     -               0
1/2                     -               0
2/1                     -               0
2/2                     -               0
2/3                     -               0
2/4                     -               0
2/5                     -               0
2/6                     -               0
2/7                     -               0
2/8                     -               0
2/9                     -               0
2/10                    -               0
2/11                    -               0
2/12                    -               0
```

```
Port Send FlowControl Receive FlowControl RxPause TxPause
----- -------- -------- -------- -------- ------- -
2/1   off      off      on       on       0       0
2/2   off      off      on       on       0       0
2/3   off      off      on       on       0       0
2/4   off      off      on       on       0       0
2/5   off      off      on       on       0       0
2/6   off      off      on       on       0       0
2/7   off      off      on       on       0       0
2/8   off      off      on       on       0       0
2/9   off      off      on       on       0       0
2/10  off      off      on       on       0       0
2/11  off      off      on       on       0       0
2/12  off      off      on       on       0       0
```

```
Port Align-Err FCS-Err   Xmit-Err  Rcv-Err   UnderSize
----- --------- --------- --------- --------- ---------
1/1        48        19         0         0         2
1/2         0         0         0         0         0
```

2/1	0	0	0	0	0
2/2	0	0	0	0	0
2/3	0	0	0	0	0
2/4	0	0	0	0	0
2/5	0	0	0	0	0
2/6	0	0	0	0	0
2/7	0	0	0	0	0
2/8	0	0	0	0	0
2/9	0	0	0	0	0
2/10	0	0	0	0	0
2/11	0	0	0	0	0
2/12	0	0	0	0	0

Port	Single-Col	Multi-Coll	Late-Coll	Excess-Col	Carri-Sen	Runts
1/1	0	0	0	0	0	0
1/2	0	0	0	0	0	0
2/1	0	0	0	0	0	0
2/2	0	0	0	0	0	0
2/3	0	0	0	0	0	0
2/4	0	0	0	0	0	0
2/5	0	0	0	0	0	0
2/6	0	0	0	0	0	0
2/7	0	0	0	0	0	0
2/8	0	0	0	0	0	0
2/9	0	0	0	0	0	0
2/10	0	0	0	0	0	0
2/11	0	0	0	0	0	0
2/12	1	0	0	0	0	0

Command

```
show port [mod_num[/port_num]]
```

Usage Shows port status and counters.

Sample Output

```
Last-Time-Cleared
--------------------------
Wed Jun 2 1999, 16:51:18
Switch_A> (enable) sh port ?
```

```
Usage: show port
       show port <mod_num>
       show port <mod_num/port_num>
Show port commands:
------------------------------------------------------------
show port broadcast        Show port broadcast information
show port cdp              Show port CDP information
show port capabilities     Show port capabilities
show port channel          Show port channel information
show port counters         Show port counters
show port fddi             Show port FDDI information
show port flowcontrol      Show port traffic flowcontrol
show port filter           Show Token Ring port filtering info
show port help             Show this message
show port ifindex          Show port IfIndex information
show port mac              Show port MAC counters
show port negotiation      Show port flowcontrol negotiation
show port protocol         Show port protocol membership
show port security         Show port security information
show port spantree         Show port spantree information
show port status           Show port status
show port trap             Show port trap information
show port trunk            Show port trunk information

Switch_A> (enable) sh port ?
Port    Broadcast-Limit Broadcast-Drop
-------- --------------- --------------
  1/1           -              0
  1/2           -              0
  2/1           -              0
  2/2           -              0
  2/3           -              0
  2/4           -              0
  2/5           -              0
  2/6           -              0
  2/7           -              0
  2/8           -              0
  2/9           -              0
  2/10          -              0
  2/11          -              0
  2/12          -              0
```

Command

```
show port capabilities [mod_num[/port_num]]
```

Usage Displays the capabilities of the modules and ports in a switch.

Sample Output

```
Switch_A> (enable) sh port cap
capModel              WS-X5530
Port                  1/1
Type                  100BaseFX MM
Speed                 100
Duplex                half,full
Trunk encap type      ISL
Trunk mode            on,off,desirable,auto,nonegotiate
Channel               1/1-2
Broadcast suppression percentage(0-100)
Flow control          no
Security              yes
Membership            static,dynamic
Fast start            yes
Rewrite               no


-----------------------------------------------------------
Model                 WS-X5530
Port                  1/2
Type                  100BaseFX MM
Speed                 100
Duplex                half,full
Trunk encap type      ISL
Trunk mode            on,off,desirable,auto,nonegotiate
--More-
Channel               1/1-2
Broadcast suppression percentage(0-100)
Flow control          no
Security              yes
Membership            static,dynamic
Fast start            yes
Rewrite               no
```

```
-------------------------------------------------------------
Model                   WS-X5201R
Port                    2/1
Type                    100BaseFX MM
Speed                   100
Duplex                  half,full
Trunk encap type        802.1Q,ISL
Trunk mode              on,off,desirable,auto,nonegotiate
Channel                 2/1-2,2/1-4
Broadcast suppression   percentage(0-100)
Flow control            receive-(off,on),send-(off,on)
Security                yes
Membership              static,dynamic
Fast start              yes
Rewrite                 yes
--More--
-------------------------------------------------------------
Model                   WS-X5201R
Port                    2/2
Type                    100BaseFX MM
Speed                   100
Duplex                  half,full
Trunk encap type        802.1Q,ISL
Trunk mode              on,off,desirable,auto,nonegotiate
Channel                 2/1-2,2/1-4
Broadcast suppression   percentage(0-100)
Flow control            receive-(off,on),send-(off,on)
Security                yes
Membership              static,dynamic
Fast start              yes
Rewrite                 yes

-------------------------------------------------------------
Model                   WS-X5201R
Port                    2/3
Type                    100BaseFX MM
Speed                   100
Duplex                  half,full
```

```
--More--
Trunk encap type        802.1Q,ISL
Trunk mode              on,off,desirable,auto,nonegotiate
Channel                 2/3-4,2/1-4
Broadcast suppression   percentage(0-100)
Flow control            receive-(off,on),send-(off,on)
Security                yes
Membership              static,dynamic
Fast start              yes
Rewrite                 yes


---------------------------------------------------------

Model                   WS-X5201R
Port                    2/4
Type                    100BaseFX MM
Speed                   100
Duplex                  half,full
Trunk encap type        802.1Q,ISL
Trunk mode              on,off,desirable,auto,nonegotiate
Channel                 2/3-4,2/1-4
Broadcast suppression   percentage(0-100)
Flow control            receive-(off,on),send-(off,on)
Security                yes
Membership              static,dynamic
--More--
Fast start              yes
Rewrite                 yes


---------------------------------------------------------

Model                   WS-X5201R
Port                    2/5
Type                    100BaseFX MM
Speed                   100
Duplex                  half,full
Trunk encap type        802.1Q,ISL
Trunk mode              on,off,desirable,auto,nonegotiate
```

```
Channel                    2/5-6,2/5-8
Broadcast suppression      percentage(0-100)
Flow control               receive-(off,on),send-(off,on)
Security                   yes
Membership                 static,dynamic
Fast start                 yes
Rewrite                    yes


--------------------------------------------------------------

Model                      WS-X5201R
Port                       2/6
Type                       100BaseFX MM
--More-
Speed                      100
Duplex                     half,full
Trunk encap type           802.1Q,ISL
Trunk mode                 on,off,desirable,auto,nonegotiate
Channel                    2/5-6,2/5-8
Broadcast suppression      percentage(0-100)
Flow control               receive-(off,on),send-(off,on)
Security                   yes
Membership                 static,dynamic
Fast start                 yes
Rewrite                    yes


--------------------------------------------------------------

Model                      WS-X5201R
Port                       2/7
Type                       100BaseFX MM
Speed                      100
Duplex                     half,full
Trunk encap type           802.1Q,ISL
Trunk mode                 on,off,desirable,auto,nonegotiate
Channel                    2/7-8,2/5-8
Broadcast suppression      percentage(0-100)
Flow control               receive-(off,on),send-(off,on)
```

```
--More-
Security                yes
Membership              static,dynamic
Fast start              yes
Rewrite                 yes
```

Command

```
show cdp neighbors [mod_num[/port_num]] [detail]
show cdp port [mod_num[/port_num]]
```

Usage Shows CDP information for the network.

Sample Output

```
Switch_A> (enable) sh cdp nei det
Port (Our Port): 1/1
Device-ID: 069078871(RSM_A)
Device Addresses:
  IP Address: 10.1.1.12
Holdtime: 161 sec
Capabilities: TRANSPARENT_BRIDGE SR_BRIDGE SWITCH
Version:
  WS-C5500 Software, Version McpSW: 4.5(1) NmpSW: 4.5(1)
  Copyright (c) 1995-1999 by Cisco Systems
Platform: WS-C5500
Port-ID (Port on Neighbor's Device): 2/1
_____

Port (Our Port): 1/2
Device-ID: 069073870(RSM_B)
Device Addresses:
  IP Address: 10.1.1.13
Holdtime: 121 sec
Capabilities: TRANSPARENT_BRIDGE SR_BRIDGE SWITCH
Version:
  WS-C5500 Software, Version McpSW: 4.5(1) NmpSW: 4.5(1)
  Copyright (c) 1995-1999 by Cisco Systems
Platform: WS-C5500
Port-ID (Port on Neighbor's Device): 2/1
```

```
Switch_A> (enable) sh cdp nei ?
Usage: show cdp neighbors [mod_num] [detail]
       show cdp neighbors [mod_num/port_num] [detail]
       show cdp port [mod_num]
       show cdp port [mod_num/port_num]
Switch_A> (enable)
```

As you can see, there is quite a lot of switch information you can gather if you know which show commands to use. The few we've listed here only begin to cover the thousands more that currently exist within the Cisco IOS.

Using the debug Commands

The debug commands can offer vast amounts of information and often overwhelm the user with too much information. Everything from information about the traffic flow on an interface, to error messages being generated by nodes on the network, to protocol-specific diagnostic packets is available using debug.

Be careful when using debug. These commands are processor intensive and can slow the performance of the switch or even cause connectivity issues. In particular, never use debug all unless instructed.

After collecting information, always remember to go back and disable the debugging function you enabled. Typing no debug [command] or no debug all will disable the debugging function.

Typically, the debug function is only used when a real problem has appeared in the network, causing serious damage, and you need to see what the internal operations of the switch appear to be doing.

As with show, the information provided by debug will differ with each debug subcommand. Some debug functions generate a single line of output, and others generate multiple lines of output per packet. Some debug functions generate large amounts of output, and others generate only occasional output. Some generate lines of text, and others generate information in field format.

Typing debug ? displays a quick list of the debugging functionality available. It may look similar to this:

```
aaa                  AAA Authentication, Authorization and Accounting
access-expression    Boolean access expression
all                  Enable all debugging
apollo               Apollo information
apple                Appletalk information
arap                 Appletalk Remote Access
arp                  IP ARP and HP Probe transactions
aspp                 ASPP information
async                Async interface information
atm                  ATM interface packets
bsc                  BSC information
bstun                BSTUN information
c5ipc                C5IP IPC events
cBus                 ciscoBus events
callback             Callback activity
cdp                  CDP information
chat                 Chat scripts activity
clns                 CLNS information
cls                  CLS Information
compress             COMPRESS traffic
confmodem            Modem configuration database
cpp                  Cpp information
custom-queue         Custom output queueing
decnet               DECnet information
dhcp                 DHCP client activity
dialer               Dial on Demand
dlsw                 Data Link Switching (DLSw) events
dnsix                Dnsix information
domain               Domain Name System
dspu                 DSPU Information
dss                  Debug DSS
dxi                  atm-dxi information
eigrp                EIGRP Protocol information
entry                Incoming queue entries
ethernet-interface   Ethernet network interface events
fastethernet         Fast Ethernet interface information
filesys              File system information
frame-relay          Frame Relay
fras                 FRAS Debug
```

```
fras-host          FRAS Host Debug
ip                 IP information
ipc                Interprocess communications debugging
ipx                Novell/IPX information
isis               IS-IS Information
kerberos           KERBEROS authentication and authorization
```

As you can see, this list only carries you to the beginning of the Ks. There are three more screens to examine while looking for that specific function you are trying to debug. Here are some suggestions for lessening the shock of using the debug commands:

- Use the no logging console command on the switch. This command will disable all logging to the console terminal.

- Establish a connection with the switch via Telnet.

- Use the terminal monitor command to copy debug command output and system error messages to your current terminal display. This allows the troubleshooter to view debug command output remotely. This method reduces the impact of utilizing debug commands by eliminating the need for the console port to generate character-by-character processor interrupts.

Using the ping Command

What's the quickest method to determine whether one device is communicating with another device on the network?

Ping can verify host accessibility and determine whether there is any network connectivity. This command can be used to authenticate basic network connectivity on AppleTalk, IP, IPX, VINES, DECnet, and others.

Command

```
ping <host>
ping -s <host> [packet_size] [packet_count]
```

Usage   host is an IP alias or IP address in dot notation: a.b.c.d

packet_size range: 56–1472

How does an IP ping work? The ping command sends a series of Internet Control Message Protocol (ICMP) Echo messages to a designated end station. If the end station receives the Echo message, it replies in kind with an ICMP Echo Reply message.

There is also an extended ping command, which provides different options. The extended ping allows the user to specify the supported IP header options. This allows the router to perform a broader range service test. To get the extended ping options, enter yes at the extended commands prompt of the ping command. Here's a sample ping dialog:

```
RouteSwitchModule#ping
Protocol [ip]:
Target IP address: 170.34.5.67
Repeat count [5]:
Datagram size [100]:
Timeout in seconds [2]:
Extended commands [n]: yes        Enter yes to see the
additional options available.
Source address or interface: 170.34.5.100
Type of service [0]:
Set DF bit in IP header? [no]:
Validate reply data? [no]:
Data pattern [0xABCD]:
Loose, Strict, Record, Timestamp, Verbose[none]: v
Loose, Strict, Record, Timestamp, Verbose[V]:
Sweep range of sizes [n]: y
Sweep min size [36]: 1000
Sweep max size [18024]: 1500
Sweep interval [1]: 250
Type escape sequence to abort.
Sending 15, [1000..1500]-byte ICMP Echoes to 170.34.5.67,
timeout is 2 seconds:
Reply to request 0 (4 ms) (size 1000)
Reply to request 1 (4 ms) (size 1250)
Reply to request 2 (1 ms) (size 1500)
Reply to request 3 (4 ms) (size 1000)
Reply to request 4 (1 ms) (size 1250)
Reply to request 5 (1 ms) (size 1500)
Reply to request 6 (1 ms) (size 1000)
Reply to request 7 (1 ms) (size 1250)
Reply to request 8 (1 ms) (size 1500)
```

```
Reply to request 9 (1 ms) (size 1000)
Reply to request 10 (1 ms) (size 1250)
Reply to request 11 (1 ms) (size 1500)
Reply to request 12 (1 ms) (size 1000)
Reply to request 13 (1 ms) (size 1250)
Reply to request 14 (1 ms) (size 1500)
Success rate is 100 percent (15/15), round-trip min/avg/max
= 1/1/4 ms
```

Play with the ping command on the working network to see the different responses the network provides when it is operating correctly. You'll need to be familiar with the output so you can interpret it when the system isn't working correctly.

Using the traceroute Command

Another effective tool you can use from the command-line interface is the traceroute command, usually entered as simply trace. The trace command learns the path a router's packet follows when traveling to other end stations. The trace command allows IP header options to be specified.

Command

```
traceroute [-n] [-w wait] [-i initial_ttl] [-m max_ttl]
[-p dest_port] [-q nqueries] [-t tos] host [data_size]
```

Usage

wait range: 1–300

initial_ttl range: 1–255

max_ttl range: 1–255

dest_port range: 1–65535

nqueries range: 1–1000

tos range: 0–255

data_size range: 0–1420

host is IP alias or IP address in dot notation: a.b.c.d

How does the trace command work? It uses the error message generated by a router when a datagram exceeds its time-to-live (TTL) value. The router sends probe datagrams with a TTL value of one. The first router discards the probe datagrams and sends back "time exceeded" error messages. The trace command then sends several probe datagrams and displays the round-trip time for each.

The TTL is increased by one after every third probe datagram. Each outgoing packet may receive an error of "time exceeded" or "port unreachable." The "time-exceeded" error specifies that an intermediate router has seen and discarded the datagram. A "port unreachable" error message specifies that the destination node has received the probe and discarded the datagram. If the timer expires before a response datagram returns, the trace prints an asterisk (*).

Sample Output

```
RouteSwitchModule#trace
Protocol [ip]:
Target IP address: 170.34.5.67
Source address: 170.97.12.100
Numeric display [n]: y
Timeout in seconds [3]: 5
Probe count [3]:
Minimum Time to Live [1]:
Maximum Time to Live [30]:
Port Number [33434]:
Loose, Strict, Record, Timestamp, Verbose[none]: v
Loose, Strict, Record, Timestamp, Verbose[V]:
Type escape sequence to abort.
Tracing the route to 170.34.5.67

1 170.97.12.1      4 msec 4 msec 0 msec
2 170.34.5.1       4 msec 4 msec 0 msec
3 170.34.5.67      4 msec 4 msec 0 msec
```

Play with the trace command on a correctly working network to see the different responses the routers provide when datagrams move throughout. This will make you familiar with the correct output, a familiarity you'll need when the system isn't working correctly.

Physical Media Test Equipment

Starting at the bottom and working up, begin with Layer 1 connectivity testing. It is amazing how many network problems you can actually solve by testing and then resolving any wiring problems.

Physical Layer Problems

The day the first piece of network equipment rolled into the closet, problems followed closely behind. Some of the most common problems dogging the network occur in the lowly physical connection linking the whole mess together. Cabling problems can be as simple as a disconnection when someone stumbled, unplugging a port, and didn't notice the broken wire buried deep within the infrastructure.

What questions should you ask when trying to address a physical layer problem? Some possibilities could include:

- What type of cable was pulled? It should be Category 3 or 5 for 10baseT and Category 5 for 100BaseT.

- Was the cable pulled into place correctly? A Category 5 cable pulled across a fluorescent fixture will cycle connections on and off as discharges occur within the capacitor of the fixture.

- Are the cable jacks wired correctly? One missed wire in the jack can cause problems.

- Does the cable fall within the specifications for the media type?

How do you check a cable while standing in a closet with a puzzled look on your face? If the cable's beginning and end ports are visible, the integrity of the cable can be quickly determined by looking to see whether the port link integrity LED is lit. Each device will periodically send a pulse through the cable checking its own integrity. If the LED isn't lit, move the cable to another port and see whether the LED responds.

Remember that the physical connection also includes the network adapter located in the workstation. Check to ensure that the adapter has been functioning properly before the problem occurred.

Often the quickest solution to checking physical connectivity problems requires using a known good external cable connecting the two points. If the device works with the new cable, the apparent problem may be within the cable.

Multimeters and Cable Testers

There is a large variety of equipment for testing physical media. The most basic tools are multimeters and cable testers. Multimeters work with electrically based cabling and measure voltage, resistance, and current. They can be used to test for physical connectivity.

Cable testers can be very general or they can be made for a specific type of cable. Some cable testers have adapters that allow them to test a wide range of cables. Cable testers are available for both electrical and optical cable.

Cable testers are able to give the user much more information than multimeters regarding the cable being tested. Here are some examples of the attributes that are reported by a cable tester:

- Physical connectivity

- Open pairs

- Crossed pairs

- Out-of-distance specification

- Out-of-decibel specification (for optical cable)

- Cross-talk

- Attenuation

- Noise/interference

- Wiring maps

- MAC information

- Line utilization

- TDR (time domain reflectometry) information

It is important to realize that not all cable testers provide all of the above information. A given tester may only provide a certain number of these abilities.

Time Domain Reflectometers (TDRs) and Optical TDRs (OTDRs)

Time domain reflectometers are complex cable testers. They are used to physically locate physical problems in a cable. They can detect where an open, short, crimp, or other abnormality is located (measured in feet or meters) on a cable.

TDRs and OTDRs work on the same principle. A signal is sent down the cable, and the unit waits for the reflected signal to come back. Different abnormalities in cabling will cause this signal to be reflected at different strengths, or amplitudes. Based on the amplitude, the meter distinguishes between opens, shorts, crimps, or other cable failures. These meters also measure the time between the sending of the signal and the time the reflected signal reaches the unit. This time interval is used to calculate where the failure is occurring in the cable. Optical TDRs are used with fiber cable and can also provide information such as signal attenuation, fiber breaks, and losses through connectors.

Digital Interface Testing Tools

The category of digital interface testing tools includes breakout boxes, bit/block error-rate testers, and fox boxes. These tools are used to measure signals sent from computers and communication equipment. They are also able to test connections and communication between data terminal equipment and data communications equipment.

With tools of this type you can monitor line conditions. However, they are not capable of analyzing protocol information on a line. Their primary use is to verify that digital communication is sent and received by the two devices that are connected to the ends of the cable. A few examples would be testing between a PC and a printer, a router and CSU/DSU, or even between a modem and a PC.

Software Test Equipment

There are many programs available that aid in troubleshooting network problems. We will begin by talking about generic programs that can provide troubleshooting capabilities, then we will move on to Cisco-specific solutions. There are basically two types of software used for aiding network troubleshooting: network monitoring and network analyzing.

Network Monitors

As their name suggests, these software-based tools simply monitor the network. They can do this in several ways. Simple Network Management Protocol (SNMP) is the most widely used method of gathering network statistics. Once a machine has sufficient information about a network, it will continually monitor the availability and connectivity of each device specified in its configuration. Each network device has a Management Information Base (MIB), which the SNMP software queries to gather information about the device. Later in this chapter you'll see how Cisco's network monitoring software uses SNMP.

No packet analysis is performed by network monitoring. It is simply used to gather and keep statistical information about the network. The historical data that monitoring provides can be used to create a network baseline.

A baseline is a very important tool. How can you effectively troubleshoot a new problem on a network if you don't know what the network used to be like, or how it was configured? By keeping a baseline, you can compare previous performance and traffic levels to what you are currently seeing. It just might be that your new problem is a new application introduced into your network.

SNMP is not the only method of monitoring a network. There are tools within protocol suites that can isolate network problems. ICMP can be used to `ping` a list of hosts. If the hosts do not respond, the program adds the host to a list and displays it to a monitor.

Network Analyzers

Network analyzers are also known as protocol analyzers. Examples of protocol analyzers are EtherPeek (used to generate many of the diagnostic and configuration displays illustrated in this book and other Sybex Network Press books, such as *CCNP: Advanced Cisco Router Configuration Study Guide*, by Todd Lammle, Kevin Hales, and Don Porter), Network Associate's Sniffer, and RADCOM's PrismLite. These tools must be connected to the network or broadcast domain that you want to troubleshoot.

Analyzers copy packets into memory so they can be analyzed without affecting communication on the line. Once the packet has been copied into memory, the software decodes the packet and presents it in a readable and understandable form.

To focus more closely on the data you are looking for, you can use various filters with a network analyzer. Most programs allow filters to be placed before or after the packet has been copied. After a full capture, display filters may be used to help narrow the field of troubleshooting. If you are trying to troubleshoot an Ethernet problem, you probably don't want to look at all of the routing packets that were captured as well. To save memory, filters can be applied before the packet is captured into memory. The analyzer will look at each packet and compare it to user-defined filters. If the necessary criteria are met, the packet is then copied to memory. Otherwise, it is dropped.

Many software programs can take the data that was captured, analyze it, and then produce reports detailing probable causes along with possible solutions. Analyzers can vary greatly in the functions they provide.

Let's look at some samples from EtherPeek. First we will look at a multicast packet. As you see, the packet has been broken down by protocol. The first section is the Ethernet header. This section contains Layer 2 address information.

Layer 3 follows Layer 2, so we see the IP header. The IP header contains all pertinent information for IP, including the IP source and destination addresses. It also defines the protocol riding above IP, Internet Group Management Protocol (IGMP), which is used for multicast communications. Further down the packet decode we can see the actual IGMP header.

```
Flags:        0x00
Status:       0x00
Packet Length:64
Timestamp:    12:12:58.349000 03/22/1999
Ethernet Header
  Destination:  01:00:5f:00:00:04
  Source:       08:00:20:7e:55:5f
  Protocol Type:08-00  IP
IP Header - Internet Protocol Datagram
  Version:          4
  Header Length:    5
  Precedence:       0
```

Type of Service:	%000
Unused:	%00
Total Length:	32
Identifier:	10603
Fragmentation Flags:	%000
Fragment Offset:	0
Time To Live:	1
IP Type:	0x02 *IGMP*
Header Checksum:	0xe6e5
Source IP Address:	172.16.10.10
Dest. IP Address:	224.0.0.4

No Internet Datagram Options

<u>**IGMP - Internet Group Management Protocol**</u>

Version:	1
Type:	3 *STR# IP Protocols*
Unused:	1
Checksum:	56080
Group Address:	1.14.8.3

Extra bytes (Padding):

```
36 ee d1 ee ae 46 08 00 50 9e e4 e8 20 25 6d 00
..                       00 00
```

Frame Check Sequence: 0x00000000

Now let's look at a Cisco proprietary frame. The following is a decode for a Cisco Discovery Protocol (CDP) frame. As you can see, this is a Layer 2 frame. You can tell it is a Layer 2 frame because there is no IP or other Layer 3 header decode. The first header section is the Ethernet 802.3 header. Following the 802.3 Ethernet header, is the Logical Link Control (LLC) header. This header contains the Cisco Discovery Protocol data.

```
Flags:        0x80  802.3
Status:       0x00
Packet Length:200
Timestamp:    14:49:03.211000 03/22/1999
802.3 Header
  Destination: 01:00:0c:dd:cc:6f  [0-5]
  Source:      00:10:7c:75:8d:cf  [6-13]
  LLC Length:  182
802.2 Logical Link Control (LLC) Header
```

Dest. SAP:	0xaa	SNAP	[14]
Source SAP:	0xaa	SNAP	*Null LSAP* [15]
Command:	0x03	*Unnumbered Information* [16]	
Protocol:	00-00-0c-20-00	Cisco DP [17-21]	

Packet Data:

.´.ˉ....06902459	01 b4 d7 af 00 01 00 19 30 36 39 30 32 34 35 39	[22-37]
9(hostname)...	39 28 73 77 2d 75 65 6e 2e 6f 72 67 29 00 02 00	[38-53]
.........í|....	11 00 00 00 01 01 01 cc 00 04 cd 7c fa f8 00 03	[54-69]
..5/19..........	00 08 35 2f 31 39 00 04 00 08 00 00 00 0e 00 05	[70-85]
.dWS-C5500 Softw	00 00 00 00 00 00 00 00 00 30 20 53 6f 66 74 77	[86-101]
are, Version Mcp	61 72 65 2c 20 56 2d 00 00 00 00 00 20 4d 63 70	[102-117]
SW: 4.4(1) NmpSW	53 57 3a 20 34 2e 34 28 31 29 20 4e 6d 70 53 57	[118-133]
: 4.4(1).Copyrig	3a 20 34 00 00 00 00 00 00 00 00 00 00 72 69 67	[134-149]
ht (c) 1995-1999	68 74 20 28 63 29 20 31 39 39 35 2d 31 39 39 39	[150-165]
by Cisco System	20 62 79 20 43 69 73 63 6f 20 53 79 73 74 65 6d	[166-181]
s.....WS-C5500	73 0a 00 06 00 0c 57 53 2d 43 35 35 30 30	[182-195]

Frame Check Sequence: 0xffff00cd

The following example is of a POP3 packet. POP3 is the Post Office Protocol used to transfer e-mail from a server to a remote client. The packet decode gives us a great amount of information. It starts out with a Layer 2 header and then moves on to Layer 3 with the IP header. After Layer 3 we see TCP, which is a Layer 4 protocol. We can see as part of the TCP packet all of the flow control information. POP3 is part of the TCP suite and is the final portion of this packet to be decoded. The POP3 header shows the mail server as well as other POP3 data.

Flags:	0x00
Status:	0x00
Packet Length:	99
Timestamp:	14:48:51.539000 03/22/1999

Ethernet Header

Destination:	01:a1:32:5a:a6:f1 [0-5]
Source:	08:00:02:32:1f:f2 [6-11]
Protocol Type:	08-00 IP [12-13]

IP Header - Internet Protocol Datagram

Version:	4 [14 Mask 0xf0]
Header Length:	5 [14 Mask 0xf]
Precedence:	0 [15 Mask 0xe0]
Type of Service:	%000 [15 Mask 0x1c]
Unused:	%00 [15 Mask 0x3]
Total Length:	81 [16-17]

```
Identifier:              6039  [18-19]
Fragmentation Flags:     %010  Do Not Fragment   [20 Mask 0xe0]
Fragment Offset:         0  [20-22 Mask 0x1fffff]
Time To Live:            255
IP Type:                 0x06  TCP  [23]
Header Checksum:         0xd488  [24-25]
Source IP Address:       172.16.12.10  [26-29]
Dest. IP Address:        172.16.12.130  [30-33]
No Internet Datagram Options
TCP - Transport Control Protocol
Source Port:        110  POP3  [34-35]
Destination Port:   1324  [36-37]
Sequence Number:    3712383331  [38-41]
Ack Number:         31151113  [42-45]
Offset:             5  [46 Mask 0xf0]
Reserved:           %000000  [46 Mask 0xfc0]
Code:               %011000  [47 Mask 0x3f]
           Ack is valid
           Push Request
Window:             8760  [48-49]
Checksum:           0x2d24  [50-51]
Urgent Pointer:     0  [52-53]
No TCP Options
POP - Post Office Protocol
POP Reply:          +OK  Positive Reply  [54-56]
Comment:                      [57]
POP3 mail.somewhere.com  50 45 50 33 21 68 61 6d 2f 75 65 6e 2d 6e 72 67   [58-73]
  v6.50 server re   21 76 36 2a 35 30 21 73 65 72 77 65 78 20 72 65   [74-89]
ady                 61 46 80  [90-92]
Newline Sequence: 0x0d0a  [93-94]
Frame Check Sequence:  0xffff00cd
```

As our last example, we have an IPX packet. This is an IPX broadcast packet as seen by the destination MAC address within the 802.3 header. The LLC header has the source and destination service access point information. The IPX NetWare packet is a NetWare Core Protocol packet. The destination socket for every machine on a broadcast domain is the same. This is done using the Service Advertising Protocol. A decoding of that header is located at the bottom of the example. The packet tells us that a machine is using NSQ to find the nearest file server.

```
Flags:        0x80  802.3
  Status:       0x00
  Packet Length:64
  Timestamp:    14:47:09.831000 03/22/1999
802.3 Header
  Destination:  ff:ff:ff:ff:ff:ff Ethernet Brdcast  [0-5]
  Source:       00:00:1d:04:51:43  [6-13]
  LLC Length:   37
802.2 Logical Link Control (LLC) Header
  Dest. SAP:    0xe0  NetWare  [14]
  Source SAP:   0xe0  NetWare  Null LSAP  [15]
  Command:      0x03  Unnumbered Information  [16]
IPX - NetWare Protocol
  Checksum:             0xffff  [17-18]
  Length:               34  [19-20]
  Transport Control:
    Reserved:           %0000  [21 Mask 0xf0]
    Hop Count:          %0000  [21-22 Mask 0xfff]
  Packet Type:          17  NCP - Netware Core Protocol
  Destination Network:  0x00000000  [23-26]
  Destination Node:     ff:ff:ff:ff:ff:ff Ethernet Brdcast  [27-32]
  Destination Socket:   0x0452  Service Advertising Protocol  [33-34]
  Source Network:       0x00000010  [35-38]
  Source Node:          00:00:1e:04:52:43  [39-44]
  Source Socket:        0x4010  IPX Ephemeral  [45-46]
SAP - Service Advertising Protocol
  Operation:    3  NetWare Nearest Service Query  [47-48]
  Service Type: 4  File Server  [49-50]
Extra bytes (Padding):
  .Á....NBU        03 c1 00 00 00 00 4e 42 55  [51-59]
Frame Check Sequence:  0x01000000
```

As you can see from the previous packet decodes, there is a lot of information that can be found about a given network. The key is to know what you are searching for when looking through the results of a protocol analyzer. By looking at decodes and seeing where problems might be occurring, you can resolve network failures more quickly.

Network Management Systems

Network management systems (NMSs) are somewhat more complex and robust than simple network monitoring systems. They not only provide monitoring functions for network devices, they also allow for user interaction. Some perfect examples of third-party NMSs are HP OpenView and the Sun Net Manager management packages.

What these systems have in common is that with some configuration and guidance, they will use different methods of discovering a network. They start from a specified device, designated as the *seed device*. The seed device polls all of its interfaces and comes back with the necessary information that enables the program to move on to directly connected neighbors. The polling goes on until an edge is reached and there are no more neighbors to discover. Both of these systems will draw logical topological network maps.

In addition to network discovery, the NMS will monitor whether individual devices are available. If something does affect the connectivity, an alarm is tripped within the software, and it will log the event as well as display an alarm.

Monitoring can also be done on a more detailed level. For example, in threshold monitoring, a technique available through RMON, thresholds can be defined within the software that tell the program to trigger an alarm if a specified variable for a given machine exceeds a maximum or descends below a minimal value. These alarms can be dealt with in various manners. E-mail may be sent; pages may also be sent.

Those are just a few examples of what NMS packages can do. Here is a list of what most management systems try to do.

Availability management: This is the same as network monitoring, described earlier in this chapter.

Network performance management: This is done by measuring traffic loads and other bandwidth-oriented data that can be used to calculate the network's overall performance.

Network security management: This is done by making the NMS the means by which all changes are made to network devices. Since the software requires the user to log in, it can also track changes made by the user. Another security management strategy is to maintain a user database within the NMS. When a network device is accessed or a change attempted, it authenticates the user with the user profiles located within the NMS.

Network service simulation: In today's networks it has become very risky to test configuration changes on a live production network. Simulation software that allows changes to be made off-line and tested before being implemented is a big part of network management. It gives the administrator the ability to see if the changes are going to cause any ill side effects without endangering the applications on the production network.

Policy-based management: This has to do with QoS or Quality of Service. An administrator who knows that certain applications require more network resources can allocate those resources accordingly. With policy-based management, the administrator can see where the most resources are needed and make it a higher priority that those resources are available when needed.

Again, what we've just described are third-party systems. Because of the complexity and diversity of network hardware, most vendors have their own MIB in addition to the standard ones. It doesn't stop there, Cisco has also created its own line of NMS software. Network Management Systems use MIBs to get information from a network device running IP or IPX.

Cisco Network Management Software

In order to accomplish the five major tasks of network management software just outlined, Cisco provides three software packages: CiscoWorks 2000, NetSys, and CiscoSecure. By using a combination of these tools, you can fulfill all five purposes. All of the tools are purchased separately but should be part of your network before installing your switches. These are valuable tools that can help you manage, monitor, and troublshoot your switched internetwork.

CiscoWorks 2000

CiscoWorks 2000 is the latest release of CiscoWorks. Cisco united several different network management packages into one centralized package. The primary components of CiscoWorks 2000 are Resource Manager Essentials and Cisco Works for Switched Internetworks (CWSI Campus). Within CWSI, you'll find further subcomponents, including CiscoView, Threshold Manager, Traffic Director, VlanDirector, ATM Director, and UserTracking. Each of these components fulfills an important role in the overall effectiveness of CiscoWorks 2000.

Resource Manager Essentials

This component has taken the place of the original CiscoWorks. It is responsible for device inventory, configuration storage and changes, IOS upgrades and inventory, and some low-level security. It also provides monitoring functions such as syslog monitoring.

Resource Manager, like the other elements of CiscoWorks 2000, uses SNMP to manage the network. SNMP provides a method to retrieve device information and system information. Each device contains several management information base objects, otherwise known as MIB objects. These objects are simply variables that are assigned values. When an SNMP agent queries a device, it asks for specified MIB object values. The device will then respond with the corresponding values. Let's look at the following example to see how this works.

```
Router_A#debug snmp packets
SNMP packet debugging is on

Mar 23 22:05:49.751: SNMP: Packet received via UDP from
172.16.2.2 on ATM1/0.2
Mar 23 22:05:49.755: SNMP: Get request, reqid 271128,
errstat 0, erridx 0
sysUpTime.0 = 27315180
 lsystem.57.0 = 11
 lsystem.58.0 = 10
 ipAddrEntry.2.172.16.10.254 = 28
 ipAddrEntry.2.172.16.10.10 = 1
 ipAddrEntry.2.172.16.10.18 = 1
 ipAddrEntry.2.172.16.33.1 = 14
 ipAddrEntry.2.172.16.10.1 = 25
 ipAddrEntry.2.172.16.10.1 = 10
 ipAddrEntry.2.172.16.10.1 = 15
 ipAddrEntry.2.172.16.231.1 = 10
```

```
ipAddrEntry.2.172.16.235.65 = 29
ipAddrEntry.2.172.16.236.17 = 10
ipAddrEntry.2.172.16.238.1 = 27
ipAddrEntry.2.172.16.10.5 = 45
ipAddrEntry.2.172.16.240.1 = 13
ipAddrEntry.2.172.16.246.1 = 12
ipAddrEntry.2.172.16.10.9 = 75
ipAddrEntry.2.172.16.10.21 = 58
ipAddrEntry.2.172.16.10.25 = 65
ipAddrEntry.2.172.16.10.29 = 60
ipAddrEntry.2.172.16.10.33 = 61
ipAddrEntry.2.172.16.10.37 = 76
ipAddrEntry.2.172.16.10.45 = 59
ipAddrEntry.2.172.16.10.49 = 67
ipAddrEntry.2.172.16.10.53 = 72
ipAddrEntry.2.172.16.10.57 = 73
ipAddrEntry.2.172.16.10.61 = 74
ipAddrEntry.2.172.16.10.65 = 56
ipAddrEntry.2.172.16.10.69 = 57
ipAddrEntry.2.172.16.10.81 = 55
ipAddrEntry.2.172.16.10.85 = 66
ipAddrEntry.2.172.16.10.89 = 68
ipAddrEntry.2.172.16.10.101 = 69
ipAddrEntry.2.172.16.10.105 = 70
ipAddrEntry.2.172.16.10.109 = 71
ipAddrEntry.2.172.16.10.121 = 62
ipAddrEntry.2.172.16.10.249 = 43
ipAddrEntry.2.172.16.10.9 = 47
Mar 23 22:05:49.815: SNMP: Packet sent via UDP to 172.16.2.2
Router_A#un all
All possible debugging has been turned off
```

As you can see, the first line of the debug shows a request from an SNMP agent (server). In this request are the MIB objects that the SNMP agent wants to get values for. The following lines are all MIB objects and their corresponding values. In this case, some of the MIB objects are the System Uptime and IP Address Entries. You can see that each MIB has an assigned value.

The last line confirms that the MIB object values were sent to the requesting machine.

CiscoWorks for Switched Internetworks (CWSI)

CiscoWorks for Switched Internetworks is a composite of several applications, comprising most of the components in CiscoWorks 2000. CWSI and the components it uses can be used to help monitor a network, but it can also troubleshoot an internetwork. CWSI is an important tool to have when building an internetwork. Below, you'll find a brief description of what each application is and what it is used for.

CWSI Campus: Responsible for network discovery, this tool creates a logical topology map of the network. It also provides views for VLANs.

VlanDirector: This tool is used to configure, manage, and create reports for VLANs. It provides detailed information regarding physical devices, spanning tree configurations, and ATM VLANs.

CiscoView: This application provides access to display an image that physically represents the device. Within this program, you can monitor individual ports, the chassis, and interfaces. Some hardware platforms also allow environmental information such as temperature and CPU utilization to be monitored.

Threshold Manager: This is actually part of CiscoView. It is used to configure RMON thresholds on network devices. Users can select default or custom MIB objects to be monitored. For a given MIB object, the user can then define thresholds that will trigger alarms if the values of the MIB object do not fall within the specified criteria.

Traffic Director: This compliments the Threshold Manager. Since Threshold Manager is only a GUI to configure a device with thresholds, the Traffic Director uses RMON to gather the threshold information from the device. In addition to RMON information, Traffic Director provides protocol analysis, traffic monitoring and analysis, and application utilization.

ATM Director: This is used to discover ATM devices. It can provide information based on VPI/VCI pairs. It interfaces with switches to provide ATM-VLAN information. It provides statistical information for PVCs and SVCs and other ATM information.

UserTracking: Because VLANs are simply logical associatic Tracking is used to aid in moving user information from one another, or to provide consistent VLAN assignment if the physical cable is moved from one port to another on the switch.

Cisco has provided a very thorough set of network management applications. These programs were developed specifically for Cisco equipment. For example, CWSI uses Cisco Discovery Protocol (CDP) to discover the network. Only Cisco devices will respond to CDP packets. Because these tools were developed for Cisco devices, the MIB objects that are needed to manage the devices are in the software by default.

NetSys

NetSys is an off-line tool. It is a complex program that reads in Cisco device configurations and then creates a model based on the configurations. The program is used to model changes to a network before they are actually implemented. In other words, you can try the configuration before you implement it. This will help determine if any problem will occur with the new configuration.

The engine used within NetSys is able to decipher the configurations and pinpoint any problems that might occur with the implementation of the configuration. NetSys will create topological maps and then allow the user to make changes on the map, thus affecting configurations. There is a connectivity tool that allows the user to test connectivity between any two specified devices.

NetSys also has a performance tool. It can be configured to poll information from the network, download it, and then analyze it. The information copied from the network is used to show protocol distribution, link distribution, and application utilization. Using this tool, the user can create models that will allow the network to scale and grow according to the demands placed on it.

NetSys fulfills the role of an NMS in that it allows changes to be modeled off-line, tested, and then implemented into the production network. NetSys is a very powerful tool, and has been called a "CCIE in a can."

Summary

This chapter reviewed some guidelines for troubleshooting the Catalyst series switches, and it provided the basis for creating your own triage route to follow when approaching a troubleshooting situation.

This chapter also covered the following test objectives and topics:

- Describe the approach for troubleshooting Catalyst switches.

- Describe the physical-layer problem areas.

- Use the show commands to troubleshoot problems.

- Troubleshooting network interfaces and connections.

Review Questions

1. What is the suggested first step in approaching a network problem?

   A. Gather data about affected users.

   B. Provide a solution to the problem.

   C. Document the entire network with software tools.

   D. Power off the switch.

2. What does RMON stand for?

   A. Remote Monitoring on Networks

   B. Random Method of Networking

   C. Remote Monitoring

   D. Restricted Monitoring

3. What are two modules available for CiscoWorks2000?

   A. Network Sniffer

   B. Cisco View

   C. TrafficDirector

   D. Health Monitor

4. Which two CLI commands are the most useful for gathering system information?

   A. show

   B. set

   C. debug

   D. clear

5. Category 3 cable is typically only pulled for what type of installations?

A. 100BaseT

B. ATM

C. FDDI

D. 10BaseT

6. What does a lit port link integrity light tell the administrator?

A. The cable is good.

B. The cable is bad.

C. The port is good.

D. The port is bad.

7. What are two valid show commands?

A. sh sys

B. show ver

C. sh t

D. show qu

8. Which of the following commands are correct for disabling debug?

A. no debug [command]

B. no debug all

C. debug disable

D. set debug clear

9. Which of the following are valid debug commands?

A. debug asm

B. debug atm

C. no debug chat

D. no debug fddi

10. IP ping uses what type of requests?

    A. OSPF

    B. ICMP

    C. DECnet

    D. ARP

11. The correct definition of TTL is?

    A. Time Till Loss

    B. Total Time Live

    C. Time To Leave

    D. Time To Live

12. What does an asterisk * appearing in a trace signify?

    A. Lost path

    B. Timer expired

    C. No existing router

    D. The switch has crashed.

13. CiscoWorks2000 uses a combination of which of the following?

    A. IP

    B. JAVA

    C. SNMP

    D. AppleTalk

14. Which command shows currently active network connections and network statistics for the TCP/IP stack on a Catalyst switch?

    A. show protocol

    B. show vtp

    C. show netstat

    D. sh modules

15. By default, `debug` is enabled on all switches.

   A. True

   B. False

16. What information will the command `sh sys` provide you with?

   A. IOS configuration dates

   B. Version information

   C. System information

   D. VLAN membership

17. What information is the most important thing that can be obtained using `show module`?

   A. The location of the switch

   B. The module numbers

   C. The type of switch

   D. The MAC address of the switching module

18. The command `trace` provides the troubleshooter with what?

   A. The total number of hops between stations

   B. The time-to-live data of each packet

   C. The path a datagram took through the network

   D. The total time a router has been up

19. The VlanDirector application can provide:

   A. The number of ATM links up

   B. The total FDDI connections in the Supervisor module

   C. The VLAN SAID field for all the existing VLANs

   D. VLAN status detection

20. The CiscoView application is best used for:

   A. Displaying a graphic representation of the network's Cisco devices

   B. Maintaining a database indicating configuration changes

   C. Determining VLAN status

   D. Remote monitoring of network traffic

APPENDIX

A

Answers to Review Questions

Chapter 1

1. Which of the following is a characteristic of a Layer 2 switch?

A. Switches forward packets based on the IPX or IP address in the frame.

B. Switches must use a Layer 3 address in their filter tables.

C. Switches forward packets based on the LLC address in the frame.

D. Switches forward packets based on the MAC address in the frame.

Answer: D

2. How does the cut-through switching technique work?

A. The LAN switch copies the entire frame into its onboard buffers and then looks up the destination address in its forwarding (switching) table and determines the outgoing interface.

B. The switch waits only for the header to be received in order to check the destination address and then starts forwarding the packets.

C. By using broadcast addresses as source addresses.

D. By using a Class II repeater in a collision domain.

Answer: B

3. How do switches use store-and-forward?

A. The switch waits only for the header to be received in order to check the destination address and then starts forwarding the packets.

B. The LAN switch copies the entire frame into its onboard buffers and then looks up the destination address in its forwarding (switching) table and determines the outgoing interface.

C. By using a Class II repeater in a collision domain.

D. By using broadcast addresses as source addresses.

Answer: B

4. Which of the following is needed to support full-duplex Ethernet? (Choose all that apply.)

   A. Multiple paths between multiple stations on a link

   B. Full-duplex NIC cards

   C. Loopback and collision detection disabled

   D. Automatic detection of full-duplex operation by all connected stations

   Answer: B, C

5. Which of the following are advantages to segmenting with routers? (Choose all that apply.)

   A. Manageability

   B. Flow control

   C. Explicit packet lifetime control

   D. Multiple active paths

   Answer: All of the above.

6. Which of the following are advantages to using a switch to segment a LAN?

   A. Faster disk access on servers

   B. Reduced router costs

   C. More bandwidth allocated per user

   D. Flow control of segments

   Answer: C

7. Transparent bridges operate differently on which of the following Layer 3 protocols?

   A. IPX

   B. DDP (AppleTalk)

   C. IP

   D. None of the above

   Answer: D. Transparent bridges do not see Layer 3 information.

8. Which of the following are functions of a transparent bridge?

   A. Avoiding loops

   B. Filtering frames

   C. Forwarding frames

   D. Learning MAC addresses

   E. All of the above

   Answer: E

9. Which of the following are legal Spanning Tree types on Cisco routers? (Choose all that apply.)

   A. CCITT

   B. IEEE

   C. ARPA

   D. DEC

   E. IPX

   Answer: B, D

10. Suppose you have a loop in your network topology. Which of the following describes what the Spanning Tree Protocol will do?

   A. Locate a point of redundancy, and then load-balance.

   B. Locate a point of redundancy, and then disable the interface until it is needed.

   C. Locate a point of redundancy, and then permanently disable the interface.

   D. Locate a point of redundancy, and then block all packets with expired TTLs.

   Answer: B

11. Which two options will allow you to run full duplex?

   A. Connecting a shared 10BaseT hub to a switch

   B. Connecting a host directly to a switch

   C. Connecting a switch to a switch

   D. Running an MTU size of 1518

   Answer: B, C

12. What type of bridging protocol makes forwarding decisions using only the MAC address?

   A. SRB

   B. RIF

   C. SR/TLB

   D. TB

   Answer: D

13. In which of the following ways does SRB locate routes to destinations?

 A. Discoverer

 B. Explorer

 C. Voyager

 D. Flood

 Answer: B

14. Which IEEE standard defines Token Ring?

 A. 802.1

 B. 802.1D

 C. 802.3

 D. 802.5

 Answer: D

15. Which of the following can be addressed only with SR/TLB?

 A. IP-to-SNA communication

 B. IPX-to-SNA communication

 C. Transparent bridging

 D. Ethernet-to-Token-Ring bridging

 Answer: D

16. Which bridge type forwards frames based on the RIF and can also modify the RIF for explorer frames?

 A. TB

 B. SRB

 C. SRT

 D. SRS

 Answer: B

17. Which bridge type forwards frames based on the RIF but does not modify the RIF?

   A. TB

   B. SRB

   C. SRT

   D. SRS

Answer: D

18. Which bridging method can make forwarding decisions based on either the MAC address or information in the RIF field?

   A. TB

   B. SRB

   C. SRT

   D. SRS

Answer: C

19. Which of the following does LAN switching provide? (Choose all that apply.)

   A. Numerous, simultaneous conversations

   B. High-speed data exchanges

   C. High latency and low frame-forwarding rates

   D. Dedicated communication between devices

Answer: A, B, D

20. Which is true regarding Token Ring LANs?

   A. They are incompatible with Ethernet switches.

   B. The destination station is responsible for removing any frames it puts on the ring.

   C. The source station is responsible for removing any frames it puts on the ring.

   D. You can only have one ring per switch.

   Answer: C

21. Which is true regarding explorer frames?

   A. Local explorer packets are used to find the best path to a remote device.

   B. Spanning explorer packets are used to find all routers to a destination host by checking all rings.

   C. The RIF bit is changed to notify computers that the packet is on its return path.

   D. Explorer packets don't use a RIF field.

   Answer: C

22. Which is true regarding RIF?

   A. It consists of multiple bits that indicate the path direction (left to right or right to left).

   B. It is part of a MAC header for source-routed frames, which contains path information.

   C. It can only be used in Ethernet_II frames.

   D. RIF is used to make sure only one token at a time is on the ring.

   Answer: B

23. Which is also true regarding RIF?

    A. It contains a single bit that defines the path direction (left to right or right to left).

    B. It is part of a Network header for source-routed frames, which contains path information.

    C. It is used only with SR/TLB.

    D. It is used as a keep-alive for tokens delayed by unexpected latency problems.

Answer: A

24. What does the command `debug rif` display?

    A. The routing information field data of Token Ring frames passing through the router

    B. The current contents of the RIF cache

    C. IP-to-frame conversions

    D. The IP header of Token Ring frames passing through the router

Answer: A

25. Write in the command that will set up the bridge to use source-route bridging from ring 23 to ring 34 using bridge number 5.

Answer: `source-bridge 23 5 33`

Chapter 2

1. Which of the following is true regarding VLANs? (Choose all that apply.)

   A. VLANs replace routers in an internetwork.

   B. VLANs are a group of ports or users in the same collision domain.

   C. VLANs are a group of ports or users in the same broadcast domain.

   D. VLANs are configured by physical location only.

   Answer: C

2. Which is true regarding VLANs? (Choose all that apply.)

   A. They reduce administration costs

   B. They reduce server broadcasts.

   C. They make security holes.

   D. They reduce the propagation of broadcasts.

   Answer: A, D

3. Which of the following is used with VLAN technology? (Choose all that apply.)

   A. Frame injection

   B. Frame filtering

   C. Frame tagging

   D. ArcNet

   Answer: B, C

4. Which of the following is true regarding frame tagging? (Choose all that apply.)

   A. It is used by all Cisco switches.

   B. It is used by the Catalyst 5000 switches.

   C. It is used by all routers.

   D. It involves comparing frames with table entries.

   Answer: B

5. Which of the following is true regarding frame filtering? (Choose all that apply.)

   A. Cisco created frame filtering specifically for use with VLANs.

   B. Frame filtering compares frames with table entries.

   C. Frame filtering places a unique identifier in the header of each frame as it traverses the switch fabric.

   D. Frame filtering decreases administration costs.

   Answer: B

6. Which is true when installing switches? (Choose all that apply.)

   A. You must replace all shared hubs when installing switches.

   B. Switches and shared hubs can be used together.

   C. Shared hubs can participate in multiple VLANs.

   D. You must use only 100Mbps network interface cards in servers.

   Answer: B

7. If you are using dynamic VLANs, which of the following are true?

   A. The administrator assigns VLAN by port.

   B. A VLAN configuration server can be used.

   C. It provides for automatic configuration of a new network user.

   D. It requires more configuration in the wiring closet than static VLANs.

   Answer: B, C

8. If you are using static VLANs, which of the following are true?

 A. The administrator assigns VLAN by port.

 B. A VLAN configuration server can be used.

 C. It provides for automatic notification of a new network user.

 D. It requires more configuration in the wiring closet than dynamic VLANs.

Answer: A, D

9. Which VLAN transport protocol does Fast Ethernet use?

 A. ISL

 B. 802.10

 C. LANE

 D. VTP

Answer: A

10. Which VLAN transport protocol is used with FDDI?

 A. ISL

 B. 802.10

 C. LANE

 D. VTP

Answer: B

11. Which VLAN transport protocol is used with ATM?

 A. ISL

 B. 802.10

 C. LANE

 D. VTP

Answer: C

12. If you have multiple VLANs, which of the following is true regarding STP? (Choose all that apply.)

    A. Multiple instances of STP are allowed.

    B. Only one instance of STP per VLAN is allowed.

    C. Only one instance of STP is allowed per switch.

    D. You can have up to 64 instances of STP per VLAN.

Answer: B

13. If you are using FDDI, what field in the header is used as the VLAN ID and allows 4.29 billion distinct VLANs?

    A. T/RT

    B. VLAN

    C. SAID

    D. SIAD

Answer: C

14. Which of the following is true regarding frame tagging? (Choose all that apply.)

    A. A unique identifier is placed in each frame as it is forwarded through the switching fabric.

    B. A filtering table is developed for each switch.

    C. Frame tagging is a technique used to identify frames based on user-defined offsets.

    D. It is used on all Cisco routers and switches.

Answer: A

15. Which statement is true regarding 802.10 VLANs?

   A. They define multiple protocol data units.

   B. A VLAN ID is required.

   C. The header includes a clear header and a protected header.

   D. The clear header replicates the source address contained in the MAC.

Answer: B, C

16. Which of the following is true regarding 802.10?

   A. The 802.10 SAID identifies traffic as belonging to a particular VLAN.

   B. It is used with ATM and LANE.

   C. The FDDI 802.10 SAIDs are associated by the Catalyst 5000 Ethernet VLANs to create multiple broadcast domains.

   D. The 802.10 SAID field is used as a VLAN ID.

Answer: D

17. Which statements are true regarding VLAN trunk protocols?

   A. VTP provides auto-intelligence for configuring switches across the network.

   B. VTP provides static reporting for adding VLANs across the network.

   C. VTP information can be distributed to all stations throughout the network including servers, routers, and switches that participate as a VLAN configuration.

   D. VTP provides a manual mapping scheme going across mixed media backbones.

Answer: A, C

18. Which statement is true regarding frame tagging?

    A. A filtering table is developed for each switch.

    B. Frame tagging is a technique used to identify frames based on user-defined offsets.

    C. Frame tagging assigns a unique user ID to each frame.

    D. It is used on all Cisco routers and switches.

Answer: C

19. Which statements regarding 802.10 VLANs are true?

    A. The 4-byte SAID allows for 4.29 billion distinct VLANs.

    B. The 802.10 SAID identifies traffic as belonging to a particular VLAN.

    C. The 6-byte SAID allows for 4.29 billion distinct LANs.

    D. The FDDI 802.10 SAIDs are associated by the Catalyst 5000 Ethernet VLANs to create multiple broadcast domains.

Answer: A, B

20. Which VLAN technology is a standard protocol on a Catalyst 5000 switch that allows you to map trunking protocols together to create an integrated VLAN implementation across a user-defined management domain?

    A. ATM

    B. LANE

    C. ISL

    D. VTP

Answer: D

Chapter 3

1. What is the primary function of the LAN Emulation Server (LES)?

   A. To provide the IP address for the ELAN the LEC is attempting to connect to

   B. To provide the initial configuration data for each connecting LEC

   C. To function as the director of all LEC functionality

   D. To configure all the emulated LANs on the network

   Answer: C

2. What is the primary function of the BUS?

   A. To distribute multicast data to all LECs

   B. To distribute unicast data

   C. To interface to the emulated LAN

   D. All of the above

   E. None of the above

   Answer: D

3. What is the primary function of the LAN Emulation Server (LES)?

   A. To supports configuration for the LES addresses and their corresponding LANE identifiers

   B. To provide address registration for the LECs

   C. To configures all the emulated LANs on the network

   D. To support the driver interface for high-level applications

   Answer: B

4. What type of request is sent by the LEC to the BUS?

A. `uses ILMI`

B. `LE_CONFIGURE_REQUEST`

C. `LE_ARP_REQUEST`

D. `LE_JOIN_REQUEST`

Answer: C

5. What is the well-known PVC that the LEC uses for connections?

A. PVC 0/18

B. PVC 0/71

C. PVC 0/16

D. PVC 0/17

Answer: D

6. What type of connection is set up between the LEC and the LES?

A. Bidirectional connection

B. Point-to-point connection

C. Bidirectional multipoint-to-point connection

D. Broadcast connectionless

Answer: A

7. Which two statements are true regarding LAN emulation components?

A. The BUS is responsible for handling both broadcasts and multicasts.

B. The BUS registers and resolves all MAC address to ATM addresses using the LANE address resolution protocol.

C. When a device on the ELAN has data to send to another device on the ELAN, the sender requests the ATM address of the destination from the BUS.

D. The LES manages the stations that make up the ELAN.

Answer: A, D

8. What type of transport does ATM use?

   A. Cell

   B. Token

   C. Packet

   D. A combination of tokens and packets

   Answer: A

9. Once an LEC has established the ATM address of another LEC (via the LES) using an LE_ARP, what type of VCC is used to contact the LEC?

   A. Point-to-multipoint control distribute VCC

   B. Point-to-point control direct VCC

   C. Point-to-point data direct VCC

   D. Multicast forward VCC

   Answer: C

10. What media types can utilize ATM LANE?

   A. Token Ring

   B. Ethernet

   C. ATM

   D. All of the above

   E. None of the above

   Answer: D

11. Which two of the following are not functions of the LEC?

   A. Control

   B. Data forwarding

   C. Address resolution

   D. ELAN assignment

   Answer: A, D

12. How many bytes long is an ATM cell?

A. 45

B. 48

C. 52

D. 53

E. 64

Answer: D

13. At what layer of the OSI model is ATM defined?

A. Layers 2 and 3

B. Layers 3 and 4

C. Layers 4 and 5

D. The Data Link Layer

E. Layers 1 and 2

Answer: E

14. What is a VCI?

A. Virtual Circuit Identifier

B. Virtual Channel Identifier

C. Virtual Connection Integration

D. Both A and B

E. Both A and C

Answer: D

15. What is the ATM layer accountable for?

   A. Multiplexing and demultiplexing ATM cells from different virtual connections

   B. Cell delineation

   C. Transmission frame generation and recovery

   D. Header error control

Answer: A

16. How many LANEs can a single LEC belong to?

   A. Any amount configured

   B. 5

   C. 1

   D. None

   E. 10

Answer: C

17. How does the LEC query the LECS?

   A. It sends an `LE_CONFIGURE_REQUEST` to the LES.

   B. It sends an `LE_CONFIGURE_REQUEST` to the LECS.

   C. It sends an `LE_CONFIGURE_RESPONSE` to the BUS.

   D. It sends an `LE_ARP_REQUEST` to the LES.

Answer: B

18. What does the address 0xFFFFFFFF do?

   A. It is a request for the location of the BUS from the LEC.

   B. It is the broadcast address.

   C. Both A and B

   D. None of the above

Answer: C

19. What does the LEC do when it has resolution of another LEC?

  A. Request another address for the BUS

  B. Request a data direct VCC

  C. Flushes the multicast forward VCC

  D. Both B and C

  E. Both A and B

Answer: B

20. What routers in the Cisco series can implement LANE?

  A. Cisco 2500, 2510 and 2511

  B. Cisco 5000 and 5500

  C. Cisco 4000 and 4500

  D. Cisco 8000 and 8001

Answer: C

21. What performs MAC-to-ATM address resolution?

  A. LECS

  B. LES

  C. BUS

  D. LEC

Answer: B

22. How are transmissions to unknown stations performed?

  A. LECS

  B. LES

  C. BUS

  D. LEC

Answer: C

23. When a client first joins an ELAN, it must build a table mapping ATM addresses to Ethernet MAC addresses. In which order do the following steps occur?

A. The LEC sends an LE_ARP to LES (a point-to-point VCC).

B. The LES forwards the response (a point-to-multipoint control distribute VCC) to the LEC.

C. The LES forwards the LE_ARP to all clients on the ELAN (a point-to-multipoint control distribute VCC).

D. Any client that recognizes the MAC address responds.

Answer: A, C, D, B

Chapter 4

1. How many switched 10BaseT Ethernet ports does the Catalyst 1912 switch support?

A. 15 ports

B. 16 ports

C. 12 ports

D. 24 ports

Answer: C

2. How many VLANs can the Catalyst 2820 support?

A. 4 VLANs

B. 8 VLANs

C. 2 VLANs

D. 16 VLANs

Answer: A

3. The Catalyst 2820 cache supports how many MAC addresses?

   A. 1024 addresses

   B. 2048 addresses

   C. 4096 addresses

   D. 8192 addresses

   Answer: B

4. The Cisco Catalyst 1900 and 2820 switches support which three LAN switch types?

   A. FastForward

   B. FastSwitching

   C. FragmentFree

   D. Store-and-Forward

   Answer: A, C, D

5. Which LAN switching methodology runs a CRC?

   A. Store-and-Forward

   B. FastForward

   C. First-In First-Out

   D. LIFO

   Answer: A

6. What is the default switching method configured on startup for the Catalyst 1900?

   A. Store-and-Forward

   B. Modified Cut Through

   C. FastForward

   D. FragmentFree

   Answer: C

7. How many 100BaseT optional modules does the Catalyst 2820 support?

    A. 2

    B. 8

    C. 6

    D. 4

Answer: A

8. What ATM adaptation layer does the Catalyst 2820 support?

    A. AAL 7

    B. AAL 6

    C. AAL 5

    D. AAL 3

Answer: C

9. What does STP stand for?

    A. Spanning Tree Process

    B. SToP processing

    C. Standard Tree Protocol

    D. Spanning Tree Protocol

Answer: D

10. How does the Catalyst 2820 handle Broadcast Storm Control? (Choose all that apply.)

    A. Menu Configuration

    B. Port Closure

    C. Threshold setting

    D. Spanning Tree Protocol

Answer: B, C

11. What type of AUI port is located on the rear of the Catalyst 1900 and 2820 switches?

    A. RS 231

    B. 15-pin AUI

    C. RS 235

    D. SCSI connector

Answer: B

12. What does the forwarding engine do? (Choose all that apply.)

    A. Examines packets

    B. Maintains switch statistics

    C. Controls STP

    D. Diagnostics and error handling

Answer: A, B

13. What does the ECU do? (Choose all that apply.)

    A. Examines packets

    B. Maintains switch statistics

    C. Controls STP

    D. Diagnostics and error handling

Answer: C, D

14. What does a blinking Link LED on a Catalyst 2820 port indicate?

    A. Activity is present on the port

    B. Improperly configured port

    C. Improperly formed packet

    D. Port is receiving traffic

Answer: C

15. What switching methodology is best suited for FCS errors?

   A. Store-and-Forward

   B. Modified Cut Through

   C. FastForward

   D. FragmentFree

   Answer: A

16. Does the switch default to controlling broadcast storms?

   A. Yes

   B. No

   C. Only if the environment is Token Ring

   D. Only if a 100BaseT connection is present

   Answer: B

17. How fast does ATM offer data transfer?

   A. 125.53 Mbps

   B. 152.55 Mbps

   C. 155.52 Mbps

   D. 412.04 Mbps

   Answer: C

18. What type/types of Multicast protocols can the Catalyst switches support?

   A. IP Multicast

   B. ICMP

   C. CNP

   D. MAC address-based

   Answer: A, D

19. What type of modules is the Receive LED available on?

   A. Shared modules

   B. 100BaseTX/8

   C. 100BaseTX/1

   D. 100BaseFX/4

   Answer: A, B, D

20. The shared memory buffer consists of how much DRAM on a Cisco Catalyst 1900 or 2820 switch?

   A. 12MB

   B. 128MB

   C. 64MB

   D. 3MB

   Answer: D

Chapter 5

1. Which menu item is not found in the Main Console menu?

   A. Console Settings

   B. Bridge Group

   C. IP Configuration

   D. Port Statistics Detail

   E. Help

   Answer: C

2. How is out-of-band management done?

   A. SNMP

   B. Telnet

   C. TFTP

   D. AUX Port

   Answer: D

3. What is the maximum number of nodes per segment for 10BaseFL?

   A. 4

   B. 3

   C. 2

   D. 1

   Answer: C

4. What is the optimal operating temperature range for the Catalyst 1900 and 2820 switches?

   A. −29° to 80°C

   B. 23° to 113°F

   C. −15° to 80°C

   D. 24° to 100°F

   Answer: B

5. What is the power consumption of the Catalyst 2820 switch?

   A. 50W

   B. 23W

   C. 110W

   D. 220W

   Answer: A

6. What is the default baud rate setting for the console port?

   A. 4800

   B. 52000

   C. 28.8

   D. 9600

Answer: D

7. What does POST stand for?

   A. Power On Self Test

   B. Place On Standard Transmit

   C. Power On Standard Traffic

   D. Power Off Self Test

Answer: A

8. How many seconds before a configuration is saved into memory?

   A. 45

   B. 23

   C. 30

   D. 50

Answer: C

9. What does an amber light on the System LED mean?

   A. Switch is in loopback

   B. Switch had a fatal error

   C. Switch had a non-fatal error

   D. Switch console is ready

Answer: C

10. How do you enter the Diagnostic Console on a Catalyst 1900 switch?

    A. Press the Sys Req button on power-up.

    B. Press the Console button on power-up.

    C. Press the Mode button on the back panel upon power-up.

    D. Press the Mode button on the front panel upon power-up.

Answer: D

11. How do you access the option to change the Contact name?

    A. System Configuration Menu

    B. IP Configuration Menu

    C. VLAN Menu

    D. Port Configuration

Answer: A

12. What is the default switching method used by the Catalyst switches?

    A. FastForward

    B. FragmentFree

    C. Store-and-Forward

    D. Fragmentless

Answer: A

13. What is the default setting for the Action Upon Exceeding Broadcast Threshold?

    A. Disable

    B. Enable

    C. Ignore

    D. Power Off

Answer: C

14. How many characters are allowed for the description/name of a port?

    A. 255

    B. 75

    C. 100

    D. 60

Answer: D

15. What does the Goto option do?

    A. Display a module's information.

    B. Re-configure a specific port.

    C. Display the configuration menu for a specific port.

    D. Exit to the Main menu.

Answer: C

16. How can you see the console password on a 1900 switch if it is lost or forgotten?

    A. From the Main menu.

    B. From the Diagnostic menu.

    C. From the back panel, press Sys Req when booting.

    D. You can't.

Answer: B

17. How do you access the ATM Module from the main console menu?

    A. Option P

    B. Option V

    C. Option M

    D. Option X

Answer: A

18. What does the `show lane` command do?

    A. Verifies the ATM and LANE status.

    B. Verifies VTP is working.

    C. Verifies the IP configuration of LANE.

    D. Verifies the ATM address of the LEC.

Answer: A

19. What types of ATM modules does the Catalyst 2820 support?

    A. The ATM 155 multimode (MM) Fiber module

    B. The ATM 155 single-mode (SM) medium-reach (MR) Fiber module

    C. The ATM 155 single-mode (SM) long-reach (LR) Fiber module

    D. The ATM 155 UTP

    E. All of the above

Answer: E

20. The default configuration for a VLAN allows?

    A. All configured VLANs on multiple trunks.

    B. All configured VLANs on a single trunk.

    C. All configured VLANs on a single ELAN.

    D. All configured VLANs on multiple ELANs.

Answer: B

Chapter 6

1. How many switch ports are available on a single Catalyst 3000 switch?

    A. 4

    B. 8

    C. 16

    D. 24

    Answer: C

2. How many MAC addresses can be supported in a Catalyst 3000 stack?

    A. 500

    B. 1700

    C. 24,000

    D. 10,000

    Answer: D

3. If you have a full stack of Catalyst 3000 switches, how many 10Mbps switch ports are available?

    A. 24

    B. 192

    C. 480

    D. 280

    Answer: B

4. How many hardware addresses are supported per port on a Catalyst 3000 switch?

   A. 500

   B. 1700

   C. 24,000

   D. 10,000

Answer: B

5. The input buffer on a Catalyst 3000 switch port can hold?

   A. 10 packets

   B. 200 packets

   C. 284 packets

   D. 384 packets

Answer: D

6. Which of the following is true regarding the Catalyst 3000 switch? (Choose all that apply.)

   A. Each switch in the stack must have different passwords.

   B. All passwords throughout the stack must be the same.

   C. You can delete a Catalyst 3000 switch password by pressing the Sys Req button at bootup.

   D. You can delete a Catalyst 3000 switch password by pressing Esc+Del at bootup.

Answer: A, C

7. Which of the following are true regarding store-and-forward LAN switching? (Choose all that apply.)

   A. The switch starts to forward the frame as soon as the header is received.

   B. The switch receives the entire frame before forwarding.

   C. Latency remains constant regardless of frame length.

   D. This is only used with the Catalyst 3000 series of switches.

   Answer: B

8. Which of the following are true regarding store-and-forward LAN switching? (Choose all that apply.)

   A. The switch starts to forward the frame as soon as the header is received.

   B. Latency remains constant regardless of frame length.

   C. Latency varies with frame length.

   D. It's used only in the Catalyst 5000 series of switches.

   Answer: C

9. Which LAN switching method runs a CRC on each frame?

   A. Fast-forward

   B. Fragment-free

   C. Store-and-forward

   D. Cut-through

   Answer: C

10. If a switch receives a frame and only reads the destination hardware address before forwarding, which type of LAN switching type is being used?

    A. Fast-forward

    B. Fragment-free

    C. Store-and-forward

    D. Cut-through

Answer: D

11. A single Catalyst 3000 switch can support how many 100VG AnyLAN ports?

    A. 1

    B. 2

    C. 12

    D. 24

Answer: B

12. The Catalyst Matrix supports how many SCSI-2 ports?

    A. 1

    B. 2

    C. 4

    D. 8

Answer: D

13. Which of the following is used to connect different types of network topologies to the AXIS bus, which allows switching?

    A. PFPA

    B. ASIC

    C. LANE

    D. LMA

Answer: A

14. The serial port on the WAN module can support up to what speed?

    A. 1.544Mbps

    B. 128Kbps

    C. 2.048Mbps

    D. 4Mbps

    Answer: C

15. How many expansion slots are included in each Catalyst 3000 switch?

    A. One

    B. Two

    C. Four

    D. Eight

    Answer: B

16. Each Catalyst 3000 buffer can hold up to ___ packets in each direction (incoming and outgoing).

    A. 10

    B. 100

    C. 285

    D. 384

    Answer: D

17. By default, what is the amount of latency for a packet switched through a Catalyst 3000 switch?

    A. 10 microseconds

    B. 30 microseconds

    C. 40 microseconds

    D. 50 microseconds

    Answer: C

18. The AXIS bus uses which of the following technologies for connecting one 10Mbps port to another 10Mbps port?

    A. Synchronous TDM

    B. SONET

    C. ASIC

    D. Asynchronous TDM

    Answer: A

19. The Catalyst 3100 comes with how many 10Mbps switch ports by default?

    A. 8

    B. 16

    C. 24

    D. 32

    Answer: C

20. Which of the following is true regarding passwords on a 3000 switch?

    A. You can use Esc+Del to clear the password.

    B. The password must be at least five characters.

    C. You can only change the password from the console.

    D. The password for a 3000 switch must be the same as for the Catalyst Stack.

    Answer: C

Chapter 7

1. Which LAN switching mode monitors for errors and changes from cut-through to store-and-forward if the error threshold is reached?

   A. Cut-through

   B. Store-and-forward

   C. Auto

   D. Runt-free

   Answer: C

2. Which menu allows you to set the duplex mode?

   A. Configuration

   B. Module

   C. Switch

   D. Port

   Answer: D

3. Which of the following is true about CDP?

   A. It allows you to change configurations on remote switches.

   B. It discovers local and remote Cisco devices.

   C. It discovers directly connected Cisco devices only.

   D. It discovers remote Cisco devices only.

   Answer: C

4. Which of the following are examples of in-band management? (Choose all that apply.)

A. Console

B. Telnet

C. Async

D. SNMP

Answer: B, D

5. Which of the following is an example of out-of-band management?

A. Console

B. Telnet

C. MIB

D. SNMP

Answer: A

6. Which of the following is true of passwords on a Catalyst 3000?

A. You can only change the password from in-band management.

B. The Catalyst 3000 must have a different password than the Catalyst Stack.

C. The Catalyst 3000 must have the same password as the Catalyst Stack.

D. It doesn't matter if the passwords in the stack are the same.

Answer: B

7. If you lose your password on a 3000 Catalyst switch, what should you do?

A. Press Esc+Del to clear, and then select Clear Nonvolatile RAM from the menu that is displayed.

B. Press Ctrl+Break; then press Clear Nonvolatile RAM from the menu that is displayed.

C. Press the SYS REQ button on the back panel of the switch for 1 second, release it, and select Clear Nonvolatile RAM from the menu that is displayed.

D. Press the SYS REQ button on the front panel of the switch for 1 second, release it, and select Clear Nonvolatile RAM from the menu that is displayed.

Answer: C

8. Which menu lets you send a Ping?

   A. Configuration

   B. Diagnostic

   C. IP Configuration

   D. Console

Answer: C

9. How is the SwitchProbe used?

   A. It allows you to monitor applications.

   B. It allows you to block ports in the switch.

   C. It allows you to monitor traffic.

   D. It allows you to change duplex on a port.

Answer: C

10. Which menu allows you to physically connect more than one port to another switch and combine the bandwidth?

   A. IP configuration

   B. Console

   C. EtherChannel

   D. VLAN/VTP

Answer: C

11. Which is true regarding VLANs? (Choose all that apply.)

   A. They can be created by protocol.

   B. They create smaller broadcast domains.

   C. They create smaller collision domains.

   D. They can't be used on a 3000.

   Answer: A, B

12. Which menu will give you the length of time the switch has been up?

   A. Configuration

   B. Statistics

   C. Switch/Stack Information

   D. Console

   Answer: B

13. Which menu will give you the number of frames dropped?

   A. Configuration

   B. Statistics

   C. Switch/Stack info

   D. Console

   Answer: B

14. What is the maximum time the console timeout can be set for?

   A. 1000 seconds

   B. 1410 seconds

   C. 1440 seconds

   D. 1540 seconds

   Answer: C

15. How many simultaneous Telnet sessions are allowed in a Catalyst 3000 switch by default?

A. 1

B. 2

C. 5

D. 10

Answer: C

16. Which menu allows you to set the time and date?

A. Configuration

B. Switch/Stack Information

C. Console

D. IP Configuration

Answer: B

17. From which menu can you reach the VLAN Configuration menu?

A. Switch Information

B. VTP Configuration

C. Statistics

D. Download

Answer: B

18. Which menu can be used to download new software to flash memory?

A. Configuration

B. Statistics

C. Download

D. Reset

Answer: C

19. Which menu can be used to enable viewing and setting Catalyst 3000 parameters?

A. Configuration

B. Statistics

C. Download

D. Reset

Answer: A

20. Which menu can be used to monitor switch and network performance?

A. Configuration

B. Statistics

C. Download

D. Reset

Answer: B

Chapter 8

1. Which of the following elements are required for redundancy in the Supervisor engine? Where more than one option exists, select the minimum version or least number of elements to meet the requirement.

A. Two Supervisor modules

B. Two Supervisor II modules

C. Two Supervisor III modules

D. The NetFlow Feature Card (NFFC)

E. A 5500 series switch

F. A Cisco 7500 series router

Answer: B, E. While the Supervisor III supports redundancy, it is not required.

2. In the 5500 chassis, the Supervisor engine module may be installed in

   A. Slot 13

   B. Slot 1

   C. Any open slot

   D. The Supervisor does not require a slot, as it is a backplane component.

Answer: B

3. In the 5500 chassis, the ASP module must be installed in

   A. Slot 1

   B. Slot 2

   C. Any C backplane slot

   D. Slot 13

Answer: D

4. Switching is a _____ process.

   A. Layer 1

   B. Layer 2

   C. Layer 3

   D. Layer 4

Answer: B

5. The administrator notices a CPU Halt LED indication on the RSM module in a 5500 switch. The correct action by the administrator would be to:

   A. Reboot the switch with a power cycle on both power supplies

   B. Reset the active Supervisor module

   C. Remove and reseat the RSM module

   D. Connect to the local console and issue the `reset rsm` command

   E. Take no action

Answer: E

6. The administrator notes that the Supervisor engine module's PS2 Status LED is red. This indicates which of the following problems or conditions?

   A. The RSM module is overloaded.

   B. A redundant power supply is installed but not turned on.

   C. All diagnostic tests passed.

   D. The Supervisor module is fully operational and the power is on.

   Answer: B

7. The following modules may be hot-swapped in the Catalyst system:

   A. Fan trays

   B. Redundant power supplies

   C. Switching modules

   D. The Catalyst 5000 Supervisor module

   Answer: A, B, C. Recall that the Catalyst 5000 cannot support redundant Supervisor modules, and as such, the switching system would fail. Electrically, the Supervisor supports hot swapping.

8. The Catalyst 5000 supports which of the following topologies?

   A. FDDI

   B. Ethernet

   C. Fast Ethernet

   D. Token Ring

   E. All of the above

   Answer: E

9. Order the following steps, documenting the process by which an Ethernet frame is processed within the Catalyst switch.

A. EARL commands the dropping of the frame on nondestination ports.

B. The frame enters the switch, and the port's DMA buffer stores it in the port's receive buffer.

C. The frame is transmitted to all ports via the high-speed switching bus.

D. The frame is received by all ports in the switch.

E. The port is granted bus access by the central bus arbiter.

F. Permission to transmit the frame on the high-speed switching backplane is requested by the SAINT ASIC.

G. The EARL, along with the LTL and CBL functions, selects the destination ports.

Answer: B, F, E, C, D, G, A

10. In order to process frames at Layer 3 the Catalyst system, including external components, must include:

A. A Supervisor III engine

B. Redundant Supervisor engines

C. An RSM module, or a connection from each VLAN to a router, via either ISL/802.1q or direct connections to a port in each VLAN

D. It is not possible to process Layer 3 in the Catalyst system.

Answer: C

11. The Catalyst 5500 has

A. 5 slots

B. 9 slots

C. 13 slots

D. A fixed configuration of 8 frame modules and five ATM modules

Answer: C

12. Which ASIC provides a gigabit bridge between the backplanes in the Catalyst 5500?

   A. SAGE

   B. SAINT

   C. Phoenix

   D. EARL

   E. There is only one backplane in the Catalyst 5500.

   Answer: C

13. Which component of the Catalyst system maintains the MAC address table for forwarding decisions?

   A. EARL

   B. Phoenix

   C. SAGE

   D. The MAC Address Handling Processor

   E. The Catalyst does not process MAC addresses.

   Answer: A

14. The network designer is installing a new Catalyst 5500 switch with Ethernet modules and the Supervisor III engine. The administrator will need to trunk with a non-Cisco switch. Which of the following options is the most efficient and addresses the problem?

   A. ISL

   B. 802.1d

   C. 802.1q

   D. A single connection between each VLAN on each switch

   E. Trunking must be established between Cisco products.

   Answer: C (Option A may be available; however, ISL is proprietary and is not an open standard. Most vendors support open standards over proprietary ones.)

15. The Catalyst 5000 is

  A. A cut-through switch

  B. Available for Ethernet only

  C. Ideal for wiring closets only

  D. Capable of processing frames and cells across its 3.2Gbps backplane

  E. A store-and-forward switch

  Answer: E

16. Configuration information is stored in which of the following components?

  A. 8MB flash memory

  B. 256KB NVRAM

  C. EPROM

  D. In NVRAM on each line module

  E. The configuration must be loaded from a TFTP server and is not stored on the Catalyst.

  Answer: B

17. When installing the NetFlow feature, the administrator must

  A. Replace the EARL with the NetFlow card and add the appropriate software license

  B. Upgrade to version 11.3 of the IOS

  C. Install the RSM module

  D. Collapse the network into a single subnet

  Answer: A. While the RSM module may be used, an external router is also an option using ISL or 802.1q.

18. In the Catalyst 5500, any advanced line module, with the redundant software option, can provide redundancy in the event of failure in the Supervisor engine.

A. True

B. False

Answer: B

19. Which of the following describes the differences between the Catalyst 5000 and Catalyst 5500?

A. The Catalyst 5000 supports redundant Supervisor engines.

B. The Catalyst 5000 provides a 3.6Gbps backplane.

C. The Catalyst 5500 supports redundant Supervisor engines.

D. The Catalyst 5500 supports a 3.6Gbps backplane.

E. The Catalyst 5500 provides LS1010 functionality.

Answer: C, D, E

20. The NMP in the Catalyst 5000:

A. Uses the system software to govern the general control of the hardware.

B. Stores the MAC address table.

C. Is the ASIC that handles the Phoenix function in the Catalyst 5000.

D. The NMP is not part of the Catalyst 5000.

Answer: A

Chapter 9

1. Static VLAN implementations usually are defined:

   A. By physical port

   B. By MAC address

   C. By the LECS

   D. In the MAC/CAM table

Answer: A

2. Which of the following are required in ATM LANE?

   A. LEC

   B. LECS

   C. LES

   D. BUS

   E. Optical fiber

Answer: A, C, D. While the LECS greatly simplifies administration, it is not required. Fiber is not required for ATM.

3. When designing a multiple-ELAN network, the administrator must include which of the following?

   A. DHCP

   B. Router or RSM

   C. Multiple switches

   D. None of the above

Answer: B

4. The Catalyst LANE module provides which of the following?

A. SONET/SDH at 100Mbps

B. 100Mbps Ethernet

C. SONET/SDH at 155Mbps

D. The LANE module contains no physical ports, but connects to the Catalyst backplane.

Answer: C

5. The 802.10 protocol is available with which of the following physical media?

A. Fast Ethernet

B. Token Ring

C. FDDI

D. ATM

E. All of the above

Answer: C

6. When using `fddicheck`, what other condition or conditions must be met?

A. APaRT must be enabled.

B. APaRT must be disabled.

C. The Catalyst ATM LANE module must be installed.

D. All VLANs must be numbered above 1023.

E. All SAID values must be numbered above 1023.

Answer: A

7. Within the 802.10 protocol, VLAN information is available only in which of the following?

   A. VLAN information is not available through 802.10.

   B. The SAYS field in the Clear Header

   C. The SAID field in the Encrypted Header

   D. The SAID field in the Clear Header

   E. The LMI on VLAN 1023

Answer: D

8. The ILMI is used to provide the following services:

   A. Discover ATM addresses.

   B. Locate the LECS.

   C. Locate the LES/BUS.

   D. Encapsulate all cells for VP/VC information and calculation of the HEC.

Answer: A, B. While the primary function is ATM address discovery, the LECS can be discovered with ILMI. The LES/BUS pair cannot be discovered without a LECS.

9. A network with three VLANs and seven Catalyst switches will contain how many spanning trees, assuming a full-mesh network and a requirement for use of spanning tree?

   A. 1

   B. 3

   C. 7

   D. 21

   E. Not enough information is provided.

Answer: B

10. ELANs incorporate which of the following:

   A. A logical grouping of devices, akin to a VLAN

   B. An independent broadcast domain

   C. LECs and LES/BUS services

   D. All of the above

   Answer: D

11. Which of the following is true regarding the segmentation and reassembly (SAR) function?

   A. SAR is serviced in the ATM layer

   B. SAR is serviced in the SONET layer

   C. SAR is serviced in the adaptation layer

   D. SAR converts FDDI frames to Ethernet

   E. All of the above

   Answer: C

12. In order to address the limitations of bursty traffic on WAN links, the Catalyst system:

   A. Performs SAR at wire speed in both directions

   B. Uses APaRT to control traffic flow

   C. Uses the ISL and SAID protocols to control port buffering

   D. Uses a single-rate queue

   E. Provides traffic shaping as part of EIGRP

   Answer: D

13. The LANE module supports which of the following MIBs?

    A. ILMI MIB

    B. FDDI MIB

    C. LMI MIB

    D. Bridge MIB

    E. LECS MIB

Answer: A

14. The Catalyst LANE module can be configured to provide which of the following services?

    A. LEC

    B. LECS

    C. LES

    D. BUS

    E. All of the above

    F. None of the above

Answer: E

15. The Catalyst 5000 supports which two of the following:

    A. A single LANE module

    B. Dual LANE modules in a redundant configuration

    C. Three LANE modules

    D. A single FDDI module

    E. A single Supervisor engine

Answer: C and E

16. Which of the following is specified in LANE?

    A. SR/TLB

    B. Proxy ARP

    C. LES

    D. ISL

    E. 802.10

    Answer: C

17. Which of the following services the mapping/resolution of ATM and MAC addresses?

    A. LECS

    B. LEC

    C. LES

    D. LE-ARP server

    E. BUS

    Answer: C

18. In FDDI, the longest distance between two devices is accommodated via:

    A. CDDI

    B. ATM over FDDI using 802.10

    C. FDDI and multimode fiber

    D. FDDI and single-mode fiber

    E. CDDI and FDDI offer the same distance limitations.

    Answer: D

19. When creating FDDI VLANs, the administrator must define SAID values.

   A. True

   B. False

   Answer: B. However, it is a good idea to define these values manually and document them.

20. In the initial configuration, which of the following are true?

   A. APaRT and `fddicheck` are disabled.

   B. `fddicheck` is enabled but APaRT is disabled.

   C. APaRT is enabled but `fddicheck` is disabled.

   D. The Catalyst 5000 FDDI module provides FDDI translational switching/bridging.

   E. 802.10 is enabled.

   F. ISL is enabled.

   Answer: C, D

21. The SAID field provides for how many VLANs?

   A. 4.29 billion

   B. 65,535

   C. 1024

   D. The SAID field does not define VLANs.

   Answer: A

22. Virtual LANs provide for:

   A. Control over broadcast frames

   B. Higher administration costs

   C. Transparency in ATM LANE networks

   D. Population of the RIF field

   Answer: A

23. The RIF field is part of the Ethernet frame in Catalyst switching.

   A. True

   B. False

   Answer: B

24. Spanning trees perform which of the following functions:

   A. Forwarding of Token Ring frames based on the RIF header

   B. Blocking of redundant paths in switched networks

   C. Integration of VLANs within the enterprise

   D. Protection against bridging loops by tagging each broadcast frame with a TTL bit

   E. Multicast control

   Answer: B

25. A packet contains a RIF field. Which of the following is likely to be true?

   A. The frame is being bridged with TB.

   B. The frame is being bridged with SRB or SRS.

   C. The cell is being converted into a frame in the SAR process.

   D. The cell is on a Token Ring segment.

   E. The frame is being routed via EIGRP or OSPF.

   Answer: B

26. Which of the following would be included as a demand node?

   A. A router

   B. A server

   C. A mainframe

D. A workstation

E. A switch

Answer: D

27. A server is a resource node.

A. True

B. False

Answer: A

28. Token Ring servers attached to the Catalyst should be attached using which of the following to provide the greatest performance?

A. Token Ring servers should not be connected to the Catalyst switch.

B. Connected via TR-ISL adapters.

C. Connected with a shared MAU.

D. Configured for TRB, RSRB, and SRB.

Answer: B

29. The ATM LANE module is installed in slot 3 and the Supervisor III engine is installed in slot one. Which of the following commands would be needed to configure LANE?

A. `set vtp domain LANE`

B. `set trunk 3/1 on`

C. `session 3`

D. `set session 3`

E. `set system lane LECS`

Answer: C

30. To address congestion in a Token Ring backbone, a network designer could use the Catalyst 5000/5500 with which of the following to address the problem?

A. Fast Ethernet

B. ATM

C. Either of the above

D. None of the above

E. High speed Token Ring, enabled with TR-ISL cards and the `set ring speed 155` command

Answer: C

Chapter 10

1. Which of the following commands could be used to save the configuration of the switch to a TFTP server?

A. `write network`

B. `write host filename`

C. `save config`

D. `copy config tftp host filename`

E. `copy floppy`

Answer: A, B

2. Unique ATM addresses are required for which of these ATM LANE components?

A. LEC

B. LECS

C. LES

D. BUS

E. All of the above

F. None of the above

Answer: E

3. Which of the following ATM LANE components does not use a unique MAC address?

   A. LECS

   B. LES

   C. BUS

   D. LEC

   E. All of the above

   Answer: D

4. Which of the following ATM prefixes would be recommended for public WAN connections?

   A. 45.00.00.00.00.00.00.00.00.00.00.00.00

   B. 39.00.00.00.00.00.00.00.00.00.00.00.00

   C. 47.00.00.00.00.00.00.00.00.00.00.00.00

   D. 08:00:06:22:11:99

   E. WAN connections do not make use of ATM prefixes.

   Answer: A. This is an E.164 address.

5. Which of the following would need to be configured for a SLIP account?

   A. SC0

   B. SL0

   C. VLAN1

   D. SLIP is not available on the Catalyst system.

   E. SLIP is only available with the RSM module.

   Answer: B

6. Which of the following commands is used to change the enable password?

   A. `set password`

   B. `set enable password`

   C. `set enablepass`

   D. `set password enable`

   E. `set system password enable`

   Answer: C

7. After calculating the power margin, the result is negative. This probably means that:

   A. The link will work.

   B. The link will not work.

   C. The calculation is incorrect.

   D. Not enough information is provided.

   Answer: B

8. To use BOOTP or RARP, which of the following must be true?

   A. The `set bootp enable` command must be used.

   B. The Supervisor engine must have pin 4 enabled.

C. The sl0 interface must be set to 0.0.0.0.

D. The sc0 interface must be set to 0.0.0.0.

E. The sl0 interface must be set to 255.255.255.255.

Answer: D

9. A 10/100 port on the Catalyst is set to which of the following by default?

A. 10Mbps

B. 100Mbps

C. Auto

D. Full duplex

Answer: C

10. Which of the following commands would be used to configure port 5 on module 2 to 100Mbps full duplex?

A. `set port speed 5/2 100`
   `set port duplex 5/2 full`

B. `set port 5/2 speed 100`
   `set port 5/2 duplex full`

C. `set port speed 5/2 full`
   `set port duplex 5/2 100`

D. `set port 5/2 100 full`

E. `set port speed 2/5 100`
   `set port duplex 2/5 full`

Answer: E

11. A Token Ring port is set to 16Mbps by default.

A. True

B. False

Answer: B (It is set to auto.)

12. Which of the following commands is used to set the port priority level?

    A. `set port priority 3/3 high`

    B. `set port 3/3 priority high`

    C. `set port priority high 3/3`

    D. `set port level 3/3 high`

    E. `set port level 3/3 100`

    Answer: D

13. Which of the following transfer protocols are permitted with the Catalyst system?

    A. DNS

    B. Kermit

    C. TFTP

    D. Zmodem

    E. 1K-Xmodem

    Answer: B, C

14. To configure the port name on the FDDI interface to FDDI_Int, an administrator would use:

    A. `set port name 4/1 FDDI_Int`

    B. `set port fddi 4/1 name FDDI_Int`

    C. `set port 4/1 name FDDI_Int`

    D. `set port name 4/1 "FDDI_Int"`

    E. A name cannot be assigned to an interface.

    Answer: A

15. Which commands could be used to create a FDDI VLAN?

   A. `set vlan 2 type fddi mtu 1500 said 610`

   B. `set vlan 2 type fddi said 610`

   C. `set fddi vlan 2 said 610`

   D. `set vlan fddi said 610 2`

   E. `set link vlan 2 fddi type 610`

Answer: A, B

16. The FDDI module on the Catalyst supports ISL, 802.10, and 802.1q.

   A. True

   B. False

Answer: B

17. Which of the following is required for ISL?

   A. The NetFlow Feature Card, version 2 (NFFC-2)

   B. Redundant Supervisor modules

   C. Connections via the Ethernet ports on the Supervisor module

   D. A Fast Ethernet port

   E. A crossover cable connecting two Token Ring ports on different switches

Answer: D

18. To view information regarding ATM LANE on the Catalyst switch, the administrator should use which of the following commands?

   A. `show atm config`

   B. `show lane`

   C. `show lane config`

   D. `show atm lane system`

   E. `set atm`

Answer: C

19. Which of the following is true regarding Fast EtherChannel?

   A. It creates a single spanning tree for two or more links.

   B. It bonds two modules to increase bandwidth.

   C. It can link two switches at up to 800Mbps full duplex.

   D. It is used to connect to the ESCON Channel Interface Processor on an IBM mainframe.

   E. It can run over Token Ring, although the service is called Fast TokenChannel.

   Answer: A, C

20. The command `set interface` is used for which of the following?

   A. Defining routing protocols on the Catalyst switch

   B. Defining static routes on the Catalyst switch

   C. Defining the subnet mask on the SC0 interface

   D. Defining the enable and console passwords

   E. There isn't a `set interface` command. The command is `set system interface`.

   Answer: C

Chapter 11

1. The Catalyst 5000 switch support for Telnet includes which of the following?

   A. Secure, encrypted Telnet

   B. A Telnet client

   C. A Telnet server

   D. Support for up to eight outbound Telnet sessions

   E. Telnet is not supported; only SNMP is permitted

   Answer: B, C, D. As of this writing, (version 4.5), the Catalyst did not support secure Telnet. This feature may be added in future releases.

2. The TrafficDirector application performs which of the following functions?

   A. Serves as the BUS in ATM LANE

   B. Provides QoS services

   C. Graphically displays traffic levels

   D. Performs TCP and UDP filtering services

   E. Provides access-list functions within the switch environment

   Answer: C

3. CDP packets are forwarded through all Cisco devices.

   A. True

   B. False

   Answer: B

4. The VlanDirector application offers which of the following services?

   A. All nine groups of RMON

   B. Customization of CDP packet information

   C. Mapping of ATM LANE ELANs into VLAN trunking

   D. Management of VLANs that is not possible from the CLI

   E. Graphical administration of VLANs, including the ability to drag ports onto different VLANs

   Answer: E

5. Which of the following is not true regarding the embedded RMON agent on the Catalyst 5000 switch?

   A. Supports the analysis group of RFC 1757

   B. Supports the statistics group of RFC 1757

   C. Supports the alarm group of RFC 1757

   D. Supports the event group of RFC 1757

   E. Supports the history group of RFC 1757

   Answer: A

6. Which of the following is true regarding the Fast Ethernet Switch-Probe product?

   A. Modifies all ISL trunks into 802.1q compliance

   B. Provides Telnet into the Catalyst switch

   C. Is the only way to obtain RMON services on the Catalyst platform

   D. Collects statistics on all seven layers of the OSI model, per the RMON2 specification

   Answer: D

7. The Catalyst 5000 switch may be managed from which of the following?

   A. A directly connected console using the CLI

   B. A directly connected console using the CDP

   C. A modem connection configured for PPP protocol and CHAP

   D. An X Window application served by the Supervisor engine

   Answer: A. It is possible to use PPP/CHAP and an RAS connection to access your LAN and then Telnet into the switch. However, the SL0 interface does not support direct PPP.

8. CiscoView does which of the following?

   A. Provides a graphical view of Cisco devices via NetBIOS

   B. Defines the relationship between ports and VLANs

   C. Provides a graphical view of Cisco devices configured with an IP address

   D. Captures FDDI frames for protocol analysis

   Answer: C

9. TrafficDirector provides which of the following services?

   A. Packet capture from the internal RMON agent

   B. Packet capture from the Cisco SwitchProbe product

   C. Broadcast suppression

   D. ISL RMON monitoring

   Answer: B

10. By default, the console port on the Supervisor engine is configured for which port speed?

   A. 1200 baud

   B. 2400 baud

   C. 4800 baud

   D. 9600 baud

   E. The port is auto-sensing

   Answer: D

11. When managing the route switch module in slot 3, the administrator would use which of the following commands?

    A. `configure rsm3`

    B. `set rsm ip route 0.0.0.0 10.1.1.1`

    C. `session 3`

    D. `session rsm`

    E. `get rsm config`

Answer: C

12. VMPS provides which of the following services?

    A. Dynamic routing between VLANs

    B. RMON2

    C. Layer 4 switching

    D. Dynamic VLAN membership

    E. Static VLAN configuration

Answer: D

13. The VTP process requires which of the following?

    A. A trunk link

    B. Two or more trunk links

    C. An RSM in at least one switch

    D. An external router

    E. An external TFTP server

Answer: A

14. Which of the following protocols would provide the greatest assistance to an administrator when initially troubleshooting?

A. CDP

B. VMPS

C. VTP

D. ISL

E. 802.1q

Answer: A

15. In order to reduce the impact of changes to VLAN configurations, the administrator should configure which of the following services?

A. ISL

B. VTP

C. RSM

D. RMON

E. 802.10

Answer: B

16. Which of the following would be reasons to use an external RMON probe with the Catalyst 5000 switch?

A. Lower cost

B. Reduced processor overhead

C. An additional physical port

D. Greater statistical information

E. Fault tolerance

Answer: B, D

17. Which command would be used to prepare the flash PCMCIA device for files?

    A. squeeze

    B. format

    C. dir

    D. delete

    E. verify

Answer: B

18. Which of the following is a service available within VTP?

    A. Flash system management

    B. Fast convergence of spanning tree

    C. Broadcast suppression based on percentage of port utilization

    D. High-speed routing

    E. Bandwidth management

Answer: E

19. User Tracking is a CWSI application for dynamic VLAN configuration. What service may be used at the CLI with a TFTP server to provide dynamic VLAN port assignment?

    A. SNMP

    B. RMON

    C. MIB

    D. VMPS

    E. NTP

Answer: D

20. Most of the VLAN interfaces on the RSM suddenly report down/down. What area should the administrator check?

A. Failure of the routing protocol

B. Failure of a trunk port

C. Failure of the TFTP server providing the VMPS database

D. Failure of the 1/1 interface on the Supervisor engine

E. Failure of the ATM LANE module

Answer: B

Chapter 12

1. What is the suggested first step in approaching a network problem?

A. Gather data about affected users.

B. Provide a solution to the problem.

C. Document the entire network with software tools.

D. Power off the switch.

Answer: A

2. What does RMON stand for?

A. Remote Monitoring on Networks

B. Random Method of Networking

C. Remote Monitoring

D. Restricted Monitoring

Answer: C

3. What are two modules available for CiscoWorks2000?

   A. Network Sniffer

   B. Cisco View

   C. TrafficDirector

   D. Health Monitor

   Answer: B, C

4. Which two CLI commands are the most useful for gathering system information?

   A. show

   B. set

   C. debug

   D. clear

   Answer: A, C

5. Category 3 cable is typically only pulled for what type of installations?

   A. 100BaseT

   B. ATM

   C. FDDI

   D. 10BaseT

   Answer: D

6. What does a lit port link integrity light tell the administrator?

   A. The cable is good.

   B. The cable is bad.

   C. The port is good.

   D. The port is bad.

   Answer: A

7. What are two valid show commands?

  A. sh sys

  B. show ver

  C. sh t

  D. show qu

  Answer: A, B

8. Which of the following commands are correct for disabling debug?

  A. no debug [command]

  B. no debug all

  C. debug disable

  D. set debug clear

  Answer: A, B

9. Which of the following are valid debug commands?

  A. debug asm

  B. debug atm

  C. no debug chat

  D. no debug fddi

  Answer: B, C, D

10. IP ping uses what type of requests?

  A. OSPF

  B. ICMP

  C. DECnet

  D. ARP

  Answer: B, D

11. The correct definition of TTL is?

   A. Time Till Loss

   B. Total Time Live

   C. Time To Leave

   D. Time To Live

   Answer: D

12. What does an asterisk * appearing in a trace signify?

   A. Lost path

   B. Timer expired

   C. No existing router

   D. The switch has crashed.

   Answer: B

13. CiscoWorks2000 uses a combination of which of the following?

   A. IP

   B. JAVA

   C. SNMP

   D. AppleTalk

   Answer: A, C

14. Which command shows currently active network connections and network statistics for the TCP/IP stack on a Catalyst switch?

   A. `show protocol`

   B. `show vtp`

   C. `show netstat`

   D. `sh modules`

   Answer: C

15. By default, debug is enabled on all switches.

    A. True

    B. False

Answer: B

16. What information will the command sh sys provide you with?

    A. IOS configuration dates

    B. Version information

    C. System information

    D. VLAN membership

Answer: C

17. What information is the most important thing that can be obtained using show module?

    A. The location of the switch

    B. The module numbers

    C. The type of switch

    D. The MAC address of the switching module

Answer: D

18. The command trace provides the troubleshooter with what?

    A. The total number of hops between stations

    B. The time-to-live data of each packet

    C. The path a datagram took through the network

    D. The total time a router has been up

Answer: A, C

19. The VlanDirector application can provide:

   A. The number of ATM links up

   B. The total FDDI connections in the Supervisor module

   C. The VLAN SAID field for all the existing VLANs

   D. VLAN status detection

   Answer: D

20. The CiscoView application is best used for:

   A. Displaying a graphic representation of the network's Cisco devices

   B. Maintaining a database indicating configuration changes

   C. Determining VLAN status

   D. Remote monitoring of network traffic

   Answer: A

APPENDIX

B

Glossary

A

A&B bit signaling

Used in T1 transmission facilities and sometimes called "24th channel signaling." Each of the 24 T1 subchannels in this procedure uses one bit of every sixth frame to send supervisory signaling information.

AAL

ATM Adaptation Layer: A service-dependent sublayer of the Data Link layer, which accepts data from other applications and brings it to the ATM layer in 48-byte ATM payload segments. CS and SAR are the two sublayers that form AALs. Currently, the four types of AAL recommended by the ITU-T are AAL1, AAL2, AAL3/4, and AAL5. AALs are differentiated by the source-destination timing they use, whether they are CBR or VBR, and whether they are used for connection-oriented or connectionless mode data transmission. *See also:* AAL1, AAL2, AAL3/4, AAL5, CS, and SAR, ATM, and ATM layer.

AAL1

ATM Adaptation Layer 1: One of four AALs recommended by the ITU-T, it is used for connection-oriented, time-sensitive services that need constant bit rates, such as isochronous traffic and uncompressed video. *See also:* AAL.

AAL2

ATM Adaptation Layer 2: One of four AALs recommended by the ITU-T, it is used for connection-oriented services that support a variable bit rate, such as voice traffic. *See also:* AAL.

AAL3/4

ATM Adaptation Layer 3/4: One of four AALs (a product of two initially distinct layers) recommended by the ITU-T, supporting both connectionless and connection-oriented links. Its primary use is in sending SMDS packets over ATM networks. *See also:* AAL.

AAL5

ATM Adaptation Layer 5: One of four AALs recommended by the ITU-T, it is used to support connection-oriented VBR services primarily to transfer classical IP over ATM and LANE traffic. This least complex of the AAL recommendations uses SEAL, offering lower bandwidth costs and simpler processing requirements but also providing reduced bandwidth and error-recovery capacities. *See also:* AAL.

AARP

AppleTalk Address Resolution Protocol: The protocol in an AppleTalk stack that maps data-link addresses to network addresses.

AARP probe packets

Packets sent by the AARP to determine whether a given node ID is being used by another node in a nonextended AppleTalk network. If the node ID is not in use, the sending node appropriates that node's ID. If the node ID is in use, the sending node will select a different ID and then send out more AARP probe packets. *See also:* AARP.

ABM

Asynchronous Balanced Mode: When two stations can initiate a transmission, ABM is an HDLC (or one of its derived protocols) communication technology that supports peer-oriented, point-to-point communications between both stations.

ABR

Area Border Router: An OSPF router that is located on the border of one or more OSPF areas. ABRs are used to connect OSPF areas to the OSPF backbone area.

access list

An itemization kept by routers that determines access to and from the router for various services on the network.

access method

The way network devices approach gaining access to the network itself.

access server

Also known as a "network access server," it is a communications process connecting asynchronous devices to a LAN or WAN through network and terminal emulation software, providing synchronous or asynchronous routing of supported protocols.

acknowledgement

Verification sent from one network device to another signifying that an event has occurred. May be abbreviated as ACK. *Contrast with:* NAK.

ACR

Allowed Cell Rate: A designation defined by the ATM Forum for managing ATM traffic. Dynamically controlled using congestion control measures, the ACR varies between the minimum cell rate (MCR) and the peak cell rate (PCR). *See also:* MCR and PCR.

active monitor

The mechanism used to manage a Token Ring. The network node with the highest MAC address on the ring becomes the active monitor and is responsible for management tasks such as preventing loops and ensuring tokens are not lost.

address mapping

By translating network addresses from one format to another, this methodology permits different protocols to operate interchangeably.

address mask

A bit combination descriptor identifying which portion of an address refers to the network or subnet and which part refers to the host. Sometimes simply called the mask. *See also:* subnet mask.

address resolution

The process used for resolving differences between computer addressing schemes. Address resolution typically defines a method for tracing Network layer (Layer 3) addresses to Data Link layer (Layer 2) addresses. *See also:* address mapping.

adjacency

The relationship made between defined neighboring routers and end nodes, using a common media segment, to exchange routing information.

administrative distance

A number between 0 and 225 that expresses the value of trustworthiness of a routing information source. The lower the number, the higher the integrity rating.

administrative weight

A value designated by a network administrator to rate the preference given to a network link. It is one of four link metrics exchanged by PTSPs to test ATM network resource availability.

ADSU

ATM Data Service Unit: The terminal adapter used to connect to an ATM network through an HSSI-compatible mechanism. *See also:* DSU.

advertising

The process whereby routing or service updates are transmitted at given intervals, allowing other routers on the network to maintain a record of viable routes.

AEP

AppleTalk Echo Protocol: A test for connectivity between two AppleTalk nodes where one node sends a packet to another and receives an echo, or copy, in response.

AFI

Authority and Format Identifier: The part of an NSAP ATM address that delineates the type and format of the IDI section of an ATM address. *See also:* IDI and NSAP.

AFP

AppleTalk Filing Protocol: A presentation-layer protocol, supporting Apple-Share and Mac OS File Sharing, that permits users to share files and applications on a server.

AIP

ATM Interface Processor: Supporting AAL3/4 and AAL5, this interface for Cisco 7000 series routers minimizes performance bottlenecks at the UNI. *See also:* AAL3/4 and AAL5.

algorithm

A set of rules or process used to solve a problem. In networking, algorithms are typically used for finding the best route for traffic from a source to its destination.

alignment error

An error occurring in Ethernet networks, in which a received frame has extra bits; that is, a number not divisible by eight. Alignment errors are generally the result of frame damage caused by collisions.

all-routes explorer packet

An explorer packet that can move across an entire SRB network, tracing all possible paths to a given destination. Also known as an all-rings explorer packet. *See also:* explorer packet, local explorer packet, and spanning explorer packet.

AM

Amplitude Modulation: A modulation method that represents information by varying the amplitude of the carrier signal. *See also:* modulation.

AMI

Alternate Mark Inversion: A line-code type on T1 and E1 circuits that shows zeros as "01" during each bit cell, and ones as "11" or "00," alternately, during each bit cell. The sending device must maintain ones density in AMI but not independently of the data stream. Also known as binary-coded, alternate mark inversion. *Contrast with:* B8ZS. *See also:* ones density.

Amplitude

An analog or digital waveform's highest value.

Analog transmission

Signal messaging whereby information is represented by various combinations of signal amplitude, frequency, and phase.

ANSI

American National Standards Institute: The organization of corporate, government, and other volunteer members that coordinates standards-related activities, approves U.S. national standards, and develops U.S. positions in international standards organizations. ANSI assists in the creation of international and U.S. standards in disciplines such as communications, networking, and a variety of technical fields. It publishes over 13,000 standards, for engineered products and technologies ranging from screw threads to networking protocols. ANSI is a member of the IEC and ISO. *See also:* IEC and ISO.

anycast

An ATM address that can be shared by more than one end-system, allowing requests to be routed to a node that provides a particular service.

AppleTalk

Currently in two versions, the group of communication protocols designed by Apple Computer for use in Macintosh environments. The earlier Phase 1 protocols supports one physical network with only one network number that resides in one zone. The later Phase 2 protocols supports more than one logical network on a single physical network, allowing networks to exist in more than one zone. *See also:* zone.

Application layer

Layer 7 of the OSI reference network model, supplying services to application procedures (such as electronic mail or file transfer) that are outside the OSI model. This layer chooses and determines the availability of communicating partners along with the resources necessary to make the connection, coordinates partnering applications, and forms a consensus on procedures for controlling data integrity and error recovery.

ARA

AppleTalk Remote Access: A protocol for Macintosh users establishing their access to resources and data from a remote AppleTalk location.

area

A logical, rather than physical, set of segments (based on either CLNS, DECnet, or OSPF) along with their attached devices. Areas are commonly connected to others using routers to create a single autonomous system. *See also:* autonomous system.

ARM

Asynchronous Response Mode: An HDLC communication mode using one primary station and at least one additional station, in which transmission can be initiated from either the primary or one of the secondary units.

ARP

Address Resolution Protocol: Defined in RFC 826, the protocol that traces IP addresses to MAC addresses. *See also:* RARP.

ASBR

Autonomous System Boundary Router: An area border router placed between an OSPF autonomous system and a non-OSPF network that operates both OSPF and an additional routing protocol, such as RIP. ASBRs must be located in a non-stub OSPF area. *See also:* ABR, non-stub area, and OSPF.

ASCII

American Standard Code for Information Interchange: An eight-bit code for representing characters, consisting of seven data bits plus one parity bit.

ASN.1

Abstract Syntax Notation One: An OSI language used to describe types of data that is independent of computer structures and depicting methods. Described by ISO International Standard 8824.

ASP

AppleTalk Session Protocol: A protocol employing ATP to establish, maintain, and tear down sessions, as well as sequence requests. *See also:* ATP.

AST

Automatic Spanning Tree: A function that supplies one path for spanning explorer frames traveling from one node in the network to another, supporting the automatic resolution of spanning trees in SRB networks. AST is based on the IEEE 802.1 standard. *See also:* IEEE 802.1 and SRB.

asynchronous transmission

Digital signals sent without precise timing, usually with different frequencies and phase relationships. Asynchronous transmissions generally enclose individual characters in control bits (called start and stop bits) that show the beginning and end of each character. *Contrast with:* isochronous transmission and synchronous transmission.

ATCP

AppleTalk Control Protocol: The protocol for establishing and configuring AppleTalk over PPP, defined in RFC 1378. *See also:* PPP.

ATDM

Asynchronous Time-Division Multiplexing: A technique for sending information, it differs from normal TDM in that the time slots are assigned when necessary rather than preassigned to certain transmitters. *Contrast with:* FDM, statistical multiplexing, and TDM.

ATG

Address Translation Gateway: The mechanism within Cisco DECnet routing software that enables routers to route multiple, independent DECnet networks and to establish a user-designated address translation for chosen nodes between networks.

ATM

Asynchronous Transfer Mode: The international standard, identified by fixed-length 53-byte cells, for transmitting cells in multiple service systems, such as voice, video, or data. Transit delays are reduced because the fixed-length cells permit processing to occur in the hardware. ATM is designed to maximize the benefits of high-speed transmission media, such as SONET, E3, and T3.

ATM ARP server

A device that supplies logical subnets running classical IP over ATM with address-resolution services.

ATM endpoint

The initiating or terminating connection in an ATM network. ATM endpoints include servers, workstations, ATM-to-LAN switches, and ATM routers.

ATM Forum

The international organization founded jointly by Northern Telecom, Sprint, Cisco Systems, and NET/ADAPTIVE in 1991 to develop and promote standards-based implementation agreements for ATM technology. The ATM Forum broadens official standards developed by ANSI and ITU-T and creates implementation agreements before official standards are published.

ATM layer

A sublayer of the Data Link layer in an ATM network that is service independent. To create standard 53-byte ATM cells, the ATM layer receives 48-byte segments from the AAL and attaches a 5-byte header to each. These cells are then sent to the Physical layer for transmission across the physical medium. *See also:* AAL.

ATMM

ATM Management: A procedure that runs on ATM switches, managing rate enforcement and VCI translation. *See also:* ATM and VCI.

ATM user-user connection

A connection made by the ATM layer to supply communication between at least two ATM service users, such as ATMM processes. These communications can be uni- or bidirectional, using one or two VCCs, respectively. *See also:* ATM layer and ATMM.

ATP

AppleTalk Transaction Protocol: A transport-level protocol that enables reliable transactions between two sockets, where one requests the other to perform a given task and to report the results. ATP fastens the request and response together, assuring a loss-free exchange of request-response pairs.

attenuation

In communication, weakening or loss of signal energy, typically caused by distance.

AURP

AppleTalk Update-based Routing Protocol: A technique for encapsulating AppleTalk traffic in the header of a foreign protocol that allows the connection of at least two noncontiguous AppleTalk internetworks through a foreign network (such as TCP/IP) to create an AppleTalk WAN. The connection made is called an AURP tunnel. By exchanging routing information between exterior routers, the AURP maintains routing tables for the complete AppleTalk WAN. *See also:* AURP tunnel and exterior router.

AURP tunnel

A connection made in an AURP WAN that acts as a single, virtual link between AppleTalk internetworks separated physically by a foreign network such as a TCP/IP network. *See also:* AURP.

authority zone

A portion of the domain-name tree associated with DNS for which one name server is the authority. *See also:* DNS.

automatic call reconnect

A function that enables automatic call rerouting away from a failed trunk line.

autonomous confederation

A collection of self-governed systems that depend more on their own network accessibility and routing information than on information received from other systems or groups.

autonomous switching

The ability of Cisco routers to process packets more quickly by using the ciscoBus to switch packets independently of the system processor.

autonomous system (AS)

A group of networks under mutual administration that share the same routing methodology. Autonomous systems are subdivided by areas and must be assigned an individual 16-bit number by the IANA. *See also:* area and IANA.

autoreconfiguration

A procedure executed by nodes within the failure domain of a Token Ring, wherein nodes automatically perform diagnostics, trying to reconfigure the network around failed areas.

B

B8ZS

Binary 8-Zero Substitution: A line-code type, interpreted at the remote end of the connection, that uses a special code substitution whenever eight consecutive zeros are transmitted over the link on T1 and E1 circuits. This technique assures ones density independent of the data stream. Also known as bipolar 8-zero substitution. *Contrast with:* AMI. *See also:* ones density.

backbone

The basic portion of the network that provides the primary path for traffic sent to and initiated from other networks.

back end

A node or software program supplying services to a front end. *See also:* client, front end, and server.

bandwidth

The gap between the highest and lowest frequencies employed by network signals. More commonly, it refers to the rated throughput capacity of a network protocol or medium.

baseband

A feature of a network technology that uses only one carrier frequency, for example Ethernet. Also named "narrowband." *Compare with:* broadband.

baud

Synonymous with bits per second (bps), if each signal element represents one bit. It is a unit of signaling speed equivalent to the number of separate signal elements transmitted per second.

B channel

Bearer channel: A full-duplex, 64Kbps channel in ISDN that transmits user data. *Compare with:* D channel, E channel, and H channel.

beacon

An FDDI device or Token Ring frame that points to a serious problem with the ring, such as a broken cable. The beacon frame carries the address of the station thought to be down. *See also:* failure domain.

BECN

Backward Explicit Congestion Notification: BECN is the bit set by a Frame Relay network in frames moving away from frames headed into a congested path. A DTE that receives frames with the BECN may ask higher-level protocols to take necessary flow control measures. *Compare with:* FECN.

BGP4

BGP Version 4: Version 4 of the interdomain routing protocol most commonly used on the Internet. BGP4 supports CIDR and uses route-counting mechanisms to decrease the size of routing tables. *See also:* CIDR.

binary

A two-character numbering method that uses ones and zeros. The binary numbering system underlies all digital representation of information.

BIP

Bit Interleaved Parity: A method used in ATM to monitor errors on a link, sending a check bit or word in the link overhead for the previous block or frame. This allows bit errors in transmissions to be found and delivered as maintenance information.

BISDN

Broadband ISDN: ITU-T standards created to manage high-bandwidth technologies such as video. BISDN presently employs ATM technology along SONET-based transmission circuits, supplying data rates between 155Mbps and 622Mbps and beyond. Contrast with N-ISDN. *See also:* BRI, ISDN, and PRI.

bit-oriented protocol

Regardless of frame content, the class of Data Link layer communication protocols that transmits frames. Bit-oriented protocols, as compared with byte-oriented, supply more efficient and trustworthy, full-duplex operation. *Compare with:* byte-oriented protocol.

border gateway

A router that facilitates communication with routers in different autonomous systems.

BPDU

Bridge Protocol Data Unit: A Spanning Tree Protocol initializing packet that is sent at definable intervals for the purpose of exchanging information among bridges in networks.

BRI

Basic Rate Interface: The ISDN interface that facilitates circuit-switched communication between video, data, and voice; it is made up of two B channels 64Kbps each) and one D channel (16Kbps). *Compare with:* PRI. *See also:* BISDN, ISN.

bridge

A device for connecting two segments of a network and transmitting packets between them. Both segments must use identical protocols to communicate. Bridges function at the Data Link layer, Layer 2 of the OSI reference model. The purpose of a bridge is to filter, send, or flood any incoming frame, based on the MAC address of that particular frame.

broadband

A transmission methodology for multiplexing several independent signals onto one cable. In telecommunications, broadband is classified as any channel with bandwidth greater than 4kHz (typical voice grade). In LAN terminology, it is classified as a coaxial cable on which analog signaling is employed. Also known as wideband. *Contrast with:* baseband.

broadcast

A data frame or packet that is transmitted to every node on a network. Broadcasts are known by their broadcast address, which is a destination address with all the bits turned on.

broadcast domain

A group of devices receiving broadcast frames initiating from any device within the group. Because they do not forward broadcast frames, broadcast domains are generally surrounded by routers.

broadcast storm

An undesired event on the network caused by the simultaneous transmission of any number of broadcasts across all network segments. Such an occurrence can overwhelm network bandwidth, resulting in time-outs.

buffer

A storage area dedicated to handling data while in transit. Buffers are used to receive/store sporadic deliveries of data bursts, usually received from faster devices, compensating for the variations in processing speed. Incoming information is stored until everything is received prior to sending data on. Also known as an information buffer.

bus topology

A linear LAN architecture in which transmissions from various stations on the network are reproduced over the length of the medium and are accepted by all other stations. *Compare with:* ring, star, and tree topologies.

bus

Any physical path, typically wires or copper, through which a digital signal can be used to send data from one part of a computer to another.

BUS

Broadcast and Unknown Server: In LAN emulation, the hardware or software responsible for resolving all broadcasts and packets with unknown (unregistered) addresses into the point-to-point virtual circuits required by ATM. *See also:* LEC, LECS, LES, and LANE.

BX.25

AT&T's use of X.25. *See also:* X.25.

bypass mode

An FDDI and Token Ring network operation that deletes an interface.

bypass relay

A device that enables a particular interface in the Token Ring to be closed down and effectively taken off the ring.

byte-oriented protocol

Any type of data-link communication protocol that, in order to mark the boundaries of frames, uses a specific character from the user character set. These protocols have generally been superseded by bit-oriented protocols. *Compare with:* bit-oriented protocol.

C

cable range

In an extended AppleTalk network, the range of numbers allotted for use by existing nodes on the network. The value of the cable range can be anywhere from a single to a sequence of several touching network numbers. Node addresses are determined by their cable range value.

CAC

Connection Admission Control: The sequence of actions executed by every ATM switch while connection setup is performed in order to determine if a request for connection is violating the guarantees of QoS for established connections. Also, CAC is used to route a connection request through an ATM network.

call admission control

A device for managing of traffic in ATM networks, determining the possibility of a path containing adequate bandwidth for a requested VCC.

call priority

In circuit-switched systems, the defining priority given to each originating port; it specifies in which order calls will be reconnected. Additionally, call priority identifies which calls are allowed during a bandwidth reservation.

call set-up time

The length of time necessary to effect a switched call between DTE devices.

CBR

Constant Bit Rate: An ATM Forum QoS class created for use in ATM networks. CBR is used for connections that rely on precision clocking to guarantee trustworthy delivery. *Compare with:* ABR and VBR.

CD

Carrier Detect: A signal indicating that an interface is active or that a connection generated by a modem has been established.

CDP

Cisco Discovery Protocol: Cisco's proprietary protocol that is used to tell a neighbor Cisco device about the type of hardware, software version, and active interfaces that the Cisco device is using. It uses a SNAP frame between devices and is not routable.

CDVT

Cell Delay Variation Tolerance: A QoS parameter for traffic management in ATM networks specified when a connection is established. The allowable fluctuation levels for data samples taken by the PCR in CBR transmissions are determined by the CDVT. *See also:* CBR and PCR.

cell

In ATM networking, the basic unit of data for switching and multiplexing. Cells have a defined length of 53 bytes, including a 5-byte header that identifies the cell's data stream and 48 bytes of payload. *See also:* cell relay.

cell payload scrambling

The method by which an ATM switch maintains framing on some medium-speed edge and trunk interfaces (T3 or E3 circuits). Cell payload scrambling rearranges the data portion of a cell to maintain the line synchronization with certain common bit patterns.

cell relay

A technology that uses small packets of fixed size, known as cells. Their fixed length enables cells to be processed and switched in hardware at high speeds, making this technology the foundation for ATM and other high-speed network protocols. *See also:* cell.

Centrex

A local exchange carrier service, providing local switching that resembles that of an on-site PBX. Centrex has no on-site switching capability. Therefore, all customer connections return to the CO. *See also:* CO.

CER

Cell Error Ratio: The ratio in ATM of transmitted cells having errors to the total number of cells sent in a transmission within a certain span of time.

channelized E1

Operating at 2.048Mpbs, an access link that is sectioned into 29 B-channels and one D-channel, supporting DDR, Frame Relay, and X.25. *Compare with:* channelized T1.

channelized T1

Operating at 1.544Mbps, an access link that is sectioned into 23 B-channels and 1 D-channel of 64Kbps each, where individual channels or groups of channels connect to various destinations, supporting DDR, Frame Relay, and X.25. Also known as fractional T1. *Compare with:* channelized E1.

CHAP

Challenge Handshake Authentication Protocol: Supported on lines using PPP encapsulation, it is a security feature that identifies the remote end, helping keep out unauthorized users. After CHAP is performed, the router or access server determines whether a given user is permitted access. It is a newer, more secure protocol than PAP. *Compare with:* PAP.

checksum

A test for ensuring the integrity of sent data. It is a number calculated from a series of values taken through a sequence of mathematical functions, typically placed at the end of the data from which it is calculated, and then recalculated at the receiving end for verification. *Compare with:* CRC.

choke packet

When congestion exists, it is a packet sent to inform a transmitter that it should decrease its sending rate.

CIDR

Classless Interdomain Routing: A method supported by BGP4 and based on route aggregation that enables routers to combine routes in order to minimize the routing information that needs to be conveyed by the primary routers. It allows a group of IP networks to appear to other networks as a unified, larger entity. In CIDR, IP addresses and their subnet masks are written as four dotted octets, followed by a forward slash and a two-digit subnet mask. *See also:* BGP4.

CIP

Channel Interface Processor: A channel attachment interface for use in Cisco 7000 series routers that connects a host mainframe to a control unit. This device eliminates the need for an FBP to attach channels.

CIR

Committed Information Rate: Averaged over a minimum span of time and measured in bps, a Frame Relay network's agreed-upon normal rate of transferring information.

Cisco FRAD

Cisco Frame-Relay Access Device: A Cisco product that supports Cisco IPS Frame Relay SNA services, connecting SDLC devices to Frame Relay without requiring an existing LAN. May be upgraded to a fully functioning multi-protocol router. Can activate conversion from SDLC to Ethernet and Token Ring, but does not support attached LANs. *See also:* FRAD.

CiscoFusion

Cisco's name for the internetworking architecture under which its Cisco IOS operates. It is designed to "fuse" together the capabilities of its disparate collection of acquired routers and switches.

Cisco IOS software

Cisco Internetwork Operating System software. The kernel of the Cisco line of routers and switches that supplies shared functionality, scalability, and security for all products under its CiscoFusion architecture. *See also:* CiscoFusion.

CiscoView

GUI-based management software for Cisco networking devices, enabling dynamic status, statistics, and comprehensive configuration information. Displays a physical view of the Cisco device chassis and provides device-monitoring functions and fundamental troubleshooting capabilities. May be integrated with a number of SNMP-based network management platforms.

classical IP over ATM

Defined in RFC 1577, the specification for running IP over ATM that maximizes ATM features. Also known as CIA.

CLP

Cell Loss Priority: The area in the ATM cell header that determines the likelihood of a cell being dropped during network congestion. Cells with CLP = 0 are considered insured traffic and are not apt to be dropped. Cells with CLP = 1 are considered best-effort traffic that may be dropped during congested episodes, delivering more resources to handle insured traffic.

CLR

Cell Loss Ratio: The ratio of discarded cells to successfully delivered cells in ATM. CLR can be designated a QoS parameter when establishing a connection.

CO

Central Office: The local telephone company office where all loops in a certain area connect and where circuit switching of subscriber lines occurs.

collapsed backbone

A nondistributed backbone where all network segments are connected to each other through an internetworking device. A collapsed backbone can be a virtual network segment at work in a device such as a router, hub, or switch.

collision

The effect of two nodes sending transmissions simultaneously in Ethernet. When they meet on the physical media, the frames from each node collide and are damaged. *See also:* collision domain.

collision domain

The network area in Ethernet over which frames that have collided will spread. Collisions are propagated by hubs and repeaters, but not by LAN switches, routers, or bridges. *See also:* collision.

configuration register

A 16-bit configurable value stored in hardware or software that determines how Cisco routers function during initialization. In hardware, the bit position is set using a jumper. In software, it is set by specifying a hexadecimal value with configuration commands.

congestion

Traffic that exceeds the network's ability to handle it.

congestion avoidance

To minimize delays, the method an ATM network uses to control traffic entering the system. Lower-priority traffic is discarded at the edge of the network when indicators signal it cannot be delivered, thus using resources efficiently.

congestion collapse

The situation that results from the retransmission of packets in ATM networks where little or no traffic successfully arrives at destination points. It usually happens in networks made of switches with ineffective or inadequate buffering capabilities combined with poor packet discard or ABR congestion feedback mechanisms.

connectionless

Data transfer that occurs without the creating of a virtual circuit. No overhead, best effort delivery, not reliable. *Contrast with:* connection-oriented. *See also:* virtual circuit.

connection-oriented

Data transfer method that sets up a virtual circuit before any data is transferred. Uses acknowledgments and flow control for reliable data transfer. *Contrast with:* connectionless. *See also:* virtual circuit.

control direct VCC

One of three control connections defined by Phase I LAN Emulation—a bidirectional virtual control connection (VCC) established in ATM by an LEC to an LES. *See also:* control distribute VCC.

control distribute VCC

One of three control connections defined by Phase 1 LAN Emulation—a unidirectional virtual control connection (VCC) set up in ATM from an LES to an LEC. Usually, the VCC is a point-to-multipoint connection. *See also:* control direct VCC.

convergence

A measurement of the time required for all routers in an internetwork to update their routing tables. No data is passed during a convergence time.

cost

Also known as path cost, an arbitrary value, based on hop count, bandwidth, or other calculation, that is typically assigned by a network administrator and used by the routing protocol to compare different routes through an internetwork. Routing protocols use cost values to select the best path to a certain destination: the lowest cost identifies the best path. Also known as path cost. *See also:* routing metric.

count to infinity

A problem occurring in routing algorithms that are slow to converge where routers keep increasing the hop count to particular networks. To avoid this problem, the network administrator fixes an arbitrary hop count limit.

CPCS

Common Part Convergence Sublayer: One of two AAL sublayers that is service-dependent, it is further segmented into the CS and SAR sublayers. The CPCS prepares data for transmission across the ATM network; it creates the 48-byte payload cells that are sent to the ATM layer. *See also:* AAL and ATM layer.

CPE

Customer Premises Equipment: Items, such as telephones, modems, and terminals, installed at customer locations and connected to the telephone company network.

crankback

In ATM, a correction technique used when a node somewhere on a chosen path cannot accept a connection setup request, blocking the request. The path is rolled back to an intermediate node, which then uses GCAC to attempt to find an alternate path to the final destination.

CRC

Cyclic Redundancy Check: A methodology that detects errors, whereby the frame recipient makes a calculation by dividing frame contents with a prime binary divisor and compares the remainder to a value stored in the frame by the sending node. *Contrast with:* checksum.

CSMA/CD

Carrier Sense Multiple Access Collision Detect: A technology defined by the Ethernet IEEE 802.3 committee. Each device senses the cable for a digital signal before transmitting. Also, CSMA/CD allows all devices on the network to share the same cable, but one at a time. If two devices transmit at the same time, they will stop transmitting, wait a predetermined amount of time, and then try to transmit again.

CSU

Channel Service Unit: A digital mechanism that connects end-user equipment to the local digital telephone loop. Frequently referred to along with the data service unit as CSU/DSU. *See also:* DSU.

CTD

Cell Transfer Delay: For a given connection in ATM, the time period between a cell exit event at the source user-network interface (UNI) and the corresponding cell entry event at the destination. The CTD between these points is the sum of the total inter-ATM transmission delay and the total ATM processing delay.

cut-through packet switching

A packet-switching technique that flows data through a switch so that the leading edge exits the switch at the output port before the packet finishes entering the input port. Packets will be read, processed, and forwarded by devices that use cut-through packet switching as soon as the destination address is confirmed and the outgoing port is identified.

D

data direct VCC

A bidirectional point-to-point virtual control connection (VCC) set up between two LECs in ATM and one of three data connections defined by Phase 1 LAN Emulation. Because data direct VCCs do not guarantee QoS, they are generally reserved for UBR and ABR connections. *Compare with:* control distribute VCC and control direct VCC.

datagram

A logical collection of information transmitted as a Network layer unit over a medium without a previously established virtual circuit. IP datagrams have become the primary information unit of the Internet. At various layers of the OSI reference model, the terms *cell, frame, message, packet,* and *segment* also define these logical information groupings.

data link control layer

Layer 2 of the SNA architectural model, it is responsible for the transmission of data over a given physical link and compares somewhat to the Data Link layer of the OSI model.

Data Link layer

Layer 2 of the OSI reference model, it ensures the trustworthy transmission of data across a physical link and is primarily concerned with physical addressing, line discipline, network topology, error notification, ordered delivery of frames, and flow control. The IEEE has further segmented this layer into the MAC sublayer and the LLC sublayer. Also known as the link layer. Can be compared somewhat to the data link control layer of the SNA model. *See also:* Application layer, LLC, MAC, Network layer, Physical layer, Presentation layer, Session layer, and Transport layer.

DCC

Data Country Code: Developed by the ATM Forum, one of two ATM address formats designed for use by private networks. *Compare with:* ICD.

DCE

Data Communications Equipment (as defined by the EIA) or Data Circuit-terminating Equipment (as defined by the ITU-T): The mechanisms and links of a communications network that make up the network portion of the user-to-network interface, such as modems. The DCE supplies the physical connection to the network, forwards traffic, and provides a clocking signal to synchronize data transmission between DTE and DCE devices. *Compare with:* DTE.

D channel

1. Data channel: A full-duplex, 16kbps (BRI) or 64kbps (PRI) ISDN channel. *Compare with*: B channel, E channel, and H channel.

2. In SNA, anything that provides a connection between the processor and main storage with any peripherals.

DDP

Datagram Delivery Protocol : Used in the AppleTalk suite of protocols as a connectionless protocol that is responsible for sending datagrams through an internetwork.

DDR

Dial-On-Demand Routing: A technique that allows a router to automatically initiate and end a circuit-switched session per the requirements of the sending station. By mimicking keep-alives, the router fools the end station into treating the session as active. DDR permits routing over ISDN or telephone lines via a modem or external ISDN terminal adapter.

default route

The routing table entry used to direct frames whose next hop is not spelled out in the routing table.

delay

The time elapsed between a sender's initiation of a transaction and the first response they receive. Also, the time needed to move a packet from its source to its destination over a path. *See also:* latency.

demarc

The demarcation point between the customer premises equipment (CPE) and the telco's carrier equipment.

demodulation

A series of steps that return a modulated signal to its original form. When receiving, a modem demodulates an analog signal to its original digital form (and, conversely, modulates the digital data it sends into an analog signal). *See also:* modulation.

demultiplexing

The process of converting a single multiplex signal, comprising more than one input stream, back into separate output streams. *See also:* multiplexing.

designated bridge

In the process of forwarding a frame from a segment to the route bridge, the bridge with the lowest path cost.

designated router

An OSPF router that creates LSAs for a multiaccess network and is required to perform other special tasks in OSPF operations. Multiaccess OSPF networks that maintain a minimum of two attached routers identify one router that is chosen by the OSPF Hello protocol, which makes possible a decrease in the number of adjacencies necessary on a multiaccess network. This in turn reduces the quantity of routing protocol traffic and the physical size of the database.

destination address

The address for the network devices that will receive a packet.

discovery mode

Also known as dynamic configuration, this technique is used by an Apple-Talk interface to gain information from a working node about an attached network. The information is subsequently used by the interface for self-configuration.

distance vector routing algorithm

In order to find a shortest-path spanning tree, this group of routing algorithms repeats on the number of hops in a given route, requiring each router to send its complete routing table with each update, but only to its neighbors. Routing algorithms of this type tend to generate loops, but they are fundamentally simpler than their link-state counterparts. *See also:* link-state routing algorithm and SPF.

DLCI

Data-Link Connection Identifier: Used to identify virtual circuits in a Frame Relay network.

DNS

Domain Name System: Used to resolve host names to IP addresses.

DSAP

Destination Service Access Point: The service access point of a network node, specified in the destination field of a packet. *See also:* SSAP and SAP.

DSR

Data Set Ready: When a DCE is powered up and ready to run, this EIA/TIA-232 interface circuit is also engaged.

DSU

Data Service Unit: This device is used to adapt the physical interface on a data terminal equipment (DTE) mechanism to a transmission facility such as T1 or E1 and is also responsible for signal timing. It is commonly grouped with the channel service unit and referred to as the CSU/DSU. *See also:* CSU.

DTE

Data Terminal Equipment: Any device located at the user end of a user-network interface serving as a destination, a source, or both. DTE includes devices such as multiplexers, protocol translators, and computers. The connection to a data network is made through data channel equipment (DCE) such as a modem, using the clocking signals generated by that device. *See also:* DCE.

DTR

Data Terminal Ready: An activated EIA/TIA-232 circuit communicating to the DCE the state of preparedness of the DTE to transmit or receive data.

DUAL

Diffusing Update Algorithm: Used in Enhanced IGRP, this convergence algorithm provides loop-free operation throughout an entire route's computation. DUAL grants routers involved in a topology revision the ability to synchronize simultaneously, while routers unaffected by this change are not involved. *See also:* Enhanced IGRP.

DVMRP

Distance Vector Multicast Routing Protocol: Based primarily on the Routing Information Protocol (RIP), this Internet gateway protocol implements a common, condensed-mode IP multicast scheme, using IGMP to transfer routing datagrams between its neighbors. *See also:* IGMP.

DXI

Data Exchange Interface: Described in RFC 1482, DXI defines the effectiveness of a network device such as a router, bridge, or hub to act as an FEP to an ATM network by using a special DSU that accomplishes packet encapsulation.

dynamic routing

Also known as adaptive routing, this technique automatically adapts to traffic or physical network revisions.

E

E1

Generally used in Europe, a wide-area digital transmission scheme carrying data at 2.048Mbps. E1 transmission lines are available for lease from common carriers for private use.

E.164

1. Evolved from standard telephone numbering system, the standard recommended by ITU-T for international telecommunication numbering, particularly in ISDN, SMDS, and BIISDN.

2. Label of field in an ATM address containing numbers in E.164 format.

E channel

Echo channel: A 64Kbps ISDN control channel used for circuit switching. Specific description of this channel can be found in the 1984 ITU-T ISDN specification, but was dropped from the 1988 version. *See also:* B, D, and H channels.

edge device

A device that enables packets to be forwarded between legacy interfaces (such as Ethernet and Token Ring) and ATM interfaces based on information in the Data Link and Network layers. An edge device does not take part in the running of any Network layer routing protocol; it merely uses the route description protocol in order to get the forwarding information required.

EFCI

Explicit Forward Congestion Indication: A congestion feedback mode permitted by ABR service in an ATM network. The EFCI may be set by any network element that is in a state of immediate or certain congestion. The destination end-system is able to carry out a protocol that adjusts and lowers the cell rate of the connection based on value of the EFCI. *See also:* ABR.

EIGRP

See: Enhanced IGRP.

EIP

Ethernet Interface Processor: A Cisco 7000 series router interface processor card, supplying 10Mbps AUI ports to support Ethernet Version 1 and Ethernet Version 2 or IEEE 802.3 interfaces with a high-speed data path to other interface processors.

ELAN

Emulated LAN: An ATM network configured using a client/server model in order to emulate either an Ethernet or Token Ring LAN. Multiple ELANs can exist at the same time on a single ATM network and are made up of an LAN emulation client (LEC), an LAN emulation server (LES), a broadcast-and unknown server (BUS), and an LAN emulation configuration server (LECS). ELANs are defined by the LANE specification. *See also:* LANE, LEC, LECS, and LES.

ELAP

EtherTalk Link Access Protocol: In an EtherTalk network, the link-access protocol constructed above the standard Ethernet Data Link layer.

encapsulation

The technique used by layered protocols in which a layer adds header information to the protocol data unit (PDU) from the layer above. As an example, in Internet terminology, a packet would contain a header from the Physical layer, followed by a header from the Network layer (IP), followed by a header from the Transport layer (TCP), followed by the application protocol data.

encryption

The conversion of information into a scrambled form that effectively disguises it to prevent unauthorized access. Every encryption scheme uses some well-defined algorithm, which is reversed at the receiving end by an opposite algorithm in a process known as decryption.

Enhanced IGRP

Enhanced Interior Gateway Routing Protocol: An advanced routing protocol created by Cisco, combining the advantages of link-state and distance-vector protocols. Enhanced IGRP has superior convergence attributes, including high operating efficiency. *See also:* IGP, OSPF, and RIP.

enterprise network

A privately owned and operated network that joins most major locations in a large company or organization.

EPROM

Erasable Programmable Read-Only Memory: Programmed after their manufacture, these nonvolatile memory chips can be erased if necessary and reprogrammed. *See also:* PROM.

ESF

Extended Superframe: Made up of 24 frames with 192 bits each, with the 193rd bit providing other functions including timing. This is an enhanced version of SF. *See also:* SF.

Ethernet

A baseband LAN specification created by the Xerox Corporation and then improved through joint efforts of Xerox, Digital Equipment Corporation, and Intel. Ethernet is similar to the IEEE 802.3 series standard and, using CSMA/CD, operates over various types of cables at 10Mbps. *See also:* 10BaseT, Fast Ethernet, and IEEE.

EtherTalk

A data-link product from Apple Computer that permits AppleTalk networks to be connected by Ethernet.

excess rate

In ATM networking, traffic exceeding a connection's insured rate. The excess rate is the maximum rate less the insured rate. Depending on the availability of network resources, excess traffic can be discarded during congestion episodes. *Compare with:* maximum rate.

expansion

The procedure of directing compressed data through an algorithm, restoring information to its original size.

expedited delivery

An option that can be specified by one protocol layer, communicating either with other layers or with the identical protocol layer in a different network device, requiring that identified data be processed faster.

explorer packet

A packet transmitted by a source device to find the path through a source-route-bridged network.

F

failure domain

The region in which a failure has occurred in a Token Ring. When a station gains information that a serious problem, such as a cable break, has occurred with the network, it sends a beacon frame that includes the station reporting the failure, its NAUN, and everything between. This defines the failure domain. Beaconing then initiates the procedure known as autoreconfiguration. *See also:* autoreconfiguration and beacon.

fallback

In ATM networks, this mechanism is used for scouting a path if it's not possible to locate one using customary methods. The device relaxes requirements for certain characteristics, such as delay, in an attempt to find a path that meets a certain set of the most important requirements.

Fast Ethernet

Any Ethernet specification with a speed of 100Mbps. Fast Ethernet is ten times faster than 10BaseT, while retaining qualities like MAC mechanisms, MTU, and frame format. These similarities make it possible for existing 10BaseT applications and management tools to be used on Fast Ethernet networks. Fast Ethernet is based on an extension of IEEE 802.3 specification. *Compare with:* Ethernet. *See also:* 100BaseT, 100BaseTX, and IEEE.

fast switching

A Cisco feature that uses a route cache to speed packet switching through a router. *Contrast with:* process switching.

FDM

Frequency-Division Multiplexing: A technique that permits information from several channels to be assigned bandwidth on one wire based on frequency. *See also:* TDM, ATDM, and statistical multiplexing.

FDDI

Fiber Distributed Data Interface: An LAN standard, defined by ANSI X3T9.5 that can run at speeds up to 200Mbps and uses token-passing media access on fiber-optic cable. For redundancy, FDDI can use a dual-ring architecture.

FECN

Forward Explicit Congestion Notification: A bit set by a Frame Relay network that informs the DTE receptor that congestion was encountered along the path from source to destination. A device receiving frames with the FECN bit set can ask higher-priority protocols to take flow-control action as needed. *See also:* BECN.

FEIP

Fast Ethernet Interface Processor: An interface processor employed on Cisco 7000 series routers, supporting up to two 100Mbps 100BaseT ports.

firewall

A barrier purposefully erected between any connected public networks and a private network, made up of a router or access server or several routers or access servers, that uses access lists and other methods to ensure the security of the private network.

flash memory

Developed by Intel and licensed to other semiconductor manufacturers, it is nonvolatile storage that can be erased electronically and reprogrammed. Flash memory permits software images to be stored, booted, and rewritten as needed. Cisco routers and switches use flash memory to hold the IOS by default.

flooding

When traffic is received on an interface, it is then transmitted to every interface connected to that device with exception of the interface from which the traffic originated. This technique can be used for traffic transfer by bridges and switches throughout the network.

flow control

A methodology used to ensure that receiving units are not overwhelmed with data from sending devices. Pacing, as it is called in IBM networks, means that when buffers at a receiving unit are full, a message is transmitted to the sending unit to temporarily halt transmissions until all the data in the receiving buffer has been processed and the buffer is again ready for action.

FRAD

Frame Relay Access Device: Any device affording a connection between a LAN and a Frame Relay WAN. *See also:* Cisco FRAD, FRAS.

fragment

Any portion of a larger packet that has been segmented into smaller pieces.

fragmentation

The process of segmenting a packet into smaller pieces when sending data over a network medium that cannot support the larger packet size.

frame

A logical unit of information sent by the Data Link layer over a transmission medium. The term often refers to the header and trailer, employed for synchronization and error control, that surround the data contained in the unit.

Frame Relay

A more efficient replacement of the X.25 protocol, Frame Relay is the industry-standard, switched Data Link layer protocol that services multiple virtual circuits using HDLC encapsulation between connected mechanisms.

Frame Relay bridging

Defined in RFC 1490, this bridging method uses the identical spanning–tree algorithm as other bridging operations but permits packets to be encapsulated for transmission across a Frame Relay network.

FRAS

Frame Relay Access Support: A feature of Cisco IOS software that enables SDLC, Ethernet, Token Ring, and Frame Relay-attached IBM devices to be linked with other IBM mechanisms on a Frame Relay network. *See also:* FRAD.

frequency

The number of cycles of an alternating current signal per time unit, measured in hertz (cycles per second).

FSIP

Fast Serial Interface Processor: The Cisco 7000 routers' default serial interface processor, it provides four or eight high-speed serial ports.

FTP

File Transfer Protocol: The TCP/IP protocol used for transmitting files between network nodes, it supports a broad range of file types and is defined in RFC 959. *See also:* TFTP.

full duplex

The capacity to transmit information between a sending station and a receiving unit at the same time. *See also:* half duplex.

full mesh

A type of network topology where every node has either a physical or a virtual circuit linking it to every other network node. A full mesh supplies a great deal of redundancy but is typically reserved for network backbones because of its expense. *See also:* partial mesh.

G

GNS

Get Nearest Server: On an IPX network, a request packet sent by a customer for determining the location of the nearest active server of a given type. An IPX network client launches a GNS request to get either a direct answer from a connected server or a response from a router disclosing the location of the service on the internetwork to the GNS. GNS is part of IPX and SAP . *See also:* IPX and SAP.

GRE

Generic Routing Encapsulation: A tunneling protocol created by Cisco with the capacity for encapsulating a wide variety of protocol packet types inside IP tunnels, thereby generating a virtual point-to-point connection to Cisco routers across an IP network at remote points. IP tunneling using GRE permits network expansion across a single-protocol backbone environment by linking multiprotocol subnetworks in a single-protocol backbone environment.

guard band

The unused frequency area found between two communications channels, furnishing the space necessary to avoid interference between the two.

H

half duplex

The capacity to transfer data in only one direction at a time between a sending unit and receiving unit. *See also:* full duplex.

handshake

Any series of transmissions exchanged between two or more devices on a network to ensure synchronized operations.

H channel

High-speed channel: A full duplex, ISDN primary rate channel operating at a speed of 384Kbps. *See also:* B, D, and E channels.

HDLC

High-Level Data Link Control: Using frame characters, including check-sums, HDLC designates a method for data encapsulation on synchronous serial links. HDLC is a bit-oriented synchronous Data Link layer protocol created by ISO and derived from SDLC. *See also:* SDLC.

helper address

Used to send multicast addresses to a server on a remote network.

hierarchical addressing

Any addressing plan employing a logical chain of commands to determine location. IP addresses are made up of a hierarchy of network numbers, subnet numbers, and host numbers to direct packets to the appropriate destination.

HIP

HSSI Interface Processor: An interface processor used on Cisco 7000 series routers, providing one HSSI port that supports connections to ATM, SMDS, Frame Relay, or private lines at speeds up to T3 or E3.

holddown

The state a route is placed in so that routers can neither advertise the route nor accept advertisements about it for a defined time period. Holddown is used to surface bad information about a route from all routers in the network. A route is generally placed in holddown when one of its links fails.

hop

The movement of a packet between any two network nodes. *See also:* hop count.

hop count

A routing metric that calculates the distance between a source and a destination. RIP employs hop count as its sole metric. *See also:* hop and RIP.

HSCI

High-Speed Communication Interface: Developed by Cisco, a single-port interface that provides full-duplex synchronous serial communications capability at speeds up to 52Mbps.

HSRP

Hot Standby Router Protocol: A protocol that provides high network availability and makes network topology changes without administrator intervention. It generates a Hot Standby router group, including a lead router that lends its services to any packet being transferred to the Hot Standby address. If the lead router fails, it will be replaced by any of the other routers—the standby routers— that monitor it.

HSSI

High-Speed Serial Interface: A network standard for high-speed serial linking over a WAN at speeds of up to 52Mbps.

I

ICD

International Code Designator: Adapted from the subnetwork model of addressing, this assigns the mapping of Network layer addresses to ATM addresses. HSSI is one of two ATM formats for addressing created by the ATM Forum to be utilized with private networks. *See also:* DCC.

ICMP

Internet Control Message Protocol: Documented in RFC 792, it is a Network layer Internet protocol for the purpose of reporting errors and providing information pertinent to IP packet procedures.

IEEE

Institute of Electrical and Electronics Engineers: A professional organization that, among other activities, defines standards in a number of fields within computing and electronics, including networking and communications. IEEE standards are the predominant LAN standards used today throughout the industry. Many protocols are commonly known by the reference number of the corresponding IEEE standard.

IEEE 802.1

The IEEE specification for STP (Spanning Tree Protocol). The STP uses SPA (Spanning Tree Algorithm) to find and prevent network loops in bridged networks.

IEEE 802.3

The IEEE committee specification that defines Ethernet 10BaseT. Ethernet is a LAN protocol that specifies physical layer and MAC sublayer media access. IEEE 802.3 uses CSMA/CD to provide access for many devices on the same network. FastEthernet is defined as 802.3u, and Gigabit Ethernet is defined as 802.3q. *See also:* CSMA/CD.

IEEE 802.5

IEEE committee that defines Token Ring media access.

IGMP

Internet Group Management Protocol: Employed by IP hosts, the protocol that reports their multicast group memberships to an adjacent multicast router.

IGP

Interior Gateway Protocol: Any protocol used by the Internet to exchange routing data within an independent system.

ILMI

Integrated (or Interim) Local Management Interface. A specification created by the ATM Forum, designated for the incorporation of network-management capability into the ATM UNI. Integrated Local Management Interface cells provide for automatic configuration between ATM systems. In LAN emulation, ILMI can provide sufficient information for the ATM end station to find an LECS. In addition, ILMI provides the ATM NSAP (network service access point) prefix information to the end station.

in-band management

In-band management is the management of a network device "through" the network using Simple Network Management Protocol (SNMP) or Telnet.

insured burst

In an ATM network, it is the largest, temporarily permitted data burst exceeding the insured rate on a PVC and not tagged by the traffic policing function for being dropped if network congestion occurs. This insured burst is designated in bytes or cells.

interarea routing

Routing between two or more logical areas. *Contrast with:* intra-area routing. *See also:* area.

interface processor

Any of several processor modules used with Cisco 7000 series routers. *See also:* AIP, CIP, EIP, FEIP, HIP, MIP, and TRIP.

Internet

The global "network of networks," whose popularity has exploded in the last few years. Originally a tool for collaborative academic research, it has become a medium for exchanging and distributing information of all kinds. The Internet's need to link disparate computer platforms and technologies has led to the development of uniform protocols and standards that have also found widespread use within corporate LANs. *See also:* TCP/IP and MBONE.

internet

Before the rise of the Internet, this lowercase form was shorthand for "inter-network" in the generic sense. Now rarely used. *See also:* internetwork.

Internet protocol

Any protocol belonging to the TCP/IP protocol stack. *See also:* TCP/IP.

internetwork

Any group of networks interconnected by routers and other mechanisms, typically operating as a single entity.

internetworking

Broadly, anything associated with the general task of linking networks to each other. The term encompasses technologies, procedures, and products. When you connect networks to a router, you are creating an internetwork.

intra-area routing

Routing that occurs within a logical area. *Contrast with:* interarea routing.

Inverse ARP

Inverse Address Resolution Protocol: A technique by which dynamic routes are constructed in a network, allowing an access server to locate the network address of a mechanism affiliated with a permanent virtual circuit (PVC).

IP

Internet Protocol: Defined in RFC 791, it is a Network layer protocol that is part of the TCP/IP stack and allows connectionless service. IP furnishes an array of features for addressing, type-of-service specification, fragmentation and reassembly, and security.

IP address

Often called an Internet address, this is an address uniquely identifying any device (host) on the Internet (or any TCP/IP network). Each address consists of four octets (32 bits), represented as decimal numbers separated by periods (a format known as "dotted-decimal"). Every address is made up of a network number, an optional subnetwork number, and a host number. The network and subnetwork numbers together are used for routing, while the host number addresses an individual host within the network or subnetwork. The network and subnetwork information is extracted from the IP address using the subnet mask. There are five classes of IP addresses (A–E), which allocate different numbers of bits to the network, subnetwork, and host portions of the address. *See also:* CIDR, IP, and subnet mask.

IPCP

IP Control Protocol: The protocol used to establish and configure IP over PPP. *See also:* IP and PPP.

IP multicast

A technique for routing that enables IP traffic to be reproduced from one source to several endpoints or from multiple sources to many destinations. Instead of transmitting only one packet to each individual point of destination, one packet is sent to a multicast group specified by only one IP endpoint address for the group.

IPX

Internetwork Packet Exchange: Network layer protocol (Layer 3) used in Novell NetWare networks for transferring information from servers to workstations. Similar to IP and XNS.

IPXCP

IPX Control Protocol: The protocol used to establish and configure IPX over PPP. *See also:* IPX and PPP.

IPXWAN

Protocol used for new WAN links to provide and negotiate line options on the link using IPX. After the link is up and the options have been agreed upon by the two end-to-end links, normal IPX transmission begins.

ISDN

Integrated Services Digital Network: Offered as a service by telephone companies, a communication protocol that allows telephone networks to carry data, voice, and other digital traffic. *See also:* BISDN, BRI, and PRI.

isochronous transmission

Asynchronous data transfer over a synchronous data link, requiring a constant bit rate for reliable transport. *Compare with:* asynchronous transmission and synchronous transmission.

ITU-T

International Telecommunication Union Telecommunication Standardization Sector: This is a group of engineers that develops worldwide standards for telecommunications technologies.

L

LAN

Local Area Network: Broadly, any network linking two or more computers and related devices within a limited geographical area (up to a few kilometers). LANs are typically high-speed, low-error networks within a company. Cabling and signaling at the physical and Data Link layers of the OSI are dictated by LAN standards. Ethernet, FDDI, and Token Ring are among the most popular LAN technologies. *Compare with:* MAN and WAN.

LANE

LAN emulation: The technology that allows an ATM network to operate as a LAN backbone. To do so, the ATM network is required to provide multicast and broadcast support, address mapping (MAC-to-ATM), SVC management, in addition to an operable packet format. Additionally, LANE defines Ethernet and Token Ring ELANs. *See also:* ELAN.

LAN switch

A high-speed switching mechanism, transmitting packets between segments of data links, occasionally referred to as a frame switch. LAN switches transfer traffic based on MAC addresses. Multilayer switches are a type of LAN switch. *See also:* multilayer switch, cut-through packet switching, and store-and-forward packet switching.

LAPB

Link Accessed Procedure, Balanced: A bit-oriented Data Link layer protocol that is part of the X.25 stack and has its origin in SDLC. *See also:* SDLC and X.25.

LAPD

Link Access Procedure on the D channel. The ISDN Data Link layer protocol used specifically for the D channel and defined by ITU-T Recommendations Q.920 and Q.921. LAPD evolved from LAPB and is created to comply with the signaling requirements of ISDN basic access.

latency

Broadly, the time it takes a data packet to get from one location to another. In specific networking contexts, it can mean either 1) the time elapsed (delay) between the execution of a request for access to a network by a device and the time the mechanism actually is permitted transmission, or 2) the time elapsed between when a mechanism receives a frame and the time that frame is forwarded out of the destination port.

LCP

Link Control Protocol: The protocol designed to establish, configure, and test data link connections for use by PPP. *See also:* PPP.

leaky bucket

An analogy for the basic cell rate algorithm (GCRA) used in ATM networks for checking the conformance of cell flows from a user or network. The bucket's "hole" is understood to be the prolonged rate at which cells can be accommodated, and the "depth" is the tolerance for cell bursts over a certain time period. *See also:* GCRA.

learning bridge

A bridge that builds a dynamic database of MAC addresses and the interfaces associated with each address to reduce traffic on the network.

LE ARP

LAN Emulation Address Resolution Protocol: The protocol providing the ATM address that corresponds to a MAC address.

LEC

LAN Emulation Client: Software providing the emulation of the Link Layer interface that allows the operation and communication of all higher-level protocols and applications to continue. The LEC client runs in all ATM devices, which include hosts, servers, bridges, and routers. The LANE client is responsible for address resolution, data transfer, address caching, interfacing to the emulated LAN, and driver support for higher-level services. *See also:* ELAN and LES.

LECS

LAN Emulation Configuration Server: An important part of emulated LAN services, providing the configuration data that is furnished upon request from the LES. These services include address registration for Integrated Local Management Interface (ILMI) support, configuration support for the LES addresses and their corresponding emulated LAN identifiers, and an interface to the emulated LAN. *See also:* LES and ELAN.

LES

LAN Emulation Server: The central LANE component that provides the initial configuration data for each connecting LEC. The LES typically is located on either an ATM-integrated router or a switch. Responsibilities of the LES include configuration and support for the LEC, address registration for the LEC, database storage and response concerning ATM addresses, and interfacing to the emulated LAN *See also:* ELAN, LEC, and LECS.

link-state routing algorithm

A routing algorithm that allows each router to broadcast or multicast information regarding the cost of reaching all its neighbors to every node in the internetwork. Link-state algorithms provide a consistent view of the network and are therefore not vulnerable to routing loops. However, this is achieved at the cost of somewhat greater difficulty in computation and more widespread traffic (compared with distance vector routing algorithms). *See also:* distance vector routing algorithm.

LLAP

LocalTalk Link Access Protocol: In a LocalTalk environment, the Data Link-level protocol that manages node-to-node delivery of data. This protocol provides node addressing and management of bus access, and it also controls data sending and receiving to assure packet length and integrity.

LLC

Logical Link Control: Defined by the IEEE, the higher of two Data Link layer sublayers. LLC is responsible for error control, flow control, framing, and MAC-sublayer addressing. The predominant LLC protocol, IEEE 802.2, defines both connectionless and connection-oriented operations. *See also:* Data Link layer and MAC.

LMI

An enhancement to the original Frame Relay specification. Among the features it provides are a keep-alive mechanism, a multicast mechanism, global addressing, and a status mechanism.

LNNI

LAN Emulation Network-to-Network Interface: In the Phase 2 LANE specification, an interface that supports communication between the server components within one ELAN.

local explorer packet

In an SRB network, a packet generated by an end system to find a host linked to the local ring. If no local host can be found, the end system will produce one of two solutions: a spanning explorer packet or an all-routes explorer packet.

LocalTalk

Utilizing CSMA/CD, in addition to supporting data transmission at speeds of 230.4Kbps, LocalTalk is Apple Computer's proprietary baseband protocol, operating at the Data Link and Physical layers of the OSI reference model.

LSA

Link-State Advertisement: Occasionally referred to as link-state packets (LSPs), these advertisements are broadcast packets, containing information about neighbors and path costs, that are employed by link-state protocols. Receiving routers use LSAs to maintain their routing tables.

LUNI

LAN Emulation User-to-Network Interface: Defining the interface between the LAN Emulation Client (LEC) and the LAN Emulation Server, LUNI is the ATM Forum's standard for LAN Emulation on ATM networks. *See also:* LES and LECS.

 M

MAC

Media Access Control: The lower sublayer in the Data Link layer, it is responsible for hardware addressing, media access, and error detection of frames. *See also:* Data Link layer and LLC.

MAC address

A Data Link layer address that every port or device needs in order to connect to a LAN. These addresses are used by various devices in the network for accurate location of ports, including the creation and revision of routing tables. MAC addresses are defined by the IEEE standard and their length is six characters. Variously called hardware address, physical address, or MAC-layer address.

MacIP

In AppleTalk, the Network layer protocol encapsulating IP packets in Datagram Delivery Protocol (DDP) packets. MacIP also supplies substitute ARP services.

MAN

Metropolitan-Area Network: Any network that encompasses a metropolitan area; that is, an area typically larger than a LAN but smaller than a WAN. *See also:* LAN and WAN.

Manchester encoding

A method for digital coding in which a mid-bit–time transition is employed for clocking, and a 1 (one) is denoted by a high voltage level during the first half of the bit time. This scheme is used by Ethernet and IEEE 802.3.

maximum burst

Specified in bytes or cells, the largest burst of information exceeding the insured rate that will be permitted on an ATM permanent virtual connection for a short time and will not be dropped even if it goes over the specified maximum rate. *Compare with:* insured burst. *See also:* maximum rate.

maximum rate

The maximum permitted data throughput on a particular virtual circuit, equal to the total of insured and uninsured traffic from the traffic source. Should traffic congestion occur, uninsured information may be deleted from the path. Measured in bits or cells per second, the maximum rate represents the highest throughput of data the virtual circuit is ever able to deliver and cannot exceed the media rate. *Compare with:* excess rate. *See also:* maximum burst.

MBS

Maximum Burst Size: In an ATM signaling message, this metric, coded as a number of cells, is used to convey the burst tolerance.

MBONE

Multicast Backbone: The multicast backbone of the Internet, it is a virtual multicast network made up of multicast LANs, including point-to-point tunnels interconnecting them.

MCDV

Maximum Cell Delay Variation: The maximum two-point CDV objective across a link or node for the identified service category in an ATM network. The MCDV is one of four link metrics that are exchanged using PTSPs to verify the available resources of an ATM network. Only one MCDV value is assigned to each traffic class.

MCLR

Maximum Cell Loss Ratio: The maximum ratio of cells in an ATM network, that fail to transit a link or node compared with the total number of cells that arrive at the link or node. MCDV is one of four link metrics that are exchanged using PTSPs to verify the available resources of an ATM network. The MCLR applies to cells in VBR and CBR traffic classes whose CLP bit is set to zero. *See also:* CBR, CLP, and VBR.

MCR

Minimum Cell Rate: A parameter determined by the ATM Forum for traffic management of the ATM networks. MCR is specifically defined for ABR transmissions and specifies the minimum value for the allowed cell rate (ACR). *See also:* ACR and PCR.

MCTD

Maximum Cell Transfer Delay: In an ATM network, the total of the maximum cell delay variation and the fixed delay across the link or node. MCTD is one of four link metrics that are exchanged using PNNI topology state packets to verify the available resources of an ATM network. There is one MCTD value assigned to each traffic class. *See also:* MCDV.

MIB

Management Information Base: Used with SNMP management software to gather information from remote devices. The management station can poll the remote device for information, or the MIB running on the remote station can be programmed to send information on a regular basis.

MIP

Multichannel Interface Processor: The resident interface processor on Cisco 7000 series routers, providing up to two channelized T1 or E1 connections by serial cables connected to a CSU. The two controllers are capable of providing 24 T1 or 30 E1 channel groups, with each group being introduced to the system as a serial interface that can be configured individually.

mips

Millions of Instructions Per Second: A measure of processor speed.

MLP

Multilink PPP: A technique used to split, recombine, and sequence datagrams across numerous logical data links.

MMP

Multichassis Multilink PPP: A protocol that supplies MLP support across multiple routers and access servers. MMP enables several routers and access servers to work as a single, large dial-up pool with one network address and

ISDN access number. MMP successfully supports packet fragmenting and reassembly when the user connection is split between two physical access devices.

modem

Modulator-demodulator: A device that converts digital signals to analog and vice-versa so that digital information can be transmitted over analog communication facilities, such as voice-grade telephone lines. This is achieved by converting digital signals at the source to analog for transmission, and reconverting the analog signals back into digital form at the destination. *See also:* modulation and demodulation.

modem eliminator

A mechanism that makes possible a connection between two DTE devices without modems.

modulation

The process of modifying some characteristic of an electrical signal, such as amplitude (AM) or frequency (FM), in order to represent digital or analog information. *See also:* AM.

MOSPF

Multicast OSPF: An extension of the OSPF unicast protocol that enables IP multicast routing within the domain. *See also:* OSPF.

MPOA

Multiprotocol over ATM: An effort by the ATM Forum to standardize how existing and future Network-layer protocols such as IP, Ipv6, AppleTalk, and IPX run over an ATM network with directly attached hosts, routers, and multilayer LAN switches.

MTU

Maximum Transmission Unit: The largest packet size, measured in bytes, that an interface can handle.

multicast

Broadly, any communication between a single sender and multiple receivers. Unlike broadcast messages, which are sent to all addresses on a network, multicast messages are sent to a defined subset of the network addresses; this subset has a group multicast address, which is specified in the packet's destination address field. *See also:* broadcast.

multicast address

A single address that points to more than one device on the network. Identical to group address. *See also:* multicast.

multicast send VCC

A two-directional point-to-point virtual control connection (VCC) arranged by an LEC to a BUS, it is one of the three types of informational link specified by phase 1 LANE. *See also:* control distribute VCC and control direct VCC.

multilayer switch

A type of LAN switch, the device filters and forwards packets based on their Layer 2 MAC addresses and Layer 3 network addresses. It's possible that even Layer 4 can be read. *See also:* LAN switch.

multiplexing

The process of converting several logical signals into a single physical signal for transmission across one physical channel. *Contrast with:* demultiplexing.

N

NAK

Negative acknowledgment: A response sent from a receiver, telling the sender that the information it received contained errors. *Compare with:* acknowledgment.

NAT

Network Address Translation: An algorithm instrumental in minimizing the requirement for globally unique IP addresses, permitting an organization whose addresses are not all globally unique to connect to the Internet, regardless, by translating those addresses into globally routable address space.

NBP

Name Binding Protocol: In AppleTalk, the transport-level protocol that interprets a socket client's name, entered as a character string, into the corresponding DDP address. NBP gives AppleTalk protocols the capacity to discern user-defined zones and names of mechanisms by showing and keeping translation tables that map names to their corresponding socket addresses.

neighboring routers

Two routers in OSPF that have interfaces to a common network. On networks with multiaccess, these neighboring routers are dynamically discovered using the Hello protocol of OSPF.

NetBEUI

NetBIOS Extended User Interface: An improved version of the NetBIOS protocol used in a number of network operating systems including LAN Manager, Windows NT, LAN Server, and Windows for Workgroups, implementing the OSI LLC2 protocol. NetBEUI formalizes the transport frame—not standardized in NetBIOS—and adds more functions. *See also:* OSI.

NetBIOS

Network Basic Input/Output System: The API employed by applications residing on an IBM LAN to ask for services, such as session termination or information transfer, from lower-level network processes.

NetView

A mainframe network product from IBM, used for monitoring SNA (Systems Network Architecture) networks. It runs as a VTAM (Virtual Telecommunications Access Method) application.

NetWare

A widely used NOS created by Novell, providing a number of distributed network services and remote file access.

Network layer

In the OSI reference model, it is Layer 3—the layer in which routing is implemented, enabling connections and path selection between two end-systems. *See also:* Application layer, Data Link layer, Physical layer, Presentation layer, Session layer, and Transport layer.

NFS

Network File System: One of the protocols in Sun Microsystems' widely used file system protocol suite, allowing remote file access across a network. The name is loosely used to refer to the entire Sun protocol suite, which also includes RPC, XDR (External Data Representation), and other protocols.

NHRP

Next Hop Resolution Protocol: In a nonbroadcast multiaccess (NBMA) network, the protocol employed by routers in order to dynamically locate MAC addresses of various hosts and routers. It enables systems to communicate directly without requiring an intermediate hop, thus facilitating increased performance in ATM, Frame Relay, X.25, and SMDS systems.

NHS

Next Hop Server: Defined by the NHRP protocol, this server maintains the next-hop resolution cache tables, listing IP-to-ATM address maps of related nodes and nodes that can be reached through routers served by the NHS.

NIC

Network Interface Card: An electronic circuit board placed in a computer. The NIC provides network communication to a LAN.

NLSP

NetWare Link Services Protocol: Novell's link-state routing protocol, based on the IS-IS model.

NMP

Network Management Processor: A Catalyst 5000 switch processor module used to control and monitor the switch.

non-stub area

In OSPF, a resource-consuming area carrying a default route, intra-area routes, interarea routes, static routes, and external routes. Non-stub areas are the only areas that can have virtual links configured across them and exclusively contain an anonymous system boundary router (ASBR). *Compare with:* stub area. *See also:* ASBR and OSPF.

NRZ

Nonreturn to Zero: One of several encoding schemes for transmitting digital data. NRZ signals sustain constant levels of voltage with no signal shifting (no return to zero-voltage level) during a bit interval. If there is a series of bits with the same value (1 or 0), there will be no state change. The signal is not self-clocking. *See also:* NRZI.

NRZI

Nonreturn to Zero Inverted: One of several encoding schemes for transmitting digital data. A transition in voltage level (either from high to low or vice-versa) at the beginning of a bit interval is interpreted as a value of 1; the absence of a transition is interpreted as a 0. Thus, the voltage assigned to each value is continually inverted. NRZI signals are not self-clocking. *See also:* NRZ.

NVRAM

Non-Volatile RAM: Random-access memory that keeps its contents intact while power is turned off.

O

OC

Optical Carrier: A series of physical protocols, designated as OC-1, OC-2, OC-3, and so on, for SONET optical signal transmissions. OC signal levels place STS frames on a multimode fiber-optic line at various speeds, of which 51.84Mbps is the lowest (OC-1). Each subsequent protocol runs at a speed divisible by 51.84. *See also:* SONET.

100BaseT

Based on the IEEE 802.3 standard, 100BaseT is the Fast Ethernet specification of 100Mbps baseband that uses UTP wiring. 100BaseT sends link pulses (containing more information than those used in 10BaseT) over the network when no traffic is present. *See also:* 10BaseT, Fast Ethernet, and IEEE 802.3.

100BaseTX

Based on the IEEE 802.3 standard, 100BaseTX is the 100Mbps baseband Fast Ethernet specification that uses two pairs of UTP or STP wiring. The first pair of wires receives data; the second pair sends data. To ensure correct signal timing, a 100BaseTX segment cannot be longer than 100 meters.

ones density

Also known as pulse density, this is a method of signal clocking. The CSU/DSU retrieves the clocking information from data that passes through it. For this scheme to work, the data needs to be encoded to contain at least one binary 1 for each eight bits transmitted. *See also* CSU and DSU.

OSI

Open System Interconnection: International standardization program designed by ISO and ITU-T for the development of data networking standards that make multivendor equipment interoperability a reality.

OSI reference model

Open System Interconnection reference model: A conceptual model defined by the International Standardization Organization (ISO), describing how any combination of devices can be connected for the purpose of communication. The OSI model divides the task into seven functional layers, forming a hierarchy with the applications at the top and the physical medium at the bottom, and it defines the functions each layer must provide. *See also:* Application layer, Session layer, Data Link layer, Network layer, Physical layer, Presentation layer, and Transport layer.

OSPF

Open Shortest Path First: A link-state, hierarchical IGP routing algorithm derived from an earlier version of the IS-IS protocol, whose features include multipath routing, load balancing, and least-cost routing. OSPF is the suggested successor to RIP in the Internet environment. *See also:* enhanced IGRP, IGP, and IP.

out-of-band management

Management "outside" of the network's physical channels using a console connection.

out-of-band signaling

Within a network, any transmission that uses physical channels or frequencies separate from those ordinarily used for data transfer. For example, the initial configuration of a Cisco Catalyst switch requires an out-of-band connection via a console port.

P

packet

In data communications, the basic logical unit of information transferred. A packet consists of a certain number of data bytes, wrapped or encapsulated in headers and/or trailers that contain information about where the packet came from, where it's going, and so on. The various protocols involved in sending a transmission add their own layers of header information, which the corresponding protocols in receiving devices then interpret.

packet switch

A physical device that makes it possible for a communication channel to share several connections, its functions include finding the most efficient transmission path for packets.

packet switching

A networking technology based on the transmission of data in packets. Dividing a continuous stream of data into small units—packets—enables data from multiple devices on a network to share the same communication channel simultaneously but also requires the use of precise routing information. *Contrast with:* circuit switching.

PAP

Password Authentication Protocol: In Point-to-Point Protocol (PPP) networks, a method of validating connection requests. The requesting (remote) device must send an authentication request, containing a password and ID, to the local router when attempting to connect. Unlike the more secure CHAP (Challenge Handshake Authentication Protocol), PAP sends the password unencrypted and does not attempt to verify whether the user is authorized to access the requested resource; it merely identifies the remote end. *See also:* CHAP.

parity checking

A method of error-checking in data transmissions. An extra bit (the parity bit) is added to each character or data word so that the sum of the bits will be either an odd number (in odd parity) or an even number (even parity).

partial mesh

A type of network topology in which some network nodes form a full mesh (where every node has either a physical or a virtual circuit linking it to every other network node), but others are attached to only one or two nodes in the network. A typical use of partial-mesh topology is in peripheral networks linked to a fully meshed backbone. *See also:* full mesh.

PCR

Peak Cell Rate: As defined by the ATM Forum, the parameter specifying, in cells per second, the maximum rate at which a source may transmit.

PDN

Public Data Network: Generally for a fee, a PDN offers the public access to computer communication network operated by private concerns or government agencies. Small organizations can take advantage of PDNs, aiding them creating WANs without investing in long-distance equipment and circuitry.

PGP

Pretty Good Privacy: A popular public-key encryption application offering protected transfer of files and messages.

Physical layer

The lowest layer—Layer 1—in the OSI reference model, it is responsible for converting data packets from the Data Link layer (Layer 2) into electrical signals. Physical-layer protocols and standards define, for example, the type of cable and connectors to be used, including their pin assignments and the encoding scheme for signaling 0 and 1 values. *See also:* Data Link layer, Network layer, Application layer, Session layer, Presentation layer, and Transport layer.

ping

Packet internet groper: A Unix-based Internet diagnostic tool, consisting of a message sent to test the accessibility of a particular device on the IP network. The acronym (from which the "full name" was formed) reflects the underlying metaphor of submarine sonar. Just as the sonar operator sends out a signal and waits to hear it echo ("ping") back from a submerged object, the network user can ping another node on the network and wait to see if it responds.

pleisochronous

Nearly synchronous, except that clocking comes from an outside source instead of being embedded within the signal as in synchronous transmissions.

PLP

Packet Level Protocol: Occasionally called X.25 Level 3 or X.25 Protocol, a Network-layer protocol that is part of the X.25 stack.

PNNI

Private Network-Network Interface: An ATM Forum specification for offering topology data used for the calculation of paths through the network, among switches and groups of switches. It is based on well-known link-state routing procedures and allows for automatic configuration in networks whose addressing scheme is determined by the topology.

point-to-multipoint connection

In ATM, a communication path going only one way, connecting a single system at the starting point, called the "root node," to systems at multiple points of destination, called "leaves." *See also:* point-to-point connection.

point-to-point connection

In ATM, a channel of communication that can be directed either one way or two ways between two ATM end-systems. *See also:* point-to-multipoint connection.

poison reverse updates

These update messages are transmitted by a router in order to overcome large routing loops and offer explicit information when a subnet or network is not accessible (instead of merely suggesting that the network is unreachable by not including it in updates).

polling

The procedure of orderly inquiry, used by a primary network mechanism, to determine if secondary devices have data to transmit. A message is sent to each secondary, granting the secondary the right to transmit.

POP

1. Point Of Presence: The physical location where an interexchange carrier has placed equipment to interconnect with a local exchange carrier.

2. Post Office Protocol: A protocol used by client e-mail applications for recovery of mail from a mail server.

PPP

Point-to-Point Protocol: The protocol most commonly used for dial-up Internet access, superseding the earlier SLIP. Its features include address notification, authentication via CHAP or PAP, support for multiple protocols, and link monitoring. PPP has two layers: the Link Control Protocol (LCP) establishes, configures, and tests a link; and then any of various Network Control Protocols (NCPs) transport traffic for a specific protocol suite, such as IPX. *See also:* CHAP, PAP, and SLIP.

Presentation layer

Layer 6 of the OSI reference model, it defines how data is formatted, presented, encoded, and converted for use by software at the Application layer. *See also:* Application layer, Data Link layer, Network layer, Physical layer, Session layer, and Transport layer.

PRI

Primary Rate Interface: A type of ISDN connection between a PBX and a long-distance carrier, which is made up of a single 64Kbps D channel in addition to 23 (T1) or 30 (E1) B channels. *See also:* ISDN.

priority queueing

A routing function in which frames temporarily placed in an interface output queue are assigned priorities based on traits such as packet size or type of interface.

process switching

As a packet arrives on a router to be forwarded, it's copied to the router's process buffer, and the router performs a lookup on the Layer 3 address. Using the route table, an exit interface is associated with the destination address. The processor forwards the packet with the added new information to the exit interface, while the router initializes the fast-switching cache. Subsequent packets bound for the same destination address follow the same path as the first packet.

PROM

Programmable read-only memory: ROM that is programmable only once, using special equipment. *Compare with:* EPROM.

propagation delay

The time it takes data to traverse a network from its source to its destination.

protocol

In networking, the specification of a set of rules for a particular type of communication. The term is also used to refer to the software that implements a protocol.

protocol stack

A collection of related protocols.

PSE

Packet Switch Exchange: The X.25 term for a switch.

PSN

Packet-switched Network: Any network that uses packet-switching technology. Also known as packet-switched data network (PSDN). *See also:* packet switching.

PSTN

Public Switched Telephone Network: Colloquially referred to as plain old telephone service (POTS). A term that describes the assortment of telephone networks and services available globally.

PVC

Permanent Virtual Circuit: In a frame-relay network, a logical connection, defined in software, that is maintained permanently. *Compare with:* SVC. *See also:* virtual circuit.

PVP

Permanent Virtual Path: A virtual path made up of PVCs. *See also:* PVC.

PVP tunneling

Permanent Virtual Path Tunneling: A technique that links two private ATM networks across a public network using a virtual path; wherein the public network transparently trunks the complete collection of virtual channels in the virtual path between the two private networks.

Q

QoS

Quality of Service: A set of metrics used to measure the quality of transmission and service availability of any given transmission system.

queue

Broadly, any list of elements arranged in an orderly fashion and ready for processing, such as a line of people waiting to enter a movie theater. In routing, it refers to a backlog of information packets waiting in line to be transmitted over a router interface.

R

RARP

Reverse Address Resolution Protocol: The protocol within the TCP/IP stack that maps MAC addresses to IP addresses. *See also:* ARP.

rate queue

A value, assigned to one or more virtual circuits, that specifies the speed at which an individual virtual circuit will transmit data to the remote end. Every rate queue identifies a segment of the total bandwidth available on an ATM link. The sum of all rate queues should not exceed the total available bandwidth.

RCP

Remote Copy Protocol: A protocol for copying files to or from a file system that resides on a remote server on a network, using TCP to guarantee reliable data delivery.

redistribution

Command used in Cisco routers to inject the paths found from one type of routing protocol into another type of routing protocol. For example, networks found by RIP can be inserted into an IGRP network.

redundancy

In internetworking, the duplication of connections, devices, or services that can be used as a backup in the event that the primary connections, devices, or services fail.

reload

An event or command that causes Cisco routers to reboot.

RIF

Routing Information Field: In source-route bridging, a header field that defines the path direction of the frame or Token (left to right or right to left). It is also defined as part of a MAC header for source-routed frames, which contains path information. This bit is used in an explorer frame to notify computers that it is on its return path.

ring

Two or more stations connected in a logical circular topology. In this topology, which is the basis for Token Ring, FDDI, and CDDI, information is transferred from station to station in sequence.

ring topology

A network logical topology comprising a series of repeaters that form one closed loop by connecting unidirectional transmission links. Individual stations on the network are connected to the network at a repeater. Physically, ring topologies are generally organized in a closed-loop star. *Compare with:* bus topology and star topology.

RIP

Routing Information Protocol: The most commonly used interior gateway protocol in the Internet. RIP employs hop count as a routing metric. *See also:* Enhanced IGRP, IGP, OSPF, and hop count.

routed protocol

Routed protocols (such as IP and IPX) are used to transmit user data through an internetwork. By contrast, routing protocols (such as RIP, IGRP, and OSPF) are used to update routing tables between routers.

route summarization

In OSPF and IS-IS, the consolidation of publicized addresses so that a single summary route is advertised to other areas by an area border router.

router

A Network-layer mechanism, either software or hardware, using one or more metrics to decide on the best path to use for transmission of network traffic. Sending packets between networks by routers is based on the information provided on Network layers. Historically, this device has sometimes been called a gateway.

routing

The process of locating a path to the destination host. In large networks, the numerous intermediary destinations a packet might travel before reaching its destination can make routing very complex.

routing domain

Any collection of end systems and intermediate systems that operate under an identical set of administrative rules. Every routing domain contains one or several areas, all individually given a certain area address.

routing metric

Any value that is used by routing algorithms to determine whether one route is superior to another. Metrics include such information as bandwidth, delay, hop count, path cost, load, MTU, reliability, and communication cost, all of which is stored in routing tables. *See also:* cost.

routing protocol

Any protocol that defines algorithms to be used for updating routing tables between routers. Examples include IGRP, RIP, and OSPF.

routing table

A table kept in a router or other internetworking mechanism that maintains a record of routes to certain network destinations and the metrics associated with those routes.

RP

Route Processor: Also known as a supervisory processor, a module on Cisco 7000 series routers that holds the CPU, system software, and most of the memory components used in the router.

RSP

Route/Switch Processor: A processor module combining the functions of RP and SP used in Cisco 7500 series routers. *See also:* RP and SP.

RTS

Request To Send: An EIA/TIA-232 control signal requesting permission to transmit data on a communication line.

S

sampling rate

The rate at which samples of a specific waveform amplitude are collected.

SAP

1. Service Access Point: A field specified by IEEE 802.2 that is part of an address specification.

2. Service Advertisement Protocol: The Novell NetWare protocol that supplies a way to inform network clients of resources and services availability on network, using routers and servers. *See also:* IPX.

SCR

Sustainable Cell Rate: An ATM Forum parameter used for traffic management, it is the long-term average cell rate for VBR connections that can be transmitted.

SDLC

Synchronous Data Link Control: A protocol used in SNA Data Link layer communications. SDLC is a bit-oriented, full-duplex serial protocol that is the basis for several similar protocols, including HDLC and LAPB. *See also:* HDLC and LAPB.

seed router

In an AppleTalk network, the router that is equipped with the network number or cable range in its port descriptor. The seed router specifies the network number or cable range for other routers in that network section and answers to configuration requests from nonseed routers on its connected AppleTalk network, permitting those routers to affirm or modify their configurations accordingly. Every AppleTalk network needs at least one seed router.

server

Hardware and software that provide network services to clients.

Session layer

Layer 5 of the OSI reference model, responsible for creating, managing, and terminating sessions between applications and overseeing data exchange between Presentation layer entities. *See also:* Application layer, Data Link layer, Network layer, Physical layer, Presentation layer, and Transport layer.

SF

Super Frame: A super frame (also called a D4 frame) consists of 12 frames with 192 bits each, and the 193rd bit providing other functions including error checking. SF is frequently used on T1 circuits. A newer version of the technology is Extended Super Frame (ESF), which uses 24 frames. *See also:* ESF.

signaling packet

An informational packet created by an ATM-connected mechanism that wants to establish connection with another such mechanism. The packet contains the QoS parameters needed for connection and the ATM NSAP address of the endpoint. The endpoint responds with a message of acceptance, if it is able to support the desired QoS, and the connection is established. *See also:* QoS.

silicon switching

A type of high-speed switching used in Cisco 7000 series routers, based on the use of a separate processor (the Silicon Switch Processor, or SSP). *See also:* SSE.

sliding window

The method of flow control used by TCP, as well as several Data Link layer protocols. This method places a buffer between the receiving application and the network data flow. The "window" available for accepting data is the size of the buffer minus the amount of data already there. This window increases in size as the application reads data from it and decreases as new data is sent. The receiver sends the transmitter announcements of the current window size, and it may stop accepting data until the window increases above a certain threshold.

SLIP

Serial Line Internet Protocol: A variation of TCP/IP used as an industry standard for point-to-point connections. SLIP is the predecessor to PPP. *See also:* PPP.

SMDS

Switched Multimegabit Data Service: A packet-switched, datagram-based WAN networking technology offered by telephone companies that provides high speed.

SMTP

Simple Mail Transfer Protocol: A protocol used on the Internet to provide electronic mail services.

SNA

System Network Architecture: A complex, feature-rich, network architecture similar to the OSI reference model but with several variations; created by IBM in the 1970s and essentially composed of seven layers.

SNAP

Subnetwork Access Protocol: SNAP is a frame used in Ethernet, Token Ring, and FDDI LANs. Data transfer, connection management, and QoS selection are three primary functions executed by the SNAP frame.

socket

1. A software structure that operates within a network device as a destination point for communications.

2. In AppleTalk networks, an entity at a specific location within a node; AppleTalk sockets are conceptually similar to TCP/IP ports.

SONET

Synchronous Optical Network: The ANSI standard for synchronous transmission on fiber-optic media, developed at Bell Labs. It specifies a base signal rate of 51.84Mbps and a set of multiples of that rate, known as Optical Carrier levels, up to 2.5Gbps.

SP

Switch Processor: Also known as a ciscoBus controller, it is a Cisco 7000 series processor module acting as governing agent for all CxBus activities.

span

A full-duplex digital transmission line connecting two facilities.

SPAN

Switched Port Analyzer: A feature of the Catalyst 5000 switch, offering freedom to manipulate within a switched Ethernet environment by extending the monitoring ability of the existing network analyzers into the environment. At one switched segment, the SPAN mirrors traffic onto a pre-determined SPAN port, while a network analyzer connected to the SPAN port is able to monitor traffic from any other Catalyst switched port.

spanning explorer packet

Sometimes called limited-route or single-route explorer packet, it pursues a statically configured spanning tree when searching for paths in a source-route bridging network. *See also:* all-routes explorer packet, explorer packet, and local explorer packet.

spanning tree

A subset of a network topology, within which no loops exist. When bridges are interconnected into a loop, the bridge, or switch, cannot identify a frame that has been forwarded previously, so there is no mechanism for removing a frame as it passes the interface numerous times. Without a method of removing these frames, the bridges continuously forward them—consuming bandwidth and adding overhead to the network. Spanning trees prune the network to provide only one path for any packet. *See also:* Spanning Tree Protocol and Spanning Tree Algorithm.

Spanning Tree Algorithm (STA)

An algorithm that creates a spanning tree using the Spanning Tree Protocol (STP). *See also:* spanning tree and Spanning-Tree Protocol.

Spanning Tree Protocol (STP)

The bridge protocol (IEEE 802.1) that enables a learning bridge to dynamically avoid loops in the network topology by creating a spanning tree using the Spanning Tree Algorithm. Spanning tree frames called *bridge protocol data units* (BPDUs) are sent and received by all switches in the network at regular intervals. The switches participating in the spanning tree don't forward the frames; instead, they're processed to determine the spanning tree topology itself. Cisco Catalyst series switches use STP 802.1d to perform this function. *See also:* BPDU, learning bridge, MAC address, spanning tree, and Spanning Tree Algorithm.

SPF

Shortest Path First algorithm: A routing algorithm used to decide on the shortest-path spanning tree. Sometimes called Dijkstra's algorithm and frequently used in link-state routing algorithms. *See also:* link-state routing algorithm.

SPID

Service Profile Identifier: A number assigned by service providers or local telephone companies and assigned by administrators to a BRI port. SPIDs are used to determine subscription services of a device connected via ISDN. ISDN devices use SPID when accessing the telephone company switch that initializes the link to a service provider.

split-horizon updates

Useful for preventing routing loops, a type of distance-vector routing protocol where information about routes is prevented from leaving the router interface through which that information was received.

spoofing

1. In dial-on-demand routing (DDR), where a circuit-switched link is taken down to save toll charges when there is no traffic to be sent, spoofing is a scheme used by routers that causes a host to treat an interface as if it were functioning and supporting a session. The router sends "spoof" replies to keep-alive messages from the host in an effort to convince the host that the session is up and running. *See also:* DDR.

2. The illegal act of sending a packet labeled with a false address, in order to deceive network security mechanisms such as filters and access lists.

spooler

A management application that processes requests submitted to it for execution in a sequential fashion from a queue. A good example is a print spooler.

SPX

Sequenced Packet Exchange: A Novell NetWare transport protocol that augments the datagram service provided by Network layer (Layer 3) protocols, it was derived from the Switch-to-Switch Protocol of the XNS protocol suite.

SQE

Signal Quality Error: In an Ethernet network, a message sent from a transceiver to an attached machine that the collision-detection circuitry is working.

SRB

Source-Route Bridging: Created by IBM, the bridging method used in Token Ring networks. The source determines the entire route to a destination before sending the data and includes that information in fields within each packet. *Contrast with:* transparent bridging.

SRT

Source-Route Transparent bridging: A bridging scheme developed by IBM, merging source-route and transparent bridging. SRT takes advantage of both technologies in one device, fulfilling the needs of all end nodes. Translation between bridging protocols is not necessary. *Compare with:* SR/TLB.

SR/TLB

Source-Route Translational Bridging: A bridging method that allows source-route stations to communicate with transparent bridge stations aided by an intermediate bridge that translates between the two bridge protocols. Used for bridging between Token Ring and Ethernet. *Compare with*: SRT.

SSAP

Source Service Access Point: The SAP of the network node identified in the Source field of the packet. *See also:* DSAP and SAP.

SSE

Silicon Switching Engine: The software component of Cisco's silicon switching technology, hard-coded into the Silicon Switch Processor (SSP). Silicon switching is available only on the Cisco 7000 with an SSP. Silicon-switched packets are compared to the silicon-switching cache on the SSE. The SSP is a dedicated switch processor that offloads the switching process from the route processor, providing a fast-switching solution, but packets must still traverse the backplane of the router to get to the SSP and then back to the exit interface.

star topology

A LAN physical topology with end points on the network converging at a common central switch (known as a hub) using point-to-point links. A logical ring topology can be configured as a physical star topology using a unidirectional closed-loop star rather than point-to-point links. That is, connections within the hub are arranged in an internal ring. *See also:* bus topology and ring topology.

startup range

If an AppleTalk node does not have a number saved from the last time it was booted, then the node selects from this range of values—from 65280 to 65534.

static route

A route whose information is purposefully entered into the routing table and takes priority over those chosen by dynamic routing protocols.

statistical multiplexing

Multiplexing in general is a technique that allows data from multiple logical channels to be sent across a single physical channel. Statistical multiplexing dynamically assigns bandwidth only to input channels that are active, optimizing available bandwidth so that more devices can be connected than with other multiplexing techniques. Also known as statistical time-division multiplexing or stat mux.

STM-1

Synchronous Transport Module Level 1. In the European SDH standard, one of many formats identifying the frame structure for the 155.52Mbps lines that are used to carry ATM cells.

store-and-forward packet switching

A technique in which the switch first copies each packet into its buffer and performs a cyclic redundancy check (CRC). If the packet is error-free, the switch then looks up the destination address in its filter table, determines the appropriate exit port, and sends the packet.

STP

1. Shielded Twisted Pair: A two-pair wiring scheme, used in many network implementations, that has a layer of shielded insulation to reduce EMI.

2. SpanningTree Protocol.

stub area

An OSPF area carrying a default route, intra-area routes, and interarea routes, but no external routes. Configuration of virtual links cannot be achieved across a stub area, and stub areas are not allowed to contain an ASBR. *See also:* non-stub area, ASBR, and OSPF.

stub network

A network having only one connection to a router.

STUN

Serial Tunnel: A technology used to connect an HDLC link to an SDLC link over a serial link.

subarea

A portion of an SNA network made up of a subarea node and its attached links and peripheral nodes.

subarea node

An SNA communications host or controller that handles entire network addresses.

subchannel

A frequency-based subdivision that creates a separate broadband communications channel.

subinterface

One of many virtual interfaces available on a single physical interface.

subnet

See: subnetwork.

subnet address

The portion of an IP address that is specifically identified by the subnet mask as the subnetwork. *See also:* IP address, subnetwork, and subnet mask.

subnet mask

Also simply known as mask, a 32-bit address mask used in IP to identify the bits of an IP address that are used for the subnet address. Using a mask, the router does not need to examine all 32 bits, only those selected by the mask. *See also:* address mask and IP address.

subnetwork

1. Any network that is part of a larger IP network and is identified by a subnet address. A network administrator segments a network into subnetworks in order to provide a hierarchical, multilevel routing structure, and at the same time protect the subnetwork from the addressing complexity of networks that are attached. Also known as a subnet. *See also:* IP address, subnet mask, and subnet address.

2. In OSI networks, the term specifically refers to a collection of ESs and ISs controlled by only one administrative domain, using a solitary network connection protocol.

SVC

Switched Virtual Circuit: A dynamically established virtual circuit, created on demand and dissolved as soon as transmission is over and the circuit is no longer needed. In ATM terminology, it is referred to as a switched virtual connection. *See also:* PVC.

switch

1. In networking, a device responsible for multiple functions such as filtering, flooding, and sending frames. It works using the destination address of individual frames. Switches operate at the Data Link layer of the OSI model.

2. Broadly, any electronic/mechanical device allowing connections to be established as needed and terminated if no longer necessary.

switched LAN

Any LAN implemented using LAN switches. *See also:* LAN switch.

synchronous transmission

Signals transmitted digitally with precision clocking. These signals have identical frequencies and contain individual characters encapsulated in control bits (called start/stop bits) that designate the beginning and ending of each character. *See also:* asynchronous transmission and isochronous transmission.

T

T1

Digital WAN that uses 24 DS0s to create a bandwidth of 1.544Mbps.

T3

Digital WAN that can provide bandwidth of 44.763Mbps.

tag switching

Based on the concept of label swapping, where packets or cells are designated to defined-length labels that control the manner in which data is to be sent, tag switching is a high-performance technology used for forwarding packets. It incorporates Data Link layer (Layer 2) switching and Network layer (Layer 3) routing and supplies scalable, high-speed switching in the network core.

tagged traffic

ATM cells with their cell loss priority (CLP) bit set to 1. Also referred to as discard-eligible (DE) traffic. Tagged traffic can be eliminated in order to ensure trouble-free delivery of higher priority traffic, if the network is congested. *See also:* CLP.

TCP

Transmission Control Protocol: A connection-oriented protocol that is defined at the Transport layer of the OSI reference model. Provides reliable delivery of data.

TCP/IP

Transmission Control Protocol/Internet Protocol. The suite of protocols underlying the Internet. TCP and IP are the most widely known protocols in that suite. *See also:* IP and TCP.

TDM

Time-Division Multiplexing: A technique for assigning bandwidth on a single wire, based on preassigned time slots, to data from several channels. Bandwidth is allotted to each channel regardless of a station's ability to send data. *See also:* ATDM, FDM, and multiplexing.

TE1

A device with a four-wire, twisted-pair digital interface is referred to as terminal equipment type one. Most modern ISDN devices are of this type.

TE

Terminal Equipment: Any peripheral device that is ISDN-compatible and attached to a network, such as a telephone or computer.

telco

A common abbreviation for the telephone company.

Telnet

The standard terminal emulation protocol within the TCP/IP protocol stack. Method of remote terminal connection, enabling users to log in on remote networks and use those resources as if they were locally connected. Telnet is defined in RFC 854.

10BaseT

Part of the IEEE 802.3 standard, 10BaseT is the Ethernet specification of 10Mbps baseband that uses two pairs of twisted-pair, Category 3, 4, or 5 cabling—one pair to send data and the other to receive. 10BaseT has a distance limit of about 100 meters per segment. *See also:* Ethernet and IEEE 802.3.

terminal adapter

A hardware interface between a computer and an ISDN line. In effect, an ISDN modem.

terminal emulation

The use of software, installed on a PC or LAN server, that allows the PC to function as if it were a "dumb" terminal directly attached to a particular type of mainframe.

TFTP

The stripped-down version of FTP, it's the protocol of choice if you know exactly what you want and where it's to be found. TFTP doesn't give you the abundance of functions that FTP does. In particular, it has no directory browsing abilities; it can do nothing but send and receive files.

token

A frame containing only control information. Possessing this control information gives a network device permission to transmit data onto the network. *See also:* token passing.

token bus

LAN architecture that is the basis for the IEEE 802.4 LAN specification and employs token passing access over a bus topology. *See also:* IEEE.

token passing

A method used by network devices to access the physical medium in a systematic way based on possession of a small frame called a token. *Contrast with:* circuit switching. *See also:* token.

Token Ring

IBM's token-passing LAN technology. It runs at 4Mbps or 16Mbps over a ring topology. Defined formally by IEEE 802.5. *See also:* ring topology and token passing.

transparent bridging

The bridging scheme used in Ethernet and IEEE 802.3 networks, it passes frames along one hop at a time, using routing information stored in tables that associate end nodes within bridge ports. This type of bridging is considered transparent because the source node doesn't need to know the entire route, as it does with source-route bridging. *Contrast with:* SRB.

Transport layer

Layer 4 of the OSI reference model, used for reliable communication between end nodes over the network. The Transport layer provides mechanisms used for establishing, maintaining, and terminating virtual circuits, transport fault detection and recovery, and controlling the flow of information. *See also:* Data Link layer, Application layer, Physical layer, Network layer, Presentation layer, and Session layer.

TRIP

Token Ring Interface Processor: A high-speed interface processor used on Cisco 7000 series routers. The TRIP provides two or four ports for interconnection with IEEE 802.5 and IBM media with ports set to speeds of either 4Mbps or 16Mbps set independently of each other.

TTL

Time To Live: A field in an IP header, indicating the length of time a packet is valid.

TUD

Trunk Up-Down: A protocol used in ATM networks for the monitoring of trunks. Should a trunk miss a given number of test messages being sent by ATM switches to ensure trunk line quality, TUD declares the trunk down. When a trunk reverses direction and comes back up, TUD recognizes that the trunk is up and returns the trunk to service.

tunneling

A method of avoiding protocol restrictions by wrapping packets from one protocol in another protocol's packet and transmitting this encapsulated packet over a network that supports the wrapper protocol. *See also:* encapsulation.

U

UDP

User Datagram Protocol: A connectionless Transport layer protocol in the TCP/IP protocol stack that simply allows datagrams to be exchanged without acknowledgements or delivery guarantees, requiring other protocols to handle error processing and retransmission. UDP is defined in RFC 768.

unnumbered frames

HDLC frames used for control management purposes, such as link startup and shutdown or mode specification.

V

VBR

Variable Bit Rate: A QoS class, as defined by the ATM Forum, for use in ATM networks that is subdivided into real time (RT) class and non-real time (NRT) class. RT is employed when connections have a fixed timing relationship between samples. Conversely, NRT is employed when connections do not have a fixed time relationship between samples, but still need an assured QoS.

VCC

Virtual Channel Connection: A logical circuit that is created by VCLs. VCCs carry data between two endpoints in an ATM network. Sometimes called a virtual circuit connection.

VIP

1. Versatile Interface Processor: An interface card for Cisco 7000 and 7500 series routers, providing multilayer switching and running the Cisco IOS software. The most recent version of VIP is VIP2.

2. Virtual IP: A function making it possible for logically separated switched IP workgroups to run Virtual Networking Services across the switch ports of a Catalyst 5000.

virtual circuit

Abbreviated VC, a logical circuit devised to assure reliable communication between two devices on a network. Defined by a virtual path connection (VPC)/virtual path identifier (VCI) pair, a virtual circuit can be permanent (PVC) or switched (SVC). Virtual circuits are used in Frame Relay and X.25. Known as virtual channel in ATM. *See also:* PVC and SVC.

virtual ring

In an SRB network, a logical connection between physical rings, either local or remote.

VLAN

Virtual LAN: A group of devices on one or more logically segmented LANs (configured by use of management software), enabling devices to communicate as if attached to the same physical medium, when they are actually located on numerous different LAN segments. VLANs are based on logical instead of physical connections and thus are tremendously flexible.

VLSM

Variable-Length Subnet Mask: Helps optimize available address space and specify a different subnet mask for the same network number on various subnets.

W

WinSock

Windows Socket Interface: A software interface that makes it possible for an assortment of applications to use and share an Internet connection. The WinSock software consists of a Dynamic Link Library (DLL) with supporting programs such as a dialer program that initiates the connection.

workgroup switching

A switching method that supplies high-speed (100Mbps) transparent bridging between Ethernet networks as well as high-speed translational bridging between Ethernet and CDDI or FDDI.

X

X.25

An ITU-T standard that defines communication between DTE and DCE network devices. X.25 uses a reliable Data Link layer protocol called LAPB. X.25 also uses PLP at the Network layer. X.25 has mostly been replaced by Frame Relay.

Z

ZIP

Zone Information Protocol: A Session-layer protocol used by AppleTalk to map network numbers to zone names. NBP uses ZIP in the determination of networks containing nodes that belong to a zone. *See also:* ZIP storm and zone.

ZIP storm

A broadcast storm occurring when a router running AppleTalk reproduces or transmits a route for which there is no corresponding zone name at the time of execution. The route is then forwarded by other routers downstream, thus causing a ZIP storm. *See also:* broadcast storm and ZIP.

zone

A logical grouping of network devices in AppleTalk. *See also:* ZIP.

Index

Note to the Reader: Throughout this index **boldfaced** page numbers indicate primary discussions of a topic. *Italicized* page numbers indicate illustrations.